SURVIVING THE UNIPOLAR ERA

SURVIVING THE UNIPOLAR ERA

North Korea's 35-Year Standoff with the United States

A. B. Abrams

Clarity Press, Inc.

ISBN: 978-1-963892-12-3
EBOOK ISBN: 978-1-963892-13-0

In-house editor: Diana G. Collier
Book design: Becky Luening

Library of Congress Control Number: 2024944099

Clarity Press, Inc.
2625 Piedmont Rd. NE, Ste. 56
Atlanta, GA 30324, USA
https://www.claritypress.com

Table of Contents

Abbreviations

AFRICOM – United States Africa Command

CFR – Council on Foreign Relations

CIA – Central Intelligence Agency

CIVD – Complete Irreversible Verifiable Denuclearization

DMZ – Korean Demilitarized Zone

DNI – Director of National Intelligence

DPRK – Democratic People's Republic of Korea

GMD – Ground-Based Midcourse Defense

IAEA – International Atomic Energy Agency

ICBM – Intercontinental Range Ballistic Missile

KCNA – Korean Central News Agency

KPA – Korean People's Army

NATO – North Atlantic Treaty Organisation

NPT – Treaty on the Non-Proliferation of Nuclear Weapons

THAAD – Terminal High Altitude Area Defense

UN – United Nations

UNSC – United Nations Security Council

US – United States

USSR – Union of Soviet Socialist Republics

WMD – weapons of mass destruction

A Note on Naming Missiles

Since North Korea first began to field ballistic missiles in the early 1980s, considerable uncertainty regarding the names of new missile types has consistently led Western sources to create new names for those missiles seen, which have often continued to be used even after their Korean names have been revealed. These names have often been based on the locations from which the missiles have launched, an example being North Korea's first intermediate range ballistic missile the Hwasong-10 which was referred to in the West as the Musudan as it was first launched near the village of Musudan.

For the purposes of this book all missiles will be referred to by their Korean names. The sole exception are the country's solid fueled short range ballistic missiles, including the Hwasong-11, 11A, 11B, 11C, as these refer to entirely different missiles rather than new variants of the same missile which can cause significant confusion. Thus the original Hwasong-11 will be referred to as such, while the 11A, 11B, 11C will be referred to by their U.S. Forces Korea designations KN-23, KN-24 and KN-23B.

INTRODUCTION

A Unique Adversary

Origins of the U.S.–North Korean Conflict

On August 14, 1945, in anticipation of the imminent formal surrender of the Japanese Empire, officials from the Pentagon's Strategy Policy Committee proposed the division of the Korean Peninsula into American and Soviet trusteeships, using the 38th parallel to grant Washington the southern half and Moscow the northern. Korea had been under effective Japanese rule for four decades from 1905, and in the immediate aftermath of Tokyo's defeat had seen popular people's committees formed across its territory to establish a People's Republic of Korea – a short-lived state that would be abolished once Soviet and U.S. forces fully took control. The beginnings of a distinction between the two halves of the Korean Peninsula would emerge with the vastly diverging policies between the Soviets and the Americans, with the former allowing the people's committees to remain and granting a great deal of autonomy to local nationalist forces which had previously resisted Japanese rule. The latter employed military force extensively against those associated with the People's Republic, instead relying on Koreans who had governed under the Japanese, and a number who had resided in the West, to form a new state.

Opposition to the new order in the south resulted in five years of intensive civil war, which at the most conservative estimates killed two percent of the population as insurrections broke out across the country. Entire population centers were either massacred or placed in concentration camps, which by 1950 housed up to 1.2 million people or over five percent of the population.[1] With the new establishment solidifying its authority, headed by 20-year resident of Washington, D.C. Syngman Rhee, who had been handpicked to rule by the U.S. Army, it was able to declare the formation of the Republic of Korea on August 15, 1948. Rhee's administration claimed to be the sole government of the entire Korean nation including all territory north of the 38th parallel. The government in the north, headed by the leaders of the guerrilla movement that had for decades fought Japanese rule, subsequently declared the Democratic People's Republic of Korea (DPRK) on September 9. With the division of Korea thereby officialized, two further years of civil war in the south and the escalation of tensions along the 38th parallel culminated in the outbreak of full scale war between the rival governments on June 25, 1950, for which each side blamed the other.

With South Korean forces effectively disintegrating within 72 hours, the United States would play a central role in fighting North Korea over the next three years, leading a vast coalition of predominantly Western militaries. In September, Washington made the controversial decision to invade the north in an attempt to abolish the state and extend the authority of Syngman Rhee's government. The invasion would in hindsight widely be seen as a reckless error, particularly after U.S. forces pushed up to the Chinese border and provoked Beijing to intervene on North Korea's side. The magnitude of the costs this incurred were such that, even 40 years later, the fallout from the invasion was considered a primary factor inclining Washington towards caution when considering escalating the Gulf War and invading Iraq.[2] The result after almost three more years of fighting was a stalemate roughly along the 38th parallel and the conclusion of hostilities in an armistice. While Chinese forces completely withdrew from North Korea once reconstruction was complete in 1958, and Beijing would normalize relations with South Korea in 1992, U.S. forces would remain in the south indefinitely with Washington continuing to refuse to form diplomatic ties with North Korea or to recognize its existence. It thereby implicitly continued to endorse the south's claim of sovereignty over the north.

North Korea and the United States have remained officially at war for over seven decades, representing by far the longest war between any two industrial powers in history. With the U.S. having since 1950 waged well over a dozen other hot wars, from Panama and Grenada to Iraq and Somalia, all of which were resolved in small fractions of the time of the yet unresolved Korean conflict, this aspect alone has made North Korea stand out among America's adversaries. This book explores the evolution of the conflict in the 35 years following the end of the Cold War in 1989, after it entered an entirely new phase with North Korea's isolation and the emergence of a unipolar post-Soviet global order, before gradually moving on into an era characterized by decline in U.S. and Western power.

This introductory chapter provides background to four core aspects of the conflict between North Korea and the United States that are key to understanding its course and nature and the rationales for the policies enacted by both states. It first observes the history and thought behind North Korean foreign and security policies aimed at countering the United States, and the shaping of American perceptions of its adversary's resolve and military strength over more than seven decades. The second and third sections then explore North Korean rationales for two weapons programs which have been at the center of shaping the course of conflict since the end of the Cold War, namely the development of ballistic missiles and nuclear weapons, tracing the histories of both back to the Korean War. Finally, a fourth section highlights the overarching rationale behind the imperative for Pyongyang to deter the United States, and the perceived dangers posed to the state and its population should they fail to prevent the U.S. from placing them under its control.

A Unique Adversary Confronting American Power

The armed forces of North Korea, the Korean People's Army (KPA), made their first major demonstration of their capabilities during the Korean War, and within ten days of its outbreak on June 25, 1950 had seen their first engagements with U.S. Army units. Their performance would leave a lasting impression on the United States and the wider Western world which would continue to influence policy towards the country decades into the next century. Assessments of KPA capabilities would transform rapidly in the conflict's initial weeks, with Pulitzer Prize winning American journalist David Halberstam observing: "almost everyone, from top to bottom, seemed to share the view that the moment the North Koreans saw they were fighting Americans rather than the ROKs [South Koreans] they would cut and run. It was arrogance born of racial prejudice."[3] Supreme Commander General Douglas MacArthur boasted that if he only deployed the U.S. Army 1st Cavalry to Korea: "why, heavens, you'd see these fellows [KPA] scuttle up to the Manchurian border so quick, you would see no more of them."[4]

Although being far better armed, and often having a numerical advantage, U.S. forces faced loss after loss after their first engagements with the North Koreans, with their forces quickly falling into disorder as they retreated often chaotically.[5] The threat was such that all of the U.S. Army's combat ready divisions, other than the 82nd Airborne Division in Germany, were deployed to Korea.[6] As a result by late August the North Koreans were outnumbered 179,300 to 98,000, with their tanks outnumbered by a five-to-one ratio.[7] The U.S. was delivering more firepower from the air than any other three countries combined could, with tremendous fire support from its navy further tipping the balance in its favor. The KPA by contrast, as reported by the U.S military headquarters, at times relied on obsolete "World War 1 rifles" and did not receive "any post-[Second World] war Soviet weapons,"[8] with its arms and supply shortages being extreme.[9]

Despite overwhelming material disadvantages, North Korean forces were still making consecutive weeks of "startling gains" in late August, bringing the U.S. and allied perimeter around Pusan "near breaking point." Contingency plans had to be made for a total American withdrawal and continuation of the campaign from offshore islands.[10] By mid-September America and its allies "had just barely turned back the great North Korean offensive," taking tens of thousands of casualties in the process,[11] with U.S. military assessments consistently concluding that if the North Koreans had received supplies from their neighbors, they very likely would have won. Their very scarce supplies had placed them at a major disadvantage from the outset.[12] It took the landing of 80,000 U.S. Marines behind North Korean lines at the port city of Inchon from

September 15–19 to decisively turn the tide and make the numerical discrepancy significantly more overwhelming still.

Even after September, the performance of North Korean forces continued to make a very strong impression. With no artillery, tanks or air power KPA units put up a tenacious defense of Seoul, fighting to the last man and giving up no street without a fight, which left the U.S. Marine advance very far behind schedule. The Marines took ten days to advance just twenty miles towards Seoul, and only the indiscriminate raising of the entire city dislodged the defenders,[13] with the fighting being so intense that all North Korean personnel captured were summarily executed by the Marines.[14] After pulling back to the Sino-Korean border, the KPA shocked the Chinese with the speed at which they reconstituted their forces, including creating three new corps for a renewed effort to take Seoul.[15]

The strong North Korean performance against overwhelming odds made a lasting impression, with commander of the U.S. Eighth Army General Matthew Ridgway observing: "we had never...imagined that the NKPA [same as KPA] was a force so well-trained, so superbly disciplined, so battle-ready."[16] Supreme Commander MacArthur warned of the dangers of underestimating the KPA, stating: "The North Korean soldier must not be underestimated. He is a tough opponent, well-led, and has combined the infiltration tactic of the Japanese with the tank tactics of the Russian of World War II. He is able to march and manoeuvre and to attack at night with cohesion... tank work is extremely efficient and skillful."[17] Generals and other officers widely voiced similar assessments.[18] For Western intelligence agencies, too, the country would make a very strong impression for the unique challenge it presented, with their inability to infiltrate it considered among their most staggering failures throughout the Cold War.[19]

In subsequent Cold War conflicts the North Koreans would consistently remain true to their reputation gained in wartime. Whereas in the Korean War the country was wholly unprepared for conflict with the United States, after the July 1953 armistice it quickly turned into a fortress with massive supply and munitions stockpiles, some of the most densely defended airspace in the world, and a vast network of tunnels, bunkers and fortifications to provide cover against possible American air or nuclear strikes.

North Korea stood out among Western Bloc adversaries for its wholly disproportionate provision of aid and military support to other Western targets. During the Cuban Missile Crisis the country reportedly heavily militarized its diplomatic mission in Havana, appointing senior KPA officers to top diplomatic posts. At the height of tensions it had its embassy staff don Cuban military uniforms and pledge to fight with local forces in the event of a U.S. invasion. Subsequently during the Vietnam War, referred to by North Korean President Kim Il Sung as "the focal point" in global struggle against Western empire,[20] KPA pilots and air defense crews played extensive roles securing North Vietnamese skies. The president stressed the importance of "supporting Vietnam as if it were our own war. When Vietnam has a request, we will disrupt our own plans in order to try to meet their demands."[21] As North Vietnam suffered severe fighter pilot shortages, with these being costly and time consuming to train, Vietnamese sources reported that between 87 and 96 North Korean pilots served in the conflict, during which time they downed 26 American aircraft and took 14 losses.[22] North Koreans manned two MiG-17 companies and one MiG-21 company, providing a 50 percent increase to North Vietnam's fighter strength,[23] which was particularly important as the U.S. escalated its bombardment of population centers under Operation Rolling Thunder.[24] With President Kim having told KPA pilots to "defend the skies of Vietnam as if they were the skies of Korea,"[25] former Vietnamese Deputy Defense Minister Tran Hanh recalled: "We found them to be very brave. Their national pride was so high… They feared nothing, even death."[26] U.S. and South Korean sources also reported KPA training had been provided for Viet Cong insurgents in South Vietnam, and that KPA psychological warfare specialists played a particularly prominent role in supporting them.[27]

During the Arab-Israeli Wars, as the United States provided material and intelligence support to Israel on a tremendous scale, North Korean veteran pilots, many with more than 2,000 hours flight experience, flew Egyptian and Syrian MiG-21 fighters and engaged Israeli forces multiple times. KPA personnel also reportedly operated air defense systems for the two countries.[28] Pyongyang had previously provided considerable economic aid to Egypt after its military defeats by Western and Israeli forces in 1956 and 1967.[29] Military contingents in Syria were bolstered by 200 North Korean tank crewmen, 53 pilots and 140 missile technicians in 1970, which were reinforced by 75 air force instructors in 1975 and 40 trained fighter pilots in 1976.[30] Subsequently, as Syria engaged U.S. and Israeli forces during the Lebanon War in the 1980s, the Korean People's Army permanently stationed additional pilots, tank operators, missile technicians and officers, and reportedly saw its artillery personnel killed in Israeli air strikes.[31] Elsewhere in the Arab world, as the Libyan Armed Forces engaged U.S. and French forces multiple times from the late 1970s, several reports also indicated that the country's top interceptors, its MiG-25s, were operated by North Korean pilots.[32] On the other side of Africa, the People's Movement for the Liberation of Angola was supported in the 1980s by 1500 KPA advisors, and according to some reports several thousand regular troops as well, as part of an effort to counter the U.S. and apartheid South Africa in the Angolan Civil War.[33] Military deployments to bolster Western adversaries continued well into the 21st century, and were interpreted in U.S. reports as a sign of Pyongyang's resolve for "resolutely combating imperialism and actively supporting liberation struggle" globally.[34]

Central to North Korea's strategy for countering Western challenges to its security was the imperative of meeting pressure with pressure. This meant that in incidents ranging from the shootdown of a U.S. Navy EC-121 surveillance plane in 1969, to the multiple nuclear and missile crises of the post–Cold War years, Pyongyang attached great importance to retaliating strongly to deter its adversaries. North Korean Deputy Foreign Minister Heo Dam referred to this policy as being "ready to respond to retaliation with retaliation, and total war with total war," making the U.S. "draw the proper lesson" from KPA operations against U.S. forces accused of infringing on its territory. He elaborated regarding the rationale behind it:

> If the Americans had decided to fight then [after the EC-121 shootdown], we would have fought… we wage firefights with the Americans in the area of the 38th parallel almost every day. When they shoot, we also shoot… But no special aggravation arises from this… we've also shot down American planes before, and similar incidents are possible in the future… It's good for them to know that we won't sit with folded arms… If we sit with folded arms when a violator intrudes into our spaces, two planes will appear tomorrow, then four, five, etc. This would lead to an increase of the danger of war. But if a firm rebuff is given, then this will diminish the danger of an outbreak of war. When the Americans understand that there is a weak enemy before them they will start a war right away. If, however, they see that there is a strong partner before them, this delays the beginning of war.[35]

The EC-121 shootdown served to reinforce the messages sent by multiple other shootdowns in the preceding years, among them the downing of an RF-4C reconnaissance plane on August 31, 1967, an F-105D fighter five months later on January 14, 1968 and an F-4B fighter the following month on February 12. KPA ground forces' active taking to the offensive in skirmishes in the Demilitarized Zone at the time was assessed to have also been intended to convey resolve to the United States in order to deter another possible invasion attempt.[36] The KPA Navy, too, was far from inactive, and a year before the EC-121 downing it seized a U.S. Navy surveillance warship on January 23, 1968, which had been carrying out surveillance operations in what Pyongyang alleged were its territorial waters. A submarine chaser, three torpedo boats and a pair of MiG-21 fighters were involved in the first stages of the operation, followed by other warships. The USS *Pueblo* was escorted to Wonsan Harbor and its 82 crew imprisoned, to be later released on December 23.

The *Pueblo* seizure occurred six days after President Lyndon Johnson's State of the Union address, which focused heavily on the state of conflict in Southeast Asia, and was speculated to have been coordinated with the Viet Minh, who just seven days later launched the large-scale Tet Offensive against U.S. and allied forces. Minister Heo Dam would later refer to the shootdown of the EC-121 the following year as being part of a specific effort to condition American behavior, to make them "draw the proper lesson from the *Pueblo*."[37] This appeared to have been at least somewhat successful, as after the EC-121 downing the Richard Nixon White House decided against plans to respond with escalation and air strikes. This was specifically due to its awareness that North Korea would respond with major offensives of its own, resulting in all-out war on the peninsula.[38] A strong belief had been instilled in Washington that Pyongyang could not be deterred from responding to attacks on its territory, with this on multiple occasions significantly influencing considerations for possible attacks on the country both during the Cold War and in the three decades that followed.

On August 26, 1981 the U.S. alleged that North Korean S-75 air defense systems had fired on an SR-71 surveillance aircraft, which Pyongyang alleged had violated "the territorial air of the northern half of our republic."[39] This was the only shootdown attempt against an SR-71 ever reported by the U.S. government, and although not bringing down the world's fastest aircraft, it came close to doing so, with pilots reporting that the missiles passed to the right of their cockpit windows after having their guidance systems jammed. SR-71s from then on gave North Korean airspace a much wider berth. When the possibility was subsequently raised in early 1994 of bringing the SR-71 back into service to survey North Korean nuclear sites, the Pentagon notably decided against it, with the KPA having since then also operatiaonlized much more capable S-200D air defense systems that could pose a far greater threat.[40]

Beyond demonstrations of North Korean resolve, and of its willingness to retaliate even at great risk and against great odds, American and South Korean military sources have frequently highlighted the high morale and professionalism which the KPA has consistently demonstrated.[41] As was the case for many militaries, the expanded scope of special forces operations meant these were the most frequently tested, burnishing the reputation the country's armed forces had gained during the Korean War. Korean People's Army special forces were described in a 1988 British assessment as "highly motivated, politically well indoctrinated and well trained.... units are expected to seek the initiative continuously, to turn all unforeseen events to their advantage, and advance all to achieve their objectives regardless of cost." Their notoriously rigorous training programs reportedly included "skills, such as abseiling, mountain climbing, swimming, martial arts, airborne, demolition, and rigorous physical fitness, and training designed to produce individual initiative, creativity, flexibility and aggressiveness."[42]

Insight into the capabilities of North Korean special forces was provided eight years later when three of these personnel became trapped in South Korea following a submarine accident on September 17, 1996. Although South Korean military search parties comprised of tens of thousands of personnel were extremely thorough, the three North Koreans were successful in evading them for a full 49 days, and during that time killed 12 South Korean soldiers and caused 27 more military casualties. Two of the North Koreans were eventually captured on November 5, with the third never found and assumed to have successfully returned to North Korea. This unplanned operation served as a highly potent demonstration of the capabilities of KPA elite units, with its significance being particularly great considering that North Korea deployed far more special forces than any other country at an estimated 180,000–200,000 personnel.[43] As summarized in a Council on Foreign Relations assessment regarding the lessons extrapolated from the incident: "the conduct of the North Korean special forces team stranded in the South last fall suggests that there is no shortage of courage in the North, even against long odds," highlighting signs in the country of "a toughness of spirit that allows them to overcome conditions that might break another population."[44] The reputation of North Korean special forces was further bolstered in the 2010s when they were deployed to support Syrian counterinsurgency efforts against a range of Western-backed insurgent groups, with a report from the insurgent Syrian National Council stating that two special forces units named Chalma-1 and Chalma-7 proved "fatally dangerous" on the battlefield.[45,i] This reputation built up by North Korea over three quarters of a century of conflict with the United States, both in regard to its defense policies and the capabilities of its armed forces, has consistently been a vital contributor to its security.

Deterring America: Why Develop Missiles

As North Korea's long conflict with the United States entered a new phase following the end of the Cold War, the country's development of ballistic missiles became an increasingly central aspect of their standoff. Having reverse engineered and improved the Soviet R-17 Scud-B design in the 1980s, the North Korean defense sector's building on these technologies to develop increasingly sophisticated missile classes with greater precision, survivability, mobility and much longer reaches became a central factor shifting the balance of power between it and the United States. Overshadowing relations for over three decades, an understanding of the primary rationales for the country's ballistic missile program, many of which date back to the Korean War, are key to a fuller comprehension of the conflict between Pyongyang and Washington.

Four days after the Korean War's outbreak, the newly formed U.S. Air Force began bombing North Korea from June 29, 1950. The air campaign frequently targeted civilians, including repeated

---

i On the opposite end of the spectrum of North Korean manpower, the country's civilian sailors themselves contributed to the reputation of North Koreans as particularly capable fighters eleven years later in October 2007 after Somali pirates attacked and seized one of the country's cargo vessels in the Indian Ocean near Mogadishu. While no military personnel were aboard, the unarmed sailors were able to kill two pirates and capture the remainder, seizing their weapons. Another notable aspect of the incident was that medical care was subsequetnly provided by the U.S. Navy, leading North Korean state media to publish unusual praise for American actions, namely that on behalf of the Korean people: "We feel grateful to the United States for its assistance given to our crewmen." ('DPRK's Consistent Principled Stand to Fight against All Forms of Terrorism Reiterated,' *KCNA*, November 11, 2007.)

strafing and bombing of South Korean refugee columns,[46] with tolerance for Korean civilian deaths, both southern and northern, remaining extremely high. Entire villages were wiped out by napalm saturation and strafing if it was suspected that even a small number of KPA personnel were present. This worsened from November 5 when Supreme Commander MacArthur initiated the strategic bombing of North Korea,[47] ordering the bombing of "every means of communication, every installation, factory, city and village" in the country.[48] Assistant State Secretary Dean Rusk later elaborated that bombers would attack "everything that moved in North Korea, every brick standing on top of another."[49] As journalist Robert Jackson stated regarding the shift: "the B-29s were [now] to carry full loads of incendiaries and their task was to burn the selected cities from end to end."[50] Attacking population centers became a goal in and of itself regardless of whether they housed enemy personnel or contributed to the war effort.

Having been a correspondent in North Korea during the war, the anti-communist Hungarian writer Tibor Meray recalled years later after defecting to the West: "I saw destruction and horrible things committed by the American forces... Everything which moved in North Korea was a military target, peasants in the fields were machine gunned by pilots who, this was my impression, amused themselves to shoot the targets which moved." He witnessed "a complete devastation between the Yalu River and the capital [Pyongyang]." There were simply "no more cities in North Korea... my impression was that I am travelling on the moon, because there was only devastation."[51] Following his capture by North Korean forces U.S. Army Major General William Dean recalled: "The town of Huichon amazed me. The city I'd seen before – two storied buildings, a prominent main street – wasn't there anymore." He encountered only "unoccupied shells" of town after town. Villages were reduced to rubble or "snowy open spaces." Nothing more remained.[52] Air Force General Curtis LeMay stated to much the same effect: "we burned down just about every city in North Korea and South Korea both… we killed off over a million civilian Koreans and drove several million more from their homes."[53]

By late 1950 the U.S. Air Force alone was dropping 800 tons of munitions on North Korea daily, much of it pure napalm,[54] with considerable further sorties flown by the Navy and by British, Australian and South African air units. Air Force communiques consistently showed mass indiscriminate targeting of population centers,[55] with 635,000–698,000 tons of bombs dropped on North Korea,[56] compared to 503,000 tons dropped on the entire Japanese Empire, a land mass 25 times larger, during the Pacific War.[57] The Air Force saw napalm as a highly destructive "wonder weapon,"[58] although British Prime Minister Winston Churchill was among the vocal opponents of its mass use against civilian targets on moral grounds. "I do not like this napalm bombing at all. A fearful lot of people must be burned, not by ordinary fire, but by the contents of the bomb... Napalm in the war was devised by us and used by fighting men in action... No one ever thought of splashing it all over the civilian population," he observed.[59] Reports on the effects[ii] of napalm,[iii] including from American units hit by friendly fire, were consistently horrific, with 32,557 tons of the incendiary dropped on North Korea throughout the war.[60] U.S. bombings succeeded in wiping out a significant percentage

---

ii Physician Richard Perry, having spent years treating its victims, would write years later regarding napalm's effects on civilian targets: *"I have been an orthopedic surgeon for a good number of years, with a rather wide range of medical experience. But nothing could have prepared me for my encounters with... women and children burned by napalm. It was shocking and sickening, even for a physician, to see and smell the blackened flesh. One continues for days afterward getting sick when he looks at a piece of meat on his plate because the odour of burning flesh lingers so long in the memory. And one never forgets the bewildered eyes of the silent, suffering, napalm-burned child. What could anyone possibly say to such a child?"* (Perry, Richard E. and Levin, Robert J., 'Where the Innocent Die,' *Redbook*, January 1967 (p. 103).)

iii British war correspondent Alfred Winnington, who wrote from North Korea, reported of napalm: "Many people die horribly from the burns and shock, and still more survive as walking monstrosities sickened by their own images… the hands become drawn backward like claws of birds, the eyelids are pulled up and down, leaving bulbous eyeballs staring, apparently terrified, from wide red frames of the out-turned eyeball itself." He speculated that mass dousing of population centers with napalm was intended to produce "living corpses whose appearance will strike terror into others, and to break morale." (*Daily Worker*, July 26, 1952.)

of the Korean population on a scale without precedent or equal in recent history, with the air campaign killing the bulk of the 3–4 million North Koreans estimated to have died in the war.[61] Unexploded American ordnance has continued to endanger North Korean civilians, and the cleanup operation is expected to last for over 100 years.[62]

While the United States could launch bombing raids both from southern Korea miles behind the frontlines, as well as from Japan, North Korean and allied Chinese forces were wholly incapable of threatening the bases from which the attacks were launched. Had the Soviet Union not provided a small number of MiG-15 fighters, which flew from bases in China, the two countries would have been almost totally helpless against high flying bombers, although even with the fighters, enemy bombers were still far harder to destroy when airborne than they were when at their bases.

The asymmetry between America's ability to bomb Korea with impunity, and if needed to do the same to China, and the East Asian countries' inability to threaten airbases even in South Korea or Japan, let alone cities on the U.S. mainland, was exploited to the full at considerable cost to Pyongyang and Beijing. Leading calls to use strategic bombing to force concessions in armistice negotiations, Defense Secretary Robert Lovett stated: "If we can stay firm [in our terms for negotiation] we can tear them up by air. We are hurting them badly… If we keep on tearing the place apart, we can make it a most unpopular affair for the North Koreans. We ought to go right ahead."[63] From July 1952 the new supreme commander Mark Clark accordingly oversaw an intensification of the bombardment of North Korea's civilian infrastructure under Operation Pressure Pump, and advocated a similar targeting of Chinese cities to force concessions,[64] which was supported by the State Department at the most senior levels.[65]

As negotiations on an armistice entered an indefinite recess from October 8, 1952, the U.S. was able to respond with further intensified bombardment of North Korea and threats of similar attacks on China. This included the largest air attack of the war in which over 1200 sorties were launched to bomb, napalm and strafe Pyongyang and its surroundings, destroying 1500 buildings and causing mass civilian casualties.[66] A further stalling of negotiations in May 1953 saw the U.S. escalate by bombing irrigation dams. Attacks on the Yalu River dams, on which 75 percent of North Korea's rice crop relied,[67] envisioned destroying 250,000 tons of rice and causing huge floods and mass starvation – a severe war crime.[68] The official U.S. Air Force history claimed that two of the larger attacks on irrigation dams were the most devastating air operations of the entire war, and "portended the devastation of the most important segment of the North Korean agricultural economy,"[69] bringing the DPRK's ability to sustain the war effort or feed its population into serious doubt.[70] This was pursued in parallel to the targeting of agriculture and of relief supplies entering Korea to further exacerbate famine.[71] Days after the bombing of the dams, Supreme Commander of U.S.-led coalition forces Mark Clark warned the North Korean and Chinese negotiators that terms for an armistice were "final,"[72] with Beijing warned through multiple channels that failure to accept armistice terms would result in an expanded of bombing to target its territory.[73] With China and North Korea quickly accepting an armistice on terms that were far from favorable, State Secretary John Foster Dulles would cite their awareness of America's ability to expand strategic bombing to China as the primary factor forcing this outcome.[74]

Not only could America's new B-36 bombers strike North Korea and China from U.S. territories, but its older B-29s could deliver tremendous payloads from forward bases in Japan, while its blue water navy was well positioned to deliver considerable further firepower against cities across the two countries. Thus the North Koreans and Chinese had no means of mounting a remotely comparable response to the targeting of their cities. When American aviation intensified its bombardment to increase pressure during negotiations, even U.S.-aligned populations in Japan and South Korea remained well out of reach of retaliatory strikes, much less the American mainland itself for a fully proportional response.

This lesson was subsequently repeatedly reinforced by American demonstrations of its ability to bring ruin from the air and sea to other targets that were wholly unable to respond proportionally with attacks on American territory or its major bases, from Vietnam and Yugoslavia to Iraq, Syria and Libya. Indeed, taking this argument further back, had Imperial Japan had a significant strike capability against American cities, the United States would have likely accepted its surrender months earlier, foregoing the firebombing of 67 cities and nuclear strikes on two more. After winning the war, the U.S.' ability to devastate its adversary to push for six months for a total and unconditional surrender, while making a major show of force in the process at almost no cost to its own forces, was primarily facilitated by the total lack of mutual vulnerability. Like all the targets that came after them, the best the Japanese could hope for in the war's final six months was to shoot down a number of American bombers, killing a few dozen airmen in the process, while a successful American bombing operation could kill over 100,000 civilians in just hours. The rationale for North Korea's pursuit of a long-range strike capability can thus be traced back to years before the state had itself been founded.

With no blue water navy, no overseas military bases, and no strategic bomber fleet, ballistic missiles emerged as the only means for North Korea to hold American bases across the Pacific, and eventually the American mainland itself, within the line of fire, much as the U.S. had done to it from the 1940s onward, with its military expansion into the Western Pacific. The KPA's ability to strike Japan would ensure not only that Tokyo would press Washington towards greater caution when considering attacks on North Korea from its territory, but also that bases hosting American warships, aircraft and supplies could be targeted – a capability that would have been a major game changer in the Korean War. As the Korean War era B-29's successors the B-52, B-1 and B-2 strategic bombers were widely used in shows of force against North Korea, with B-52s considered for use in nuclear strikes multiple times, the ability to strike facilities across the Pacific that could host these aircraft, from Guam and Wake Island to Darwin and Hawaii, was highly valued. While accidents at American bomber bases demonstrated that units could be forced out of action for weeks by relatively minor disruptions at their facilities, the potential for putting the fleet out of action with minor strikes, including on the American mainland itself, was invaluable to North Korea's security and the safety of its population centers.

Alongside their strategic importance, ballistic missiles also had significant tactical benefits in allowing North Korea to asymmetrically counter advances in enemy conventional forces. While during the Cold War North Korea had consistently been supplied with aircraft capable of challenging their top Western rivals of their time, from MiG-15s in the 1950s to MiG-29s three decades later, after the USSR's disintegration the emergence of a tremendous capability disadvantage against the latest American aircraft made the ability to target the bases which hosted them all the more important. Facing new generations of American assets such as F-35 stealth fighters and B-21 stealth bombers, this was far more feasible for the small country's defense sector than developing cutting edge stealth aircraft of its own. With a cornerstone of the post–Cold War Western-led order being Western states' ability to reshape the world with military force, where their adversaries could do little to retaliate, the ability of long-range missile arsenals to act as something of an equalizer, albeit a highly asymmetric one, made the Western world particularly sensitive to the development of such assets by countries outside its sphere of influence.

Why Develop Nuclear Weapons

Within two years of the foundation of the Democratic People's Republic of Korea on September 8, 1948, the country had not only been intensively firebombed by the U.S. Air Force, but also faced a serious threat of American nuclear attacks. Nuclear strikes against two Japanese population centers in August 1945 and the resulting deaths of over 200,000 had cast a long shadow over the Western Bloc's new Cold War adversaries, indicating that their own cities could face similar attacks, with the events of the Korean War making this threat appear all the more imminent. As early as July 1950 just days into the war, Supreme Commander MacArthur began calling for the Pentagon to consider nuclear strikes on North Korea.[75] Components for nuclear bombs were subsequently flown to Guam for storage, which would allow them to be employed within 72 hours should the White House authorize it.[76] As U.S.-led coalition forces faced repeated defeats, nuclear attacks were increasingly widely reported to be under more serious consideration, with this confirmed by President Harry Truman on November 30.[77] Such attacks were recommended by a committee of the Joint Chiefs of Staff.[78] Described by British military historian Max Hastings as "instilled with a yearning for crude revenge upon the people who had brought all his hopes and triumphs in Korea to nothing,"[79] MacArthur's calls for nuclear attacks grew as defeats mounted, and on December 9 he requested authority to launch them. Fifteen days later he submitted a list of targets across northern Korea and China for 26 nuclear strikes, 18 of which would hit industrial centers, although the plan was not approved by Washington.[80]

Defeats in the final months of 1950 led MacArthur to propose contaminating northern Korea and northeast China with a "radioactive by-product cordon," devastating all life across a vast area and rendering it uninhabitable for generations.[81] On March 10, 1951 MacArthur asked for "D-Day atomic capability," demanding that up to 50 nuclear weapons be dropped on northeast China. At the end of March atomic bomb loading pits at Kadena Air Base on Okinawa were operational,[82] with bombs intended to target military facilities and industrial centers in China.[83] On April 5 the Joint Chiefs of Staff gave MacArthur the authority to use nuclear weapons,[84] and ordered nuclear attacks against bases in northeast China if large Chinese forces entered the theatre or if bombers were launched against American assets from there. Mk. 4 nuclear capsules were transferred to the Air Force's 9th Bomb Group designated to carry nuclear weapons, which was authorized by President Truman who signed an order to use them against Chinese and Korean targets. The nuclear warheads would remain deployed within bombing range of Korea and under military control.[85]

Although MacArthur was dismissed on April 11, seventeen days later President Truman increased deployments of nuclear-configured bombers to East Asia and authorized reconnaissance flights over airfields in northeast China to obtain targeting data for potential strikes.[86] U.S. envoys conveyed that MacArthur's dismissal did not mean that Washington had ruled out nuclear attacks.[87] Two primary factors prevented the use of nuclear weapons in the Korean theatre: the threat of intervention by Soviet forces, which had their own intercontinental range strike capabilities and nuclear weapons, and the fact that the nuclear warheads of the era were found not to have practical applications against ground forces or fortifications.[88] The latter point was verified by the results of Operation Hudson Harbor, which had been initiated by the U.S. Air Force in October 1951 to ascertain the viability of nuclear attacks largely by dropping dud nuclear bombs on North Korea.[89] A third factor was that firebombing had already destroyed all meaningful strategic targets in Korea, meaning while a nuclear attack on a North Korean city as a show of force to China was an attractive policy option, and had been recommended by the Joint Chiefs of Staff, it was never taken.[90]

The threat to escalate to nuclear strikes grew from January 1953 with the inauguration of the new Dwight D. Eisenhower administration,[91] with Chinese state media having highlighted that month that escalated nuclear threats were expected under the new president.[92] Even in the Korean War's opening days General Eisenhower had suggested that the Pentagon ought to "consider the use of one or two atomic bombs" in Korea, among other expressions of support for nuclear strikes, and as president he would continue to support options for such escalation.[93] On March 27 the new president and his state secretary John Foster Dulles agreed "that somehow or other the taboo which surrounds the use of atomic weapons would have to be destroyed." Dulles stated that "in the present state of world opinion, we could not use an A-bomb, we should make every effort now to dissipate this feeling."[94] After the war the president repeatedly stated that the threat of "a full-scale atomic attack" had been the primary factor forcing Beijing and Pyongyang to agree to American terms.[95]

Nuclear coercion provided both China and North Korea with strong incentives to pursue means of retaliating against and thus deterring American nuclear attacks in future, with the Chinese state run *People's Daily* concluding that American "atomic militarism" needed a Chinese nuclear deterrent to contain it.[96] A spokesman for the Chinese Scientific Association similarly observed regarding armistice negotiations that "only when we ourselves have the atomic weapon, and are fully prepared, is it possible for the frenzied warmongers to listen to our just and reasonable proposals."[97] While North Korea was over 30 years behind China in developing a nuclear deterrent, the rationales expressed were highly similar, with the country's Foreign Ministry highlighting in 2010 regarding the need for this deterrent that "no nation in the world has been exposed to the nuclear threat so directly and for so long as the Koreans."[98]

Despite the State Department finding North Korea and China to be in full compliance with the armistice agreement,[99] the U.S. in June 1957 unilaterally abrogated article 13 (d) which had prohibited the introduction of nuclear weapons into the theatre and deployed its first nuclear warheads in South Korea in January the following year. The arsenal would gradually rise to reach 950 warheads. The Joint Chiefs of Staff recommended that any renewal of hostilities should be immediately followed by a "massive atomic air strike" against North Korean targets, with directives given to launch them in short order.[100] With South Korean President Syngman Rhee having called on the U.S. Congress to use thermonuclear strikes to facilitate a new invasion of North Korea,[101] the Eisenhower administration's new Korea policy under NSC 5702/2 from August 1957 allowed U.S. nuclear forces to provide "support for a unilateral ROK [Republic of Korea] military initiative" against the north.[102]

Pyongyang would be threatened with nuclear attacks following its seizure of the U.S. Navy surveillance ship the USS *Pueblo* in January 1968, with cables declassified years later showing that the Pentagon was ready to use nuclear weapons to force it to release the ship and its crew.[103] As American historian Peter Hayes noted: "the initial reaction of American decisionmakers was to drop a nuclear weapon on Pyongyang… The fact that all the U.S. F-4 fighter planes held on constant alert on [South] Korean airfields were loaded only with nuclear weapons did not help the leaders to think clearly."[104] With U.S. President Lyndon Johnson widely advised to respond with an attack, planned offensives notably involved nuclear strikes against the North Korean leadership and military facilities. The need to avoid another war as conflict in Vietnam went increasingly unfavorably, and concerns regarding a Soviet or Chinese response, were primary factors preventing this.[105]

Following the KPA Air Force's downing of an American EC-121 surveillance plane in 1969, President Nixon authorized plans for a massive counterattack – Operation Plan Freedom Drop – which envisaged "strikes against military targets in North Korea employing one nuclear weapon on each target," using over a dozen nuclear warheads against command centers and airfields across the country.[106] The CIA's top Vietnam specialist George Carver reported that the president went so far as to authorize a nuclear attack when inebriated, observing: "Nixon became incensed and ordered a tactical nuclear strike... The Joint Chiefs were alerted and asked to recommend targets, but [National Security Advisor Henry] Kissinger got on the phone to them. They agreed not to do anything until Nixon sobered up in the morning."[107] Nuclear-armed Air Force units in South Korea were placed on high alert and ordered to prepare for nuclear attacks on North Korea using 330-kiloton B61 thermonuclear bombs, which were 22 times as powerful as the Little Boy bomb dropped on Hiroshima. F-4 pilot Bruce Charles recalled after preparing for a nuclear attack: "The order to stand down was just about dusk, and it was not a certainty. The colonel said, 'It looks like from the messages I'm getting, we will not do this today. I do not know about tomorrow.'"[108] Attack plans were supported by Kissinger, but opposed by the U.S. ambassador in Seoul, the Joint Chiefs of Staff chairman, the CIA director and the commander of U.S. forces in Korea, who warned of the dangers of escalation.[109] The factors deterring nuclear strikes were almost identical to those which had deterred the Johnson administration the previous year, with Nixon later recalling that "as long as we were involved in Vietnam, we simply did not have the resources or public support for another war in another place."[110]

Although President Nixon proved highly willing to consider nuclear strikes on North Korea, Secretary Kissinger recalled that he was consistently unwilling to launch nuclear retaliation against the Soviet Union even in the event of a Soviet conventional attack on NATO due to fears that nuclear war could devastate America.[111] This highlighted the value nuclear weapons would have for North Korea, as the administration's calculus in 1969 would likely have been entirely different had the KPA fielded a nuclear deterrent at the time.[112] The nuclear threat further grew from the 1980s when the Pentagon applied the Air Land Battle warfighting doctrine to the Korean Peninsula, which stipulated extensive use of specialized penetrative nuclear weapons to neutralize hardened facilities preceding a ground invasion, as well as a further lowering of the threshold for nuclear attacks on North Korea to well below levels seen in Europe. As summarized in an assessment published by the *Bulletin of Atomic Scientists:* "The logic was that we dared not use nuclear weapons in Europe, because the other side had them, except in the greatest extremity, but we could use them in Korea because the other side didn't have such weapons. South Korean commanders...had gotten used to the idea that the United States would use nuclear weapons at an early point in a war with North Korea."[113,iv]

---

iv A key facilitator of a lower nuclear threshold was the incorporation into war plans of plans for use of neutron bombs against Korean population centers – thermonuclear warheads also known as "enhanced radiation weapons" designed to maximize emissions of lethal neutron radiation while minimizing explosive yield. These warheads caused a process of neutron activation, turning body tissues radioactive causing a slow and painful death, but causing minimal damage to buildings or industry. In one of the earliest reports on the new weapons, the *Washington Post* referred to them as: "specifically designed to kill people through the release of neutrons rather than to destroy military installations through heat and blast." The concept originated in Korean War evaluations by American nuclear scientists of the feasibility of nuclear attacks, which led to the conclusion that a weapon that could target a population while leaving cities standing would be optimal. Neutron bombs were considered to have a lower threshold for use than other nuclear weapons, and in the event of war in Korea were to also be used against South Korean cities including Seoul should they be captured by northern forces. (Pincus, Walter, 'Neutron Killer Warhead Buried in ERDA Budget,' *Washington Post,* June 6, 1977.) ('Thaw in the Koreas?,' *Bulletin of Atomic Scientists,* vol. 48, no. 3, April 1992 (p. 20).)

The danger of nuclear attacks on North Korea escalated considerably after the Cold War. Under the U.S. post–Cold War nuclear doctrine, classified as maximum deterrence, nuclear weapons could be used to achieve military victory, were not considered distinct from conventional weapons, and their use could be limited with the intention of tactical gain as a means to win a war. First strikes were permissible.[114] Senior officials, such as Air Force Chief of Staff General Norton Schwartz, and organizations such as the Defense Science Board, thus widely alluded to a battlefield role for nuclear weapons to win wars of the future.[115] Nuclear weapons expert Susan Turner Haynes described this doctrine as "premised on the belief that it is possible to win a nuclear war... war should be conducted similarly regardless of the weapons employed. Nuclear weapons present more risk but do not shift the entire calculus of war. Such a strategy requires what is known as a 'first strike capability.'"[116] While rejecting a no first use policy, the U.S. also rejected the Nuclear Non-Proliferation Treaty linked negative security assurances banning the use of nuclear weapons against non-nuclear states.[117]

United States Strategic Command reports from the 1990s stressed avoiding "portray[ing] ourselves as too rational or cool-headed," while emphasizing the benefits of appearing an irrational superpower able to strike at will at any time including with nuclear weapons.[118] The threat this presented was increased considerably by advances in the capabilities of precision-guided low-yield tactical nuclear weapons, which significantly lowered America's nuclear threshold. As summarized by James Cartwright, a veteran nuclear strategist, in 2016, "what going smaller" with lower yield tactical nuclear weapons did was "to make the weapon more thinkable."[119]

Among targets for potential American military assaults in the post–Cold War years, North Korea appeared by far the most likely to be targeted with tactical nuclear weapons. Not only were its conventional forces by far the most capable among potential U.S. adversaries other than China and Russia, but they were consistently assessed to be well positioned to win a non-nuclear war. Nuclear strikes could be seen as necessary to nullify many of

North Korea's conventional advantages, in particular its very deep and extensive fortifications that were near unrivalled elsewhere in the world and very difficult to destroy with most conventional weapons. The types of targets heavily fortified deep underground ranged from command centers to armaments factories and air defense and ballistic missile sites.[120] Indeed, in the 1990s continued funding for the B-2 bomber program, and its new B61-11 nuclear bomb, were justified on the basis of a continued need to strike "rogue" states, with the new bomb particularly optimized for neutralizing fortified underground facilities such as those that were particularly widespread in North Korea.[121]

For North Korea nuclear weapons provided a valuable asset for managing possible escalation with the United States and deterring conventional or nuclear attacks against it. In contrast to the U.S., however, the country's existential deterrence strategy meant nuclear weapons could not be used as a means to military victory or material gain, while its forces' negligible investment in power projection capabilities and highly defensive orientation left them poorly suited to taking territory or launching invasions that could be supported by nuclear strikes.[122] As observed by defensive neorealist scholar Steven Walt, states could: "construct military postures that are less threatening to others, that don't have the capacity to conquer others easily, that are primarily good for defending your own soil but not for doing much of anything else," with such states having little offensive utility for nuclear weapons, but valuing them as deterrents to aggression.[123]

With North Korea facing a vast Western-led alliance system with the United States Armed Forces at its core, the sustainment of a vast conventional force to deter potential aggression became particularly costly in the post–Cold War years as the country's economy declined and pressure on its defenses grew. With Pyongyang having been under tight Western economic sanctions since long before its nuclear weapons development, which were expected to remain in place regardless of its nuclear activities (see Chapter 7), developing a nuclear deterrent had significant economic benefits. Nuclear weapons have since the 1950s been considered a facilitator of lower defense spending levels. A notable example was the

Soviet Union, which from 1945 had been forced to retain a much larger conventional force in Europe to counterbalance America's nuclear advantage,[124] before the expansion of its own nuclear arsenal in the 1950s facilitated deep cuts.[125] The United States, too, was able to make significant cuts to spending on conventional forces through a greater reliance on nuclear weapons, with a notable example being the reductions to its massive presence in post-war Korea after deploying nuclear weapons from 1958.[126] Israel was similarly able to make major cuts to defense spending as a portion of GDP after obtaining nuclear weapons in the late 1960s.[127] A highly economical asset type, nuclear weapons could provide much greater "bang for their buck" for both offensive purposes and as deterrents.

North Korea was able to make significant reductions to spending on conventional forces from 2009,[128] with spending cuts increasing as the nuclear program further matured.[129] These cuts were cited by analysts as a contributing factor to the country's ability to weather intensifying Western economic warfare efforts.[130] The very low cost of the nuclear program was facilitated by highly modest labor costs and the diversity of the domestic economy, which could produce almost all necessary inputs cheaply particularly if calculated in dollar terms. This was highlighted by North Korean diplomat Kim Min Gyu, who after defecting in 2009 stated: "Actually, what they spend isn't that much. Their workforce works for free and, except for a few key imported parts, they make everything else."[131] Nuclear weapons thus in part represented a response to the post–Cold War challenge of shouldering a much heavier defense burden following the loss of Soviet protection, with economic decline and growing pressure on government spending from that time leading them to be highly prized as a much more cost-effective means of doing so.

The Need to Deter America: The Price of Failure for the North Korean People

The perception in Pyongyang that it remains imperative to maximize capabilities to deter and if necessary combat a potential U.S.-led invasion is firmly rooted both in the country's experience and collective historical memory of the previous U.S.-led invasion launched in September 1950, and in the reinforcing lessons from U.S. and Western forces' conduct in more recent military campaigns. The context of the North Korean population's experience in the Korean War, and the subsequent experiences of other populations placed under the power of North Korea's adversaries, is thus vital to a full comprehension of the 21st century standoff between Pyongyang and Washington and the rationales for the decisions made by DPRK policymakers.

Preceding the invasion of North Korea, Western reports showed a high level of awareness of the widespread welcome that the advancing Korean People's Army received across South Korea in the war's first three months, with southern villagers interviewed perceiving them as liberators and particularly emphasizing their respect for local women.[132] In major cities CIA intelligence reports highlighted that most of the student population actively worked with and welcomed the arrival of the North Koreans.[133] This aligned with reports from the CIA and American observers consistently emphasizing that the results of any fair nationwide elections would almost certainly strongly favor the northern government, despite two thirds of the population living in the south.[134] Knowledge of these popular sympathies may have influenced the decision to order American units to massacre South Korean civilians from the war's earliest days. This was confirmed as official policy in a letter from Ambassador John Muccio to the State Department,[135] and would later be confirmed by the Pentagon's own records.[136] This included orders for Air Force and Navy aviation to strafe civilians, and for ground forces to use handheld weapons to wipe them out, with such orders continuing to be given well into the war.[137]

One of the massacres that gained most publicity was in the village of No Gun Ri, the details of which were revealed in an extensive investigation in the 1990s that included interviews with survivors and with several U.S. Army servicemen.[138] Joe Jackman from the Army 7th Cavalry, 2nd Battalion, for one, recalled being ordered to: "'kill them all.' Then of course there was a lieutenant who was screaming like a mad man: 'fire on everything, kill them all'... Kids, there was kids out there. It didn't matter what it was. 8 to 80, blind, crippled or crazy they [U.S. personnel] shot them. It just seemed like all Koreans were the enemy."[139] Cavalryman Delos Flint described the targets as "civilians just trying to hide."[140]

Survivor Yang Hae Chan recalled: "people piled up the dead like a barricade and hid behind the bodies as a shield against the bullets... I can still see bodies writhing in agony,"[141] with U.S. Army soldiers continuing to fire as the villagers fled and sought cover.[142] George Early of the 7th Cavalry recalled: "Everybody just ceased moving... Because if they move they know they're gonna be fired at some more."[143] Buddy Wenzel of the 7th Cavalry recalled: "Word came through the line, open fire on them [civilians]. They were running toward us and we opened fire... We understood that we were fighting for these people, but we had orders to fire on them and we did."[144] Journalists accompanying the KPA, who arrived at No Gun Ri in the wake of the U.S. Army's withdrawal, reported finding "indescribably gruesome scenes." North Korean journalist Chun Wook reported: "Shrubs and weeds in the area and a creek running through the tunnels were drenched in blood and the area was covered with two or three layers of bodies. About 400 bodies of old and young people and children covered the scene so that it was difficult to walk around without stepping on corpses."[145]

Interviews with American personnel and South Korean survivors provided insight into the widespread massacres ordered across the country, from civilians wading across the Naktong River after the U.S. Army blew the bridges – with many civilians still on them – to those sheltering in a Confucian shrine massacred by the 25th Infantry Division.[146] Thousands taking refuge on a sheltered beach were bombarded without warning on September 1 by the U.S. Navy, despite no North Korean forces being nearby. A South Korean government investigation 40 years later confirmed that the naval units involved had been fully aware that they were targeting civilians and had been under orders to do so.[147]

These accounts were corroborated by other observers on the ground. British writer Elizabeth Comber, who accompanied American forces in the early stages of the war, wrote on July 14, 1950, regarding U.S. conduct: "they think every Korean is an enemy, firing at, and sometimes killing refugees." Two weeks later she wrote: "Day after day with their aircraft the Americans are laying waste towns and cities, killing fifty civilians for every one soldier."[148] Observers sent by the International Association of Democratic Lawyers found that civilians "clearly distinguishable as refugees, whole families including women and children" were "systematically exterminated... refugees were deliberately exterminated in their thousands by American forces."[149] *New York Times* correspondent Charles Grutzner reported "the slaughter of hundreds of South Korean civilians, women as well as men, by some U.S. troops and police of the Republic [of Korea]."[150] The American Newark *Star-Ledger* in July 1950 reported: "It's not the time to be a Korean, for the Yankees are shooting them all." This was corroborated by several other Western sources.[151] The London *Times* observed: "The U.S. Army is falling back before the onslaught, and the retreating army is venting its frustrations, fears, and hate in a deadly way, on any and all Koreans. Troops do not know who are their friends and enemies, and increasingly regard all as enemies."[152]

Journalists with U.S. units described growing hatred towards the supposedly allied local population.[153] Commander of the 1st Cavalry Division Major General Hobart Gay, for one, referred to South Korean refugees as "trash" that "clutter up the roads,"[154] while South Korean soldiers recalled being "repelled by the racism they see and hear every day," and by the rapacious nature of U.S. forces towards Korean women.[155] A *New York Times* correspondent noted that the population saw the KPA "had left their homes and schools standing," while America and its allies "left only blackened spots where towns once stood,[156] with a London *Times* report coming to much the same conclusion.[157]

Gil Insham from the U.S. Army 7th Infantry Division recalled his sergeant organized patrols into villages for the sole purpose of raping Korean women, and once watched him pistol-whip a village elder for not leading him to young women and then rape the old man's wife in front of him. He recalled GIs tortured captured North Koreans for amusement, poking the exposed brains of the wounded and laughing, or tying them to trees and pulling them apart. "I don't know why some of our people did things like that. Maybe they were just like that inside, sadistic," he recalled.[158] South Korean soldiers returned home to stories of their sisters and other family members being targeted for rapes by Western soldiers,[159] while Chinese soldiers recalled finding pictures of naked Korean rape victims in the helmets of dead American personnel.[160]

These resentments built up further from November after the U.S. Armed Forces were forced into the longest retreat in their history by intervening Chinese forces, resulting in "looting, rape and assaults on civilians" as the local population was blamed for the defeat.[161] Officers on the frontlines recalled receiving orders to "to fire directly upon groups of old men, women and children."[162] *New York Times* reporter George Barrett observed that widespread rapes by U.S. and Canadian forces "have created a deep animosity among large sections of the Korean populace," where by contrast Chinese forces "have impressed many Koreans with the discipline of their troops. Many residents of Seoul seem to go out of their way to tell about the good Chinese behaviour, and especially about executions of two rapists the Chinese are said to have held."[163] Koreans on both sides were generally impressed with Chinese conduct and their high level of discipline.[164]

Widespread reports of U.S. and allied forces' massacres across South Korea were strongly corroborated by separate reports of very similar conduct towards the population across North Korea, which was if anything significantly more extreme. Having been forced into almost three months of retreat at the hands of a scantly armed and seriously outnumbered "peasant army," U.S. and other Western forces' conduct was influenced by a strong element of retribution, which was meted out as soon as northern population centers were placed under their power. Multiple sources consistently pointed to widespread rapes and extreme sexual violence by U.S. forces, brutalization of the general population, and destruction and deliberate targeting of cultural and religious heritage. The Women's International Democratic Federation founded in Paris in 1945, a consultant to the United Nations Economic and Social Council considered the most influential women's organization of the post-war era,[165] sent a commission to Korea during the war which concluded, following a detailed survey: "in the period of occupation, hundreds of thousands of civilians, entire families, from old men to little children, have been tortured, beaten to death, burned and buried alive. Thousands of others have perished from hunger and cold in overcrowded prisons in which they were thrown without charges being leveled against them, without investigation, trial or sentence." The commission's report on conduct in the occupied northern capital elaborated:

> The Americans made the Opera and the remains of the adjoining house into an Army-brothel. To this brothel they took by force women and young girls caught in the streets... Many other residents of Pyongyang recounted the atrocities by Americans. Kim Sun Ok, 37, the mother of four children killed by a bomb, stated that she was evacuated in the village by the Americans, among them the secretary of the local women's organization. The Americans led her naked through the streets and later killed her by pushing a red-hot iron bar into her vagina. Her small son was buried alive.

Similar punishments were frequently given to women who resisted rape. In Mih Yen village three women who defended themselves against rape by American soldiers had their breasts cut off. Hot irons were thrust into their vaginas which killed them. Similar incidents were found to have occurred widely, with members of the ruling Korean Workers' Party and affiliated women's organizations consistently singled out for particularly severe torture. These reports were strongly corroborated by a separate parallel investigation by a commission from the International Association of Democratic Lawyers.[166]

British and Australian journalists Alan Winnington and Wilfred Burchett, who gained access to North Korea during the war, closely corroborated the two commissions' findings. Their testimonies were considered invaluable by Western reporters who otherwise had very restricted access to information on military operations in the north due to wartime censorship,[167] with

Burchett considered highly reliable[168] and later consulting White House National Security Advisor Henry Kissinger on the Vietnam War.[169] Interviewing North Korean women captured by U.S. forces one woman, Kim Kyong Suk, gave the following account as several others who had been detained with her sat at the interview, affirmed her story and corrected various dates and details. Kim had been put into a prison for juveniles at Kaesong under the U.S. military occupation, then held with a large group of around 150 women at Inchon. She recalled:

> The Americans treated us like animals from the day we were captured. On the pretext of searching us, they forced us to strip nude. They hurled insults at us. They paraded us naked in the streets with their bayonets prodding us along and almost bursting through our skin. They brought along photographers and took pictures which they later posted on our prison compound notice board. Americans would come with ROK troops and select girls for raping... No one was safe from their bestialities. They even violated one 14-year-old girl whom they had rounded up as a "prisoner of war." At the Inchon camp, two mothers with babies on their backs were repeatedly dragged off at bayonet-point. The children had their mouths gagged while the mothers were taken into the American guards' quarters and raped.

Kim reported that at least one young girl who had suffered from rape and torture lost her mind as a result of the psychological trauma.[170] Winnington and Burchett observed evidence of the North Korean women's testimonies. Where they alleged they had suffered from torture, including nails being put under their fingernails, severe beatings or electric torture, they had the physical scars and burn marks to prove it.[171] The fact that the testimonies of North Korean survivors were so similar to those separately collected from South Korean survivors of similar massacres by the same perpetrators, as well as the testimonies of U.S. personnel themselves, lent them considerable weight. A wide range of sources pointed to very similar conduct, including mass rapes, by Canadian[172] and British personnel.[173]

The sheer scale and extreme nature of the atrocities committed against the civilian population was such that multiple sources concluded that a genocide was being committed against the Korean people. The report of the International Association of Democratic Lawyers commission concluded: "Taking the view that the extensive murders are not the result of individual excesses, but indicate a pattern of behaviour by the U.S. forces throughout the areas occupied by them... the Commission is of the opinion that the American forces are guilty of the crime of Genocide as defined by the [UN] Genocide Convention of 1948."[v] Professor at Song Kong Hoe University in Seoul and a leading member of the government's Truth and Reconciliation Commission Kim Dong Choon published his findings in an article for the *Journal of Genocide Research* in 2004, concluding that the United States Military committed genocide during the Korean War. He cited orders to commit indiscriminate and widespread massacres, such as at No Gun Ri, as evidence, highlighting that vilification of North Korea had "served to justify any methods that the U.S. and South Korean army employed to oppose it."[174] Citing orders to "wipe out all life in tactical sites" when targeting population centers and the intentional targeting of irrigation dams at the onset of rice growing season to starve the North Korean population, among other aspects of the war, American Professor Patricia Hynes reached the same conclusion,[175] as did Ottawa University professor Michel Chossudovsky.[176] Leading American expert on Korean history Professor Bruce Cumings cited the United Nations Genocide Convention and the 1948 Red Cross Convention on the Protection of Civilians in Wartime to conclude that "neither measure had the slightest impact" on U.S. conduct, with the scale on

---

v The convention defines genocide as acts committed "with the intent to destroy, in whole or in part, a national, ethical, racial or religious group." This would include "deliberately inflicting on the group conditions of life calculated to bring about its physical destruction in whole or in part." This definition entered into force in 1951.

which civilians were intentionally targeted leaving the U.S. guilty of genocide against the Korean people.[177]

Regarding American conduct towards South Korean civilians, Kim Dong Choon reported that this was influenced by "deep racial prejudices," observing:

> With total ignorance of Asia, young soldiers regarded Koreans and Chinese as "people without history." They usually called Koreans "gooks," a term used during World War II for Pacific Islanders. The fact that many Korean women in the villages were often raped in front of their husbands and parents has not been a secret among those who experienced the Korean War. It was known that several women were raped before being shot at No Gun Ri. Some eyewitnesses say that U.S. soldiers played with their lives like boys sadistically playing with flies.[178]

A notable indicator of how the Korean War was fought was that the war crimes committed by U.S. and allied forces were used by the defense of Nazi German war criminals to argue, on the basis that their atrocities were no worse than those more recently committed in Korea, that they should have their sentences commuted. Coalition Supreme Commander Matthew Ridgeway, who after Korea served as Supreme Allied Commander in Europe, advocated pardons on the basis that he had himself given orders in Korea to commit crimes no less severe than those issued by the Nazi generals. This may well have included his commands to massacre refugees, firebomb civilian population centers across both Koreas, and "kill everything in front of us, including women and children" during advances in 1951.[179]

In the decades that followed the Korean War armistice the expansion of a vast comfort women system for American personnel in Korea, fueled by trafficking and rapes on a massive scale including of minors and a prevailing debt slavery system,[180] provided further fuel for the North Korean leadership's drive keep their population outside Western control. As a member of the Peace Corps stationed in Korea, who witnessed the comfort women system firsthand, American professor and leading expert on the country Bruce Cumings observed:

> In Seoul women were available on almost every block – in a bathhouse, massage room, restaurant, or in the ubiquitous tea houses all over the city. You could get them very young, probably around twelve; kids were shanghaied into a kind of slavery as they got off the train from the countryside, looking for work to support their peasant families. Kidnapped, gang-raped and beaten by pimps while learning their few necessary words of English, they were ready for the street in a week.... If someone called attention to the ceaseless orgy, all the usual bromine pour forth to drown out the faint cries of peasant girls yanked off a train in Seoul and thrown into a brothel, a thousand little justifications for the abasement of a thousand little girls at American hands.[181]

With South Korean police described as "actively involved in trafficking in women and smuggling them to brothels,"[182] American personnel recalled regarding their peers: "some of them *own* their girls... before leaving Korea, they sell the package to a man who is just coming in,"[183] while comfort women "were property, things, slaves... Racism, sexism – it's all there. The men don't see the women as human beings."[184] Cumings thus recalled from his time in Korea "the social construction of every Korea female as a potential object of pleasure for Americans. It is the most important aspect of the whole relationship and the primary memory of Korea for generations of young American men who have served there."[185] An estimated 1 million Korean women worked in the comfort women system from 1950 to 1971,[186] with approximately 84 percent of Americans deployed in the Korea admitting to having used local comfort women.[187]

The lessons from the Korean War regarding the price paid by populations whose governments failed to protect them from Western forces was strongly reinforced in subsequent years.

While war in Korea was ongoing, a French counterinsurgency campaign in Vietnam saw extreme atrocities committed as part of a policy of collective punishment against areas suspected of supporting Viet Minh fighters, with sexual violence forming a core part of this. "They raped women, sometimes until they died," survivors would recall years later, with villages systematically burned down, civilians blown up in their houses by grenades, and populated areas enduring heavy bombardment causing mass civilian casualties.[188,vi] Public displays of severed heads and public torture of suspected insurgents by French forces were intended to terrorize the population into submission, with beheadings and the taking of trophy skulls having long been a common practice in French colonial wars.[189] In villages suspected of aiding insurgents, French forces singled out pregnant Vietnamese women for rape as a means of cowing dissent, with these often resulting in deaths of the women and their fetuses. Regions such as Thinh Tri, known for making greater contributions to the insurgency, saw villages targeted more harshly. One survivor, Mr. Quyen, recalled that villagers "always begged the soldiers to spare pregnant women" albeit to little avail. He stated regarding one such incident: "Once, our gatekeeper signaled that the French enemy was coming. So we went down to the tunnels, but some did not [manage to come along]. Then the French burned, and killed, and also raped about 10 [pregnant] women. After the raping, the women had to go to other places [mentioning particular places] to be cured. A few of them died immediately after the raping and abuse."[190] The bayoneting of politically suspect pregnant women by colonial forces was also widely reported.[191]

Similarly extreme conduct was widely observed the following decade as U.S. forces largely took over the war effort against the Viet Minh. The most widely publicized incident of a massacre in South Vietnam was the village of Son My, where the civilian population was similarly wiped out on March 16, 1968. The BBC

---

vi For more extensive assessment of U.S. conduct during the Vietnam War see the writer's previous work: *Power and Primacy: A History of Western Intervention in the Asia-Pacific, 2023 Updated Edition,* Oxford, Peter Lang, 2022 (Chapter 8).

described the U.S. Army 23rd Infantry Division "gunning down unarmed men, women, children and babies. Families which huddled together for safety in huts or bunkers were shown no mercy. Those who emerged with hands held high were murdered." "Women were gang raped," with other civilians "beaten with fists and tortured, clubbed with rifle butts and stabbed with bayonets. Some victims were mutilated with the signature 'C Company' carved into the chest."[192] Helicopter gunner Larry Colburn recalled: "These were elders, mothers, children and babies... They [U.S. personnel] come into a town and rape the women, kill the babies, kill everyone... They were butchering people."[193] Over 500 civilians were killed without warning including infants and the elderly, with many women and young girls gang raped.[194,vii]

Alongside massacres, the torture of civilians was also highly common using fists, sticks, bats, water and electric shocks,[195] as was the rape of women and children often carried out using bottles and rifles.[196] It was also common to execute women following rapes, with perpetrators referred to as "double veterans."[197] One veteran described such an incident as follows: "After we raped her, took her cherry [virginity] from her, after we shot her in the head... we literally start stomping her body. And everybody was laughing about it. It's like seeing the lions around a just-killed zebra. You see them in these animal pictures, Wild Kingdom or something. The whole pride comes around and they start feasting on the body."[198] Serviceman John Ketwig recalled that in another

---

vii Private First Class Michael Bernhardt recalled: "I walked up and saw these guys... Setting fire to the hootches and huts and waiting for people to come out and then shooting them... going into the hootches and shooting them up... gathering people in groups and shooting them... As I walked in you could see piles of people all through the village... all over. They were gathered up into large groups. I saw them shoot an M79 [grenade launcher] into a group of people who were still alive. But it was mostly done with a machine gun. They were shooting women and children just like anybody else. We met no resistance and I only saw three captured weapons. We had no casualties. It was just like any other Vietnamese village – old papa-sans, women and kids. As a matter of fact, I don't remember seeing one military-age male in the entire place, dead or alive." (Hersh, Seymour M., 'Eyewitness accounts of the My Lai massacre; story by Seymour Hersh,' *The Plain Dealer*, November 20, 1969.)

incident when three young women were captured: "everybody circled around and they tortured these women with lit cigarettes... the one girl, they held her down and put the hose from the fire truck between her legs and turned on the water and exploded her. And the explosion of body fluids splashed across our faces." He described it as a "revenge type of thing: hate against the Vietnamese, the 'gooks.'"[199]

Regarding the tendency for personnel to target civilians in retribution for military frustrations, one veteran recalled: "in Vietnam you identify every gook with the enemy... You feel it's their fault we're there. If it weren't for the Vietnamese, we wouldn't be there."[200] Another stated to justify the rape of a Vietnamese woman: "the general attitude was, we are over here helping these people. The least they could do was lay a little leg on us."[201] Another veteran, immediately after describing how he and others had raped and murdered a Vietnamese girl in front of her father, complained that the population ought to be more appreciative of American support. "We expected them to run out and welcome us like that World War II type of thing ... But they were a little standoffish," he stated, while further implying either that the rape was punishment for this attitude or that sexual access had been an expected reward.[202]

Instructors and commanders very widely condoned and at times promoted rape, often as a means of enhancing the performances of personnel.[203] Based on widespread interviews with American veterans, researcher Elizabeth Anderson highlighted a widespread "belief that Vietnamese women's role in the war was sexual gratification of American men... an understanding of Vietnamese women as existing for the sexual gratification of Americans."[204] This went so far that "almost all of the men whose testimonies I have reviewed say that the leadership within their unit either directly encouraged sexual violence or passively allowed it to exist." In part, as a result, "sexual violence was an indisputable part of the war, and undercurrents of gendered violence appear in almost every historical account of atrocities in Vietnam."[205] Infantryman Michael Farrell, for one, recalled being instructed by his Korean War veteran commander: "'If there's a woman in a hootch, lift up her dress, you know, and tell by her sex; if it's a man, kill him; and if it's a female, rape her.'"[206] Other personnel reported that their commanders instructed units to kidnap women for "entertainment" while on patrol, who would face hours of gang rape and then death.[207] At times commanding officers saw that they had to outperform their subordinates in rapes to cement their positions of leadership, with one recalling: "I was in charge of a group of animals, and I had to be the biggest animal there."[208] Rape and threat of rape were widely used strategically as well as recreationally both to enforce submission and to obtain information from both prisoners and civilians,[209] as well as intimidating insurgents and their supporters.[210] As one veteran testified: "It makes a lasting impression on some guy – some 'zip' – that's watching his daughter get worked over. So we have a better opportunity of keeping him in line."[211]

Personnel from the 23rd Infantry Division recalled men raped Vietnamese women "on the average of once every third day,"[212] with this widely corroborated by reports from personnel from other units,[213] as well as by press reporters.[214] Rapes of pregnant women were also reported widely.[215] One Vietnamese survivor, interviewed as "Mr. Bao," recalled that in areas suspected of supporting insurgents: "The American soldiers killed every family they found in the shelters. They rounded up the women. They cut off their ears, and they raped them. They threw old people in the river."[216] Journalist and expert on the Vietnam War Nick Turse reported regarding the sexual violence committed: "I felt I didn't have the language to describe exactly what I found in the cases, because rape or even gang rape didn't seem to convey the level of sexual sadism."[217] The conduct of personnel on the ground, and a massive bombing campaign from the air targeting population centers across the country with even more ordnance than that seen in Korea, were central contributors to the death toll of 3.8 million Vietnamese during the war, the large majority of which were civilians.[218] Reports from all sides of U.S. and Western forces' conduct in Vietnam and Korea closely corroborated one another.

With the United States and its Western allies expanding their military operations considerably in the aftermath of the Cold War, conduct towards non-Western populations under their power was shown to have improved little despite the much lower intensity of the wars of the era. Examples ranged from the Rwandan refugees targeted by French personnel for gang rapes,[219] to French forces' mass rapes in the Central African Republic including forced bestiality for young women,[220] and Italian and Belgian personnel's torture of Somali civilians.[221] With an invasion of North Korea having been seriously considered by the George W. Bush administration before Iraq was decided on as the priority target (see Chapter 2), the conduct of U.S. forces once the Iraqi population was placed under their power carried particularly relevant lessons.

Notable insight into U.S. conduct was provided by Representative Duncan D. Hunter, a Marine Corps Iraq War veteran, who said his military unit "killed probably hundreds of civilians." This statement was an attempt to justify Navy SEAL chief Edward Gallagher's killing of an Iraqi teenage combatant prisoner, to which Hunter responded: "I frankly don't care if he [the prisoner] was killed. I just don't care. Even if everything that the prosecutors say is true in this case, then, you know, Eddie Gallagher should still be given a break, I think." Claiming Gallagher was not guilty of any unique crime, and implying a prevailing norm among personnel in Iraq, Hunter stated: "Well, then, how do you judge me? So, I was an artillery officer, and we fired hundreds of rounds into Fallujah, killed probably hundreds of civilians." His statement ultimately pointed to the fact that only a small fraction of war crimes committed were ever publicized, with the majority being overlooked. Gallagher had killed the wounded prisoner with a knife before posing with his corpse for photos which he sent to friends with the caption: "Good story behind this, got him with my hunting knife," with SEALs under his command subsequently warned against reporting his actions.[222] Hunter defended this on the basis that he had also posed for pictures with killed Iraqis.[223]

Regarding the conditioning personnel received preceding operations, U.S. Marine sniper Rudy Reyes recalled that before being sent to Baghdad in 2003 he was desensitized with footage of men having their heads blown off by sniper rifles, including "in slow motion, head expanding three times the size, then vacuum collapse, then brains and skull." This was part of his being "systematically programmed" to kill.[224] More extreme methods of desensitizing at the time included junior Australian personnel in Afghanistan being given civilians to kill by hand by their seniors – a mental preparation known as "blooding."[225] British special forces had a near identical practice.[226]

U.S. Army Corporal Michael Prysner was among many Iraq veterans who stressed that, much like in Korea and Vietnam, racial dehumanization of the population significantly influenced American conduct. A Marine interviewed separately observed to this effect "what's inherent to that training? Well people in the Middle East are referred to as sand niggers, hajis, camel jockeys, towel heads, barbarians, terrorists. Women [as] bitches, c***s." These prevailing attitudes which fueled misconduct, according to him, were "all firmly entrenched in the training, all firmly entrenched in the ideology. All firmly entrenched in the linguistics and lexicon within the military." The Marine recalled that on the basis of these perceptions intentionally instilled in personnel: "If they looked like an insurgent you did what you wanted for them… The Marines took it upon themselves to shoot at, beat, rob, rape, kill whomever they wanted to. And that's being proposed on the news as a few bad apples, an isolated incident."[227,viii]

Following the toppling of the Iraqi government U.S. forces made extensive use of depleted uranium weaponry in engagements with insurgents, including when firing into population centers.[228] After intensive Marine bombardment of Fallujah from 2004, Iraqi doctors observed a staggering increase in infant mortality, cancer

---

viii British personnel in 2019 recalled that rules of engagement in Iraq and Afghanistan allowed them to kill suspicious looking unarmed civilians, with one describing the result as a "killing spree." In the Iraqi city of Basra anyone holding a phone or a shovel could be considered a combatant and shot on the spot. One serviceman recalled: "We were shooting old men, young men. This is what I witnessed. I have never seen such lawlessness." They revealed instances in which young boys were killed, with weapons then planted on them to retrospectively justify this, with commanders providing assurances that they would be protected if found out. (Cobain, Ian, 'British army permitted shooting of civilians in Iraq and Afghanistan,' *Middle East Eye,* February 4, 2019.)

and leukaemia, far exceeding even rates seen among survivors of Hiroshima and Nagasaki. *The Independent* summarized in 2011:

> Iraqi doctors in Fallujah have complained since 2005 of being overwhelmed by the number of babies with serious birth defects, ranging from a girl born with two heads to paralysis of the lower limbs. They said they were also seeing far more cancers than they did before the battle for Fallujah between U.S. troops and insurgents. Their claims have been supported by a survey showing a four-fold increase in all cancers and a 12-fold increase in childhood cancer in under-14s.[229]

Highly similar effects had been seen in parts of Yugoslavia and in southern Iraq after the Gulf War, where depleted uranium rounds were also widely used by U.S. forces.[230] Professor Chris Busby, one of the authors of a survey of 4,800 Fallujah residents, stated regarding the cause of a surge in cancers and birth defects that "to produce an effect like this, some very major mutagenic exposure must have occurred in 2004 when the attacks happened." The fallout, he concluded, suggested use of uranium weapons, with the speed at which cancers affected people being particularly striking. The survey was carried out by 11 researchers who visited 711 houses in Fallujah, and concluded that the effects on the population were "similar to that in the Hiroshima survivors who were exposed to ionizing radiation from the bomb and uranium in the fallout."[231] Where the Iraqi government had given up its weapons of mass destruction, this paved the way for its adversaries to use unconventional weapons with very similar effects on its populated areas, as well as illegal use of white phosphorous in such areas.[232]

The treatment of Iraqis suspected of aiding the insurgency was extreme, with many held without charge or legal access, and severely tortured or killed in custody. The Washington Post described "prisoners forced to retrieve their food from toilets" and produced 65 pages worth of sworn statements. It reported:

> The detainees said they were savagely beaten and repeatedly humiliated sexually by American soldiers... pressed to denounce Islam or were force-fed pork and liquor. Many provided graphic details of how they were sexually humiliated and assaulted, threatened with rape, and forced to masturbate in front of female soldiers... Most of the detainees said in the statements that they were stripped upon their arrival to Tier 1A, forced to wear women's underwear, and repeatedly humiliated in front of one another and American soldiers.[233]

After her arest for suspected of ties to insurgents, Iraqi businesswoman Huda Alazawi recalled beatings and torture in custody, which included the use of dogs and extended solitary confinement in 1x1 meter spaces, as well as the sexual abuse and subsequent torture to death of her brother, whose corpse was thrown in her jail cell, and occasional rapes including of minors.[234] During the separately reported rape of a 15–18 year old boy, other prisoners heard his screams and watched the assault, with a female soldier taking pictures. "The kid was hurting very bad," one prisoner recalled. He observed other incidents of torture, including a detainee being tied to his bed and sodomized by U.S. personnel with a phosphoric light. Another recalled regarding that incident that the Iraqi victim: "was screaming for help... There was also a white female soldier, short, she was taking pictures."[235] Others recalled being beaten severely, having U.S. personnel step on their heads, and having the chemicals from phosphoric lights poured on them. "They were taking pictures of me during all these instances," one victim recalled, and that he was subsequently sodomized with a nightstick.[236]

Other detainees recalled highly similar conduct.[237] Prisoner Hiadar al-Aboodi, recalled: "They forced us to walk like dogs on our hands and knees. And we had to bark like a dog, and if we didn't do that they started hitting us hard on our face and chest with no mercy. After that, they took us to our cells, took the mattresses out and dropped water on the floor and they made us sleep on our stomachs on the floor with the bags on our head and they took pictures of everything."[238]

Only a small portion of the evidence of abuses would ever become available to the public, although journalist Seymour Hersh who gained special access to fuller evidence recalled of its contents:

> Some of the worst things that happened you don't know about, okay? Videos, um, there are women there. Some of you may have read that they were passing letters out, communications out to their men. This is at Abu Ghraib … The women were passing messages out saying, "Please come and kill me, because of what's happened" and basically what happened is that those women who were arrested with young boys, children in cases that have been recorded. The boys were sodomized with the cameras rolling. And the worst above all of that is the soundtrack of the boys shrieking that your government has.[239]

Journalist Rick Pearlstein recalled after hearing him speak that Hersh "said that after he broke Abu Ghraib people are coming out of the woodwork to tell him this stuff. He said he had seen all the Abu Ghraib pictures. He said, 'You haven't begun to see evil...' then trailed off. He said, 'horrible things done to children of women prisoners, as the cameras run.' He looked frightened."[240] Reports from U.S. military personnel, alongside photographic evidence, verified claims of severe sexual and other abuse including arranging male prisoners naked in piles and jumping on them, forcing prisoners to rape one another and simulating electric torture.[241] U.S. Army Major General Antonio Taguba, commenting on the photos, confirmed that they "show torture, abuse, rape and every indecency."[242] Much of the footage was not released, with President Obama warning that a release would "inflame anti-American public opinion."[243]

President Emeritus of the International Association of Middle East Studies and consultant to the State Department and Pentagon Raymond Baker summarized the invasion's consequences as follows: "the deaths of over 1 million civilians [by 2007]; the degradation in social infrastructure, including electricity, potable water, and sewage systems; the targeted assassination of over 400 academics and professionals and the displacement of approximately 4 million refugees and internally displaced people." This was "compounded by unprecedented levels of cultural devastation, attacks on national archives and monuments that represent the historical identity of the Iraqi people" – a conclusion widely shared.[244] Other consequences included the fleeing of approximately 40 percent of the Iraqi middle class within four years,[245] the flight of 2 million refugees abroad and internal displacement of a further 1.7 million – figures which only increased in the following years.[246] Where Iraqi women had enjoyed some of the Middle East's highest levels of rights protection and social participation, the situation deteriorated sharply from 2003 and the trafficking in women and girls both within and outside the country for sexual exploitation became widespread.[247]

Where they were not properly deterred, America and the wider Western world would not hesitate to bring ruin and immeasurable suffering to populations that remained outside their control, which was a lesson learned at cost to the peoples of both North and South Korea during the Korean War, and subsequently strongly reinforced by Western militaries' conduct over the following seven decades. While several volumes could be written on this pattern of conduct and its consistency from No Gun Ri to Abu Ghraib, and several centuries back into the colonial era, this section provides a very brief summary to highlight the understandings that have guided North Korean policymaking for over seven decades.

In contrast to the vast majority of countries, where Western dominance of the information space and the states' perceived need for positive relations with the Western world have limited education, coverage and discourse on these histories, they feature prominently in North Korean media ranging from school textbooks to museums. The experiences of the Korean War have continued to be conveyed in education, national songs, and their own dedicated museums such as the Sinchon Museum of American War Atrocities, rebuilt in 2015, and the National House of Class Education first opened in 2016. They have also remained formative influences in the lives of many in the country's leadership into the 21st century, with many of them now in their 80s or 90s. This indicates both the continuing influence of the Korean War historical memory, and its reinforcement through awareness of the many corroborating cases since then, in the leadership and across society.

Endnotes

1 McCann, David R. and Strauss, Barry S., *War and Democracy: A Comparative Study of the Korean War and the Peloponnesian War*, Abingdon, Routledge, 2015 (p. 59).

Cumings, Bruce, *The Korean War: A History*, New York, Modern Library, 2010 (pp. 70, 133).

'최소 60만명, 최대 120만명!' ['More than 600,000, less than 1,200,000!'], *Hankyoreh*, June 20, 2001.

Hanley, Charles J. and Change, Jae-Soon, 'Summer of Terror: At least 100,000 said executed by Korean ally of U.S. in 1950,' *The Asia-Pacific Journal,* vol. 7, issue 7, July 2, 2008.

2 Wolfowitz, Paul, 'The United States and Iraq,' in: Calabrese, John (ed.), *The Future of Iraq*, Washington, DC, Middle East Institute, 1997 (pp. 107–113).

3 Halberstam, David, *The Fifties*, New York, Ballantine Books, 2012 (p. 71).

4 Cumings, Bruce, *The Korean War: A History,* New York, Modern Library, 2010 (p. 27).

5 Fehrenbach, T. R., *This Kind of War: The Classic Korean War History, Fiftieth Anniversary Edition*, Lincoln, NE, Potomac Books, 2001 (pp. 71, 78).

Gugeler, Russell A., *Combat Actions in Korea*, University Press of the Pacific, 2005 (p. 16).

Cumings, Bruce, *The Korean War: A History,* New York, Modern Library, 2010 (Chapter 1).

Alexander, Bevin, *Korea: The First War We Lost*, New York, Hippocrene Books, 2003 (pp. 66, 67).

Ecker, Richard E., *Battles of the Korean War: A Chronology, with Unit-by-Unit United States Casualty Figures & Medal of Honor Citations*, Jefferson, NC, McFarland & Company, 2004 (p. 6).

'"Kill 'em All": American War Crimes in Korea,' *Timewatch,* Season 21, Episode 4, aired February 1, 2002.

Spurr, Russell, *Enter the Dragon: China's Undeclared War Against the U.S. in Korea, 1950–1951,* New York, William Morrow, 2010 (p. 21).

6 Cumings, Bruce, *The Korean War: A History,* New York, Modern Library, 2010 (p. 30).

7 Korea Institute of Military History, *The Korean War*, Lincoln, NE, University of Nebraska Press, 1997 (pp. 1, 511).

Stokesbury, James L., *A Short History of the Korean War,* New York, William Morrow, 1988 (pp. 58–61).

Levine, Alan J., *Stalin's Last War: Korea and the Approach to World War III,* Jefferson, NC, McFarland & Company, 2005 (p. 71).

Hanley, Charles J., *Ghost Flames: Life and Death in a Hidden War, Korea 1950–1953,* New York, PublicAffairs, 2020 (p. 110).

8 Stone, I. F., *The Hidden History of the Korean War*, Amazon Media, 2014 (Chapter 13).

9 Appleman, Roy E., *South to the Naktong, North to the Yalu: United States Army in the Korean War*, Washington, DC, Department of the Army, 1998 (p. 546).

10 Hanley, Charles J., *Ghost Flames: Life and Death in a Hidden War, Korea 1950–1953,* New York, PublicAffairs, 2020 (p. 209).

Hastings, Max, *The Korean War,* London, Michael Joseph, 1988 (p. 280).

Blair, Clay, *The Forgotten War: America in Korea, 1950–1953,* New York, Times Books, 1987 (pp. 528, 529).

11 Cumings, Bruce, *The Korean War: A History,* New York, Modern Library, 2010 (p. 31).

12 *TIME Magazine*, October 6, 1950.

Stone, I. F., *The Hidden History of the Korean War*, Amazon Media, 2014 (Chapter 13).

Schobell, Andrew and Sanford, John M., *North Korea's Military Threat: Pyongyang's Conventional Forces, Weapons of Mass Destruction, and Ballistic Missiles*, U.S. Army War College Strategic Studies Institute, April 2007 (p. 62).

13 Spurr, Russell, *Enter the Dragon: China's Undeclared War Against the U.S. in Korea, 1950–1951,* New York, William Morrow, 2010 (pp. 104–105).

14 Hanley, Charles J., *Ghost Flames: Life and Death in a Hidden War, Korea 1950–1953,* New York, PublicAffairs, 2020 (p. 126).

U.S. News and World Report, November 3, 2003.

15 Spurr, Russell, *Enter the Dragon: China's Undeclared War Against the U.S. in Korea, 1950–1951,* New York, William Morrow, 2010 (p. 284).

16 Hastings, Max, *The Korean War,* London, Michael Joseph, 1988 (p. 22).

17 Cumings, Bruce, *Origins of the Korean War: The Roaring of the Cataract, 1947–1950, Volume 2*, Princeton, Princeton University Press, 2004 (p. 693).

Schnabel, James F. and Watson, Robert J., *The Korean War: Part I, History of the Joint Chiefs of Staff* (pp. 178–181).

18 *United States Army in the Korean War, Volume 4*, Washington, DC, Government Printing Office, 1961 (p. 84).

19 Weiner, Tim, *Legacy of Ashes: The History of the CIA*, New York, Anchor Books, 2008 (Chapter 6).

20 *North Korean Intentions and Capabilities with Respect to South Korea*, Special National Intelligence Estimate, Number 14.2-67, Central Intelligence Agency, September 21, 1967 (p. 6).

21 Record of Conversation between Premier Kim and the Chinese Friendship Delegation, August 20, 1965, PRC FMA 106-01479-05 (pp. 46–51).

22 *Tuoi Tre Weekend Edition,* August 17, 2007 (http://tuoitre.vn/Tuoi-tre-cuoi-tuan/273979/14-chien-binh-Trieu-Tien-tren-bau-troi-Viet-Nam.html).

Nguyen, Kham and Park, Ju Min, 'From comrades to assassins, North Korea and Vietnam eye new chapter with Trump-Kim summit,' *Reuters*, February 15, 2019.

Military History Institute of Vietnam, *Lich su khang chien chong My, cuu nuoc, 1954–1975, Tap V: tong tien cong va noi day 1968* [History of the Resistance War Against the Americans to Save the Nation, 1954–1975, Volume V: The 1968 General Offensive and Uprising], Hanoi, People's Army Publishing House, 2001 (p. 271).

Kim, Jiyul, 'North Korea in the Vietnam War,' in: Sorley, Lewis and Yarborough, Tom and Celeski, Joseph, *Year of the Cock – 1969,* Houston, Radix Press, 2017 (pp. 106–145).

Sổ công tác của Đại tướng Văn Tiến Dũng [General Van Tien Dung's Work Notebook], General Staff Headquarters, Historical Review Section, vol. 20, no. 59.

23 Toperczer, István, *MiG-17 and MiG-19 Units of the Vietnam War*, Oxford, Osprey, 2001 (pp. 14–19).

24 Schlight, Colonel John, *The War in South Vietnam: The Years of the Offensive, 1965–1968*, Washington, DC, Air Force History and Museums Program, 1999 (p. 53).

25 Author's visit to the Victorious Fatherland Liberation War Museum, May 25, 2016.

26 Nguyen, Kham and Park, Ju Min, 'From comrades to assassins, North Korea and Vietnam eye new chapter with Trump-Kim summit,' *Reuters*, February 15, 2019.

27 Kim, Jiyul, 'North Korea in the Vietnam War,' in: Sorley, Lewis and Yarborough, Tom and Celeski, Joseph, *Year of the Cock – 1969,* Houston, Radix Press, 2017 (pp. 106–145).

28 El-Shazly, Saad, *The Crossing of the Suez*, American Mideast Research, 2003 (pp. 81–83).

Bechtol, Bruce and Maxwell, David, 'North Korean Military Proliferation in the Middle East and Africa: A Book Launch,' presentation at the Korea Economic Institute of America, September 25, 2018.

Golan, John W., *Lavi: The United States, Israel, and a Controversial Fighter Jet*, Sterling, VA, Potomac Books, 2016 (p. 15).

McCarthy, David, *The Sword of David: The Israeli Air Force at War*, New York, Skyhorse, 2014 (p. 9).

29 Gills, Barry K., *Korea versus Korea: A Case of Contested Legitimacy*, London, Routledge, 1996 (p. 64).

30 Mansourov, Alexandre, 'North Korea: Entering Syria's Civil War,' *38 North*, November 25, 2013.

31 Berger, Andrea, *Target Markets: North Korea's Military Customers in the Sanctions Era*, Abingdon, Routledge, 2017 (pp. 64–65).

32 Wren, Christopher S., 'Libya's Identity Blurred by Ties With East, West and Terrorism,' *New York Times*, October 14, 1979.

33 James, W. Martin III, *A Political History of the Civil War in Angola: 1974–1990*, New Brunswick, Transaction Publishers, 2011 (pp. 207–214, 239–245).

Bechtol, Bruce E., 'North Korea and Support to Terrorism: An Evolving History,' *Journal of Strategic Security*, vol. 3, no. 2, Summer 2010 (p. 47).

34 Telegram from AmEmbassy, Moscow, to SecState, Subject: North Korea, November 14, 1967. Folder POL 7, KOR N, 1/1/67. Box 2262. RG 59, General Records of the Department of State, Central Foreign Policy Files 1967–1969, Political and Defense, POL 7 KOR N to POL 7 KOR N. NARA II.

35 Record of Conversation between N.G. Sudarikov and Pak Seong Cheol, a Member of the Political Committee of the Workers' Party of Korea, April 16, 1969, History and Public Policy Program Digital Archive, Russian State Archive of Contemporary History, fond 5, opis 61, delo 466, listy 199–127.

36 Jackson, Van, *On the Brink: Trump, Kim, and the Threat of Nuclear War*, Cambridge, Cambridge University Press, 2018 (p. 22).

Jackson, Van, 'The EC-121 Shoot Down and North Korea's Coercive Theory of Victory,' *Wilson Center*, April 13, 2017.

37 Record of Conversation between N.G. Sudarikov and Heo Dam, the Leader of the Ministry of Foreign Affairs of DPRK, April 16, 1969, History and Public Policy Program Digital Archive, Russian State Archive of Contemporary History, fond 5, opis 61, delo 462, listy 71–74, obtained by Sergey Radchenko and translated by Gary Goldberg.

38 Nixon, Richard M., *RN: The Memoirs of Richard Nixon*, New York, Warner Books, 1978 (pp. 473–475).

39 Stokes, Henry Scott, 'North Korea Disputes U.S. Over Missile-Firing Incident,' *New York Times*, August 29, 1981.

40 Graham, Richard H., *The Complete Book of the SR-71 Blackbird: The Illustrated Profile of Every Aircraft, Crew, and Breakthrough of the World's Fastest Stealth Jet*, Minneapolis, Zenith Press, 2015 (p. 251).

41 Schobell, Andrew and Sanford, John M., *North Korea's Military Threat: Pyongyang's Conventional Forces, Weapons of Mass Destruction, and Ballistic Missiles*, U.S. Army War College Strategic Studies Institute, April 2007 (pp. 63–64).

Dreazen, Yochi, 'Here's what war with North Korea would look like,' *Vox*, February 8, 2018.

42 Bermudez, Joseph S., *North Korean Special Forces*, Coulsdon, Jane's Publishing, 1988 (p. 2).

43 Fitzpatrick, Mark, *North Korean Security Challenges: A Net Assessment*, London, International Institute for Strategic Studies, 2011 (p. 50).

44 Jannuzi, Frank Sampson, 'Can the United States Cause the Collapse of North Korea? Should We Try?,' *Council on Foreign Relations*, January 13, 1999.

45 Gady, Franz-Stefan, 'Is North Korea Fighting for Assad in Syria?,' *The Diplomat*, March 24, 2016.

46 '"Kill 'em All": American War Crimes in Korea,' *Timewatch,* Season 21, Episode 4, aired February 1, 2002.

Williams, Jeremy, '"Kill 'em All": The American Military in Korea,' *BBC History,* 2011.

Hanley, Charles J., 'No Gun Ri: Official Narrative and Inconvenient Truths,' *Critical Asian Studies*, vol. 42, issue 4, 2010 (pp. 589–622).

47 Stone, I. F., *The Hidden History of the Korean War*, Amazon Media, 2014 (Chapter 24).

48 Acheson, Dean G., *Present at the Creation: My Years in the State Department*, London, W. W. Norton, 1969 (pp. 463, 464).

Far Eastern Air Forces HQ to MacArthur, November 8, 1950, RG 6 Far East Command Box 1, General Files 10, Correspondence Nov.–Dec. 1950, MacArthur Memorial Library, Norfolk, VA.

49 Harden, Blaine, 'The U.S. war crime North Korea won't forget,' *Washington Post*, March 24, 2015.

50 Jackson, Robert, *Air War Over Korea*, London, Ian Allen, 1973 (p. 61).

51 Thames Television, transcript of the fifth seminar for *Korea: The Unknown War*, November 1986.

52 Dean, William F., *General Dean's Story, as told to William L. Worden*, New York, Viking Press, 1954 (p. 274).

53 LeMay, Curtis E. with MacKinlay, Kantor, *Mission with LeMay: My Story*, New York, Doubleday, 1965 (p. 382).

54 Cumings, Bruce, 'Nuclear Threats Against North Korea: Consequences of the "forgotten" war,' *The Asia-Pacific Journal*, vol. 3, issue 1, January 13, 2005 (p. 2).

55 Stone, I. F., *The Hidden History of the Korean War*, Amazon Media, 2014 (Chapter 34).

56 Garner, Dwight, 'Carpet-Bombing Falsehoods About a War That's Little Understood,' *New York Times*, July 21, 2010.

Tanaka, Yuki and Young, Marilyn, *Bombing Civilians: A Twentieth Century History*, New York, New Press, 2009 (p. 157).

57 Fifeld, Anna, 'Why Does North Korea Hate the United States? Let's go back to the Korean War,' *Washington Post,* May 17, 2017.

58 Bullene, E. F., 'Wonder Weapon: Napalm,' *Army Combat Forces Journal*, November 1952.

'Napalm Jelly Bombs Prove a Blazing Success in Korea,' *All Hands*, April 1951.

Townsend, Earle J., 'They Don't Like Hell Bombs,' *Armed Forces Chemical Journal*, January 1951.

59 Deane, Hugh, *The Korean War, 1945–1953*, San Francisco, China Books and Periodicals, 1999 (p. 144).

MacDonald, Callum A., *Korea: The War Before Vietnam*, London, Macmillan, 1986 (pp. 234, 235).

McCormack, Gavan, *Cold War, Hot War: An Australian Perspective on the Korean War*, Sydney, Hale and Iremonger, 1983 (p. 132).

60 Cumings, Bruce, *The Korean War: A History,* New York, Modern Library, 2010 (p. 152).

Williams, Christopher, *Leadership Accountability in a Globalizing World*, London, Palgrave Macmillan, 2006 (p. 185).

61 Deane, Hugh, *The Korean War, 1945–1953*, San Francisco, China Books and Periodicals, 1999 (p. 191).

62 Talmadge, Eric, '64 years after Korean War, North Korea still digging up bombs,' *Associated Press*, July 24, 2017.

'Legacy of Terror: Dozens of Unexploded American Bombs Found at Construction Site of Pyongyang General Hospital,' *Military Watch Magazine,* May 19, 2020.

63 Connelly, Matthew, Notes on Cabinet Meeting, September 12, 1952, Connelly Papers, Harry S. Truman Library.

64 G-3 381 Pacific, G-3 Staff Study, 'Capability of U.S. Army to Implement Commander in Chief, United Nations Command Operations Plan,' ca. 21, January 1953.

Levine, Alan J., *Stalin's Last War: Korea and the Approach to World War III,* Jefferson, NC, McFarland & Company, 2005 (pp. 277, 278, 280).

Edwards, Paul M., *Historical Dictionary of the Korean War,* Lanham, Scarecrow Press, 2010 (p. 212).

65 U.S. Department of State, *Foreign Relations of the United States 1951, Vol. VII, Part 1, Korea and China,* U.S. Government Printing Office, Washington, DC, 1983 (pp. 667–668, 881–882, 1106–1109).

Foot, Rosemary, *The Wrong War*, Ithaca, Cornell University Press, 1985 (pp. 148–153, 176).

Hermes, Walter, *Truce Tent and Fighting Front,* Washington, DC, Department of the Army, 1966 (pp. 56, 107).

Pogue, Forrest C., *George C. Marshall, Vol. 4: Statesman, 1945–1959,* New York, Viking, 1987 (p. 488).

66 Hanley, Charles J., *Ghost Flames: Life and Death in a Hidden War, Korea 1950–1953,* New York, PublicAffairs, 2020 (p. 387).

Daily Worker, July 21, 1952.

Futrell, Robert F., *The United States Air Force in Korea 1950–1953*, Washington, DC, Office of Air Force History, 1983 (pp. 512, 515, 517).

67 *SSSR i Korea* [The USSR and Korea], Moscow, USSR Academy of Sciences, 1988 (p. 256).

68 Callum MacDonald, *Korea: The War Before Vietnam*, London, Macmillan, 1986 (pp. 241, 242).

Chomsky, Noam, *Who Rules the World?*, London, Hamish Hamilton, 2016 (pp. 132, 133).

Cumings, Bruce, *The Korean War: A History,* New York, Modern Library, 2010 (p. 147).

69 Futrell, Robert F., *United States Air Force Operations in the Korean Conflict,* 1 July 1952–27 July 1953, USAF Historical Study no. 127, Maxwell Air Force Base, USAF Historical Division, Research Studies Institute, Air University, 1956 (pp. 93, 126).

70 Levine, Alan J., *Stalin's Last War: Korea and the Approach to World War III,* Jefferson, NC, McFarland & Company, 2005 (p. 283).

71 Merrill, Frank J., *A Study of the Aerial Interdiction of Railways during the Korean War*, Fort Leavenworth, Texas, U.S. Army Command and General Staff College, 1965 (pp. 91–93).

Futrell, Robert F., *United States Air Force Operations in the Korean Conflict,* 1 July 1952–27 July 1953, USAF Historical Study no. 127, Maxwell Air Force Base, USAF Historical Division, Research Studies Institute, Air University, 1956 (p. 473).

Armstrong, Charles K., 'The Destruction and Reconstruction of North Korea, 1950–1960,' *The Asia-Pacific Journal* 7, issue 0, March 16, 2009. Balázs Szalontai, 'The Four Horsemen of the Apocalypse in North Korea: The Forgotten Side of a Not-So-Forgotten War,' in: Springer, Chris and Szalontai, Balázs, *North Korea Caught in Time: Images of War and Reconstruction*, Reading, Garnet Publishing, 2010 (pp. xiv–xv).

72 U.S. Department of State, *Foreign Relations of the United States 1952–1954, Vol. XV, Part 1, Korea*, Washington, DC, U.S. Government Printing Office, 1984 (pp. 1082–1086).

73 *Congressional Record: Proceedings and Debates of the 86th Congress*, Vol. 105, Part 7, May 20–June 4, 1959 (p. 8703).

Futrell, Robert Frank, *The United States Air Force in Korea, 1950–1953,* Washington, DC, Office of Air Force History, 1983 (p. 667).

U.S. Department of State, *Foreign Relations of the United States 1952–1954, Vol. XV, Part 1, Korea*, Washington, DC, U.S. Government Printing Office, 1984 (p. 1068).

Levine, Alan J., *Stalin's Last War: Korea and the Approach to World War III,* Jefferson, NC, McFarland & Company, 2005 (pp. 283–284).

74 U.S. Department of State, *Foreign Relations of the United States, 1952–54, Vol. V, Part 1, Western European Security*, Washington, DC, U.S. Government Printing Office, 1983 (pp. 1811–1813).

Freedman, Lawrence, *The Evolution of Nuclear Strategy*, London, Macmillan, 1983 (p. 85).

75 Millet, Alan R., *Their War for Korea,* Washington, DC, Brassey's, 2002 (p. 169).

76 Outgoing Classified Message Joint Chiefs of Staff 87570 to Commander-in-Chief, Far East, Tokyo, July 31, 1950, Truman Library.

77 Truman, Margaret, *Harry S. Truman*, New York, William Morrow & Company, 1973 (pp. 495–496).

'Use of A-Bomb in Korea Studied by U.S. – Truman,' *Pittsburgh Press,* November 30, 1950 (p. 1).

Harry S. Truman, The President's News Conference, November 30, 1950, The American Presidency Project, University of California at Santa Barbara.

78 Grosscup, Beau, *Strategic Terror: The Politics and Ethics of Aerial Bombardment,* London, Zed Books, 2013 (Chapter 5, Part 4).

79 Hastings, Max, *The Korean War,* London, Michael Joseph, 1988 (p. 192).

80 'Thaw in the Koreas?,' *Bulletin of Atomic Scientists*, vol. 48, no. 3, April 1992 (p. 18).

Weintraub, Stanley, *MacArthur's War: Korea and the Undoing of an American Hero*, New York, Free Press, 2000 (p. 263).

81 Tucker, Spencer C., *The Encyclopaedia of the Korean War: A Political, Social, and Military History Volume I*, Santa Barbara, ABC-CLIO, 2010 (p. 645).

Smith, Robert, *MacArthur in Korea: The Naked Emperor*, New York, Simon and Schuster, 1982 (pp. 191, 192).

James, D. Clayton, *The Years of MacArthur: Volume 2, 1941–1945*, Boston, Houghton Mifflin, 1975 (pp. 578, 579).

Crane, Conrad C., *American Airpower Strategy in Korea, 1950–1953*, Lawrence, Kansas, University Press of Kansas, 2000 (p. 71).

Deane, Hugh, *The Korean War, 1945–1953*, San Francisco, China Books and Periodicals, 1999 (p. 145).

82 'Thaw in the Koreas?,' *Bulletin of Atomic Scientists*, vol. 48, no. 3, April 1992 (pp. 18, 19).

83 Anders, Roger M., *The Atomic Bomb and the Korean War: Gordon Dean and the Issue of Civilian Control*, Lexington, Society for Military History, 1988 (pp. 3, 4).

James, D. Clayton, *The Years of MacArthur: Volume 2, 1941–1945*, Boston, Houghton Mifflin, 1975 (p. 591).

84 Anders, Roger M., *The Atomic Bomb and the Korean War: Gordon Dean and the Issue of Civilian Control*, Lexington, Society for Military History, 1988 (pp. 3–4).

James, D. Clayton, *The Years of MacArthur: Volume 2, 1941–1945*, Boston, Houghton Mifflin, 1975 (p. 591).

85 Cumings, Bruce, *Korea's Place in the Sun: A Modern History*, New York, W. W. Norton & Company, 1997 (p. 149).

Rhodes, Richard, *Dark Sun: The Making of the Hydrogen Bomb*, New York, Simon and Schuster, 1995 (pp. 448–451).

Cumings, Bruce, *Origins of the Korean War: The Roaring of the Cataract, 1947–1950, Volume 2*, Princeton, Princeton University Press, 2004 (pp. 750–751).

86 Pape, Robert A., *Bombing to Win: Air Power and Coercion in War*, Ithaca, Cornell University Press, 1996 (p. 146).

87 Dingman, Roger, *Atomic Diplomacy during the Korean War*, Cambridge, The MIT Press, 1988 (pp. 75, 76).

88 Gwertzman, Bernard, 'U.S. Papers Tell of '53 Policy to Use A-Bomb in Korea,' *New York Times*, June 8, 1984.

Levine, Alan J., *Stalin's Last War: Korea and the Approach to World War III*, Jefferson, NC, McFarland & Company, 2005 (p. 279).

89 Hasbrouck, S. V., memo to file (November 7, 1951), G-3 Operations file, box 38-A, Library of Congress, 1951.

Army Chief of Staff, memo to file (November 20, 1951), G-3 Operations file, box 38-A, Library of Congress, 1951.

Cumings, Bruce, *Origins of the Korean War: The Roaring of the Cataract, 1947–1950, Volume 2*, Princeton, Princeton University Press, 2004 (p. 752).

Tucker, Spencer C., *The Encyclopaedia of the Korean War: A Political, Social, and Military*, Santa Barbara, ABC-CLIO, 2010 (p. 645).

'Thaw in the Koreas?,' *Bulletin of Atomic Scientists*, vol. 48, no. 3, April 1992 (p. 19).

90 Levine, Alan J., *Stalin's Last War: Korea and the Approach to World War III*, Jefferson, NC, McFarland & Company, 2005 (pp. 278, 280).

91 Brodie, Bernard, *War and Politics*, London, Macmillan, 1973 (p. 105).

George, Alexander L. and Smoke, Richard, *Deterrence in American Foreign Policy: Theory and Practice*, New York, Columbia University Press, 1974 (p. 239).

Rees, David, *Korea: The Limited War*, New York, St. Martin's Press, 1964 (pp. 419, 420).

92 BBC Summary, *Far East,* No. 221, January 23, 1953.

93 Blair, Clay, *The Forgotten War: America in Korea, 1950–1953,* New York, Times Books, 1987 (p. 78).

Winnington, Alan and Burchett, Wilfred, *Plain Perfidy: The Plot to Wreck the Korea Peace*, Britain-China Friendship Association, 1954 (p. 12).

Gwertzman, Bernard, 'U.S. Papers Tell of '53 Policy to Use A-Bomb in Korea,' *New York Times*, June 8, 1984.

94 Ibid.

Whitfield, Stephen J., *The Culture of the Cold War*, Baltimore, Johns Hopkins University Press, 1996 (pp. 6, 7).

95 Adams, Sherman, *Firsthand Report: The Inside Story of the Eisenhower Administration,* London, Hutchinson, 1962 (p. 102).

Eisenhower, Dwight D., *The White House Years: Mandate for Change, 1953–1956*, New York, Doubleday, 1963 (pp. 179, 180).

96 Ibid. (p. 94).

97 Harris, William R., 'Chinese Nuclear Doctrine: The Decade Prior to Weapons Development, 1945–1955,' *The China Quarterly,* no. 21, January–March 1965 (p. 94).

98 'Foreign ministry issues memorandum on N-issue,' *KCNA*, April 21, 2010.

99 MacDonald, Donald Stone, *U.S.-Korean Relations from Liberation to Self-Reliance: The Twenty-Year Record: An Interpretive Summary of Archives of the U.S. Department of State for the Period 1945 to 1965,* Boulder, Westview Press, 1992 (pp. 23, 78, 79).

100 Mizokami, Kyle, 'Everything You Need to Know: The History of U.S. Nuclear Weapons in South Korea,' *The National Interest*, September 10, 2017.

Kristensen, Hans M. and Norris, Robert S., 'A history of U.S. nuclear weapons in South Korea,' *Bulletin of Atomic Scientists*, vol. 73, no. 6, 2017 (pp. 349–357).

Memorandum of Discussion at the 173d Meeting of the National Security Council, Thursday, December 3, 1953, in: U.S. Department of State, *Foreign Relations of the United States, 1952–1954, Vol. XV, Part 2, Korea,* Washington, DC, U.S. Government Printing Office.

101 Cumings, Bruce, *Korea's Place in the Sun: A Modern History*, New York, W. W. Norton & Company, 1997 (pp. 478, 479).

102 Macdonald, Donald Stone, *U.S.-Korean Relations from Liberation to Self-Reliance: The Twenty-Year. Record: An Interpretive Summary of the Archives of the U.S. Department of State for the Period 1945 to 1965,* Boulder, Westview Press, 1992 (pp. 23, 24, 80).

103 'Inquiry Into the U.S.S. *Pueblo* and EC-121 Plane Incidents, Report of the Special Subcommittee on the U.S.S. *Pueblo* of the Committee on Armed Services House of Representatives,' Ninety-first Congress, First Session, July 28, 1969.

104 Hayes, Peter, *Pacific Powderkeg: American Nuclear Dilemmas in Korea*, Lanham, Lexington Books, 1991 (pp. 47–48).

105 Prados, John and Cheevers, Jack, 'USS *Pueblo:* LBJ Considered Nuclear Weapons, Naval Blockade, Ground Attacks in Response to 1968 North Korean Seizure of Navy Vessel, Documents Show,' National Security Archive Electronic Briefing Book no. 453, January 23, 2014.

106 McGreal, Chris, 'Papers reveal Nixon plan for North Korea nuclear strike,' *The Guardian*, July 7, 2010.

Foster, Peter, 'Richard Nixon planned nuclear strike on North Korea,' *The Telegraph*, July 8, 2010.

107 'Drunk in charge, part two,' *The Guardian*, September 2, 2000.

108 Shuster, Mike, 'Nixon Considered Nuclear Option Against N. Korea,' *NPR*, July 6, 2010.

109 Bolger, Daniel, *Scenes From a Unfinished War: Low-Intensity Conflict in Korea, 1966–1969,* Leavonworth Papers no.19, Fort Leavenworth, Kansas, Combat Studies Institute, June 1991 (p. 102).

110 Nixon, Richard M., *RN: The Memoirs of Richard Nixon*, New York, Warner Books, 1978 (pp. 473–475).

111 Graff, Garrett M., 'The Madman and the Bomb: The nuclear launch process once haunted Nixon's aides. 43 years later, is it finally time to reform the system?,' *Politico*, August 11, 2017.

112 Nixon, Richard M., *RN: The Memoirs of Richard Nixon*, New York, Warner Books, 1978 (pp. 473–475).

113 'Thaw in the Koreas?,' *Bulletin of Atomic Scientists*, vol. 48, no. 3, April 1992 (pp. 19–20).

114 Haynes, Susan Turner, *Chinese Nuclear Proliferation: How Global Politics is Transforming China's Weapons Buildup and Modernization*, Lincoln, NE, Potomac Books, 2016 (pp. 14–15)

115 Kristensen, Hans M., 'General Confirms Enhanced Targeting Capabilities of B61–12 Nuclear Bomb,' *Federation of American Scientists*, January 23, 2014.

Coyle, Philip E. and McKeon, James, 'The Huge Risk of Small Nukes,' *Politico*, March 10, 2017.

Feinstein, Dianne, 'There's no such thing as a "limited" nuclear war,' *Washington Post*, March 3, 2017.

116 Ibid. (p. 39).

117 Chomsky, Noam, *The New Military Humanism: Lessons From Kosovo*, London, Pluto Press, 1999 (Chapter 6).

Center for Defense Information, *Defense Monitor,* Washington, DC, 2000 (p. XXIX.3).

118 *Essentials of Post–Cold War Deterrence,* Policy Subcommittee of the Strategic Advisory Group (SAG) of the United States Strategic Command, 1995.

Chomsky, Noam, *The New Military Humanism: Lessons From Kosovo*, London, Pluto Press, 1999 (pp. 145–146).

119 Broad, William J. and Sanger, David E., 'As U.S. Modernizes Nuclear Weapons, "Smaller" Leaves Some Uneasy,' *New York Times*, January 11, 2016.

120 Bennett, Bruce W., 'A surgical strike against North Korea? Not a viable option,' *Fox News*, July 14, 2017.

Smith, Derek D., *Deterring America: Rogue States and the Proliferation of Weapons of Mass Destruction*, Cambridge, Cambridge University Press, 2006 (pp. 87, 108–109).

Woolf, Christopher, 'The only effective arms against North Korea's missile bunkers are nuclear weapons, says a top war planner,' *PRI*, August 10, 2017.

Sepp, Eric M., *Deeply Buried Facilities: Implications for Military Operations*, Occasional Paper no. 14, Maxwell Air Force Base, AL, Air War College, May 2000 (p. 5).

Levi, Michael A., *Fire in the Hole: Nuclear and Non-Nuclear Options for Counter-proliferation*, Working Paper no. 31, Washington, DC, Carnegie Endowment for International Peace, November 2002 (p. 8).

121 Kristensen, Hans M. and Handler, Joshua, 'The USA and Counter-Proliferation: A New Dubious Role for US Nuclear Weapons,' *Security Dialogue*, vol. 27, no. 4, December 1996 (p. 329).

122 Haynes, Susan Turner, *Chinese Nuclear Proliferation: How Global Politics is Transforming China's Weapons Buildup and Modernization*, Lincoln, NE, Potomac Books, 2016 (pp. 14–15).

123 'The New Era of Great Power Competition | John Mearsheimer & Stephen Walt' [video], *Hidden Forces* (YouTube Channel), June 6, 2022.

124 Calvocoressi, Peter, *World Politics Since 1945*, Abingdon, Routledge, 2008 (p. 18).

125 Mathers, Jennifer G., *The Russian Nuclear Shield from Stalin to Yeltsin: The Cold War and Beyond*, London, Palgrave Macmillan, 2000 (pp. 220–224).

126 U.S. Department of State, *Foreign Relations of the United States, 1955–1957, Vol. XXIII, Part 2, Korea*, Washington, DC, U.S. Government Printing Office (p. 162). *Progress Report Prepared by the Operations Coordinating Board*, July 18, 1956.

127 Beinin, Joel, 'Challenge from Israel's Military,' *MERIP Reports*, no. 92, November–December 1980 (p. 7).

128 Ha-young, Choi, 'North Korea to decrease national defense proportion this year,' *NK News*, March 31, 2016.

Conversation with retired Korean People's Army serviceman, anonymous, September 10, 2019.

Conversation with conscription age male university graduate in Pyongyang, anonymous, September 8, 2019.

Conversation with overseas diplomat from DPRK, anonymous, November 7, 2019.

129 Ha-young, Choi, 'North Korea to decrease national defense proportion this year,' *NK News*, March 31, 2016.

130 Dorell, Oren, 'North Korean economy keeps humming despite ever-tighter sanctions,' *USA Today*, November 26, 2017.

131 Pearson, James and Park, Ju-min, 'North Korea overcomes poverty, sanctions with cut-price nukes,' *Reuters*, January 11, 2016.

'Less than one aircraft carrier? The cost of North Korea's nukes,' *CNBC*, July 20, 2017.

132 Hanley, Charles J. and Choe, Sang Hun and Mendoza, Martha, *The Bridge at No Gun Ri: A Hidden Nightmare from the Korean War*, New York, Henry Holt and Company, 2001 (pp. 195, 196).

Stokesbury, James L., *A Short History of the Korean War*, New York, William Morrow and Company, 1988 (pp. 39, 42, 43).

Lowe, Peter, 'The Frustrations of Alliance: Britain, The United States and the Korean War, 1950–1951,' in: Cotton, James and Neary, Ian, *The Korean War in History*, Manchester, Manchester University Press, 1989 (pp. 80–99).

The Times, London, July 15, 1950.

MacDonald, Callum, '"So terrible a liberation" – The UN occupation of North Korea,' *Bulletin of Concerned Asian Scholars*, vol. 23, no. 2, 1991 (pp. 3–19).

Kim, Monica, *The Interrogation Rooms of the Korean War: The Untold History*, Princeton, NJ, Princeton University Press, 2019 (p. 265).

133 Hanley, Charles J. and Choe, Sang Hun and Mendoza, Martha, *The Bridge at No Gun Ri: A Hidden Nightmare from the Korean War*, New York, Henry Holt and Company, 2001 (pp. 195–196).

134 Ibid. (p. 170).

U.S. Department of State, *Foreign Relations of the United States, 1950, Volume VII, Korea*, Washington, DC, U.S. Government Printing Office, 1976 (p. 602).

Stone, I. F., *The Hidden History of the Korean War*, Amazon Media, 2014 (Chapter 17).

135 'Report: Korean War–Era Massacre Was Policy,' *CBS News*, April 14, 2007.

136 '"Kill 'em All": American War Crimes in Korea,' *Timewatch*, Season 21, Episode 4, aired February 1, 2002.

Hanley, Charles J. and Choe, Sang Hun and Mendoza, Martha, *The Bridge at No Gun Ri: A Hidden Nightmare from the Korean War*, New York, Henry Holt and Company, 2001 (pp. 140, 141).

137 Hanley, Charles J., *Ghost Flames: Life and Death in a Hidden War, Korea 1950–1953*, New York, PublicAffairs, 2020 (pp. 222, 228, 229).

Memo to General Timberlake, Fifth Air Force, Air Force Office Records 970, Unit 1, July 25, 1950, U.S. National Archives.

'"Kill 'em All": American War Crimes in Korea,' *Timewatch,* Season 21, Episode 4, aired February 1, 2002.

138 Ibid.

139 Ibid.

140 Hanley, Charles J., *Ghost Flames: Life and Death in a Hidden War, Korea 1950–1953,* New York, PublicAffairs, 2020 (p. 65).

141 Williams, Jeremy, '"Kill 'em All": The American Military in Korea,' *BBC History,* 2011.

142 Hanley, Charles J. and Choe, Sang Hun and Mendoza, Martha, *The Bridge at No Gun Ri: A Hidden Nightmare from the Korean War*, New York, Henry Holt and Company, 2001 (p. 129).

143 Williams, Jeremy, '"Kill 'em All": The American Military in Korea,' *BBC History,* 2011.

144 Hanley, Charles J. and Choe, Sang Hun and Mendoza, Martha, *The Bridge at No Gun Ri: A Hidden Nightmare from the Korean War*, New York, Henry Holt and Company, 2001 (p. 126).

145 *Chosun Min Bo*, August 19, 1950.

146 *Washington Post*, September 30, 1999 (p. 1).

Washington Post, October 14, 1999 (p. 14)

Washington Post, December 29, 1999 (p. 19).

Williams, Jeremy, '"Kill 'em All": The American Military in Korea,' *BBC History,* 2011.

Hanley, Charles J., *Ghost Flames: Life and Death in a Hidden War, Korea 1950–1953,* New York, PublicAffairs, 2020 (pp. 83, 151, 188, 189).

'"Kill 'em All": American War Crimes in Korea,' *Timewatch,* Season 21, Episode 4, aired February 1, 2002.

147 Truth and Reconciliation Commission of the Republic of Korea, Comprehensive Report, Vol. 1, Part 1, December 2010 (p. 121).

'"Kill 'em All": American War Crimes in Korea,' *Timewatch,* Season 21, Episode 4, aired February 1, 2002.

148 Suyin, Han, *A Many-Splendored Thing*, London, Jonathan Cape, 1952 (pp. 342, 349).

149 *Report on U.S. Crimes in Korea*, Commission of International Association of Democratic Lawyers, March 31, 1952 (p. 21).

150 Blakely, Ruth, *State Terrorism and Neoliberalism: The North in the South*, Abingdon, Routledge, 2009 (p. 87).

151 Nichols, Donald, *How Many Times Can I Die? The Life Story of a Special Intelligence Agent,* Pensacola, Brownsville Printing, 1981 (p. 128).

152 *The Times*, London, July 24, 1950.

153 *New York Times*, July 26, 1950.

154 Hanley, Charles J., *Ghost Flames: Life and Death in a Hidden War, Korea 1950–1953,* New York, PublicAffairs, 2020 (p. 65).

155 Ibid. (pp. 153, 154).

156 Deane, Hugh, *The Korean War, 1945–1953,* San Francisco, China Books and Periodicals, 1999 (p. 143).

157 *Times,* London, November 16, 1950.

158 Hanley, Charles J., *Ghost Flames: Life and Death in a Hidden War, Korea 1950–1953,* New York, PublicAffairs, 2020 (p. 281).

159 Ibid. (p. 290).

160 Ibid. (p. 284).

161 Macdonald, Callum, *Korea: The Last War Before Vietnam,* New York, Palgrave Macmillan, 1986 (p. 216).

162 Hanley, Charles J., *Ghost Flames: Life and Death in a Hidden War, Korea 1950–1953,* New York, PublicAffairs, 2020 (p. 250).

163 'Koreans Watch U. N. Murder Trial as Test of Curb on Unruly Behavior,' *New York Times*, August 21, 1951.

164 Hanley, Charles J., *Ghost Flames: Life and Death in a Hidden War, Korea 1950–1953,* New York, PublicAffairs, 2020 (p. 284).

165 De Haan, Francisca, *The Women's International Democratic Federation (WIDF): History, Main Agenda, and Contributions, 1945–1991*, Women and Social Movements, International – 1840 to Present, Central European University, 2012.

166 *We Accuse: Report of the Committee of the Women's International Democratic Federation in Korea, May 16–27, 1951*, Berlin, Women's International Democratic Forum, 1951.

Report on U.S. Crimes in Korea, Commission of International Association of Democratic Lawyers, March 31, 1952.

167 Winnington, Alan, *Breakfast with Mao: Memoirs of a Foreign Correspondent*, London, Lawrence and Wishart, 1986 (p. 128).

Cumings, Bruce, *The Korean War: A History,* New York, Modern Library, 2010 (p. 84).

Parrott, Lindesay, 'Peiping Radio is Busy,' *New York Times*, October 12, 1951.

168 Fromson, Murray, 'Parallels in Crisis,' *Saturday Review*, June 1, 1968 (p. 29).

'Mouthpiece for the Reds: The Strange Role of Wilfred Burchett,' *U.S. News and World Report*, February 27, 1967 (pp. 19, 20).

169 Burchett, Wilfred, *At the Barricades*, London, Quartet Books, 1980 (pp. 274–279). In the introduction to the book, Harrison Salisbury described Burchett as a "well- informed, useful source and a warm and decent friend.")

170 Winnington, Alan and Burchett, Wilfred, *Plain Perfidy, The Plot to Wreck the Korea Peace*, Britain-China Friendship Association, 1954 (pp. 69, 71, 72).

171 Jenks, John, 'The Enemy Within: Journalism, the State and the Limits of Dissent in Cold War Britain, 1950–1951,' *American Journalism,* vol. 18, no. 1, Winter, 2001.

172 Denney, Steven, 'Speaking the Truth to Power: Canadian War Crimes in Korea,' *The Diplomat*, November 3, 2014.

173 *We Accuse: Report of the Committee of the Women's International Democratic Federation in Korea, May 16–27, 1951*, Berlin, Women's International Democratic Forum, 1951.

174 Kim, Dong-Choon, 'Forgotten war, forgotten massacres – the Korean War, (1950–1953) as licensed mass killings,' *Journal of Genocide Research*, vol. 6, issue 4, December 2004 (pp. 523–544).

175 Hynes, Patricia, 'The Korean War: Forgotten, Unknown and Unfinished,' *Truthout*, July 12, 2013.

176 Chossudovsky, Michael, Presentation to the Japanese Foreign Correspondents Club on U.S. Aggression against the People of Korea, Tokyo, August 1, 2013 (https://off-guardian.org/2017/05/08/video-u-s-crimes-of-genocide-against-korea/).

177 Cumings, Bruce, *The Korean War: A History,* New York, Modern Library, 2010 (p. 154).

178 Kim, Dong-Choon, 'Forgotten war, forgotten massacres – the Korean War, (1950–1953) as licensed mass killings,' *Journal of Genocide Research* vol. 6, issue 4, December 2004 (pp. 523–544).

179 *New York Times*, February 24, 1952.

Large, David Clay, *Germans to the Front: West German Rearmament in the Adenauer Era,* Chapel Hill, University of North Carolina Press, 1996 (p. 117).

180 Moon, Katherine H. S., *Sex Among Allies*, New York, Columbia University Press, 1997 (pp. 19, 20, 23, 24, 131, 132, 310–327).

Hye Seung Chung, *Kim Ki-duk*, Champaign, University of Illinois Press, 2012 (p. 34).

Lee, Diana S. and Lee, Grace Yoonkyung, 'Camp Arirang,' *Third World Newsreel*, 1995.

Mal Magazine, vol. 26, August 1988 (p. 108).

181 Pollock, Sandra, *Let the Good Times Roll: Prostitution and the U.S. Military in Asia*, New York, New Press, 1992 (pp. 170–173).

182 Kamienski, Lukasz, *Shooting Up: A History of Drugs in Warfare*, London, C. Hurst & Co. Publishers, 2016 (p. 148).

183 'South Korea: A Hooch is Not a Home,' *Time*, October 9, 1964 (p. 48).

184 D'Amico, Francine J. and Weinstein, Laurie L., *Gender Camouflage: Women and the U.S. Military*, New York, New York University Press, 1999 (p. 212).

185 Pollock, Sandra, *Let the Good Times Roll: Prostitution and the U.S. Military in Asia*, New York, New Press, 1992 (pp. 172–173).

186 Moon, Katherine H. S., *Sex Among Allies*, New York, Columbia University Press, 1997 (p. 1).

187 Ibid. (p. 37).

188 Lewis, Norman, *A Dragon Apparent: Travels in Cambodia, Laos, and Vietnam*, London, Jonathan Cape, 1951 (pp. 184, 208).

Rydstrom, Helle, 'Politics of Colonial Violence: Gendered atrocities in French occupied Vietnam,' *European Journal of Women's Studies,* 2014 (pp. 1–17).

'Vụ thảm sát Mỹ Trạch – Nỗi đau nhức nhối suốt 66 năm' ['My Trach Massacre – Painful Suffering for 66 years'], *Da Tri*, November 28, 2013.

'Algeria buries fighters whose skulls were in Paris museum,' *AP News,* July 5, 2020.

189 Lewis, Norman, *A Dragon Apparent: Travels in Cambodia, Laos, and Vietnam*, London, Jonathan Cape, 1951 (pp. 184, 208).

Rydstrom, Helle, 'Politics of Colonial Violence: Gendered atrocities in French occupied Vietnam,' *European Journal of Women's Studies,* 2014.

'Vụ thảm sát Mỹ Trạch – Nỗi đau nhức nhối suốt 66 năm' [My Trach Massacre – Painful Suffering for 66 years].

'Algeria buries fighters whose skulls were in Paris museum,' *AP News,* July 5, 2020.

190 Rydstrom, Helle, 'Politics of Colonial Violence: Gendered atrocities in French occupied Vietnam,' *European Journal of Women's Studies,* 2014.

191 Ibid.

192 Ibid.

193 Kuznick, Peter and Stone, Oliver, *The Untold History of the United States*, London, Elbury Press, 2012 (p. 368).

194 Brownmiller, Susan, *Against Our Will: Men, Women and Rape*, London, Simon & Schuster, 1975 (pp. 103–105).

Jones, Howard, *My Lai: Vietnam, 1968, and the Descent into Darkness*, New York, Oxford University Press, 2017 (p. xxi).

195 Turse, Nick and Nelson, Deborah, 'Civilian Killings Went Unpunished,' *Los Angeles Times*, August 6, 2006.

196 Denvir, Daniel, 'The Secret History of the Vietnam War', Interview with Nick Turse, *Vice News*, April 17, 2015.

197 Belknap, Michal R., *The Vietnam War on Trial: The My Lai Massacre and the Court-Martial of Lieutenant Calley*, Lawrence, University Press of Kansas, 2002 (p. 68).

Greiner, Bernd, *War Without Fronts: The USA in Vietnam*, New Haven, Yale University Press, 2009 (pp. 152–159).

Anderson, Elizabeth, *'An Everyday Affair': Violence Against Women during the Vietnam War*, The University of Texas at Austin, May 2020.

198 Baker, Mark, *NAM: The Vietnam War in the Words of the Men and Women*

Who Fought There, New York, First Cooper Square Press, 2001 (p. 210).

199 Kendall, Bridget, *The Cold War: A New Oral History of Life Between East and West*, London, BBC Books, 2017 (p. 305).

200 Appy, Christian G., *Working Class War: American Combat Soldiers and Vietnam*, Chapel Hill, University of North Carolina Press, 1993 (p. 270).

201 Weaver, Gina Marie, *Ideologies of Forgetting: American Erasure of Women's Sexual Trauma in the Vietnam War,* Houston, Rice University, 2006 (p. 130).

Anderson, Elizabeth, *'An Everyday Affair': Violence Against Women during the Vietnam War*, The University of Texas at Austin, May 2020.

202 Baker, Mark, *NAM: The Vietnam War in the Words of the Men and Women Who Fought There,* New York, First Cooper Square Press, 2001 (p. 210).

203 Vietnam Veterans Against the War, *The Winter Soldier Investigation: An Inquiry into American War Crimes*, Boston, Beacon Press, 1972.

Bourke, Joanna, *Rape: A History from 1860 to the Present Day*, London, Virago Press, 2007 (p. 367).

Anderson, Elizabeth, *'An Everyday Affair': Violence Against Women during the Vietnam War*, The University of Texas at Austin, May 2020.

204 Ibid.

205 Ibid.

206 Vietnam Veterans Against the War, *The Winter Soldier Investigation: An Inquiry into American War Crimes*, Boston, Beacon Press, 1972.

207 Lang, Daniel, 'Casualties of War,' *The New Yorker*, October 10, 1969.

208 Bourke, Joanna, *Rape: A History from 1860 to the Present Day*, London, Virago Press, 2007 (p. 366).

209 Meger, Sarah, *Rape Loot Pillage: The Political Economy of Sexual Violence in Armed Conflict*, Oxford, Oxford University Press, 2016 (pp. 60, 61).

Askin, Kelley Dawn, *War Crimes Against Women: Prosecution in International War Crimes Tribunals*, The Hague, Kluwar Law International, 1997 (p. 50).

210 Bourke, Joanna, *Rape: A History from 1860 to the Present Day*, London, Virago Press, 2007 (p. 362).

211 Vietnam Veterans Against the War, *The Winter Soldier Investigation: An Inquiry into American War Crimes*, Boston, Beacon Press, 1972.

212 Turse, Nick, *Kill Everything That Moves: The Real American War in Vietnam*, London, Picador, 2014 (p. 167).

213 Bilton, Michael and Sim, Kevin, *Four Hours in My Lai: A War Crime and its Aftermath*, London, Viking, 1992 (p. 81).

Brownmiller, Susan, *Against Our Will: Men, Women and Rape*, New York, Fawcett Books, 1975 (p. 92).

Anderson, Elizabeth, *'An Everyday Affair': Violence Against Women during the Vietnam War*, The University of Texas at Austin, May 2020.

214 Brownmiller, Susan, *Against Our Will: Men, Women and Rape*, London, Simon & Schuster, 1975 (p. 98).

215 Ibid. (p. 159).

216 Ibid. (p. 161).

217 Denvir, Daniel, 'The Secret History of the Vietnam War', Interview with Nick Turse, *Vice News*, April 17, 2015.

218 Rummel, Rudolph Joseph, *Statistics of Democide*, Honolulu, University of Hawaii, 1997, Table 6.1A, Vietnam Democide: Estimates, Sources, and Calculations.

219 Bloomfield, Steve, 'French troops "raped girls during Rwanda genocide,"' *The Independent*, August 31, 2007.

'Witnesses: French GIs raped Rwandan women,' *NBC News,* December 14, 2006.

220 '"Forced sex with dog": 98 Central African Rep. girls report shocking abuse by UN peacekeepers,' *RT*, April 1, 2016.

221 'Photos reveal Belgian paratroopers' abuse in Somalia,' *CNN*, April 17, 1997.

'Italy Says Its Soldiers Tortured Somalis,' *New York Times*, August 9, 1997.

222 Philipps, Dave, 'Navy SEALs Were Warned Against Reporting Their Chief for War Crimes,' *New York Times,* April 23, 2019.

223 Sonmez, Felicia, 'Rep. Duncan Hunter says his unit "killed probably hundreds of civilians" in Iraq,' *Washington Post,* June 4, 2019.

224 Phakdeetham, Janine, 'Iraq War Vet says he was "shown slow-motion sniper kills to desensitize him" and was "systematically trained to kill,"' *The Sun,* July 14, 2020.

225 'Australian "war crimes": Elite troops killed Afghan civilians, report finds,' *BBC News,* November 19, 2020.

Hadid, Diaa, '"I Remember Them Screaming": Afghans Detail Alleged Killings By Australian Military,' *NPR News,* April 25, 2021.

226 Bardo, Matt and O'Grady, Hannah, 'Did UK Special Forces execute unarmed civilians?,' *BBC News,* August 1, 2020.

227 'Iraq war veteran: "The Marines took it upon themselves to shoot at, beat, rob, rape, kill whoever they wanted to. And that's being proposed on the news as a few bad apples, an isolated incident,"' *In the NOW,* December 16, 2019.

228 Edwards, Rob, 'U.S. fired depleted uranium at civilian areas in 2003 Iraq war, report finds,' *The Guardian*, June 19, 2014.

229 Cockburn, Patrick, 'Toxic legacy of US assault on Fallujah "worse than Hiroshima,"' *The Independent,* October 22, 2011.

230 '"Up to 15 tons of depleted uranium used in 1999 Serbia bombing" – lead lawyer in suit against NATO,' *RT*, June 13, 2017.

231 Cockburn, Patrick, 'Toxic legacy of US assault on Fallujah "worse than Hiroshima,"' *The Independent,* October 22, 2011.

232 Ibid.

233 Higham, Scott and Stephens, Joe, 'New Details of Prison Abuse Emerge,' *Washington Post*, May 21, 2004 (p. A01).

234 Harding, Luke, 'After Abu Ghraib,' *The Guardian*, September 20, 2004.

Taguba, Antonio, '"The Taguba Report" on Treatment of Abu Ghraib Prisoners in Iraq,' *Findlaw.com*, May 2004.

235 Higham, Scott and Stephens, Joe, 'New Details of Prison Abuse Emerge,' *Washington Post*, May 21, 2004 (p. A01).

236 Ibid.

237 Ibid.

238 Ibid.

239 Sealey, Geraldine, 'Hersh: Children sodomized at Abu Ghraib, on tape,' *Salon,* July 15, 2004.

240 Ibid.

241 Taguba, Antonio, '"The Taguba Report" on Treatment of Abu Ghraib Prisoners in Iraq,' *Findlaw.com*, May 2004.

242 Gardham, Duncan and Cruickshank, Paul, 'Abu Ghraib abuse photos "show rape,"' *The Daily Telegraph*, May 28, 2009.

243 Ibid.

244 Baker, Raymond W. and Ismael, Shereen T. and Ismael, Tareq Y., *Cultural Cleansing in Iraq*, London, Pluto Press, 2010 (p. 4).

'Iraq conflict has killed a million Iraqis: Survey,' *Reuters,* January 30, 2008.

'The Iraq We Left Behind,' *Foreign Affairs,* March/April 2012.

245 Lochhead, Carolyn, 'Conflict in Iraq – Iraq Refugee Crisis Exploding – 40% of Middle Class Believed To Have Fled Crumbling Nation,' *San Francisco Chronicle*, January 16, 2007.

246 'Millions Leave Home in Iraqi Refugee Crisis,' *NPR News,* February 17, 2007.

'UN warns of five million Iraqi refugees,' *The Independent,* December 14, 2007.

247 'At a Crossroads: Human Rights in Iraq Eight Years after the US-Led Invasion,' *Human Rights Watch*, 2010.

CHAPTER 1

The Post–Cold War Years: A New Era of Conflict

North Korea Under a New World Order

During the Cold War North Korea maintained a unique position among Western Bloc adversaries, and although the country had been a Soviet treaty ally since 1961, it had retained a degree of political, economic, military and ideological autonomy not seen elsewhere in the Soviet Bloc. While North Korean forces were a leading contributor to jointly supporting Western Bloc adversaries alongside the USSR, from Southern Africa to Vietnam, the country uniquely among Soviet allies also maintained a treaty alliance with neighboring China, in spite of pressure from Moscow to align against its northern neighbor. The country's economy was highly unique as by far the most urbanized and industrialized in Asia, as it had been since its foundation, with 70 percent of North Koreans living in cities in the 1970s representing the second highest urbanization level on the continent after Japan. This reflected the economy's strong orientation towards industry, which stood out from other Western Bloc adversaries, particularly in Asia, with less than 20 percent of Chinese or Vietnamese having lived in cities at the time as they still maintained primarily rural economies.

Another notable indicator was North Korea's particularly high number of registered industrial designs, which according to data from the Geneva-based World Intellectual Property Organization by the mid-1980s placed it far ahead of all socialist countries other than the Soviet Union itself. By 1990 the country had eclipsed the USSR to gain a global fourth place behind Japan, South Korea and the United States.[1] High levels of technical education among the workforce even in rural areas were consistently highlighted by foreign observers, with domestic industrial works such as hydroelectric dams, according to experts from companies such as the Swiss-Swedish ABB Group, having been considered nothing less than "engineering masterpieces."[2]

Although achieving impressive industrial and military standings, in an increasingly globalized world the outcome of North Korea's conflict with the United States was as much contingent on the success of the global struggle between the Western Bloc and other countries around the world outside its influence, as it was on events that occurred in Korea itself. Thus as the Western Bloc's sphere of influence encompassed the large majority of the world, from the near totality of the Americas and Oceania to the large majority of Africa and the Middle East, while gaining dominance over prized territories from Congo in 1960 to Indonesia in 1965, North Korea became increasingly isolated much as all Soviet Bloc states were. The result was a growing disadvantage for states outside the Western Bloc's sphere of influence, which were increasingly sidelined from the Western-centered global economy. This isolation would only be exacerbated when the Soviet Bloc itself disintegrated in 1990, and the USSR the following year, leaving North Korea in a very small minority of states outside Western of influence.

While the United States and the majority of Western Bloc states, from Switzerland and France to Australia and Canada, refused to form diplomatic ties to North Korea and implicitly recognized South Korean sovereignty over the entire peninsula, the growing power discrepancy between the Western and Soviet Blocs made this increasingly unfavourable. The issue only worsened when the Soviet Union recognized and formed diplomatic ties with the South Korea in September 1990, followed by China in August 1992, which marked a major milestone at the end of the Cold War to which Seoul's traditional partners did not reciprocate by recognizing Pyongyang.

Much as Moscow moved to undermine and bring about a collapse in communist East Germany as part of its rapprochement with West Germany and with the Western Bloc more broadly, so too was the Mikhail Gorbachev administration seen by a number of analysts to be doing its utmost to simulate a similar collapse of

North Korea to facilitate its absorption into the south.[3] Unlike East Germany, however, North Korea was very far from a Soviet dependency, with the contrast perhaps best demonstrated by the total absence of foreign military personnel permitted to operate on its soil compared to the 19 divisions of 340,000 Soviet personnel in Germany.[4] This left Moscow's options to place pressure on North Korea very limited, beyond cutting off the small amount of Soviet aid the country received, which Gorbachev's administration did gradually from 1985. The post-Soviet Russian government would from 1992 place additional economic pressure on Pyongyang while seeking to further bolster its ties with Seoul.

Pyongyang's strategic position would further diminish in the 1990s, with the first landmark in this regard being the Gulf War and Operation Desert Storm. The conflict saw the United States and its allies make an unprecedented projection of power against Iraq, a state which much like North Korea had been left vulnerable due to the loss of Soviet protection. Washington had from the outset of the conflict sought to avoid options for mediation,[5] and called for the removal of Iraqi President Saddam Hussein from power, the disbanding of the Iraqi Armed Forces and disarmament of strategic military assets as preconditions for a peaceful settlement.[6]

While Baghdad was itself largely to blame for leaving itself extremely exposed, not only politically and economically but also, in the literal sense, militarily, as it camped its forces at the end of long supply lines with negligible cover in a clear desert, the intensity of the U.S.-led assault deeply shook the world. Over 100,000 Iraqi personnel and thousands of civilians were killed in just 44 days,[7] with the *Washington Post* highlighting that the destruction of key infrastructure such as oil refineries, electrical plants and transportation networks, was intended to devastate local living standards. Examples ranged from the destruction of 80 percent of Iraq's power generation capabilities, to the crippling of its sewage treatment system.[8] Jane's Information Group concluded that coalition operations had worked to "bring Iraqis' infrastructure virtually back to where it was at the country's birth" – back to 1921.[9] The Western Bloc states further demonstrated mastery of the information space, and proved highly adept at concealing details of the conflict that undermined their interests, such as the gruesome massacres of retreating Iraqi personnel,[10] while at the same time using fabricated atrocities to work public opinion into a frenzy against Iraq. Narratives widely repeated by media outlets, NGOs, and officials, but later debunked as knowingly fabricated, ranged from Iraqi soldiers slaughtering premature Kuwaiti babies, to mass rapes and looting, forced relocation of hundreds of thousands of Kuwaitis and mass extrajudicial killings. This in a matter of weeks transformed the previously little known country's image into that of an imminent threat and preeminent evil.[11]

A prominent Brookings Institute paper would subsequently conclude: "The Persian Gulf War marked a new era in American power projection.... Operation Desert Storm showed that U.S. forces could quickly amass at an adversary's doorstep and project power into adversary territory."[12] It was thus far from unnoticed that in the aftermath of Iraq's defeat, and in parallel to the beginning of limited military operations by NATO members targeting Yugoslavia, Western discourse surrounding and media representations of North Korea provided growing indications that it was the next potential target for for military action under the new post–Cold War order. Former assistant secretary of state Leslie Gelb, who would two years later become president of America's most influential foreign policy think tank the Council on Foreign Relations, on April 10 set a new tone for discourse on North Korea. In an article titled "North Korea: The Next Nuclear Nightmare," he referred to the country as "the next renegade state" and "run by a vicious dictator" with "a million men under arms," a ballistic missile arsenal and very likely a nuclear weapon "in a few years." Its armed forces' size and firepower were consistently depicted not as precautions for self defense, but as signs of aggressive intent.[13]

The need to bring political change to Pyongyang began to be widely asserted, with the *Washington Quarterly*, for one, reflecting the Western consensus when it observed in the summer of 1991: "the key factor contributing to instability in the Korean Peninsula and the prolongation of the cold war structure between the two Koreas lies in the very political nature of North Korea's outdated Communist regime."[14] A February 1992 Naval War College paper, titled *Kim Il Sung (North Korea), Another Saddam Hussein (Iraq)?: Countering and Deterring Aggression in the Northern Pacific,* concluded: "the prospects for long term peace on the Korean Peninsula remain dim until the departure of the regime of [North Korean President] Kim Il Sung." As was typical of Western coverage, North Korea was referred to as "a despotic, totalitarian regime," while reflecting the immediate-post Gulf War trend, which piggybacked on the highly effective vilification of the Iraqi leadership, it referred to aspects of governance in North Korea as "chillingly similar to Saddam Hussein's regime in Iraq."[15]

The Naval War College paper effectively summarized how prevailing trends in American thought on the post–Cold War projection of U.S. military power posed an imminent threat to Pyongyang, and the strong connections drawn between Iraq and North Korea as targets, stating:

> The demise of the global Soviet threat has brought about a fundamental shift in the National Military Strategy of the United States. Future employment of American military forces must be considered through the focus of regional contingencies. The most threatening of future regional contingencies are those exacerbated by the "Hostile Proliferator," the radical and unstable regime equipped with weapons of mass destruction... Scarcely has Operation Desert Storm wound down than another potential "Hostile Proliferator" appears on the horizon. Western intelligence sources are now estimating that the Democratic People's Republic of Korea under the leadership of Kim Il Sung may be able to produce nuclear weapons in as little as a year.

The paper accordingly stressed the possible need for pre-emptive attacks.[16] References to the need for action against North Korea otherwise indicated a need to resolve a longstanding conflict decisively in the West's favor, a notable example being the reference in *The National Interest* in 1993 to a need to act against "the same evil Kim Il Sung, still all powerful in the half-country he has tortured so much." Having opposed the Western Bloc's designs for over 40 years, America's oldest state adversary was now seen to be far more vulnerable.[17]

The First Nuclear Crisis: Normalization Through Strength

The end of the Cold War closely coincided with North Korea's approach to attaining a nuclear weapons capability, with considerable uncertainty remaining as to the extent to which the global geopolitical shift which occurred from the late 1980s influenced or accelerated this process. It is also highly uncertain when the leadership of the ruling Korean Workers' Party and the Korean People's Army, the two foremost decision-making bodies in the country, resolved to develop nuclear weapons. Some sources traced these ambitions to the Korean War, and others to various standoffs with the United States where American nuclear forces had left Pyongyang at a vast disadvantage. As observed by the director of the International Security Strategies Project at the leading think tank CSIS, Michael J. Mazarr, through a long history of nuclear threats the United States "had exposed North Korea, during its infancy as a nation, to the fearsome power and enormous political value of nuclear weapons," with Pyongyang's incentive to pursue such a capability having been successively reinforced during multiple standoffs.[18]

Other sources claimed that the leadership in Pyongyang only fully resolved to develop nuclear weapons in the 2000s, citing its major concessions on nuclear activities in the preceding decade and its strong willingness to exchange its gas-graphite reactors for "proliferation proof" light water ones. This argument was supported by the fact that although North Korean gas-graphite reactors were optimal for nuclear weapons development, production of such reactors could be explained by their simplicity as they were the only reactor type which the country could build independently at the time.[19]

While the date from which a nuclear weapons program was planned remains highly uncertain, there remains little dispute that the events that followed the Cold War's end very considerably strengthened arguments for developing a nuclear deterrent, and made obtaining a cost effective counter to American military capabilities appear particularly urgent. An assessment in the Foreign Policy journal in 1991 highlighted that "possession of nuclear weapons would alleviate the requirement for alliances, thus negating North Korean's current diplomatic isolation,"[20] while a Naval War College assessment in early 1992 stressed that as Pyongyang "has lost its superpower counterbalance to the United States," nuclear weapons could be valued as a means of "providing an offset against the nuclear umbrella of the United States."[21] The latter paper highlighted "the relative low cost of nuclear weapons development, compared with the burden of supporting a large conventional military force," thereby providing Pyongyang with a solution to the increasingly unfavorable post–Cold War economic balance. It added that North Korea may have learned from the Gulf War that Iraq's "fatal mistake was taking on the [U.S.-led] coalition without nuclear weapons."[22]

Nineteen years after operationalizing its first research reactor in 1967 with Soviet support, North Korea in 1986 completed construction of a small 5 megawatt graphite-moderated nuclear reactor near the city of Yongbyon. Having initially sought to build such a facility with Soviet support, Moscow's refusal resulted in an indigenous effort which established full supply chains for a nuclear industry, with the first domestically built nuclear facility having a simple design that negated requirements for imported heavy water or highly enriched uranium, while having a not insignificant plutonium production capability. The country that year began construction of a second much larger 50 MW(e) gas-graphite reactor also at Yongbyon, and three years later in 1989 began construction of a larger 200 MW(e) facility at a separate location in Taechon.

Shortly after the first Yongbyon facility became operational, U.S. intelligence alleged that satellite surveillance had discovered a reprocessing facility at Yongbyon. There spent fuel from reactors could be dissolved to separate plutonium from uranium and fission products for production of nuclear weapons. The limited uses for plutonium in the civilian sector created a growing consensus that a nuclear weapons program was underway,[23] and by April 1991 it was expected that its annual output would be sufficient to produce a not insignificant number of nuclear warheads.[24]

In an apparent effort to reduce tensions surrounding its nuclear program, and likely influenced by awareness of its newfound vulnerability, North Korea on January 30, 1992 signed an International Atomic Energy Agency (IAEA) agreement under which it provided an initial declaration of its nuclear facilities and materials. This was ratified on April 9 by the Supreme People's Assembly in Pyongyang, and provided access for IAEA inspectors to verify this. A key condition for signing was that the United States would confirm it no longer deployed nuclear weapons in Korea, although leaked documents would later reveal that this was far from the case and that nuclear warheads remained in South Korea at least until 1998.[25] President George H. W. Bush had also pledged high level bilateral meetings and a cancellation of annual Team Spirit military exercises in South Korea should Pyongyang sign. There was no follow-through on the former pledge, however, while the latter was heavily compensated for by expanding other military exercises in the south and delaying plans to reduce U.S. deployments in the country.[26] Pyongyang's confidence in U.S. pledges to reduce military tensions was notably significantly further eroded when Team Spirit exercises were resumed in 1993 – a decision U.S. ambassador to South Korea Donald Gregg referred to as "one of the biggest mistakes" of Washington's Korea policy which did much to reverse gains made the previous year.[27] State Department Country Director for Korea Charles Kartman similarly observed that although the exercises were highly counterproductive, the "advantages of using Team Spirit as a club appealed to many people" and "the voice of caution was rather low level."[28]

After six rounds of inspections from May 1992 to February 1993, the IAEA on February 9 made an unexpected and historically unprecedented request for highly intrusive "special inspections" of North Korean sites outside its nuclear facilities, which Pyongyang refused on the basis that they were military facilities.[29] Such requests from the IAEA had not been made of other countries in the past, and appeared highly suspicious, with the agency later confirmed to have received its information and briefings on the sites from the United States.[30] Considering later revelations that U.S. used United Nations inspectors to collect intelligence on potential target states, and accessed highly sensitive intelligence gathered by the United Nations Special Commission's teams in Iraq to plan attacks on the country, the Korean response would prove to be justified in light of the considerable national security threat it faced.[31] UN inspection teams, it later emerged, had been heavily infiltrated by U.S. and British intelligence to attempt to engineer a coup in Iraq, organize the assassination of its leader and gather otherwise inaccessible high-value intelligence.[32] UN inspectors had passed on their findings and large quantities of seized Iraqi government documents to Washington before doing so to the United Nations, drawing strong criticisms from several quarters of the UN. This reflected the realities of the post–Cold War order in which Western dominance at major international organizations was wholly unchallenged.[33] Iraq's case ultimately highlighted the dangers that granting inspectors free reign in North Korea would have posed to the country's security.[i]

Much as had been the case for UN inspectors in Iraq, the IAEA passed results of its inspections of those Korean facilities to which it was granted access, including plutonium samples, to the United States. Indeed, a year before inspectors entered the country, officials in Washington had informed the *New York Times* in January 1992 that the U.S. required "a mandate to roam North Korea's heavily guarded military sites at will."[34] Clinton administration officials subsequently advocated achieving this exposure of North Korean defenses through international inspections.[35] As

---

i The Iranian government and sources affiliated with Iran's intelligence services would separately in the 2010s and 2020s repeatedly allege a highly similar campaign was being waged to that in Iraq, including using IAEA inspections to send agents from Western intelligence services into the country both for intelligence gathering and to support assassination attempts. Although no evidence was provided, the Iraqi precedent meant this possibility could not be ruled out. ('Iran says UN agency sending spies, not inspectors,' *NBC News*, December 4, 2010.) ('Khamenei Loyalist Accuses IAEA Inspectors of Spying For Mossad, CIA,' *Iran International*, April 6, 2022.)

observed by expert on Korean security at Yale, Paul Bracken, there was an "immediate threat to North Korea" from "strategic isolation leading to greater economic isolation, and opportunities for international intervention in Korean affairs. This is what is now happening, most notably with the pressure on the North to open suspect nuclear facilities to inspection by the IAEA. But such demands must surely be seen as only the first moves to open up the entire North Korean state."[36]

By 1994 the nature and full extent of American and British efforts to conduct deep espionage into Iraq in preparation for an invasion had not been exposed, nor indeed had similar inspections of Libya's military sites even begun, with the Western assault on that country which this would similarly facilitate still being 17 years away. Nevertheless, North Korea's perceptions of Washington's efforts to use very deep and extensive inspections to undermine its armed forces' ability to defend the country, while threatening continued economic sanctions if this was not provided, was effectively summarized by the following statement by President Kim Il Sung:

> The reason we refuse inspection in depth is just this: we only have secret defense systems and organizations and the Americans know, perhaps, that we have no nuclear weapons, but they want to know what exactly our defense system with conventional weapons is. That is the reason they want the UN atomic agency to make inspections in depth. Besides the question of our sovereignty and national dignity and pride, we have our secrets.
>
> Please compared us to a man: They want us to take off our shirt, our coat and now our trousers, and after that we will be nude, absolutely naked. What they want us to be is a man without defense secrets, just a naked man. We cannot accept that. We would rather accept a

> war. If they decide to make war, we accept the war, the challenge we are prepared for.[37,ii]

The IAEA notably not only passed on the information it gathered to the United States, but also relied heavily on intelligence received directly from the CIA which, with North Korea and the United States still technically at war, made it appear far from a neutral party.[38] A further cause for perceptions of the IAEA as highly partial was that it had not sought to verify American claims to have removed nuclear weapons from South Korea by December 1991, which North Korean officials asserted a need for. Much as information released over the next two decades strongly vindicated Pyongyang's concerns regarding international inspections, so too would its concerns regarding the continued presence of American nuclear weapons in South Korea prove to be far from unfounded. In 2004 documents obtained by the Japanese Kyodo news agency confirmed that an American nuclear arsenal had remained in South Korea well past 1991 and at least until 1998.[39] Thirteen years later, on November 16, 2017, the U.S. Strategic Command published a statement on Twitter claiming that the U.S. retained secret nuclear weapons silos in South Korea, although whether there was any veracity to this, or whether it was intended to play on North Korean fears remained uncertain.[40] Whichever was the case, however, it highlighted the fact that the lack of inspections to verify the withdrawal of American nuclear weapons had left the situation highly ambiguous.

Having been denied access to the two North Korean facilities requested, the IAEA called on the United Nations Security Council to authorize special ad hoc inspections. It was noted at the time in the *Executive Intelligence Review* that "The IAEA's tone vis-a-vis

---

ii State media similarly referred to expanding requests for inspections as follows: "this demand reveals its [America's] intention to disarm the DPRK," representing an effort "to stifle the DPRK militarily on the pretext of 'nuclear development'," as part of "an unreasonable act to stifle anti-imperialist independent countries including the Democratic People's Republic of Korea under the unjustifiable pretext of 'non-proliferation' of nuclear and other mass destruction weapons." (*KCNA,* June 10, June 16, June 18, 1994.)

North Korea has been uncharacteristically confrontational," and that CIA Director James Woolsey had "praised the IAEA's new 'aggressive' posture." "An eventual military strike is not excluded," the report added, stressing "the suddenness, intensity, and coordinated nature of the campaign about the 'North Korean bomb,'" and that the U.S. was " insisting on backing Pyongyang up against the wall."[41,iii] On February 24 Director Woolsey informed the Senate Governmental Affairs Committee that North Korea "is probably our most grave current concern,"[42] while the influential British weekly *The Economist*, reflecting the growing consensus at the time, warned that "North Korea is next in line for nuclear prevention" and "should expect a bloody nose."[43]

Increasingly hostile discourse was paired with a significant intensification of American military pressure, with the head of the newly formed U.S. Strategic Command General, George Butler, announcing in February that the American nuclear arsenal formerly aimed at the Soviet Union was being retargeted against North Korea and other much smaller state adversaries – a process that had long been in the making after the USSR disintegrated.[44] Subsequently on March 8 the massive Team Spirit military exercises were resumed for the first time since the USSR's disintegration, after they had been canceled by President Bush the previous year. The exerciscs took place in South Korea and the surrounding airspace and waters simulating a major military operation against the north, and involved close to 200,000 personnel, new M1 and K1 tanks, B-52H and B-1B strategic bombers, and a vast naval fleet deploying several hundred precision guided cruise missiles, among other new assets.

iii Citing "a source in the international 'non-proliferation' complex, who is not sympathetic to the North Korean regime," the *Review* article elaborated: "the problem of its nuclear facilities was being effectively discussed on a South Korea–North Korea government-to-government basis, until the United States began issuing harsh ultimative demands toward Pyongyang. This stiffened Pyongyang's attitude into a hard intransigence, embodied in its rejection of IAEA demands." (Burdman, Mark, 'North Korea set up for Iraq-style showdown,' *Executive Intelligence Review,* vol. 20, no. 11, March 12, 1993 (p. 62).)

With Soviet protection lost, the U.S. demonstrating a new degree of confidence in its military capabilities after Operation Desert Storm, and widespread calls being made in the West for military action, Pyongyang had considerable grounds to perceive an imminent threat from the massive drills on its borders. The exercises forced the Korean People's Army to divert considerable resources to maintaining a high level of combat readiness throughout their duration, which imposed a significant burden for an economy already reeling from the loss of Soviet Bloc trade. Providing insight into the degree to which the exercises were seen as provocative, U.S. Congressman Gary Ackerman, who visited North Korea that year, recalled that President Kim Il Sung's voice "quivered and his hands shook with anger" when the U.S.-led exercises were mentioned.[45]

As its security situation continued to deteriorate, North Korea announced four days after the initiation of Team Spirit that it intended to withdraw from the Treaty on the Non-Proliferation of Nuclear Weapons (NPT), giving its required three-month notice and citing its rights under Article X.[iv] With the exercises widely reported to include simulated nuclear attacks, which would violate the NPT-linked prohibition on using nuclear weapons against non-nuclear states, this provided Pyongyang with significant grounds to argue that nuclear weapons were necessary to counter nuclear threats.[v] Worsening the threat, the new Bill Clinton

---

iv The Article guaranteed the right to withdraw if "extraordinary events, related to the subject matter of this Treaty, have jeopardized the supreme interests of its country."

v Nuclear attacks on the non-nuclear East Asian country were generally considered legitimate in the United States, as they had been throughout the Cold War, with U.S. Army Lieutenant (ret.) General John Cushman summarizing one of the primary arguments as follows in 1994: "Just as the United States considered nuclear first use an option against an overwhelming Warsaw Pact advantage in Europe, it must in all realism consider that option on the Korean peninsula today, if the alternative is the loss of Seoul and a long and costly refight of the Korean War." He proposed use of eight warheads of approximately 100-kiloton yield "against selected troop and other military targets north of the DMZ." The perceived inability to decisively win a conventional war fueled support for keeping the nuclear option on the table. (Cushman, John H., 'Military Options in Korea's End Game,' *Nautilus Institute*, May 23, 1994.)

administration was widely reported to be planning a strategic nuclear expeditionary force aimed primarily at North Korea, China and Iran, redirecting much of the arsenals formerly directed at the Warsaw Pact states.[46]

Withdrawal from the NPT proved sufficient to provoke the United States into intensified negotiations, leading Pyongyang 89 days later to announced that it was suspending its withdrawal just one day before this was to take effect. While talks were underway, North Korea staged an unprecedented show of force with its first test of a ballistic missile capable of striking beyond the Korean Peninsula on May 29, 1993, with the Hwasong-7 medium ranged missile hitting a buoy floating in the Sea of Japan to demonstrate both range and precision.[47] North Korea's two previous ballistic missile classes, the Hwasong-5 and Hwasong-6, were both close derivatives of the Soviet Scud-B with short ranges of 320 and 500 kilometers. The new Hwasong-7 was a much larger missile with an estimated 1300–1500 kilometer range and a large 1000kg warhead, which represented one of the most significant early landmarks in the development of a missile deterrent. While the costs of a conflict on the peninsula were already projected as extreme, the new missile's ability to strike American military bases in Japan, which were a key staging ground for any assault on North Korea, further strengthened Pyongyang's position considerably.

Multiple reports in the 1990s would highlight that, with road mobile ballistic missiles having proven extremely difficult to locate and neutralize even over open deserts in the Gulf War, the far larger arsenal operating behind a much denser air defense network, and in Korea's highly mountainous terrain, would be extremely difficult to counter.[48] This was a particularly serious concern for the United States as a growing number of reports highlighted the severe limitations its missile defenses had faced countering even Iraq's very limited missile attacks.[49] The issue was exacerbated by the severe deficiencies the Gulf War revealed in the Tomahawk cruise missile at the heart of the American reconnaissance-strike complex, which missed the large majority of its targets and sometimes hit neighboring allied countries. This limited the Tomahawk's viability for neutralizing North Korean ballistic missiles before launch.[50]

Pyongyang's position during talks remained that it would allow continued safeguards on its nuclear facilities, but that further inspections across the country were prohibited. Meetings held from June 2–11 resulted in a joint statement in which both parties pledged not to attack or ever use nuclear weapons against the other, to respect one another's sovereignty, not to interfere in one another's internal affairs, and to continue dialogue.[51] In November the North Koreans proposed a "package deal" under which the country would renounce its entire system of graphite nuclear reactors in exchange for a supply of light water reactors which could not be used to develop nuclear weapons, for more formal security guarantees, and for full normalization of relations with the U.S., including removal of all economic sanctions. Pyongyang's proposal further called for an end to the Korean War and the signing of a conclusive peace treaty. North Korean officials had repeatedly indicated a strong interest in exchanging the country's nuclear facilities for "proliferation proof" light water reactors from as early as June 1992.[52]

With the United States refraining from accepting North Korean terms for normalization of relations, operations at Yongbyon continued, and 11 months after talks had begun on May 14, 1994, with no deal yet reached, North Korean technicians began removing the reactor's 8000 spent fuel rods.[53] This placed further pressure on Washington to reach an accommodation. All rods were placed in a temporary storage pond where they were fully accounted for – meaning there was still time to prevent them from being weaponized if a deal was reached.

While an agreement had yet to be made limiting North Korea's ability to continue operations at Yongbyon, the Bill Clinton administration responded to this development with a pledge to push for the imposition of harsher economic sanctions through the United Nations Security Council. It was intended that these would block all shipping into and out of the country and cut off all oil supplies. Pyongyang responded that "sanctions mean war, and there is no mercy in war," causing considerable concern in Washington. In response the Clinton administration considered initiating Operations Plan 5027 on June 15, which would employ F-117 stealth fighters, after having burnished their reputation for penetration strikes over Iraq, to target the Yongbyon facility supported by cruise missiles attacks from nearby destroyers and nuclear submarines. Defense Secretary William Perry and Assistant Defense Secretary for Global Strategic Affairs Ashton Carter would late recall having "readied plans for striking at North Korea's nuclear facilities and for mobilizing hundreds of thousands of American troops for the war that probably would have followed."[54] In 1993 Carter was appointed to direct a DOD task force, which West Point's Scott Silverstone reported had "drafted a paper for the National Security Council that recommended a military attack on Yongbyon." Carter's colleagues reported that he "wanted military options taken very seriously."[55,vi]

An attack on Yongbyon without authorization from the UN Security Council, and with North Korea's actions remaining in compliance with international law, would have amounted to a crime of aggression, although with preventative warfare becoming increasingly widely accepted in the Western world in the post–Cold War years, this was considered a legitimate operation domestically. A number of factors ultimately prevented the attack from being approved, primarily a combination of North Korea's significant military capabilities which made any risk of escalation to full scale war highly undesirable, as well as a strong Western consensus that the country's economic and political collapse was an inevitability with the USSR gone.

As Defense Secretary Wiliam Perry and Army Generals John Shalikashvili and Gary Luck informed President Clinton on May 19, the Pentagon projected that a war could, within its first 90 days, cause 52,000 American and 490,000 South Korean casualties and set the Treasury back $61 billion. These estimates

---

vi Carter would remain a leading advocate of an attack on North Korea into the early years of the George W. Bush administration, and when appointed secretary of defense under the second Barack Obama administration would oversee escalations that again brought Washington to the brink of war with Pyongyang.

were considered conservative.[56] The casualty predictions did not improve following the first ninety days, with over 1 million personnel and civilians from America and its allies expected to be killed, including 80,000 to 100,000 Americans. The destruction of property and interruption to business activity would cost more than one trillion dollars to the countries involved and their immediate neighbors.[57] Subsequent assessments would highlight that these war plans appeared to understate civilian casualties,[58] stressing that attacking North Korea would have been "an enormous gamble, especially from South Korea's standpoint."[59] Although Ashton Carter and his colleagues dismissed the risk of radiation contamination from bombing a then-very active nuclear facility, studies showed that a quarter of the North Korean population within a 48 kilometer radius of Yongbyon would have very likely died. The fallout would have contaminated much of the peninsula and affected both China and Japan.[60]

The threat of war, and with it by far the greatest wartime humanitarian catastrophe since the Second World War, was seen to be sufficiently serious that the Seoul stock market suffered considerably, dropping 25 percent on June 15 alone.[61] Unlike in Operation Desert Storm, however, preceding which the U.S. had built up a vast force on Iraq's doorstep for over five months, a similar military buildup in Korea never occurred and was considered far from viable.[vii] There was a near unanimous consensus that the North Koreans would not similarly allow this to occur and would launch preemptive strikes on arriving forces to ensured engagements took place while the correlation of forces was less

---

vii Although the unacceptability of the risks from an attack appeared clear to the Pentagon, this did not stop current and former civilian officials from advocating such action. The previous administration's National Security Council Advisor Brent Scowcroft and former Undersecretary of State Arnold Kanter, the latter the highest ranking official to have ever held official talks with the North Koreans, on June 15 published a *Washington Post* article titled "Korea: Time For Action," advocating attacks on its nuclear facilities. The *Wall Street Journal* that day published the article "Korea: Raise Another Desert Shield," in reference to the operation preceding Desert Storm, advocating a U.S. military buildup on North Korea's doorstep. The article advocated attacking any Chinese vessel violating an Iraq-style blockade.

unfavorable.[viii] With the Clinton administration having planned for war without consulting Seoul, which alongside Pyongyang had the most to lose from a new war on the peninsula, South Korean President Kim Young Sam insisted that his phone call with President Clinton had delayed a planned American attack, pushing the date back to mid-June.[62]

Highlighting how the threat of the U.S. initiating a war without consulting Seoul was perceived, President Kim's chief of staff Park Kwan Yong recalled: "It was truly astounding to learn that the U.S. was planning to carry out a military operation that could escalate into war without providing the slightest explanation or notification to [South] Korea, one of the parties in the conflict. I felt not so much shocked as numb at the thought that our destiny could be determined in such a way."[63] Joel Wit, Daniel Poneman and Robert Gallucci, who played central roles in U.S.-DPRK talks and held prominent State Department and National Security Council positions, highlighted that "the tougher the United States acted toward North Korea, the more unnerved the South became in understandable anxiety at the prospect of war." "In Seoul, attitudes toward North Korea and the United States have changed dramatically: many South Koreans now see their American allies as a greater threat than their North Korean rivals," they added.[64] As otherwise summarized in one CATO Institute assessment of U.S. attack plans, should Pyongyang retaliate: "It isn't clear whether the South Korean public would be angrier with North Korea or the U.S."[65]

---

viii Military leaders had widely stressed that such a massive redeployment would hardly be possible under normal conditions, with Iraq's inept diplomacy and its sacrificing of military opportunities to pursue unrealistic hopes of a diplomatic solution considered unlikely to be repeated by other U.S. adversaries. As Deputy Commander of the U.S. Transportation Command Vice Admiral Paul Butcher observed: "we ought to keep in perspective that we've had the luxury of time – 161 days to land all that stuff with nobody firing a shot," and had conditions been any less ideal "you've got a hell of a mess and the shortfalls in airlift and sealift would have been exposed." Other analysts similarly pointed to the Gulf War as a "free ride" for how ideal conditions had been. (Wilson, George C., 'Operation Highlights Weakness of U.S. Forces,' *Washington Post*, February 10, 1991 (p. A23).)

The seriousness of projections for an actual military assault remain very much in question, and there are strong indications that the Clinton administration had instead sought to use military pressure to force Pyongyang into a more favourable deal. As President Clinton would recall in his memoir, as early as the beginning of May he had "received a sobering estimate of the staggering losses both sides would suffer if war broke out," stating that the colossal fallout that was expected to ensue from an attack was the primary reason he had decided against it.[66] The fact that Washington never got as far as ordering an evacuation of American citizens from South Korea, let alone reinforcing its 37,000 personnel in the country, indicates that the administration was still much further from ordering an attack than many sources claim. Alternatives considered included pushing for further economic sanctions at the United Nations, and deploying more forces to South Korea, including 50,000 more personnel. Neither would have prevented North Korea from developing nuclear weapons and the latter option carried the significant risk of inviting preemptive strikes.[67] With no viable options other than to negotiate, the Clinton administration benefited from the mediation of former president Jimmy Carter, who on June 16 used his direct line to the White House to reach a preliminary spoken agreement.

Pyongyang appeared to have come out on top in the standoff, and under the subsequent Agreed Framework deal it did not concede anything that it had not previously expressed a willingness to, while the United States offered a great deal more than it previously had.[ix] The terms given to former president Carter were near

---

ix Much as officials under the two Bush administrations expressed significant disdain towards reports and initiatives that undermined their primary *causus belli* against Iraq, so too were Clinton administration officials by many accounts thoroughly disappointed. As a State Department official related to Leon Sigal of the Northeast Asia Cooperative Security Project: "The shocking thing about the Carter visit wasn't that people were disappointed that someone was going. It was that when he got the freeze, people here were crestfallen." As otherwise observed by scholar Aiden Warren in his study of preventative warfare, attacks on Yongbyon "commanded a wide range of support throughout the U.S. government as well as the general population. So popular was the notion that the U.S. should eliminate North Korea's nuclear capability that one high-ranking South Korean diplomat

identical to those North Korea had several months prior given to Representative Gary Ackerman during his lengthy talks with President Kim Il Sung. As recalled by Ackerman, President Kim "was very receptive. It was disappointing to me that when I returned, the Clinton administration did not accept that as real, and it was not until several months later, on Jimmy Cartner's visit... that he announced right after the meeting very publicly what then became the Framework Agreement."[68] Pyongyang's terms had not changed, but the Clinton administration's gradual coming to terms with its lack of serious alternatives had forced it to accept.

Signed on October 21, 1994 the Agreed Framework stipulated under Article 1 that the United States would "undertake to make arrangements for the provision to the DPRK of a LWR [light water reactor] project with a total generating capacity of approximately 2,000 MW(e) by a target date of 2003," with oil to be delivered by the U.S. free of charge until these reactors were operational to compensate for the loss in power generation capacity. These more complex reactors were beyond the capabilities of North Korean industry to produce, and while being more effective for electricity generation than the country's simpler gas-graphite facilities, they were effectively unusable for nuclear weapons development. In return North Korea would freeze work at Yongbyon and place the cooling ponds storing the extracted fuel rods under IAEA supervision, while suspending construction both at the second Yongbon facility and at the Taechon facility. With both facilities set to have been completed by the end of 1996, and to make much needed contributions to power generation, this was a significant concession.[69]

Under Article 2 the United States would "move toward full normalization of political and economic relations... Within

---

on his first trip to Washington was reportedly 'struck by the willingness of the American witnesses – think-tank experts and former U.S. officials – to advocate a preventive strike against North Korea.'" While military options were favored, unlike against Iraq they were never truly viable against North Korea. (Bandow, Doug, 'Laying South Korea's Kim Young-Sam to Rest: Former President Stopped Second Korean War,' *CATO Institute*, November 26, 2015.) (Warren, Aiden, *Prevention, Pre-emption and the Nuclear Option,* Abingdon, Routledge, 2012 (Chapter 3).)

three months of the date of this Document, both sides will reduce barriers to trade and investment, including restrictions on telecommunications services and financial transactions." This was to pave the way to an exchange of ambassadors. Under Article 3 Washington was also bound to "provide formal assurances to the DPRK against the threat or use of nuclear weapons by the U.S.," which alongside normalized diplomatic relations represented the security guarantees Pyongyang had long pushed for. The terms of the agreement thus appeared highly favorable to North Korea, and while under Article 4 it did concede to allow "ad hoc and routine inspections" by the IAEA "with respect to the facilities not subject to the freeze," this was only to take effect "upon conclusion of the supply contract for the provision of the LWR project" in the mid-2000s. By this time relations with the U.S. were to have been normalized and full security guarantees provided, considerably minimizing the threat from exposing its facilities.

In the three-quarter century conflict between Pyongyang and Washington, the Agreed Framework stands out as the only agreement reached that was highly favorable to North Korea, and had the potential to effectively end the conflict and allow its integration into the global economy and the post–Cold War international community. The nuclear program, combined with an ability to very seriously deter Western military action, had served to provide it with a very strong negotiating position which forced the U.S. and wider Western world to ease tensions and normalize ties, and left them unable to impose additional political and economic conditions for doing so. With the post–Cold War international order and global economy heavily centered on the power of the United States and other Western Bloc countries, this was a highly desirable breakthrough that could have heralded the beginning of a new phase in relations similar to the Sino-U.S. rapprochement of the 1970s. Where China's leverage in the 1970s had been Washington's need for a partner against the Soviet Union, North Korea's leverage had been its nuclear program that had otherwise appeared unassailable.

The Years of the Agreed Framework: Awaiting a North Korean Collapse

For the United States and wider Western world, which had long been strongly committed to the complete destruction of North Korea, the extensive concessions made under the Agreed Framework could be best understood in the context of their lack of viable alternatives. They equally significantly, however, were results of the strong confidence in the Western world that North Korea would collapse long before the terms of the deal needed to be fulfilled. As observed by the administration's Korea specialist Wendy Sherman: "At the beginning of the second Clinton administration, we had a meeting to discuss our agenda. Everyone in the room thought that North Korea would collapse within two years."[70] It was widely reported in the Western press, and privately admitted by Clinton administration officials, that Washington had agreed to the terms of the Agreed Framework only because an imminent North Korean collapse was considered highly likely.[71] North Korean officials had also suspected that the Clinton administration had committed to concessions only to buy time, freezing the nuclear program until the projected state collapse had occurred.[72] The death of President Kim Il Sung on July 8, three months before the Framework's signing, only further increased Western optimism in this regard.

The predominant Western paradigm for viewing geopolitical trends in the post–Cold War era was most prominently summarized by scholar Francis Fukuyama in his 1992 paper *The End of History,* which predicted a universalization of Western ideology, political systems and economic models unchallenged across the non-Western world. Beyond this, however, a North Korean collapse was considered even more imminent than a collapse of communist governments in China, Vietnam or Laos due to the very different way the state's identity had been perceived in the West since its founding in 1948. The DPRK had since that time been portrayed as a puppet and satellite of the Soviet Union, with such portrayals strongly encouraged particularly in the early Cold War years as part of an effort to deny it legitimacy, and thereby support the claim of the Western-aligned South Korean government to be the sole legitimate Korean government.

Thus although President Kim had had a long history of fighting Japanese colonial forces in Manchuria, and was considered a national hero when the Second World War ended, senior State Department officials would assert: "The relationship between Stalin and Kim Il Sung is exactly the same as that between Walt Disney and Donald Duck" – delegitimizing the government in Pyongyang and its leader as a Soviet puppet. South Korean state media went so far as to claim that the northern leader was an impostor using the name of the famed freedom fighter. Observations by U.S. officials on the ground in Korea, however, often strongly contradicted these conclusions.[73]

Regarding the contrast between North Korea and Eastern European communist states, prominent Korea expert at Columbia University Charles Armstrong observed: "The Soviet occupation authorities in Eastern Europe were much more heavy-handed than their American counterparts; the opposite is true in Korea," highlighting that the USSR refrained from "manipulating of North Korea's internal affairs" in sharp contrast to the U.S. military government in the south.[74] The governing people's committees in northern Korea were neither established nor run under Soviet direction,[75] and had already began to organize governing institutions, including a police force, before the Soviets arrived.[76] As Kim Namsik, a South Korean scholar who witnessed this period in North Korea firsthand, observed: "The People's Regime of North Korea was founded on the basis of the People's Committees spontaneously organized after liberation.... The People's Committees were not created from the center but organized from the bottom up."[77] The lack of Soviet influence became particularly evident in the 1950s, with overly "pro-Soviet" Koreans purged from government as part of an ideological and political break with Moscow,[78] while no similar break would have been possible in the Warsaw Pact states, nor a break with Washington in South Korea.

While predictions of a North Korean collapse based on ideological and systematic factors were increasingly acknowledged to have had little foundation, economic factors provided grounds for optimism in the West that the country could face instability after a sharp decline. The loss of the vast majority of its foreign trade as the country was cut off by the former USSR and Warsaw Pact states was a primary factor which exacerbated the effects of the Western sanctions regime, isolating it from the vast majority of opportunities for trade, tech or industrial cooperation to an unprecedented degree. With the Soviet Union cutting off aid from the mid-1980s, North Korea was required from 1990 to pay for energy imports in hard currency, which combined with an inability to generate sufficient foreign currency due to the sanctions regime led to predictions that up to 50 percent of its industry could become idle. This had added significant urgency to the development of a nuclear energy industry to mitigate reliance on imported fuel, as while North Korea lacked oil it retained significant deposits of uranium. An early response to the changed economic climate by the North Korean government was to restructure the economy and increase the emphasis on light industry.[79] Another was to shift towards partial marketization and encouragement of foreign investment, with one of the most notable examples being the opening of the Rason industrial zone near the Chinese border loosely modeled on Chinese industrial zones, which South Korean and other foreign firms were allowed to operate in. Such zones capitalized on the dollar's high purchasing power in the country, which resulted in low salaries, with this combined with a famously diligent, educated and skilled labor force making investment highly attractive.

While in the Western world Chinese leader Chairman Deng Xiaoping was widely credited with having stimulated the country's economic revival through partial marketization and opening of the country to foreign investment, with this often contrasted to the North Korean leadership portrayed as inward looking, this appeared to be out of line with the realities of Pyongyang's policies. Where China had been cut off from Soviet trade and investment since the beginning of the 1960s, thirty years before North Korea, the country had been seeking normalization of ties with the United States since 1949,[80] with normalization of political and economic ties having been primarily a result of a policy shift in Washington which, following multiple setbacks in its Cold War with the USSR and facing an increasingly unfavorable economic situation, opened to China. In much the same way, while North Korea marketized its economy significantly from the 1990s, and redoubled longstanding efforts to normalize ties with Washington that decade, no matter how similar to Deng Xiaoping's Kim Il Sung or his successor Kim Jong Il's policies and intentions were, with no equivalent to Richard Nixon or Henry Kissinger in Washington no breakthroughs were possible. With the U.S. at the height of its power having little need to use Pyongyang to counterbalance another adversary, its circumstances were entirely different. While a transformation of the North Korean economy appeared imminent when the Agreed Framework was signed, Washington would refuse to meet its obligations and left "about 99 percent" of sanctions in place,[81] meaning this could never occur. Maintaining the sanctions regime was seen to increase the chances of the state's disintegration and absorption by South Korea.

The rationale for sustaining economic pressure was effectively summarized as follows by Selig S. Harrison, who had played a central role in initiating negotiations between Washington and Pyongyang:

> While the North Korean system is not likely to "implode" or "explode" in the foreseeable future, as General [Gary] Luck predicts, it could well erode over a period of five to 10 years if the United States and its allies remain wedded to policies that exacerbate the economic problems facing the Kim Jong Il regime. In particular, the continuance of economic sanctions and a failure to give support to the U.N. food aid program in Pyongyang would undermine the prospects for a "soft landing."[82]

This rationale for economic pressure was later summarized as follows by the president of the Association of Korean Political Studies in North America Pak Kyung Ae: "a failure of a national economy undermines the legitimacy of an authoritarian regime and triggers a transition to democracy, resulting in the termination of authoritarianism or socialism. Economic catalyst has been widely accepted as the catalyst of regime collapse."[83] With North Korea having suffered considerable economic contraction from 1990, hopes for a turnaround from 1994 were dashed as the U.S. sustained its economic warfare efforts in violation of the terms of the Agreed Framework. The situation would worsen very considerably from 1995 as natural disaster struck.

Preceding the division of Korea the peninsula's southern half had been its breadbasket, with only 17 percent of land in the north being arable while soil quality remained poor.[84] As a result, according to CIA assessments, it took until 1970 for North Korea to gain full food self-sufficiency, with a growth in grain output far exceeding population growth.[85] This required particularly high levels of mechanization and fertilizer production, both of which relied on energy imports. As observed in a 1978 CIA report: "North Korean agriculture is quite highly mechanized, fertilizer application is probably among the highest in the world, and irrigation projects are extensive."[86] Although energy-intensive, agriculture programs were highly successful, with American observers visiting the country in 1980s observing: "fields were a deep green and, when I visited villages, that every inch of land was carefully tended... In the 1980s the DPRK claimed to have the highest per hectare rice output in the world; although that claim cannot be proved, experts who visited the country did not question the North's general agricultural success."[87] From 1991 the constraining of energy imports from the Soviet Union, then Russia, resulted in a steady decline in calorie intakes, which although far from catastrophic was still significant. This would change, however, in 1995.

Months after the conclusion of the Agreed Framework, the United Nations Department of Humanitarian Affairs reported: "between 30 July and 18 August 1995, torrential rains caused devastating floods in the Democratic People's Republic of Korea. In one area, in Pyongsan county in North Hwanghae province, 877mm of rain were recorded to have fallen in just seven hours, an intensity of precipitation unheard of in this area... water flow in the engorged Amnoc River, which runs along the Korea/China border, was estimated at 4.8 billion tons over a 72-hour period. Flooding of this magnitude had not been recorded in at least 70 years."[88] International observers described rain of "biblical proportions,"[89] with this unprecedented in the country's recorded history and considered by some foreign observers to be the most severe flooding of the 20th century.[90]

Before the floods of 1995 had receded, a second year of severe flooding in 1996 significantly further exacerbated the damage, with close to a million acres of paddy and dry field covered with mud and taken out of cultivation and 1.5 million tons of stored grain destroyed. Population centers were evacuated en-masse, with the military in some instances dropping down from helicopters to provide assistance. Railroads, roads, bridges, dams and irrigation systems were destroyed, coal mines were flooded, some to an extent that they had to be completely abandoned, and industries were destroyed with some torn down for scrap.[91] The areas most severely affected both years were the country's south and southwestern breadbasket provinces producing most of its grain.[92] According to the UN Development Program's 1998 report, 85 percent of North Korea's power generating capacity was lost, over a quarter of the population, or around 5.4 million people lost their homes, and transportation and communication networks were blocked by mud flows. Reserves of rice and corn fell from 3–4 and 4–5 million tons respectively in 1989 to significantly less than 1 million tons each in 1996.[93] The situation was further exacerbated by a year of severe drought in 1997.[94]

Pyongyang officially claimed 225,000–235,000 deaths, although this figure was suspected to have been exaggerated as part of efforts to gain food aid from abroad. As a proportion of the population this was relatively low, considering the extreme circumstances the country faced. To place this in perspective, it was comparable to albeit slightly lower than the proportion of Indians who died every year from infant mortality, malnutrition and starvation.[95] The material damage, however, was far greater. The fallout from the flooding would provide grounds for Western officials to claim for decades that the country was intentionally starving its population, from President George W. Bush, who referred to a policy of "starving its citizens" as an indication of the state's "true nature,"[96] to U.S. ambassadors to the UN John Bolton and Samantha Power.[97] This added to a long list of fabricated atrocities used to justify a hard line and the objective of the state's destruction. Western officials and commentators would otherwise seek to particularly strongly downplay the effects of natural disaster in order to portray the North Korean government as responsible for the country's economic crisis.[98]

While keeping North Korea's nuclear program frozen, it was vital for Washington and its allies to ensure that the economic fallout from the loss of Soviet Bloc trade, and from subsequent extreme weather, was as severe as possible. As observed in a CFR assessment: "Opponents of food aid in the U.S. Congress suggest, implicitly, that if food aid were denied, the brutal North Korean government would be overthrown by a disillusioned populace."[99] As otherwise observed by leading Russian expert on North Korea Konstantin Asmolov, the South Korean government

> began to lobby for economic sanctions against North Korea to stop all deliveries of food. It seems they calculated "the worse, the better." A representative of the conservatives who later held a respectable diplomatic post openly told the author that, in seeking to restrict the flow of food aid to Pyongyang, they were pursuing a specific policy goal. In a crisis, the North Korean masses would begin to speak out against the regime, which would leave them to fend for themselves, and if the boat was correctly shaken, the communist state in the north would collapse.[100]

From the perspective of Western geopolitical interests the timing of the unprecedentedly severe flooding and drought just after the Agreed Framework was signed appeared almost too perfect to be true. This sparked not insignificant conspiracy theories that the U.S. was using weather modification technologies to cause the disasters, much as it had initially denied but was later confirmed to have heavily manipulated rainfall patterns during the

Vietnam War,[101] and as Washington and its allies were years later repeatedly alleged to be doing to exacerbate drought in Iran to supplement the effects of economic sanctions.[102] Assertions of a man-made crisis consistently highlighted expert assessments that North Korea's extreme flooding could not be natural, although this was generally attributed by scientists to global warming. Weather modification would fit into a much broader trend of major operations to target enemy agriculture to supplement the effects of economic warfare, from the targeting of North Korean irrigation dams at the end of the Korean War, to the burning of Syrian crops in the 2010s, although beyond circumstances, motive and means, actual evidence to substantiate such theories remained absent.[103] The traction which such theories gained nevertheless reflected the extent to which the timing of sudden and extreme natural disasters from 1995 was seen as "too perfect" for Western interests.

Survival and a Second Standoff

Despite enduring a perfect storm from the Soviet disintegration, the death of its founding father, economic sanctions, sustained military pressure, political isolation, and three years of very extreme weather, the absence of signs of instability in North Korea from the end of the 1990s increasingly dissipated the Western consensus on the inevitability of a collapse. As noted in a 1999 Council on Foreign Relations assessment: "North Korea has proven amazingly resilient," citing "almost no evidence of significant popular dissatisfaction with the Kim Jong Il regime" and that "North Koreans interviewed by visiting Western food aid officials do not appear to blame the regime for their hardship." There was "no indication of a serious rift within the leadership that might threaten the current regime," it concluded.[104,x]

---

x President of the Association of Korean Political Studies in North America Park Kyung Ae lamented the absence of anti-government sentiments among the population that economic hardship had been expected to stimulate, observing: "One Korean-Chinese hotel worker in Yanji remarked: 'Even though they go hungry, North Korean [economic] refugees still continue to praise the Great Leader.' North Koreans appear to attribute their economic difficulties to outside forces such as the collapse of the socialist market,

Western observers would gradually come to acknowledge the flaws of viewing North Korea "entirely through the lens of Soviet and East European communism," increasingly highlighting factors such as the country's "anti-colonial and revolutionary nationalist origins" and "very different history." Western assessments had widely "seen North Korea as a Soviet implant comparable to the defunct European communist regimes, and especially East Germany," and as a result after 1989 "oceans of ink were spilled… on the 'German model' of Korean reunification," only for such expectations to be disappointed.[105] The shift in consensus resulted in a growing perception that Washington needed to adopt a more active stance to force the state's destruction. Author of *The End of North Korea* and leading neoconservative thinker Nicholas Eberstadt, for one, having seen his prominent predictions for an East German model collapse fail to be realized, would call on Washington to "tear down this tyranny."[106]

With U.S. intelligence sources continuing to consistently confirm North Korea's full adherence to its obligations under the Agreed Framework,[107] the agreement poised the country to make a major recovery from the economic crises of the 1990s and end its diplomatic isolation once Washington belatedly began to meet its obligations. As summarized at a Hearing Before the Select Committee on Intelligence in 1995: "we assess that the North Korean leadership under Kim Jong Il will adhere to the Agreed Framework, particularly in the near term, as they perceive their chances for survival best served by strategies that emphasize economic improvement and political-economic opening to the United States and other industrialized nations."[108] In 1998 officials testified before Congress that there had been no fundamental violations of any aspect of the agreement by the Korean side,[109] with

economic sanctions by the U.S., and natural disasters, rather than to Kim Jong Il's leadership itself." Park noted that under 10 percent of defectors cited political dissatisfaction as their reason for leaving the country, stressing that it was vital for the West and South Korea to do more to create political dissatisfaction and opposition going forward as a path to destroying the state. (Park, Kyung-Ae, 'Regime Change in North Korea?: Economic Reform and Political Opportunity Structures,' *North Korean Review,* vol. 5, no. 1, Spring 2009 (pp. 23–45).)

U.S. intelligence confirming that the fuel rods remained under international supervision and that all operations at Yongbyon had halted, while construction of the two larger reactors had ceased.[110]

While the Agreed Framework served to buy time for the United States, the disappointment of expectations for a North Korean collapse ultimately left Washington bound to concessions that were highly unfavorable to its objective of Pyongyang's absolute defeat. Although North Korea's full compliance was undisputed, the U.S. subsequently went on to violate all four articles of the agreement as part of an effort both to increase economic pressure on the country and to sustain its diplomatic isolation in the hope that this would help further stimulate a collapse. Washington also demanded additional concessions not included in the agreement as conditions for the U.S. to meet obligations to which it had already committed under the deal.

The vast majority of American economic sanctions on North Korea, including the Trading with the Enemy Act, remained in place in violation of Article II, while Washington continued to refuse to form diplomatic ties, provide security guarantees or to recognize North Korea's right to exist. Oil deliveries Washington was obliged to make began to be delayed from 1996, and by 1998 the U.S. had still not even begun to fund the light water reactors it was obliged to have constructed by 2003, placing it far behind schedule. A 1998 Senate Hearing repeatedly addressed Washington's failure to meet its requirements, although this was not corrected.[111] Pyongyang's response was to warn that it would restart work at Yongbyon,[112] while chief American negotiator Robert Gallucci warned that the framework faced serious risk of collapse unless the United States came closer to meeting its obligations.[113] Making the obliged energy exports was widely opposed in Washington on the basis that it would slow down North Korea's economic collapse, with the meeting of obligations for sanctions relief also considered out of the question for this reason.[114] Delayed energy exports and no sanctions relief thus appeared to be a compromise between the need to avoid collapsing the Agreed Framework entirely, and the need to exacerbate Pyongyang's economic difficulties.

East Asia policy expert Selig S. Harrison, who was reportedly the first to gain President Kim Il Sung's approval for a freeze on the work at Yongbyon in June 1994, was among the most notable sources to report on the state of U.S. adherence to its obligations under the Agreed Framework. An often harsh critic of Pyongyang, Harrison nevertheless observed that the U.S. was nowhere near meeting its obligations, while North Korea had fully met its own, stating:

> The removal of U.S. economic sanctions is a prerequisite for the overall liberalization of economic relations with the West and Japan that the North seeks as the key to solving its economic problems, especially its food shortage. It was primarily because the United States promised to remove these sanctions that Pyongyang decided to conclude the nuclear freeze agreement. Article II, Section One of the agreement stated that "within three months of the date of this document, both sides will reduce barriers to trade and investment." This provision was unconditional and was not linked to performance on other issues.
>
> North Korean leaders express growing impatience with the United States for its failure to honor Article II. When I visited Pyongyang in September 1995, Vice Premier and Foreign Minister Kim Yong Nam said bluntly that the United States has cheated Pyongyang out of the most important benefits promised under the freeze agreement. In December 1996, high-ranking officials who came to New York for negotiations with U.S. diplomats told me in both formal and informal meetings that hardliners in Pyongyang were pushing aggressively for revocation of the agreement. What these officials say, in effect, is, "We're living up to our side of the deal. We have frozen our nuclear program, and this has been verified by the International Atomic Energy Agency inspectors and by U.S. government experts. We've given up our nuclear independence, and we've done it for one reason: Because we thought this would lead to friendly

> relations with the United States, particularly economic relations. But you have made only token reductions in trade and investment barriers. You are not living up to your part of the deal."
>
> An objective evaluation of the sanctions issue indicates that the North Korea grievance is justified. By January 1997, all that the United States had done to implement Article II was to lift sanctions on the export of one commodity (magnesite) and to grant permission to AT&T to open up telephone and fax communications. The few U.S. companies that have shown an interest in investing cannot get Treasury Department licenses. General Motors, which looked into building an auto parts plant, is the prime example.[115]

Highlighting a further example of an American firm which had been unable to move ahead with planned projects as a result of Washington's refusal to lift sanctions, Harrison noted: "Cargill has received a license for a barter deal – North Korean minerals for grain – but sanctions prevent U.S. agencies from providing the collateral needed to get grain shipments started."[116] Pyongyang's continued unilateral adherence to the Agreed Framework bore testament to its importance to the country in the post–Cold War era.

While economic warfare continued, North Korea's emergence from the worst of its economic crisis in 1998 dimmed Western hopes for a state collapse, leading Washington to explore a broader range of policy options to increase pressure. Former Assistant Secretary of Defense for Global Strategic Affairs Ashton Carter, who had directed military planning during the 1994 crisis, would years later recall that in 1998 President Clinton had requested options for dealing with North Korea, observing regarding the proposals provided to him: "One was to undermine the North Korean regime and hasten its collapse. But we did not have evidence of significant internal dissent in this rigid Stalinist system, certainly nothing like that in Iraq, let alone Afghanistan that could provide a U.S. lever. Then there was the problem of mismatched timetables: undermining seemed a long-term prospect at best," while the administration needed near-term policy options. A further drawback of this approach, he noted, was that "adopting it openly could only worsen North Korea's behavior, prompting provocations and even war." He concluded that there were few other good options, although highlighting that "our decision not to undermine the regime could be used as a negotiating lever" and could be threatened should it resume nuclear weapons development.[117]

Three years of natural disaster passed between the signing of the Agreed Framework in 1994, and the renewed escalation of American pressure against Pyongyang from mid-1998. Military options began to again be openly raised from that time, while U.S. forces that year began simulation training exercises for nuclear attacks on North Korea.[118] In June the U.S. Congress' Commission to Assess the Ballistic Missile Threat to the United States claimed North Korea was "working hard" on an ICBM which "could be deployed rapidly" in the near future to threaten the U.S. mainland, and that its missile programs, despite a moratorium on testing, posed "a substantial and immediate danger to the U.S., its vital interests and its allies." Headed by soon-to-be defense secretary Donald Rumsfeld and many of the neoconservative hardliners who would under the next administration be leading advocates of abandoning the Agreed Framework and using military coercion against Pyongyang, the report's claims proved grossly exaggerated and were widely considered as such at the time. They nevertheless proved effective in strengthening calls for a policy shift.[119] In October Marine Lieutenant General Raymond P. Ayres spoke publicly about plans to erase North Korea from the map, stressing that should the U.S. see signs of plans by the country to attack, "the entire resources" of the Marines would be thrown into a campaign to "abolish North Korea as a state and... 'reorganize' it" under South Korean control. "We'll kill 'em all," he added regarding any North Korean resistance that might be faced.[120] Washington's refusal to hold direct bilateral negotiations and sign an official nonaggression pact, which was at the forefront of Pyongyang's demands, further increased concerns regarding American intentions.[121]

A further means of increasing pressure was through allegations from August that North Korea was building new nuclear facilities in secret at a site near the village of Kumchang not far from the Chinese border, which although far from violating the Agreed Framework was viewed as unacceptable in Washington. The Defense Intelligence Agency was quick to conclude with near certainty that construction at the site was a nuclear facility, with former Army intelligence official Charles Pritchard, who served as the deputy head of America's North Korea negotiating team, observing: "Everybody threw up their hands and said we don't know what it is, but we don't have a better explanation." The agency's adamant conclusion "turned up in the *New York Times* before we were ready," he recalled, with the Page One story fueling demands in Washington to force Pyongyang to provide access – a course of events which had caused the original 1993 crisis.[122]

Pyongyang surprised all expectations by agreeing to allow inspections of the military site at Kumchang, effectively diffusing the crisis, but also setting an unfavorable precedent for future demands by Washington to examine its military bases. The fact that the facility was still under construction and not yet operational may have been a key factor reducing opposition. Two visits by American inspectors using a range of complex equipment to examine the facility revealed that, while this was a sensitive defense facility of an undetermined nature, in Pritchard's words: "there was no way that it was nuclear." This conclusion was reaffirmed in a 2003 review of the incident.[123] The Kumchang incident foreshadowed the drama that would unfold three years later surrounding allegations of Iraqi WMD sites, with many alleged sites similarly proving to have nothing to do with such efforts.[124] It would hardly be the last time that North Korea was alleged with little foundation to be developing nuclear weapons at new sites.

On August 31, 1998 North Korea conducted its first ever attempted satellite launch, with its Paektusan launcher using the same technologies as the Hwasong-7, namely an enlarged derivative of Scud technologies, but adding a second stage enabling it to travel much further. Much like North Korea's subsequent much larger Unha series of launchers that would fly from the following decade, the Paektusan was widely referred to in the West as a ballistic missile. It was named the "Taepodong missile" based on the region from which it was fired, much as Unha launchers would be named "Taepodong 2 missiles." Although the State Department would on September 14 conclude that the Paektusan had indeed been a satellite launcher, after the administration was described as having "largely ignored official North Korean statements that the August 31 launch involved a satellite," it would continue to predominantly be referred to in the West as a missile into the 2020s.[125] Both satellite launcher types were totally unviable as ballistic missiles due primarily to their fixed launch sites and weeks of required assembly and preparation before launch.

While the launch of either a ballistic missile or a satellite remained entirely legal, and no stipulations under the Agreed Framework had restricted North Korea from doing either, the launch nevertheless further raised concerns in the United States and strengthened calls for a harder line against Pyongyang. Its misrepresentation as a missile test was a significant factor in this regard. Regarding its political implications, an assessment by the *Arms Control Association* highlighted that "the launch may also have been staged as a reminder to Washington of North Korea's dissatisfaction with U.S. performance in implementing the 1994 nuclear agreement."[126] The launch notably came five months after warnings from the Foreign Ministry that if the U.S. did not move forward with meeting its Agreed Framework obligations, Pyongyang would withdraw and resume "nuclear research," and could thus have represented a measure short of action at Yongbyon to increase pressure on Washington.[127]

With sustained economic pressure having failed to yield the political outcome intended, and with Washington's attentions at the time highly preoccupied, having just launched missile attacks on Iraq, Afghanistan and Sudan and preparing for a looming air assault on Yugoslavia, the Clinton administration ultimately again sought compromise. In talks from 1999, Washington pledged that it would better live up to its terms under the Agreed Framework, in particular normalization of economic and political ties, if North Korea agreed to a moratorium on testing of ballistic missiles, and to dismantle much of its arsenal. While the U.S. reportedly offering little beyond the terms to which it was already bound, its position was strengthened by its major show of force over Yugoslavia from March 24, 1999.

To an even greater extent than Operation Desert Storm, the assault on Yugoslavia demonstrated that the Western world could exercise military power with near total impunity, with the offensive seeing severe war crimes committed throughout its duration. The *New York Times* was among many sources to highlight that NATO had "lost the distinction between military and civilian targets and aims."[128] Examples included targeting of key civilian infrastructure such as bridges and electrical plants that had few military uses, bombing TV stations after they refused to alter their broadcasts to relay messages from NATO,[129] and scattering of cluster munitions across civilian areas, at times into crowds in broad daylight.[130] As deputy chief of the State Department's Yugoslav desk George Kenney conceded: "Dropping cluster bombs on highly populated urban areas doesn't result in accidental fatalities. It is purposeful terror bombing."[131] The house of Yugoslav President Slobodan Milosevic was singled out for targeting, a war crime,[132] as was the 23-story Belgrade high-rise housing the headquarters of the Socialist Party of Serbia and the Yugoslav United Left party. Mass targeting of civilian industry was referred to by NATO as an effort to destroy the "national assets" of Yugoslavia, ranging from car plants and tobacco concerns to petroleum refineries,[133] with the first month of attacks alone causing over $100 billion in material damage, overwhelmingly to civilian targets.[134] The *Chicago Tribune* was among the sources to observe that the campaign was waged as "a war against all of the Serbs" with the goal of taking out "the mainstays of the Serbian economy," stressing that "torturing or killing innocents in order to further a political goal is normally regarded as terrorism," but was "seen by NATO as a perfectly legitimate strategy."[135] Much like in the Gulf War, the West proved masterful in shaping the information space through atrocity narratives to justify its assault, with these similarly consistently proven false after the conflict ended.[136] The mass graves at the center of Western claims of a Yugoslav genocide,[137] referred to in 80 *New York Times* articles from June-August alone, were found to have never existed.[138]

Much like the planned strikes on North Korea five years prior, the assault on Yugoslavia was entirely illegal as acknowledged by even its strongest advocates in the Western world, highlighting that international law prohibiting crimes of aggression could be violated with impunity.[139] Although the air assault was strongly opposed by Russia, China and India, the bombing highlighted the extent of the limitations of the leading non-Western powers to respond, even in what had been the "backyard" of the USSR. This point was further made on May 7 by the bombing of the office of the military attaché at the Chinese embassy, which even within the Western world was widely believed to have been intentional, with information over the following months strongly supporting this conclusion.[140] CIA Director George Tenet subsequently confirmed that the strike had been a special mission carried out outside of NATO, and had been the only air strike of the campaign organized and directed by his agency rather than by the Pentagon.[141] With China remaining North Korea's sole treaty ally, the brazen bombing of its embassy with a precision guided weapon highlighted the West's confidence that Beijing had a very limited ability to confront Western Bloc power, and that the country knew its place in the global order and could do little more than protest when its partners from Khartoum to Belgrade were attacked.

The means by which the embassy attack was launched also represented a considerable show of force, with the new B-2 bomber that had entered service two prior years used. The aircraft combined stealth and very high precision with a massive 18,000 kilogram weapons payload, allowing each to deploy 16 conventional or B61 nuclear warheads against 16 separate targets per sortie. This revolutionized American offensive capabilities, allowing the fleet of just 21 B-2 to destroy an array of targets that would previously have required entire fleets and major military buildups. Where U.S. military leaders had highlighted in the preceding years that ballistic missiles like North Korea's could leave fighters vulnerable through strikes on their bases, including America's sole prior class of stealth aircraft, the F-117 fighter, B-2s were launched on 30-hour sorties from Whiteman Air Base, Missouri, which would be well beyond North Korea's missile reach for the next 18 years.[142,xi]

In the aftermath of the devastation of Yugoslavia, and with North Korea itself severely weakened by sanctions, isolation and natural disaster, Pyongyang proved willing to make a particularly wide range of concessions. Eighteen days after the strike on the Chinese embassy Ashton Carter and former defense secretary William Perry arrived in Pyongyang as part of the first ever visit by U.S. presidential envoys, and agreed that North Korea would impose a unilateral moratorium on missile testing. This included suspending the testing of a successor to the Paektusan satellite launcher, as well as the larger Unha launcher which U.S. intelligence has assessed as likely to fly in the near future. Significant modifications to the launch facility had already begun from the Autumn of 1998 and had just been completed by July the following year.[143] Having in Carter's words threatened that the U.S. and its allies would "resort to all means of pressure, including those that risked war, to achieve our objectives,"[144] the envoys offered that Washington would in return refrain from imposing additional sanctions and would be more inclined to meet its Agreed Framework obligations to improve diplomatic and economic ties. Progress in talks, and a lasting moratorium on missile testing, led Washington to slightly ease trade sanctions on North Korea in September 1999, although with this still very far short of the level of sanctions relief Washington was obliged to provide under the Agreed Framework, North Korea would make a case

---

xi While Iraq's ballistic missile arsenal had unperformed considerably, it had drawn attention to the fact that a more capable arsenal could seriously limit American air power. In 1996, for example, commander of coalition air forces in the Gulf War General Charles Horner told Congress that potential adversaries' ballistic missile arsenals made it necessary "to shift as much of the power projection burden as we can – as fast as we can – to long-range systems" capable of fighting from greater distances. The B-2 represented the realization of this, and was a threat against which North Korea was wholly unable to respond. (Prepared Statement of General Charles A. Horner Before the House Security Procurement Subcommittee, House Committee on National Security, U.S. Congress, September 12, 1996 (p. 81).)

for a full lifting of U.S. sanctions at the UN General Assembly on September 28.[145]

State Secretary Madeline Albright subsequently visited North Korea on October 22, 2000 holding talks with Chairman Kim Jong Il at length, with a deal expected to be finalized during a visit by President Clinton. Pyongyang was able to resist U.S. pressure to give up its entire ballistic missile arsenal, pledging only to refrain from further testing and from developing new missile classes, although ultimately the deal was never finalized due to the end of the Clinton administration's tenure. Bill Clinton would in his memoir largely blame Palestinian leader Yasser Arafat for this, claiming Arafat had delayed him at Middle East peace talks with false hopes of a deal which prevented him from flying to North Korea.[146] There was not inconsiderable speculation that Washington was again seeking to buy time against North Korean missile development efforts, and that the impending change in administration would provide a perfect pretext for ending talks with no outcome.

Endnotes

1 *The First Twenty-five Years of the World Intellectual Property Organization, from 1967 to 1992*, Geneva, International Bureau of Intellectual Property, 1992 (pp. 294–295).

2 Abt, Felix, *A Capitalist in North Korea: My Seven Years in the Hermit Kingdom*, North Clarendon, VT, Tuttle, 2014 (Chapter 2, Part 3).

3 Cumings, Bruce, 'Why Did So Many Influential Americans Think North Korea Would Collapse?,' in: Kim, Suk Hi and Roehrig, Terence and Seliger, Bernhard (eds.), *The Survival of North Korea: Essays on Strategy, Economics and International Relations*, Jefferson, NC, McFarland & Co., 2005 (p. 48).

4 International Institute for Strategic Studies, *The Military Balance,* vol. 85, 1985 (p. 26).

5 'Soviets Say Iraq Accepts Kuwait Pullout Linked to Truce and End to Sanctions; Bush Rejects Conditions: War Is to Go On,' *New York Times*, February 22, 1991.

'Gorbachev's "Diplomatic Marathon" to Prevent the 1991 Persian Gulf War,' *National Security Archive,* February 26, 2021.

Kapeliouk, Amnon, 'The U.S.S.R. and the Gulf Crisis,' *Journal of Palestine Studies,* vol. 20, no. 3, Spring 1991 (pp. 70–78).

6 Wells, Donald Arthur, *The United Nations: States vs International Laws*, New York, Algora Publishing, 2005 (p. 86).

Heikal, Mohamed, *Illusions of Triumph: An Arab View of the Gulf War*, New York, HarperCollins, 1993 (pp. 348, 352, 355, 356).

7 'Flashback: 1991 Gulf War,' *BBC News*, March 20, 2003.

8 Gellman, Barton, 'Allied Air War Struck Broadly in Iraq,' *Washington Post*, June 23, 1991.

9 Cullen, Tony and Foss, Christopher F., *Jane's Land-Based Air Defense 1992–93*, Couldson, Jane's Information Group, 1992 (p. 11).

10 DeGhett, Torie Rose, 'The Food and Agriculture Organisation War Photo No One Would Publish,' *The Atlantic*, August 8, 2014.

MacArthur, John R., *Second Front: Censorship and Propaganda in the 1991 Gulf War*, Berkeley, University of California Press, 2004 (pp. xv-xvi, 75–76).

Sloyan, Patrick J., 'What I saw was a bunch of filled-in trenches with people's arms and legs sticking out of them. For all I know, we could have killed thousands,' *The Guardian*, February 14, 2003.

11 MacArthur, John R., *Second Front: Censorship and Propaganda in the 1991 Gulf War*, Berkeley, University of California Press, 2004 (pp. 73–76).

12 'Air-Sea Battle Doctrine: A Discussion with the Chief of Staff of the Air Force and Chief of Naval Operations,' *Brookings Institute*, May 16, 2012.

13 Spector, Leonard and Smith, Jacqueline, 'North Korea: The Next Nuclear Nightmare?,' *Arms Control Today*, vol. 21, no. 2, March 1991.

14 Lee, Chung Min, 'Arms Control in the Korean Peninsula,' *Washington Quarterly*, Summer 1991 (p. 195).

15 Crumplar, Robert K., *Kim Il Sung (North Korea), Another Saddam Hussein (Iraq)? Countering and Deterring Aggression in the Northern Pacific*, United States Naval War College, February 13, 1992.

16 Ibid.

17 Cohen, Eliot A. and Iklé, Fred C. and Rostow, Eugene V., 'Three Comments,' *The National Interest*, no. 34, Winter 1993/94 (pp. 38–39).

18 Mazarr, Michael J., *North Korea and the Bomb*, New York, St. Martin's Press, 1995 (p. 16).

19 Albright, David, 'How Much Plutonium Does North Korea Have?,' *Bulletin of the Atomic Scientists*, September/October 1994 (pp. 46–53).

20 Mack, Andrew J., 'North Korea and the Bomb,' *Foreign Policy*, Summer 1991 (pp. 93–94).

21 Crumplar, Robert K., *Kim Il Sung (North Korea), Another Saddam Hussein (Iraq)? Countering and Deterring Aggression in the Northern Pacific*, United States Naval War College, February 13, 1992.

22 Ibid.

23 Spector, Leonard S. and Smith, Jacqueline R., 'North Korea: The Next Nuclear Nightmare?,' *Arms Control Today*, March 1991 (p. 9).

24 Spector, Leonard S., 'The North Korean Nuclear Threat,' *The Wall Street Journal*, April 19, 1991 (p. A:14).

25 Kristensen, Hans M. and Norris, Robert S., 'A History of US nuclear Weapons in South Korea,' *Bulletin of Atomic Scientists,* vol. 73, no. 6, 2017 (pp. 349–357).

26 Wit, Joel S. and Poneman, Daniel B. and Gallucci, Robert L., *Going Critical: The First North Korean Nuclear Crisis*, Washngton, DC, Brookings Institution Press, 2004 (p. 11).

'South Korea to Cancel 1992 "Team Spirit" Joint Military Exercise,' *Yonhap News Agency*, January 7, 1992.

27 Gregg, Donald, 'Threats and Opportunities on the Korean Peninsula,' Korean Information Center, Federal News Service, July 20, 1994.

28 Sigal, Leon V., *Disarming Strangers: Nuclear Diplomacy with North Korea,* Princeton, Princeton University Press, 1998 (pp. 46, 47).

29 'March Letter and Memorandum from the UN Permanent Representative of the DPRK to the President of the UN Security Council,' United Nations Security Council Document, March 17, 1993 (pp. 1–10).

Wit, Joel S. and Poneman, Daniel B. and Gallucci, Robert L., *Going Critical: The First North Korean Nuclear Crisis*, Washngton, DC, Brookings Institution Press, 2004 (p. 14).

30 Ibid. (pp. 20–21).

31 Weiner, Tim, 'U.S. Spied on Iraq Under U.N. Cover, Officials Now Say,' *New York Times*, January 7, 1999.

32 Ritter, Scott, 'The Coup that Wasn't,' *The Guardian*, September 28, 2005.

Edwards, David and Cromwell, David, *Propaganda Blitz: How the Corporate Media Distort Reality*, London, Pluto Press, 2018 (Chapter 5).

'Scott Ritter and Seymour Hersh: Iraq Confidential,' *The Nation*, October 26, 2005.

33 Heikal, Mohamed, *Illusions of Triumph: An Arab View of the Gulf War*, New York, HarperCollins, 1993 (pp. 414, 415).

34 'Thaw in the Koreas?,' *Bulletin of Atomic Scientists,* vol. 48, no. 3, April 1992 (p. 16).

35 Cumings, Bruce, *Korea's Place in the Sun: A Modern History*, New York, W. W. Norton & Company, 1997 (pp. 489, 490).

KCNA, February 22, 1993.

36 Bracken, Paul, 'The North Korean nuclear program as a problem of state survival,' in: Mack, Andrew (ed.), *Asian Flashpoint: Security and the Korean Peninsula*, Canberra, Allen and Unwin, 1990 (p. 91).

37 'Nude, absolutely naked,' *Far Eastern Economic Review*, June 23, 1994 (p. 15).

38 Thomas, Raju G. C., *The Nuclear Non-Proliferation Regime: Prospects for the 21st Century*, London, MacMillan, 1998 (p. 227).

39 Staines, Reuben, 'US trained for strikes on NK,' *Korea Times*, November 7, 2004.

40 United States Strategic Command on Twitter: 'The U.S.S. Kentucky is part of what is called the "nuclear triad." The triad are the three components of a nuclear defense system: land-based missiles fired from secret silos, B-1 bombers that can drop them from the air, and submarine launched ballistic missiles,' November 16, 2017.

41 Burdman, Mark, 'North Korea set up for Iraq-style showdown,' *Executive Intelligence Review,* vol. 20, no. 11, March 12, 1993 (pp. 61–62).

42 Ibid.

43 'N. Korea Inviting Bloody Nose Over Nuclear Buildup,' *The Economist*, March 7, 1993.

44 Chairman of the Joint Chiefs of Staff, 'Report on the Roles, Missions, and Functions of the Armed Forces of the United States,' Washington, DC, February 1993 (pp. II-2).

Schmitt, Eric, 'Head of Nuclear Forces Plans for a New World,' *New York Times*, January 25, 1993 (p. B7).

45 Farrell, John, 'Team Spirit: A Case Study on the Value of Military Exercises as a Show of Force in the Aftermath of Combat Operations,' *Air and Space Power Journal,* vol. 23, no. 3, Fall 2009.

46 Blair, Bruce D., 'Russia's Doomsday Machine,' *New York Times*, October 8, 1993.

47 Sanger, David E., 'Missile is Tested by North Koreans,' *New York Times*, June 12, 1993.

Cumings, Bruce, *Korea's Place in the Sun: A Modern History*, New York, W. W. Norton & Company, 1997 (p. 490).

48 Jannuzi, Frank Sampson, 'Can the United States Cause the Collapse of North Korea? Should We Try?,' *Council on Foreign Relations*, January 13, 1999.

49 Postol, Theodore A., 'Lessons of the Gulf War Experience with Patriot,' *International Security,* vol. 16, no. 3, Winter 1991–1992 (pp. 119–171).

50 Gellman, Barton, 'Gulf War Workhorses Suffer in Analysis,' *Los Angeles Times,* April 10, 1992.

51 Joint Statement of the Democratic People's Republic of Korea and the United States of America, New York, June 11, 1993.

52 Hayes, Peter, 'Should the United States Supply Light Water Reactors to Pyongyang?,' *Nautilus Institute*, November 16, 1993.

Smith, R. Jeffrey, 'North Korea May Consider Reducing Atom Program,' *Washington Post*, June 22, 1992.

53 Sanger, David E., 'North Koreans Say Nuclear Fuel Rods Are Being Removed,' *New York Times*, May 15, 1994.

Schmitt, Eric, 'U.S. Delays Taking Steps Over A-Plant,' *New York Times*, May 16, 1994 (pp. A1, A3).

54 Carter, Ashton B. and Perry, William J., 'Back to the Brink,' *Washington Post*, October 20, 2002.

55 Bandow, Doug, 'Laying South Korea's Kim Young-Sam to Rest: Former President Stopped Second Korean War,' *CATO Institute*, November 26, 2015.

56 Orcutt, Daniel J., *Carrot, Stick, or Sledgehammer: US Policy Options for North Korean Nuclear Weapons,* INSS Occasional Paper 56, U.S. Air Force Institute for National Security Studies, USAF Academy, Colorado, August 2004.

57 Ibid.

58 Bandow, Doug, 'Honoring the Man Who Prevented the Second Korean War,' *CATO Institute*, November 30, 2015.

59 Bandow, Doug, 'Laying South Korea's Kim Young-Sam to Rest: Former President Stopped Second Korean War,' *CATO Institute*, November 26, 2015.

60 Ibid.

61 Orcutt, Daniel J., *Carrot, Stick, or Sledgehammer: US Policy Options for North Korean Nuclear Weapons,* INSS Occasional Paper 56, U.S. Air Force Institute for National Security Studies, USAF Academy, Colorado, August 2004.

62 Bandow, Doug, 'Laying South Korea's Kim Young-Sam to Rest: Former President Stopped Second Korean War,' *CATO Institute*, November 26, 2015.

63 'S. Korean presidential contender claims N. Korea wouldn't have nukes if Clinton had bombed Yongbyon,' *Hankyoreh*, September 28, 2021.

64 Wit, Joel S. and Poneman, Daniel B. and Gallucci, Robert L., *Going Critical: The First North Korean Nuclear Crisis*, Washington, DC, Brookings Institution Press, 2004 (pp. xv, xvii).

65 Bandow, Doug, 'Honoring the Man Who Prevented the Second Korean War,' *CATO Institute*, November 30, 2015.

66 Clinton, Bill, *My Life*, New York, Alfred A. Knopf, 2004 (Chapter 38).

67 Erickson, Amanda, 'The last time the U.S. was on "the brink of war" with North Korea,' *Washington Post*, August 9, 2017.

68 North Korea, Briefing and Hearing Before the Committee on Foreign Affairs, House of Representatives, One Hundred Tenth Congress, First Session, Washington, DC, January 18, 2007.

69 Albright, David, 'How Much Plutonium Does North Korea Have?,' *Bulletin of the Atomic Scientists*, September/October 1994 (pp. 46–53).

70 Dinmore, Guy and Ward, Andrew, 'Hawks at Home See No Scope for a Deal with the "Axle of Evil,"' *Financial Times,* August 28, 2003 (p. 6).

71 Kessler, Glenn, 'South Korea Offers To Supply Energy if North Gives Up Arms,' *Washington Post*, July 13, 2005.

72 Kim, Ji Yong, 'DPRK Will Re-Operate Nuclear Facilities Within A Few Weeks to Produce Electricity,' *The People's Korea*, January 27, 2003.

73 Meade, Edward Grant, *American Military Government in Korea*, New York, King's Crown Press, 1952 (pp. 56, 72, 188).

74 Armstrong, Charles, *The North Korean Revolution, 1945–1950,* Ithaca, Cornell University Press, 2003 (Chapter 2).

75 *Chŏn'guk inmin wiwonhoe taep'yoja taehoe ŭisarok* [Record of the National People's Committee Representative Conference], Seoul, Chosŏn chongp'ansa, 1946 (pp. 68–70).

76 Van Ree, Eric, *Socialism in One Zone: Stalin's Policy in Korea, 1945–1947*, Oxford, Berg, 1989 (p. 89).

77 Kim, Namsik, 'Rethinking the Pre- and Post-Liberation North Korean History,' *Haebang chŏnhusa ŏi insik*, vol. 5 (pp. 21, 22).

78 Szalontai, Balazs, *The Failure of De-Stalinization in North Korea, 1953–1964: The DPRK in a Comparative Perspective*, Budapest, Central European University, 2003.

Radchenko, Sergey S., *The Soviet Union and the North Korean Seizure of the USS Pueblo: Evidence from Russian Archives*, Cold War International History Project, Working Paper #47, Washington, DC, Woodrow Wilson International Center for Scholars, 2005.

David-West, Alzo, 'Between Confucianism and Marxism-Leninism: Juche and the Case of Chong Tasan,' *Korean Studies,* vol. 35, 2011 (pp. 93–121).

Buzo, Adrian, *The Guerilla Dynasty: Politics and Leadership in North Korea,* Boulder, Westview Press, 1999 (p. 67).

79 Wit, Joel S. and Poneman, Daniel B. and Gallucci, Robert L., *Going Critical: The First North Korean Nuclear Crisis*, Washington, DC, Brookings Institution Press, 2004 (p. 17).

80 Blum, William, *Killing Hope: U.S. Military and C.I.A. Interventions Since World War II*, London, Zed Books, 2003 (p. 21).

81 Smith, Jeffrey, 'Clinton Slightly Lowers Some Bars to Trade with North Korea,' *Washington Post*, January 21, 1995 (p. A11).

82 Harrison, Selig S., 'Promoting a Soft Landing in North Korea,' *Foreign Policy*, no. 106, Spring 1997 (p. 60).

83 Park, Kyung-Ae, 'Regime Change in North Korea?: Economic Reform and Political Opportunity Structures,' *North Korean Review,* vol. 5, no. 1, Spring 2009 (pp. 23–45).

84 Food and Agriculture Organisation/ World Food Programme Crop and Food Security Assessment Mision to the Democratic People's Republic of Korea, November 28, 2013.

85 Armstrong, Charles K., *The Koreas*, Abingdon, Routledge, 2007 (p. 71).

86 Korea: The Economic Race between North and South, National Foreign Assessment Center, Central Intelligence Agency, 1978.

87 Cumings, Bruce, *Korea's Place in the Sun: A Modern History*, New York, W. W. Norton, 1997 (p. 428).

88 UN Department of Humanitarian Affairs, 'United Nations Consolidated UN Inter-Agency Appeal for Flood-Related Emergency Humanitarian Assistance to the Democratic People's Republic of Korea (DPRK), 1 July 1996–31 March 1997.'

89 Oberdorfer, Don and Carlin, Robert, *The Two Koreas: A Contemporary History,* New York, Basic Books, 2014 (p. 290).

90 Asmolov, Konstantin, 'Famine in North Korea: Causes and Myths. Part 2,' *New Eastern Outlook*, October 31, 2013.

91 Consolidated UN Inter Agency-Appeal, UN Department of Humanitarian Affairs, July 1, 1996 to March 21, 1997.

Deane, Hugh, *The Korean War, 1945–1953*, San Francisco, China Books & Periodicals, 1999 (p. 208).

92 Harrison, Selig S., 'Promoting a Soft Landing in North Korea,' *Foreign Policy*, no. 106, Spring 1997 (p. 66).

93 Asmolov, Konstantin, 'Famine in North Korea: Causes and Myths. Part 1,' *New Eastern Outlook*, October 31, 2013.

94 Crossette, Barbara, 'Relief Teams Say North Korea Faces Vast Drought Emergency,' *New York Times*, August 5, 1997.

95 Kim, Suk Hi and Roehrig, Terence and Seliger, Bernhard (eds.), *The Survival of North Korea: Essays on Strategy, Economics and International Relations*, Jefferson, NC, McFarland & Co., 2011 (p. 47).

96 Bush, George W., Second State of the Union Address, The White House, January 28, 2003.

97 Bolton, John R., 'North Korea: A Shared Challenge to the U.S. and ROK,' Speech Before the Korean-American Association, Seoul, August 29, 2002.

Power, Samantha, 'Explanation of Vote at the Adoption of UN Security Council Resolution 2270 on DPRK Sanctions,' United States Department of State, March 2, 2016.

98 Bolton, John R., 'A Dictatorship at the Crossroads,' Speech at the Seoul Hilton, Seoul, July 31, 2003.

99 Jannuzi, Frank Sampson, 'Can the United States Cause the Collapse of North Korea? Should We Try?,' *Council on Foreign Relations*, January 13, 1999.

100 Asmolov, Konstantin, 'Famine in North Korea: Causes and Myths. Part 2,' *New Eastern Outlook*, October 31, 2013.

101 Hersh, Seymour M., 'Rainmaking Is Used As Weapon by U.S.,' *New York Times*, July 3, 1972.

'Weather Modification: Hearings Before the Subcommittee on Oceans and International Environment, Committee on Foreign Relations, United States Senate, Ninety-Third Congress, Second Session on the Need for an International Agreement Prohibiting the Use of Environmental and

Geophysical Modification as Weapons of War and Briefing on Department of Defense Weather Modification Activity, January 25 and March 20, 1974,' top secret hearing held on March 20, 1974, Washington, DC, U.S. Government Printing Office, 1974.

102 Henderson, Barney, 'Mahmoud Ahmadinejad says Europe "stealing Iran's rain,"' *The Telegraph*, May 21, 2011.

Wolchover, Natalie, 'Could Iran's Enemies Really Be Destroying Its Rain Clouds?,' *NDTV*, September 12, 2012.

'Iran Accuses Israel Of Stealing Its Clouds, Snow, "Manipulating Weather,"' *NDTV World*, July 3, 2018.

'A new battleground – the rain rivalry in the Middle East,' *i24 News*, August 30, 2022.

103 'Thermal balloons dropped by US plane set fire to wheat crops in Hasaka countryside,' *Syrian Arab News Agency*, May 17, 2020.

'Syrian fighters burning crops, using food as "weapon of war": U.N.,' *Reuters*, June 4, 2019.

104 Jannuzi, Frank Sampson, 'Can the United States Cause the Collapse of North Korea? Should We Try?,' *Council on Foreign Relations*, January 13, 1999.

105 Cumings, Bruce, 'Why Did So Many Influential Americans Think North Korea Would Collapse?' in: Kim, Suk Hi and Roehrig, Terence and Seller, Bernhard (eds.), *The Survival of North Korea: Essays on Strategy, Economics and International Relations*, Jefferson, NC, McFarland & Co., 2005 (pp. 46, 47).

106 Eberstadt, Nicholas, 'Tear Down This Tyranny,' *The Weekly Standard*, November 29, 2004.

107 'Exploring the Implications of Alternative North Korean Endgames: Results From a Discussion Panel on Continuing Coexistence Between North and South Korea,' Central Intelligence Agency, January 21, 1998.

108 Worldwide Intelligence Review, Hearing Before the Select Committee on Intelligence of the United States Senate, One Hundred Fourth Congress, First Session on Worldwide Intelligence Review, January 10, 1995 (p. 164).

109 Ryan, Maria, 'Why the US's 1994 deal with North Korea failed – and what Trump can learn from it,' *The Conversation*, July 19, 2017.

110 Worldwide Intelligence Review, Hearing Before the Select Committee on Intelligence of the United States Senate, One Hundred Fourth Congress, First Session on Worldwide Intelligence Review, January 10, 1995 (pp. 103–104).

111 *KEDO and the Korean Agreed Nuclear Framework: Problems and Prospects,* Hearing Before the Subcommittee on East Asian and Pacific Affairs of the Committee on Foreign Relations, United States Senate, One Hundred Fifth Congress, Second Session, July 14, 1998.

112 'LWR Provision is U.S. Obligation: DPRK FM Spokesman,' *KCNA*, March 6, 1998.

113 Ryan, Maria, 'Why the US's 1994 deal with North Korea failed – and what Trump can learn from it,' *The Conversation*, July 19, 2017.

114 Galen Carpenter, Ted and Bandow, Doug, *The Korean Conundrum: America's Troubled Relations with North and South Korea*, New York, Palgrave Macmillan, 2004 (p. 69).

Eberstadt, Nicholas, 'The Most Dangerous Country,' *The National Interest*, no. 57, Fall 1999 (pp. 46–54).

115 Harrison, Selig S., 'Promoting a Soft Landing in North Korea,' *Foreign Policy*, no. 106, Spring 1997 (pp. 62–63).

116 Ibid.

117 Carter, Ashton, 'The Korean Nuclear Crisis,' *Harvard Magazine*, September–October 2003.

118 'North Korea's nuclear program 2003,' *Bulletin of Atomic Scientists,* vol. 59, no. 2, March/April 2003 (p. 75).

Kristensen, Hans M., 'Preemptive Posturing,' *Bulletin of Atomic Scientists,* vol. 58, no. 5, September/October 2002 (pp. 54–59).

119 Report of the Commission to Assess the Ballistic Missile Threat to the United States, July 15, 1998.

120 Smith, Hazel (ed.), *Reconstituting Korean Security: A Policy Primer,* New York, United Nations University Press, 2007 (p. 36).

121 'Pro-N. Korea Newspaper Urges U.S. to Open Two-way Talks,' *Yonhap,* May 27, 2009.

122 Lewis, Jeffrey, 'David Sanger: Two Time Loser on Kilju and Kumchang-Ri,' *Arms Control Wonk,* May 21, 2005.

123 Ibid.

124 Harding, Luke, 'Revealed: truth behind US "poison factory" claim,' *The Guardian,* February 9, 2003.

'Threats and Responses: The Evidence; Islamists in Iraq Offer a Tour of "Poison Factory" Cited by Powell,' *New York Times,* February 9, 2003.

Fleishman, Jeffrey, 'Fears Grow in Village U.S. Cited as Threat,' *Los Angeles Times,* February 18, 2003.

125 'N. Korea Launch Was Satellite, U.S. Concedes,' *Los Angeles Times*, September 15, 1998.

126 'N. Korea Launches Staged Rocket That Overflies Japanese Territory,' *Arms Control Today*, September 1998.

127 'LWR Provision Is U.S. Obligation = DPRK Foreign Ministry Spokesman,' *KCNA*, March 6, 1998.

128 Erlanger, Steven, 'Survivors of NATO Attack on Serb TV Headquarters: Luck, Pluck and Resolve,' *New York Times,* April 24, 1999.

129 Badsey, Stephen and Latawski, Paul, *Britain, NATO and the Lessons of the Balkan Conflicts, 1991–1999*, London, Frank Cass, 2004 (p. 92).

McCormack, Timothy and McDonald, Avril, *Yearbook of International Humanitarian Law – 2003*, The Hague, T.M.C. Asser Press, 2006 (p. 381).

Erlanger, Steven, 'Survivors of NATO Attack on Serb TV Headquarters: Luck, Pluck and Resolve,' *New York Times*, April 24, 1999.

130 Norton-Taylor, Richard, 'Nato cluster bombs "kill 15" in hospital and crowded market,' *The Guardian,* May 8, 1999.

131 Phillips, Peter, *Censored 2000: The Year's Top 25 Censored Stories,* New York, Seven Stories Press, 2000 (p. 208).

Los Angeles Times, May 23, 1999.

132 '22 April: Milosevic defiant as NATO bombs hit home,' *The Guardian,* April 22, 1999.

133 Richter, Paul, 'Milosevic Not Home as Nato Bombs One of His Residences,' *Los Angeles Times,* April 23, 1999.

134 Dobbs, Michael, 'NATO's Latest Target: Yugoslavia's Economy,' *Washington Post*, April 25, 1999.

135 Chapman, Steve, 'A War Against All of the Serbs,' *Chicago Tribune,* April 29, 1999.

136 Abrams, A. B., *Atrocity Fabrication and its Consequences: How Fake News Shapes World Order*, Atlanta, Clarity Press, 2023 (Chapter 5).

137 'Up to 10,000 buried in Kosovo's mass graves, British say,' *CNN,* June 17, 1999.

'The Horrors of Kosovo,' *New York Times*, June 21, 1999.

Nelson, Lars-Erik, 'Numbers in Kosovo Don't Add Up,' *Orlando Sentinel,* October 28, 1999.

138 Hammond, Philip and Herman, Edward S., *Degraded Capability: The Media and the Kosovo Crisis*, London, Pluto Press, 2000 (p. 139).

Clark, Neil, 'Fools no more,' *The Guardian,* April 19, 2008.

Descamps, Philippe, 'Kosovo's open wounds, twenty years on,' *Le Monde Diplomatique*, March 2019.

Phillips, Peter, *Censored 2000: The Year's Top 25 Censored Stories,* New York, Seven Stories Press, 2000 (p. 205).

Pilger, John, 'US and British officials told us that at least 100,000 were murdered in Kosovo. A year later, fewer than 3,000 bodies have been found,' *New Statesman,* September 4, 2000.

139 Wintour, Patrick, 'MPs say Kosovo bombing was illegal but necessary,' *The Guardian,* June 7, 2000.

Erlanger, Steven, 'Rights Group Says NATO Bombing in Yugoslavia Violated Law,' *New York Times*, June 8, 2000.

140 'Truth behind America's raid on Belgrade,' *The Guardian,* November 28, 1999.

Sweeney, John and Holsoe, Jens and Vulliamy, Ed, 'Nato bombed Chinese deliberately,' *The Guardian,* October 17, 1999.

Mizokami, Kyle, 'In 1999, America Destroyed China's Embassy in Belgrade (And Many Chinese Think It Was on Purpose),' *The National Interest,* January 21, 2017.

141 Schmitt, Eric, 'In a Fatal Error, C.I.A. Picked a Bombing Target Only Once: The Chinese Embassy,' *New York Times*, July 23, 1999.

142 Correll, John T., 'Breakthrough Force,' *Air Force Magazine*, April 1, 2001.

143 Walpole, Robert, Testimony before the Senate Governmental Affairs Subcommittee on International Security, Proliferation, and Federal Services, February 9, 2000.

144 Carter, Ashton, 'The Korean Nuclear Crisis,' *Harvard Magazine*, September–October 2003.

145 Sanger, David, 'Trade Sanctions on North Korea Are Eased by U.S.,' *New York Times*, September 18, 1999 (p. 1).

Wren, Christopher, 'North Korean, at UN, Urges US to Lift Economic Embargo,' *New York Times*, September 26, 1999.

146 Clinton, Bill, *My Life*, New York, Alfred A. Knopf, 2004 (Chapter 55).

CHAPTER 2

The George W. Bush Years: Deterring an Invasion and Becoming a Nuclear Weapons State

Washington Plans New Military Offensives

Following its inauguration in January 2001 the George W. Bush administration would oversee a significant policy shift towards North Korea, and within three years would collapse the Agreed Framework and again bring the two countries to the brink of war. Although the administration's secretary of state Colin Powell had stated on March 6, 2001 that "we do plan to engage North Korea to pick up where President Clinton left off," President Bush the following day made clear that "We will not be negotiating with North Korea."[1] This highlighted the conflicts within the administration that would shape policy over the next eight years. North Korean state media would later highlight that the policy shift had ended hopes for a nuclear deal and normalized relations, leading the country to for the first time began open pursuit of nuclear weapons, observing: "the Bush administration's DPRK policy that stemmed from its ignorance of the DPRK resulted in making the DPRK a nuclear weapons state."[2]

The Bush administration's second year in office would mark a major turning point in relations between Washington and Pyongyang, which would in hindsight appear to have pushed North Korea past the point of no return in its resolve to develop nuclear weapons and abandon hopes for normalization of relations. A year into office on January 29, 2002, President Bush in his State of the Union Address labeled North Korea a member of the "Axis of Evil"[3] alongside Iran and Iraq, which was seen to be a list of states which Washington would prioritize targeting. Within a month the president was seen at the inter-Korean Demilitarized Zone accompanied by military officials where, looking out over the north through military binoculars, he described looking at "evil" and concluded: "we are ready."[4] As observed by a South Korean official, Pyongyang felt reference to it as part of an Axis of Evil represented "a clear violation of the Agreed Framework based on mutual respect; their regime survival was threatened by the U.S. side."[5] U.S. negotiators claimed it had strengthened arguments within the North Korean leadership for a reactivation of facilities at Yongbyon and abandoning the Agreed Framework.[6]

Signs of hostility would continue to mount, with Korea expert at Columbia University Charles Armstrong being among many to conclude: "The rhetoric of the Bush administration…seemed to suggest that 'rogue states' with weapons of mass destruction were to be eliminated rather than bargained with. During the lead-up to war in Iraq, the general thrust of U.S. policy appeared to be 'regime change' in Pyongyang, not diplomacy."[7] "By 'diplomacy' the United States seemed to mean making unilateral demands on the North Koreans rather than anything resembling negotiation," he added.[8] As otherwise summarized by a former senior IAEA official, the administration "did not care much for the NPT or any other disarmament or arms control treaty," with its policymaking instead engulfed by the view that "for the strongest [power], that means not to have any legal restrictions."[9]

Pyongyang's perception of an imminent threat worsened when on September 17, 2002 the White House issued the new National Security Strategy of the United States, announcing the option of using nuclear weapons against rogue states thought to be developing weapons of mass destruction. This reaffirmed its earlier rejection of the Nuclear Non-Proliferation Treaty linked negative security assurances which had previously protected signatories from nuclear attack.[i] The United States Department of

---

i As noted by West Point Associated Professor Scott Silverstone among others, initiating wars solely to prevent other states from developing certain military capabilities, known as preventative war, was increasingly considered acceptable in the post–Cold War years. This had little if any justification in international law and was considerably more aggressive and provocative than even questionably

Defense's Nuclear Posture Review was also altered that year, and required the Pentagon to draft contingency plans for the deployment of nuclear weapons against North Korea.[10]

While the consensus that the North Korean state's destruction remained the ultimate goal of the U.S. foreign policy establishment on the peninsula was unchanged, the Bush administration in its initial years did little to leave any ambiguity regarding this. Rhetoric in Washington continued to escalate, with plans for military action against the country strongly supported by such influential figures as Donald Rumsfeld, Paul Wolfowitz, John Bolton and Nicholas Eberstadt.[11] When asked by a *New York Times* reporter what the administration's North Korea policy was, Under Secretary for Arms Control and International Security Affairs John Bolton had reportedly handed him a copy of the book *The End of North Korea* written by Eberstadt, stating in no ambiguous terms: "that's our policy."[12] U.S. Congressional Research Service East Asia specialist Larry Niksch concluded that "regime change in North Korea is indeed the Bush administration's policy objective," adding that renewed economic pressure through sanctions and interdiction of Korean shipping[ii] were intended to provoke a

---

legal pre-emptive warfare, thus representing a dramatic conceptual change in the United States' grounds for starting wars allowing for attacks on countries that had exhibited no threatening behavior. The new National Security Strategy allowing for preventative war using nuclear strikes only further worsened the threat. (Beinart, Peter, 'How America Shed the Taboo Against Preventative War,' *The Atlantic*, April 21, 2017.) (Silverstone, Scott, *Preventative War and American Democracy,* Abingdon, Routledge, 2007.) (Smith, Derek D., *Deterring America: Rogue States and the Proliferation of Weapons of Mass Destruction,* Cambridge, Cambridge University Press, 2006 (pp. 116–120).)

ii The threat that Washington would target North Korean shipping was highlighted in December 2002 by the illegal seizure of a cargo ship carrying ballistic missiles ordered by the Yemeni Defense Ministry. The White House later admitted: "There is no provision under international law prohibiting Yemen from accepting delivery of missiles from North Korea," later releasing the vessel, although with the seizure itself having been illegal, a strong enough signal had been sent that DPRK shipping could be targeted. Yemen was subsequently pressed by the U.S. to pledge not to make further arms purchases from North Korea, sending a signal that other clients for DPRK weapons systems could similarly see their cargo stopped and exposed to the world to increase pressure not to deal with America's adversary. ('Sailing on, the ship with a hold full of Scud missiles,' *The Guardian*, December 12, 2002.)

collapse of government. If this failed, Defense Secretary Donald Rumsfeld was considering “a broader plan of massive strikes against multiple targets.”[13]

Providing valuable insight into the Bush administration’s calculus regarding the possibility of military action, former U.S. Army colonel Lawrence Wilkerson, who at the time served as Chief of Staff to State Secretary Colin Powell, specifically discussed the issue in a November 2023 interview. A veteran of the Navy’s Pacific Command based in South Korea, Japan and Hawaii, Wilkerson recalled that when at the Pentagon at the beginning of the Bush administration: “I was briefed we were going to war with North Korea, we were going to war with Iraq, that’d be followed by Syria, that’d be followed by Iran, although we wouldn’t have to do probably Syria and Iran because they’d quake in their boots after we did Iraq.”[14] He recalled that Deputy Defense Secretary Paul Wolfowitz had stated at the time: “We want to end all challenges, no matter how indistinct they might be, to American power,” with attacks on all these states that remained outside the Western sphere of influence considered a means of achieving this. “These were war plans. I went to a colonel and I said: ‘are these concept plans or are these TPFDD – Time Phased Force Deployment Data – that means they’re probably going to be executed,” to which Wilkerson recalled the colonel replied: “Oh they’re fully TPFDD.”[15]

Despite North Korea having been the administration’s first target, Wilkerson recalled that the country’s significantly superior military capabilities compared to other targets led to plans for an attack being indefinitely postponed, recalling:

> Later I would come back and find out that the air force general who had briefed me on the North Korean plan had “seen the light,” if you will, and said “100,000 casualties, 30,000 of them in the first 30 days, a lot of them Americans – a quarter of a million American non-combatants in the Seoul region – maybe we shouldn’t do this one. Maybe we should put this one on a burner and do the easy ones” – he called it the “low hanging

fruit," in the Middle East. This is the authority in the Pentagon talking, at that time, to his state department representative who was absolutely floored by what they were doing.[16]

Afterwards, in the summer of 2002, State Department Director of Policy Planning Richard Hass had come into the policy planning staff and informed Wilkerson: "I think we're going to war with Iraq."[17,iii] Wilkerson's recollection was supported by those of a number of other informed sources, with South Korean President Kim Dae Jung's personal relation to President Bush of the horrors that a new Korean war would entail having reportedly played an important role in swaying him.[18] His successor in office from early 2003, President Roh Moo Hyun, recalled that in December 2002 "some U.S. officials who held considerable responsibility in the administration talked about the possibility of attacking North Korea." Only later had "opinion in the United States started to change to resolving the matter peacefully."[19]

Deterring Invasion in the Early 2000s: Conventional Prowess and Nuclear Ambiguity

Colonel Lawrence Wilkerson's recollections indicate that although North Korea had initially been intended to be targeted first, its military capabilities were sufficient to force the Bush administration to reassess its plans for an attack. While its capabilities were not sufficient to take American military options totally

iii One of the first major indications that Iraq was the likely target emerged as early as December 9, 2001,when Vice President Dick Cheney made the implausible statement that meetings between Al Qaeda and Iraqi officials were "pretty well confirmed," which was followed three months later by chairman of the influential neoconservative Project for a New American Century think tank William Kristol's statement before the Senate Foreign Relations Committee, when asked about the next step in the war on terrorism: "The short answer is that Iraq is next." Secretary Rumsfeld subsequently alluded to the possibility of Iraq harboring Al Qaeda terrorists in August 2002, claiming the following month that evidence for such ties was "bulletproof." Administration officials subsequently increasingly frequently highlighted the possibility of ties between Baghdad and the terror group.

off the table, as demonstrated by the widespread calls in the U.S. for an attack up to 2018, they were sufficient to divert attentions towards attacking other adversary states – the "low hanging fruit in the Middle East" as Wilkerson recalled they were referred to.[20]

Estimates for the fallout from a U.S.-DPRK war in the mid-2000s indicated that even if the latter had no nuclear weapons capability, it could still inflict up to 500,000 U.S. and South Korean military casualties in the first 90 days.[21] In spite of the country's economic crisis, the Korean People's Army's conventional capabilities had continued to be strengthened significantly in the 1990s and into the following decade, with Western assessments consistently highlighting its greater emphasis on "high impact" arms such as ballistic missiles.[22] A U.S. intelligence committee report on KPA activities during the period of the Agreed Framework concluded: "North Korea continues to improve and train its forward deployed forces. This underwrites their desire to maintain current conventional force capabilities and military readiness while maximizing the agreement's political-economic benefits."[23]

A particular cause for concern in planning for potential offensives against North Korea was the extreme fortification of military and industrial sites across the country, which made locating and neutralizing targets an entirely unprecedented challenge. The perceived imminent threat of American nuclear strikes since the late 1950s, and the experience of mass incendiary bombing across its territory during the Korean War, had been primary drivers of the focus on fortification, with a prominent example being the Pyongyang metro that was the deepest in the world. With three thick steel emergency doors at each entrance, its primary purpose appeared to be providing shelter from nuclear attacks in a city that had little need for underground transportation. Key industrial facilities across North Korea, from the Sinhung Machine Plant to the Kusong Machine Tool Factory, were also built largely underground, while at Yongbyon itself IAEA Director General Hans Blix had been astonished in 1992 to find "two cavernous underground shelters" which required "several minutes to descend by escalator." These had been built to provide protection against American nuclear attacks.[24]

Defense Secretary Donald Rumsfeld had himself warned of the challenges posed by North Korean underground fortifications, observing: "They are world class tunnelers. They have gone underground across that country in a way that few other nations have done. They have underground emplacements of enormous numbers of weapons."[25] Later U.S. Army reports would highlight that the country maintained "up to 300 underground munitions factories supported by numerous other civilian factories, also built underground," and that "almost all of North Korea's critical industries are now located underground." Assets ranging from artillery to air defense systems could all fire from fortified underground sites, while war materiel stockpiles, munitions plants, maintenance and refueling centers, command centers, airfields, and other key targets, were located underground. The large number of fortified subterranean facilities throughout the country allowed the KPA "to fight from prepared positions without concentrating in the cities" in ways other militaries could not, leaving them far less vulnerable.[26] Penetrative rounds were few and far between to neutralize such a massive ground force that was so heavily entrenched, and many of the best fortified sites were considered near impossible to destroy from the air without using nuclear weapons – a factor which was expected further incentivize the U.S. to employ its nuclear arsenal. Against an adversary which could redeploy entire armored regiments or ballistic missile divisions across vast distances on underground road networks, and which mounted its air defense systems and radars on lift systems so they could be withdrawn underground to avoid being targeted, a ground assault was near impossible.[iv]

---

iv The perceived potency of North Korea's underground fortifications would increase significantly from 2006, after a much smaller network put in place by KPA specialists across much of southern Lebanon in the early 2000s was credited with having been a central factor in the military successes of the local paramilitary Hezbollah against U.S.-backed Israeli forces. This was widely considered Israel's first ever lost war. Israeli experts referred to Hezbollah as "a defensive guerrilla force organized along North Korean lines," with the complexity of the network allowing mobile ballistic missile and rocket artillery systems to exit tunnels, fire, then withdraw back down and redeploy from underground, much as they were expected to do on

The effectiveness of North Korean underground fortifications was supplemented by the demonstrated difficulties Western air power had demonstrated targeting even much smaller militaries lacking such fortifications when they made effective use of terrain to conceal their assets. As noted in a later report by the Department of the Army: "The KPA takes great solace in the knowledge that 1999 NATO aerial attacks in the former Yugoslavia actually destroyed only 13 of the Serbs' 300 tanks, despite early claims that the attacks destroyed 40 percent of all Serbian armored targets. The KPA believes its underground facilities, paired with its C3D [camouflage, concealment, cover, and deception] operations, will only further reduce its units' vulnerability to aerial attacks."[27] In contrast to the open deserts in which the First Gulf War was waged, North Korea's mountainous terrain was even better suited to blunting enemy air power than Yugoslavia's had been, which when combined with the magnitude, hardness and complexity of the country's fortifications ensured that winning the war from the air would not be viable. With air power representing America's primary conventional military advantage on the peninsula, this was a game changer for its ability to shape the course of a war.

The lack of penetration of the North Korean information space was another key factor, contrasting the country sharply with Iraq and other targets. The military importance of this was effectively summarized in a study by Foreign Area Officer for Eurasia Major Ralph Peters, who was assigned responsibility for future warfare at the Office of the Deputy Chief of Staff for Intelligence. "Hollywood is 'preparing the battlefield,'" he stated in a 1997 assessment, stressing that "the image of U.S. power and the U.S.

---

the Korean Peninsula. Israel's inability to counter these capabilities when deployed on a much smaller scale highlighted the extreme difficulties which the U.S. would face if fighting the KPA. Hezbollah was seen to have had far worse odds against Israel than North Korea did against the U.S., and if Hezbollah using North Korea tactics and infrastructure could fight Israel to a standstill, then North Korea stood a good chance of doing the same or better against the United States. (Abrams, A. B., 'What Hezbollah's Fortifications Teach Us About North Korean Defenses,' *The Diplomat*, January 17, 2024.) (Schneider, Tal, 'Expert: Hezbollah has built a vast tunnel network far more sophisticated than Hamas's,' *Times of Israel*, January 2, 2024.)

military around the world is not only a deterrent, but a psychological warfare tool that is constantly at work in the minds of real or potential opponents." The "alliance of culture with killing power" was a vital "combat multiplier," he asserted, concluding: "the image of the U.S. military crippled the Iraqi army in the field, doing more to soften them up for our ground assault than did tossing bombs into the sand. Everybody is afraid of us. They really believe we can do all the stuff in the movies. If the Trojans 'saw' Athena guiding the Greeks in battle, then the Iraqis saw Luke Skywalker precede McCaffrey's tanks."[28] This was a force multiplier which North Korea's control of its information space left it relatively immune to, with the country's population as a result widely assessed to provide the highest level of resistance of any potential target for Western invasion. As observed by Ashton Carter, North Koreans: "believe in socialism. But they believe even more in being proud Koreans," stressing that "children in North Korea have several hours of political education a day. Their parents did, and their grandparents did." He referred to it ideologically as "a very tough nut to crack" in contrast to other targets such as Afghanistan.[29]

The Korean People's Army had gained a particularly strong reputation during the Korean War, and sustained this since, with high levels of training, morale and motivation, meaning its forces were considered far more capable than paper quantifications of their manpower and firepower alone would indicate. This was perhaps best summarized by former director of the South Korean Central Intelligence Agency Brigadier General Kim Hyong Uk, who in 1997 testified before the U.S. Congress:

> The discipline and the ideological zeal of the North Korean Communists is much stronger than that of the South Koreans. In fact, I feel that there is no comparison; the will of the North Koreans is almost 100 times stronger than the will of the South Koreans... Although North Korean troops are inferior in numbers (that is, 430,000 army, 20,000 navy, 45,000 Air Force, and total: 500,000), they are much stronger than South Korean troops on the battlefield because they are so

> well-disciplined both militarily and ideologically... Let's now take a look at the Vietnam War for a moment to demonstrate my point. Just before the fall of [South] Vietnam, the ratio of the South Vietnamese to the North Vietnamese was 3 to 1 in military troop strength and 7 to 1 in weapons and equipment. But in contrast with the corruption of the ruling elite and the lack of ideological conation of the South Vietnamese soldiers, because the North Vietnamese had strong ideological convictions they defeated the South.[30]

Although North Korea's particularly capable conventional forces were a significant deterrent, with global power trajectories remaining strongly in the favor of the United States and wider Western Bloc it remained uncertain how long this would be sufficient to prevent an attack on the country. The possibility of limited strikes on North Korea continued to be advocated in the West, in the belief that the threat of overwhelming force could deter the country from responding, with the significant asymmetry between DPRK and U.S. capabilities limiting the former's ability to manage such escalation. It was thus highly beneficial for Pyongyang's efforts to deter American assaults in the first terms of the Clinton and Bush administrations that its conventional forces were supplemented by an ambiguous and very limited nuclear deterrent.

Although the bulk of North Korea's known nuclear materials were monitored from 1994 by international inspectors in cooling ponds, it was still considered possible, if not likely, that the country had assembled a small nuclear arsenal from materials processed before the signing of the Agreed Framework. Indeed, some assessments concluded North Korea may have had enough materials for its first nuclear warheads as early as 1989, with the Yongbyon reactor having that year been shut for 70–100 days which might have allowed up to fifteen kilograms of plutonium to have been extracted.[31] U.S. military assets had notably detected an explosion at Yongbyon in 1990 consistent with the blast necessary to detonate a nuclear device,[32] and by 1991 the operational reactor there had been shut down three times in the past three years to remove spent fuel, which represented the first step towards reprocessing plutonium. IAEA assessments also indicated that technicians could have reprocessed plutonium from Yongbyon on three occasions in 1989, 1990, and 1991, on the basis of findings during inspections in 1992–93.[33] Regardless of whether any nuclear arsenal existed, maintaining this ambiguity capitalized on the almost unique lack of penetration which Pyongyang had allowed Western intelligence agencies to gain, which contributed considerably to its security by further complicating any potential Western attack plans.

As early as 1993 the head of the Department of Political Science at the U.S. Air Force Academy, Colonel William E. Berry Jr., reported: "There was no consensus in the Clinton administration on whether the DPRK already had enough plutonium to build a bomb. For example, former Secretary of State Lawrence Eagleberger testified before a congressional committee that he believed North Korea already had at least one nuclear weapon. R. James Woolsey Jr., the new CIA Director, believed the DPRK already enough plutonium to build a bomb but had not yet done so."[34] The consensus appeared to shift in the following years towards a belief that the country had indeed fielded nuclear weapons from the early 1990s.

At a hearing before the Select Committee on Intelligence of the United States Senate in January 1995, in which the DPRK was confirmed to be in full compliance with the Agreed Framework and to have placed its fuel rods under IAEA supervision, the possibility was again raised that it may have had enough fissile material to develop a small nuclear arsenal prior to the agreement. It was stated at the hearing: "The Intelligence Community has concluded that North Korea may have already produced enough plutonium for at least one nuclear weapon, though we cannot be sure of this."[35,v]

---

v A report from the International Institute for Strategic Studies observed that by mid-1994: "There is still no categorically confirmed information over North Korean possession of nuclear weapons. The Director of the CIA has estimated that, before the reactor closure of April 1994, North Korea had sufficient plutonium to build a nuclear device... U.S. intelligence sources

In 2001 Chairman of the ruling Korean Workers' Party Kim Jong Il reportedly informed Russian President Vladimir Putin that his country had a nuclear arsenal it could use should the United States invade. "In 2001, when I was on my way to pay a visit to Japan, I made a stop in North Korea... it was back then when he told me that they had a nuclear bomb," Putin would recall in 2017.[36] Having still maintained close ties to the Western world, the new Russian administration could be seen as one of the closest to a neutral party in the DPRK-U.S. conflict, and may thus have been intended as a conduit for messages to the West. Chairman Kim's warning to Moscow that a U.S.-led attack would likely result in nuclear war on its border also gave Russia a significant stake in preventing this.

An ambiguous nuclear weapons capability was a potent deterrent in and of itself, contrasting with the total lack of such ambiguity which Iraq and Libya would have when subjected to Western assaults in 2003 and 2011. Both had not only lacked domestic missile industries or nuclear expertise, relying on importing both of these, but had also allowed their WMD and military facilities to be thoroughly inspected and their forces comprehensively disarmed preceding the attacks. As summarized by the spokesman from the UN inspection teams in Iraq Mark Gwozdecky in September 2002, six months before the U.S. invasion: "we had concluded that we had neutralized their nuclear weapons program. We had confiscated their fissile material. We had destroyed all their key buildings and equipment."[37,vi] Thus Baghdad's ability to

---

claim to have evidence of high-explosive tests indicative of the development of implosion devices and of the conversion of plutonium nitrate to metal, necessary for bomb manufacture." (International Institute for Strategic Studies, *The Military Balance*, vol. 94, 1994 (p. 165).)

vi As otherwise summarized in a 2003 briefing report for the Project on Defense Alternatives: "Although bristling with SCUDS and weapons of mass destruction in 1991, the Hussein regime met America for its final battle in 2003 with this capability already largely disabled, destroyed or rendered ineffective. For this, America's war plan owes a debt to the UN disarmament missions to Iraq, UNSCOM and UNMOVIC, whose inspectors had plied Iraq for more than seven years. Indeed, the first and most important battle in this war was fought and won before a single shot was fired. It was the battle of sanctions and inspections, which gutted Iraq's economy and shriveled its

bluff the U.S. regarding a retaliatory strike capability, let alone meaningfully retaliate to an invasion, was non-existent.

A number of assessments concluded that North Korea's ambiguous nuclear arsenal had as early as 1994 been a contributing factor in the Clinton administration's decision to pull back from the brink of war. Nuclear proliferation expert at Oxford University Derek Smith, for one, observed: "As the bomb on North Korea's bumper became ever more real and menacing, the credibility of the United States to demand disarmament even at the risk of war diminished in kind."[38] Thus the U.S. could only invade Iraq under the pretext of disarming it of weapons of mass destruction because it was certain that Iraq had no such weapons.

When Pyongyang in 2002 announced its intention to pursue nuclear weapons development North Korean officials reportedly warned the Americans that they "have more powerful things as well," further fueling uncertainty and speculation. An unnamed senior Bush administration official quoted by the *New York Times* in October said that, given this position of ambiguity, the U.S. had to assume that North Korea may have already built some nuclear weapons.[39] Two months later in December, Secretary of State Colin Powell confirmed regarding the latest assessments of North Korean nuclear capabilities: "We now believe they have a couple of nuclear weapons and have had them for years," and that the country "probably" already had them as early as 1993.[40]

Collapse of the Agreed Framework

Although the Agreed Framework remained in place until 2002, eight years after its signing the United States had still not even made preparations for deliveries of the promised light water reactors, which the U.S. was obliged to see constructed by 2003, while the Bush administration's rhetoric made any prospect for

---

military power. Notably, since the Gulf War, the quality gap between Iraqi and U.S. forces had increased by as much as a factor of four, as measured by expenditures per soldier and by force modernization." (Conetta, Carl, 'What Colin Powell Showed Us: The End of Arms Control and the Normalization of War,' *Project on Defense Alternatives,* Briefing Report no. 14, May 5, 2003.)

normalization of relations appear even more remote. Efforts by Pyongyang to press for the opening of bilateral negotiations and provision of security guarantees, namely an ending of the Korean War, appeared unlikely from the outset to succeed. Pyongyang nevertheless showed considerable restraint through continued adherence to the Agreed Framework and to its missile testing moratorium, seemingly in the slim hope of better relations despite receiving only consistently delayed fuel deliveries in return.

While the U.S. had been able to avoid lifting sanctions or normalizing relations, and thus sustained considerable pressure on Pyongyang through economic and political isolation, full North Korean adherence to its Agreed Framework obligations was highly beneficial for Washington. Plutonium frozen at Yongbyon would, according to a number of sources, provide enough materials to build over 30 nuclear warheads,[41] and had Yongbyon been active multiple batches could have been produced by the turn of the century. Ashton Carter thus concluded in 2002 that "in the absence of the pact, the Yongbyon facility could have produced enough plutonium to make more than 50 nuclear bombs by now,"[42] elaborating the following year: "Had that not been frozen, by now North Korea would have several tens of nuclear weapons. So by that standard, it certainly did our security a service."[43]

Despite the benefits of the Agreed Framework, the Bush administration had been perceived since before taking office as highly likely to seek to withdraw. The very principle of such an agreement was seen highly unfavorably by the Republican Party, even if its terms were never lived up to, and withdrawal would allow for a full suspension of fuel deliveries and a shift to an increased focus on military pressure. The administration's means of withdrawing notably closely mirrored parallel efforts to provide pretext for its planned invasion of Iraq – namely through unevidenced allegations of an active nuclear weapons program. Although it could not be disputed that North Korea was adhering to the Agreed Framework's restrictions in full, in June 2002 U.S. intelligence reports alleged that that the country had "embarked on a program to create weapons by using highly enriched uranium."[44] Former president Clinton would comment on these reports that "by producing highly enriched uranium in a laboratory – enough, perhaps, to make one or two bombs," it could be concluded that "North Korea had begun to violate the spirit if not the letter of the agreement."[45] There was a consensus among those with knowledge of the Agreed Framework that even if allegations were correct, North Korea was still in full compliance while the U.S. was not.[46] As leading expert on the country's nuclear program Edward Howell argued: "whilst North Korea may not have strictly breached the Agreed Framework, which specified the freeze of *plutonium* production, it would have more certainly violated the spirit of the deal."[47]

Allegations of a uranium program provided the Bush administration with the pretext it needed to withdraw from the Agreed Framework, which could be portrayed as having failed, in the words of John Bolton: "because Kim Jong Il instructed his subordinates to systematically violate it in secret."[48] As President Bush himself claimed: "The United States honored its side of the agreement; North Korea didn't... North Korea was enriching uranium." All three assertions were verifiably false.[49] State Secretary Colin Powell similarly alleged that because Pyongyang "began another program to enrich uranium... the Agreed Framework was nullified by them," which was not technically true even if this unevidenced claim was correct.[50] With Yongbyon firmly under IAEA safeguards a violation of the agreement was difficult to fabricate, but a violation of the spirit of the agreement could be fabricated, and for public consumption, as with Bolton, Powell and President Bush's statements, it could then be portrayed as an actual violation.

A paper by the Institute for Science and International Security was among multiple sources that compared the near totally unevidenced claim of a Korean uranium program to the administration's claims that Iraq was developing weapons of mass destruction, which would consistently prove to be entirely fabricated.[51] The *New York Times* would in 2007 similarly observe that allegations against the two countries had very closely coincided, contributing to doubts regarding the veracity of the unevidenced North Korean case.[52] Mirroring the case of allegations against Iraq, leading WMD expert and former UN Chief Weapons Inspector David

Kay, who led the Iraq Survey Group to search for WMD in the country from 2003, stressed the administration's claims about a North Korean uranium program were far from persuasive. "They were driving it way further than the evidence indicated it should go."[53]

President of the Institute for Science and International Security David Albright, a leading expert on nuclear proliferation, was among other sources to highlight the lack of evidence for the administration's allegations, referring to it as "yet another questionable extrapolation based on aluminum tubes" as had been the case in Iraq. He highlighted that Pyongyang's refusal to acknowledge the unevidenced uranium program was consistently being used by opponents of a new arms control agreement in Washington to argue against such steps.[54] A paper in *Foreign Affairs* was among the sources to highlight the near complete lack of evidence supporting the administration's assertions,[55] which was similarly repeatedly highlighted in North Korean state media.[56] Much as the Bush administration was widely referred to as "cherry picking intelligence" to justify its policies towards Iraq,[57] so too did this appear to be the case for the North Korean program. As observed by former Congressman Lee Hamilton, who served multiple foreign affairs and intelligence committees: "the intelligence that you get is driven by the policy, rather than the policy being driven by the intelligence."[58]

A U.S. delegation which later visited Pyongyang in October 2002 claimed that North Korean representatives had admitted to the presence of uranium enrichment facilities during meetings,[59] with the North Koreans subsequently denying having made such an admission and chastising the Americans side for failing to produce evidence.[60] The DPRK Foreign Ministry later expressed a willingness to respond to any written evidence presented by the United States that it was pursuing a uranium enrichment program, stating that clarifying the issue could open the door to an improvement in relations with Washington, and calling for a non-aggression treaty to resolve any concerns.[61] Unlike in 1998, when the site at Kumchang had been singled out and access had been requested, no specific requests for access were made and no evidence was ever presented. It thus appeared that the issue raised by the allegations was not intended to be resolvable, and that it was being used as a pretext to achieve the political goal of ending the Agreed Framework.

It was only after the Agreed Framework's collapse had been achieved that U.S. intelligence officials would later downplay earlier claims that North Korea was pursuing nuclear weapons through highly enriched uranium, with an unnamed intelligence official cited by *USA Today* in 2004 noting that the CIA was not even certain the DPRK had a uranium enrichment plant.[62] Further serious uncertainties that any uranium weapons program existed were raised by several administration officials in 2007, who highlighted that these same doubts had been prevalent when the allegations were made in 2002.[63] Such admissions were not widely publicized, and as of the mid-2020s ambiguous claims regarding a uranium weapons program have continued to be repeated, with little attention paid to the tenuousness of the original allegations. With the allegations of Iraq WMD development having cast a long shadow over American credibility, providing publicity to a second set of unfounded allegations against another country, which rather than war had instead perpetuated a breakdown in relations and renewed nuclear weapons development, would hardly be in Washington's interest.[vii]

Had North Korea indeed been developing a uranium program, with the Bush administration for whatever reason failing to provide evidence or meaningful details, it could have been intended a means of exerting pressure to achieve greater U.S. compliance

---

vii As one official noted in March 2007 regarding the extent to which these highly tenuous allegations had worsened the American position: "The question now is whether we would be in the position of having to get the North Koreans to give up a sizable arsenal if this had been handled differently." Stressing the lack of evidence for a uranium program, Senator Jack Reed would similarly observe at a hearing at the Senate Armed Services Committee in 2007: "The administration appears to have made a very costly decision that has resulted in a fourfold increase in the nuclear weapons of North Korea." (Sanger, David E., and Broad, William J., 'U.S. Had Doubts on North Korean Uranium Drive,' *New York Times*, March 1, 2007.)

with the Agreed Framework without directly violating it. With highly enriched uranium being far less well suited than plutonium to the production of sophisticated miniaturized nuclear warheads that could be mounted on ballistic missiles, a number of experts argued it was highly possible that such uranium enrichment, if it did exist, was intended for use in upcoming light water reactors, and that such activities could hardly be taken as evidence of plans for weaponization. As East Asian security expert at the U.S. Naval War College, Jonathan Pollack, concluded: "it seems entirely plausible that Pyongyang envisioned the need for an indigenous enrichment capability... [because] the fuel requirements for a pair of thousand-megawatt reactors are substantial and open-ended." Indeed, South Korea and other non-nuclear weapons states were carrying out uranium enrichment programs of their own at the time that were very similar to that which North Korea was alleged to be preparing for.[64] North Korea would go on to open a facility to produce non-weaponizable low enriched uranium the following decade, but did so openly with U.S. experts invited to observe (see Chapter 6), contrasting sharply to assertions of it having a covert program for military purposes.

In line with the new administration's objectives, a former senior administration official would recall that due to the alleged uranium program: "everything went to hell, and we realized there was no need for negotiating much further."[65] The *New York Times* described the unevidenced allegations as "the root of the sharply increased tensions between Washington and Pyongyang."[66] Washington seized on the issue to halt oil deliveries under the Agreed Framework on November 14, which was one of the few obligations it had fulfilled albeit with very frequent and serious delays. Pyongyang responded by announcing a full withdrawal from the Agreed Framework, and December 12 announced the reactivation of its Yonbgyon facility.[viii] This began the following

---

viii Although Pyongyang would be repeatedly criticized in the West for having "chosen bombs over electricity," such claims appeared highly tenuous, considering that Pyongyang had agreed to fully shutter its Yongbyon facility once two light water reactors were delivered, and that it had kept work at Yongbyon suspended so long as Washington continued to meet

day after over eight years frozen.[67] Beijing, Seoul and Tokyo responded by pressing for Washington to deescalate, with Japanese Prime Minister Junichiro Koizumi stressing: "If you read the North Korean announcement carefully, their consistent stance is to seek a peaceful resolution." The Bush administration, however, did not show signs of willingness to revoke its actions or offer to return to the Agreed Framework.[68] Two weeks later the cameras and seals over the cooling ponds where the fuel rods were still being stored under surveillance were removed, preventing the IAEA from monitoring these materials.[69] On December 23 Defense Secretary Rumsfeld asserted that North Korea's response was "unacceptable," warning that the United States was able to take military action against the country despite ongoing operations in Afghanistan and the imminent invasion of Iraq.[70]

Twenty-nine days after its announced withdrawal from the Agreed Framework, North Korea on January 10 announced that it would withdraw from the NPT, citing its rights under Article X and the "dangerous situation where our nation's sovereignty and our state's security are being seriously violated" by Washington.[71] A North Korean delegate at the United Nations Disarmament Commission stated to this effect: "The DPRK's possession of nuclear weapons is a legitimate right to defend its sovereignty today when the Bush administration listed it as part of an 'Axis of Evil' and a 'tyrannical' state and it is getting all the more undisguised in its drive to overthrow it… The DPRK cannot renounce nuclear weapons when the U.S. is intensifying nuclear war rehearsals to make a pre-emptive strike."[72] This withdrawal removed the primary legal barrier to its nuclear weapons development.

For the Bush administration, the timing of the abandonment of the Agreed Framework, and the provoking of Pyongyang's withdrawal from the Framework and the NPT, could not have

---

minimal compliance with fuel deliveries despite Washington's failure to fulfil other Agreed Framework obligations. It was only once fuel was cut off, and the U.S. thus reneged on the only significant obligation that it had fulfilled, that North Korea moved ahead with its nuclear weapons program. The concessions North Korea had made to "trade bombs for electricity" had never been accepted by Washington.

been worse. Not only had tens of thousands of American personnel been deployed to Afghanistan less than two years prior, but momentum was also in full swing and preparations long underway for a full-scale invasion of Iraq. The September 11 attacks served as a valuable pretext for further attacks on targets in the Islamic world, with Afghanistan and Iraq both attacked largely under the pretext of ties to Al Qaeda – which in the latter case proved to be entirely fabricated. Military action against Muslim-majority states enjoyed particularly high approval ratings during this period, with 70 percent of Americans believing in 2003 that Saddam Hussein had a role in the attacks and links to Al Qaeda, despite this later being revealed to have no basis in reality.[73] Washington's very limited ability to respond to North Korea's actions at Yongbyon drew parallels to its position in the 1960s, when American overcommitment in Vietnam had provided the DPRK with significantly greater room for action. Thus even as Pyongyang resumed work at Yongbyon and retook its fuel rods, it could be confident that it retained a window of time to develop its deterrent before the United States could again turn its attentions eastwards.

A notable factor in Pyongyang's favor was that although the Bush administration was widely described as having a "proliferation fixation" with regards to the WMD programs of what it perceived as "unpleasant regimes,"[74] this was overshadowed by the strong inclination of leading neoconservatives both in and advising the administration towards a focus on Iraq, and on the Middle East more generally. Leading neoconservatives had sent an open letter to President Bill Clinton on January 26, 1998 urging him to work towards "the removal of Saddam Hussein's regime from power,"[75] with ten of the signatories subsequently receiving positions in the new Bush administration.[76] The neoconservatives were said to have "a focus on the Middle East and global Islam as pivotal to America's national interests."[77] Deputy State Secretary Richard Armitage had accordingly stated in February 2001 regarding possible confrontation with North Korea: "We've got other fish to fry," citing peace in the Middle East specifically.[78] Indeed, when asked about the implications for U.S. security of North Korea obtaining nuclear weapons, President Bush indicated his primary concern was that "they might choose to proliferate them, sell them. They may end up in the hands of dictators," which was widely interpreted to refer to proliferation to the Middle East.[79] The beginning of accelerated nuclear weapons development at Yongbyon thus came at a time when leading American officials were very strongly inclined to overlook or downplay it.

As observed by leading expert on the Bush administration journalist James Mann, for the neoconservatives in the administration eager to invade Iraq, North Korea's accelerated nuclear development:

> threatened to distract attention away from Iraq just when the Bush team was trying to win domestic and international support for military action against Saddam Hussein. Even worse, North Korea's admission seemed to call into question the administration's rationale for moving against Iraq. The North Korean nuclear program was more advanced and more dangerous than Iraq's, and so, critics wondered, what was the justification for going to war in one case and not in another?... If America was going to tolerate North Korea's nuclear program, treating it with patience, then what was the sense of urgency about Iraq?[80]

Three months before the invasion of Iraq President Bush notably struggled to provide a straight answer for why stopping an alleged Iraqi WMD program was more important than stopping a very real North Korean one. "Sir, why should we be more worried about Saddam Hussein, who doesn't have nuclear weapons, than Kim Jong Il, who does have them?," a member of the press asked. "Well, first of all, I think it's important to remember that Saddam Hussein was close to having a nuclear weapon. We don't know whether or not he has a nuclear weapon. We do expect him to disarm his weapons of mass destruction; that's what we expect," the president replied.[81] Two days prior on NBC's Meet the Press, State Secretary Powell had similarly been forced to evade the following question: "In North Korea, the inspectors are out. In

Iraq, inspectors in. In Korea, they are months from having more nuclear weapons. Iraq, perhaps years. Why isn't North Korea a more imminent threat? Why wouldn't we go after North Korea rather than go after Iraq?"[82]

Former secretary of state under the Clinton administration and deputy secretary of state under the Carter administration Warren Christopher was one of the few who warned that American preoccupation with the Islamic world under the Bush administration had given North Korea far more freedom to strengthen its defenses through nuclearization. Referring to threats from the country as "more imminent than those posed by Iraq," he stated:

> In foreign affairs, Washington is chronically unable to deal with more than one crisis at a time... While Defense Secretary Donald Rumsfeld may be right in saying that our military can fight two wars at the same time, my experience tells me that we cannot mount a war against Iraq and still maintain the necessary policy focus on North Korea and international terrorism. Anyone who has worked at the highest levels of our government knows how difficult it is to engage the attention of the White House on anything other than the issue of the day... A United States-led attack on Iraq will overshadow all other foreign-policy issues for at least a year.

Again referring to North Korea, Christopher concluded: "No doubt the world would be better off without Saddam Hussein reigning in Iraq, but we must recognize that the effort of removing him right now may well distract us from dealing with graver threats."[83] As otherwise summarized by *Los Angeles Times* media writer David Shaw, when observing North Korea's far more developed nuclear program poised to make much greater strides in the immediate future: "It seems the outstanding question is, Why Iraq and not North Korea?"[84]

Although bogging the United States down in a new quagmire, the invasion of Iraq was nevertheless far from reassuring for North Korea. It demonstrated again that the U.S. was willing to launch large scale invasions illegally and without a UN mandate, while the swiftness with which Baghdad was occupied and its fragile military collapsed threatened to embolden Washington to launch further campaigns. Iraq was defeated within two weeks of the invasion on March 20, with U.S. military casualties remaining negligible. The North Korean leadership appeared to have been aware of this danger, with state newspaper *Rodong Sinmun* stating just days before the war was initiated: "It is becoming certain that, in case the U.S. imperialists' invasion of Iraq is successful, they will wage a new war of aggression on the Korean Peninsula."[85]

The Threat of a Third Front Against North Korea

It had been widely predicted that once the invasion of Iraq was over, Washington would escalate threats against North Korea, which made the speed at which the country restarted work at Yongbyon particularly important. As one U.S. journalist summarized after discussions with North Korean officials, in the aftermath of the Iraq invasion: "Bolton's going around saying 'North Korea's next'; the Bush administration is pushing the doctrine of regime change; if you're North Korea thinking, how do we protect ourselves, the logic of having the bomb is irrefutable."[86] Furthering speculation of possible military action, State Secretary Powell had asserted three months before the invasion of Iraq regarding Baghdad and Pyongyang: "I would also make the point that we are really approaching both, in some ways, in the same fashion."[87] Indeed, within the intelligence community, officials up to the beginning of 2003 appeared far from convinced that military options against Pyongyang were off the table, with one intelligence official who had attended White House meetings recalling: "Bush and Cheney want [Kim Jong Il's] head on a platter... they have a plan, and they are going to get this guy after Iraq."[88] Although the more optimistic Western pre-invasion assessments had asserted that a decisive military success in Iraq could help intimidate North Korea into yielding to American terms, however, which was referred to as going "to Pyongyang through Baghdad,"[89] by the late summer of 2003 the viability of preventative military action had been significantly reduced, with

Pyongyang having made maximum use of the six month respite the war gave it.

As expected, discourse in the United States began to increasingly refocus towards North Korea shortly after the invasion of Iraq began, and much as President Kim Il Sung had been increasingly widely likened to "another Saddam Hussein" after the Gulf War,[90] so too did the Bush administration's rhetoric towards North Korea increasingly appear interchangeable with that used against Iraq. As early as April, following initial victories in Iraq, Under Secretary of State for Arms Control and International Security Affairs John Bolton explicitly called on North Korea to "draw the appropriate lesson from Iraq,"[91] with Defense Secretary Donald Rumsfeld quoted the following month as having delivered the same message.[92] Rhetoric towards the two states was often interchangeable, a notable example being Bolton's assertion four months after the invasion of Iraq that: "particularly after September 11, the world is acutely aware of the danger posed to civilian populations by weapons of mass destruction being developed by tyrannical rogue state leaders like Kim Jong Il or falling into the hands of terrorists."[93] Aside from the name of the North Korean leader, this was exactly the rhetoric used to argue for a need for action in Iraq. Vice President Cheney, for example, had declared in March 2002 that "the United States will not permit the forces of terror to gain the tools of genocide," in reference to Iraq's alleged WMD program and terror ties,[94] while President Bush stressed three months later that "containment is not possible when unbalanced dictators with weapons of mass destruction can deliver those weapons or missiles or secretly provide them to terrorist allies."[95] The interchangeability of the rhetoric towards North Korea with that towards the country that had just been invaded indicated that it faced a significant threat. Much as had been the case for Iraq, DPRK Foreign Minister Paek Nam Sun would allege that President Bush was using the shock of the September 11 attacks to turn Americans against his country.[96]

Almost immediately after Baghdad was captured U.S. air and naval assets significantly increased their operations in the Pacific aimed specifically at North Korea, with surveillance flights near the country's airspace surging in numbers which was common practice preceding an attack to gather target data.[97] On March 2 North Korea responded by deploying MiG-29s and other fighters to closely intercept a U.S. RC-135S reconnaissance plane over the Sea of Japan, more than 200 kilometers from its coast, with at least one locking on to the American aircraft with its targeting radar in a show of force.[98] The threat was particularly significant due to Pyongyang's history of ordering shootdowns of American aircraft during the Cold War, with multiple reports indicating that fighter escorts were expected to subsequently begin supporting U.S. reconnaissance flights. On March 4 *USA Today* announced in a headline that the U.S. was "repositioning bombers near North Korea" with the deployment of 12 B-52H and 12 B-1Bs to Guam allowing them to double their sortie rates against Korean targets.[99,ix] An explicit purpose of these flights was to strain the KPA Air Force's resources, forcing it to expend valuable fuel reserves and spare parts intercepting American aircraft.[100]

In early 2003 Defense Secretary Donald Rumsfeld requested revisions to Operations Plan 5030, which were considered highly provocative by members of the Bush administration who stressed that they sought to "blur the lines between war and peace" in Korea.[x] As summarized by insiders who read the revised plan, it

ix Regarding America's most dangerous bomber class, expert on B-2 operations Thomas Withington reported that "no sooner had the B-2A performed its epic service in Iraq, than the 509th Bomb Wing [BW] was back rehearsing its 'Global Power' deployments across the world . . . in September 2003, B-2As and their support personnel participated in Exercise Coronet Dragon 49. Ostensibly, the task of the exercise was to test the abilities of the 509th BW units to forward-deploy to a location such as Guam and to be able to fight," which he stressed was "vital should any conflict with North Korea flare up." Subsequent B-2 deployments to the region "sent a message to North Korea's Kim Jong Il" of America's ability to act "with maximum response." (Withington, Thomas, *B-2A Spirit Units in Combat,* Oxford, Osprey, 2006 (pp. 74–76).)

x This approach had previously been referred to in a CFR assessment as "Active Destabilization," and involved "an aggressive policy combining military pressure, economic strangulation, and political destabilization, all designed to topple the regime of Kim Jong Il and bring about the collapse of the North Korean state as soon as possible." (Jannuzi, Frank Sampson, 'Can the United States Cause the Collapse of North Korea? Should We Try?,' *Council on Foreign Relations*, January 13, 1999.)

was intended to "topple Kim's regime by destabilizing its military forces," was pushed "by many of the same administration hard-liners who advocated regime change in Iraq" and was considered by senior administration officials to be extremely aggressive.[101] The plan entailed a disruption of North Korean financial networks, and initiating strategic disinformation operations with the purpose of destabilizing and eventually dismantling the North Korean state. It also gave commanders the authority to hold surprise military exercises to force the KPA to maintain a very high level of combat readiness at great expense, which was further intended to exhaust its personnel and sow confusion among its officer corps.[102] Reports referred to the benefits of "a weeks-long surprise military exercise, designed to force North Koreans to head for bunkers and deplete valuable stores of food, water, and other resources."[103]

A significant contributor to North Korea's ability to deter the United States was the speed at which it proved capable of restarting its nuclear weapons program, with thousands of fresh fuel rods moved into the 5 MW(e) Yongbyon reactor in December 2002,[104] soon after which U.S. satellites detected a movement of the 8,000 stored rods away from the pool sites where they had formerly been under inspection. This placed the country on track to produce additional weapons grade plutonium by the end of March 2003.[105] Commercial satellite photography in March showed that the reactor was operating, confirming what North Korean officials had announced the previous month.[106] By June plutonium from the 8,000 spent fuel rods had been fully extracted, which was sufficient for 25–30 kilograms worth of new weapons material – enough for approximately three to four new warheads. Their reprocessing was announced in October to have been completed.[107] Thus even if the invasion of Iraq had gone ideally, North Korea's nuclear weapons capability would have expanded very significantly before U.S. forces were available for a new campaign.[xi]

---

xi Sending a further clear signal to Washington, Pyongyang in January 2004 permitted an unofficial American scientific delegation to visit facilities at Yongbyon, members of which reported upon returning to the U.S. that the display in the reactor control room and steam plumes from the cooling towers confirmed operations were underway, and that the reprocessing

Meeting with Assistant Secretary of State for East Asian and Pacific Affairs James Kelly in April 2003, North Korean representatives reportedly stated that their country already had nuclear weapons. At the same meeting they offered to address all of Washington's greatest concerns: abandoning nuclear weapons, accepting independent verification by inspectors, ceasing missile exports, and working within a multilateral framework to reach an accommodation. Concessions requested in return mirrored those sought under the Agreed Framework, namely a normalization of political and economic ties and the signing of a formal nonaggression treaty.[108] Pyongyang thus presented Washington with an opportunity to wind down tensions, while also warning that with the invasion of Iraq underway, the force it could deploy should the United States seek a military solution was inordinately greater than that which Iraq could. Having consistently placed blame solely on Pyongyang for the collapse of the Agreed Framework, and equated concessions with "rewarding bad behavior," "appeasement," or giving in to "nuclear blackmail," the Bush administration was predictably non-responsive.

The United States was highly capable of placing pressure on North Korea's defenses and using information and economic warfare, while its need for strategic aircraft in the Middle East was minimal after April 2003 allowing these to be redeployed to the Pacific. Nevertheless, the American manpower needed for an invasion, or for a response should a limited air and missile strike provoke limited KPA retaliation, was bogged down in Iraq. As East Asian security expert Peter Van Ness concluded, the first months of the Iraq War "put the Bush administration on the defensive with respect to considering any new military adventures." The "failure of the United States to consolidate its victories" over the next two years of operations in both Iraq and Afghanistan, he highlighted,

---

facility "appeared in good repair." Their findings thus corroborated both satellite intelligence, and North Korean statements at the time that the reactor was operating smoothly at 100 percent of its rated power. Notably, future president and then senator Joe Biden was also on the delegation. (Hecker, Siegfried, Testimony at the Senate Foreign Relations Committee, January 21, 2004.)

"means that the military option for the United States against North Korea has become increasingly untenable."[109] Alongside the rapid expansion of the DPRK's nuclear arsenal, this was a primary factor that helped guarantee the country's security.

Prospects for a major new military campaign would diminish considerably further as the course of the occupation of Iraq went increasingly against America's favor, with multiple Iraqi factions, many formed by former members of its armed forces, waging an insurgency against and bogging down U.S. forces, causing tens of thousands of casualties. Among other factors, the loss of face as details began to emerge of severe American war crimes in Iraq and the often grotesque torture of prisoners,[110] and unprecedented budget deficits to finance the costly war effort, further helped insulate North Korea from a possible attack, resulting in the growing isolation, albeit temporarily, of Washington's neoconservative advocates of further invasions.[111]

The year 2003 saw a consensus form that military options, including limited applications of military pressure short of war, could not viably be used to secure U.S. and Western objectives in Korea at least for the foreseeable future. As summarized by leading expert on the Bush administration journalist James Mann, the neoconservatives in the administration "had been preoccupied throughout their careers with military power. Yet North Korea was one case in which there seemed to be no good military solution, as they felt there was in Iraq. The Bush administration seemed to be searching for one but unable to find it." This, he highlighted, led them to consistently play down the extent and urgency of North Korea's "moving rapidly toward acquisition of a nuclear bomb," continuing to stress that non-military options were preferable and that unlike Iraq, the situation did not represent a crisis. "The administration's response instead was to be patient, hoping for an eventual capitulation or a collapse," he concluded.[112]

The shift in priorities was best summarized by President Bush, who in December 2006 stated with a view to justifying a further major surge in U.S. ground forces in Iraq to counter growing insurgent activities, which was placing even greater limitations on America's ability to exercise military force elsewhere:

"I'm not worried about a North Korean invasion of South Korea at this point. That's a potential hypothetical, might someday happen. We've got a war on our hands and we've got to win the war we've got."[113] Much as North Korea had taken the initiative to be much more militarily assertive against U.S. forces on the peninsula during the Vietnam War, while American preoccupation consistently prevented it from responding more forcefully, so too did the Iraq War provide a window to rapidly move ahead with nuclear weapons development.[114] Regarding the window the Iraq War provided Pyongyang, as well as Tehran, to strengthen their positions before Washington could turn its focus to them, former president Bill Clinton summarized in 2006: "Iranian and North Korean foreign policy is to stick it up America's ass because we're tied down in Iraq."[115]

Handling the Bush Administration

"The Bush administration plainly lacks a strategy for dealing with the North Korean regime," concluded leading neoconservative thinker Nicholas Eberstadt as it neared the end of its first term in November 2004. "Instead," he lamented "it merely confronts Pyongyang with an attitude... President Bush and his inner circle regard Kim Jong Il and his system with an admixture of loathing, contempt, and distrust – as well they might. Unfortunately, a mechanism for translating that point of view into effective action was manifestly absent from the statecraft of Bush's first-term administration." Eberstadt agreed with criticisms from within the Democratic Party that America's position in its conflict with Pyongyang had worsened considerably in the preceding four years, with this trend potentially continuing into the next term, recalling that "the administration on North Korea was at times akin to a rudderless boat on an open sea." His conclusion reflected a growing consensus that Pyongyang was effectively winning, with Washington highly constrained in its ability to reverse the trend, and appearing to have only accelerated it by derailing the Agreed Framework without options for handling its adversary's response.[116]

Lacking options in the face of resumed operations at Yongbyon, the Bush administration supported the initiation of six-party talks from August 2003 involving North Korea, the United States, South Korea, China, Japan and Russia. These came to be held in five separate rounds up to September 2007, with the goal of arranging Pyongyang's return to the Nuclear Non-Proliferation Treaty and a return of safeguards on its nuclear program. A primary reason for this format was the United States' reluctance to enter one-to-one talks with North Korean officials, in large part on the basis that this would legitimize the state which the U.S. continued to refuse to recognize. The six-party format caused multiple hindrances, with each state having its own separate agenda and ideas for possible roadmaps forward, which made progress particularly difficult.[117]

Pyongyang and Washington were fundamentally at odds over the nature of the talks themselves. For the United States, the talks were intended to rein in a rogue regime's weapons programs much as talks with Libya would in 2004, with the adversary envisaged as being forced to comply by threats of sanctions and military force. For North Korea, the talks were a forum for discussion, primarily between it and the United States, to agree on mutual concessions, as well as an opportunity to "show the world community whether the U.S. has a true willingness to make a switchover in its policy towards the DPRK or not."[118] North Korean negotiators consistently insisted that the talks should not be about one-sided denuclearization and disarmament, which was tantamount to "stripping us naked" without corresponding actions by the U.S. Instead, the talks were to discuss mutual nuclear arms reductions between two established nuclear powers, with some DPRK negotiators reportedly drawing parallels to the mutual arms reduction agreements between the U.S. and USSR during the Cold War.[119] Nevertheless, the talks provided a valuable means for North Korea both to delay escalation of economic sanctions while its economy recovered from the disaster of the 1990s, and to make further progress on its nuclear program, with policymakers perhaps perceiving a slim possibility that setbacks in Iraq could force the U.S. to more significantly revise its position. With the

United States unwilling to provide security guarantees, end the Korean War, or normalize economic or diplomatic ties, the concessions Pyongyang was willing to offer remained limited.

Tensions came to a head in 2005, after the DPRK Foreign Ministry broke from its longstanding ambiguity to confirm in February that the country had "manufactured nukes for self-defense."[120] The Yongbyon facility was shut down in April to remove fuel rods, and following their withdrawal resumed operations in July.[121] In June Vice Foreign Minister Kim Kye Gwan gave an interview with ABC News on the nuclear program in which he elaborated: "We have enough nuclear bombs to defend against a U.S. attack. As for specifically how many we have, that is a secret."[122] The Bush administration responded with increased economic sanctions, most notably the sanctioning of the Macau-based bank Banco Delta Asia for dealing with North Korean transactions, which left financial institutions across the world highly reluctant to process funds from the country. The U.S. Treasury had gone to extreme measures, using the Providing Appropriate Tools Required to Intercept and Obstruct Terrorism (PATRIOT) Act, Section 311, to put pressure on all banks doing business with the country, which represented a significant escalation of the sanctions campaign.[123] This escalation in particular was seen by a number of analysts to have caused Pyongyang to itself escalate pressure on Washington the following year.[124]

With American economic pressure mounting and the Six Party Talks stalling, U.S. and South Korean intelligence in 2006 reported the service entry of North Korea's first intermediate range ballistic missile the Hwasong-10, which represented the most significant step in expanding its missile range since the Hwasong-7's development. The missile had allegedly already been tested in and exported to Iran under North Korean supervision in January.[125] The proliferation of this missile class was a particularly sensitive issue, and while military action against North Korea was at least temporarily off the table, the Iranian arsenal of Korean missiles, already revolutionized with the transfer of the Hwasong-7 the previous decade, was serving as the leading impediment to a possible U.S.-led military assault on Iran that was at the time being considered.[126]

In an apparent effort to maximize pressure North Korea conducted its largest ever ballistic missile test on July 5, firing six missiles and one prototype satellite launch rocket in sequence. The Unha launcher was a successor to the Paektusan of 1998, and had initially been expected to be used for a launch from 1999–2001 before negotiations on a missile test moratorium prevented this.[127] Three months later on October 9, North Korea conducted its first confirmed detonation of a nuclear warhead, which was carried out at the Punggye underground test site and served to undercut remaining doubts regarding the country's status as a nuclear weapons state. Even preceding the test, remaining ambiguity was no longer whether the country had nuclear weapons, but "whether or not they have developed the ability to mate a nuclear weapon with a ballistic missile," as Defense Secretary Rumsfeld had stated in mid-July. The consensus leaned towards warheads having been sufficiently miniaturized for carriage by at least some missile classes, with a number of them able to carry large payloads of over 1000 kilograms.[128]

Pyongyang appeared to have expected that its nuclear and missile tests would place pressure on Washington to resume negotiations and offer better terms, which proved correct as the Bush administration was quick to organize a new phase of Six Party Talks to commence from December 18. Indeed, in sharp contrast to his prior position on engagement, President Bush went as far as to send a personal letter to Chairman Kim, addressed "Dear Mr. Chairman," which politely urged cooperation at a "critical juncture" in the arms control process. Setbacks in Iraq, and Pyongyang's rapid progress on its nuclear program, were widely credited with having forced the adoption of a softer line and a much less confrontational tone.[129] Although remaining steadfast in its refusal to end the Korean War, offer security guarantees or normalize ties, the administration conceded to removing Pyongyang from the list of State Sponsors of Terror, suspending application of the Trading with the Enemy Act, ceasing targeting or threatening to target third party banks, and resuming fuel deliveries. Revoking the Trading with the Enemy Act listing, which had been in place since 1950, had been a key demand since the early 1990s which the Clinton administration had been bound to meet under the Agreed Framework, and was followed through on by Washington on June 27, 2008, reducing pressure on the North Korean economy.[130]

In return for these concessions, North Korea agreed in February 2007 to freeze work at the Yongbyon facility and re-admit international inspectors, much as had been done under the Agreed Framework. Operations remained frozen for the next two years until three months into the Barack Obama administration's first term, when inspectors were expelled and work resumed. Almost immediately after the revocation of sanctions under the Trading With the Enemy Act, the cooling tower at Yongbyon was also destroyed on June 27, 2008. Pyongyang also provided a declaration of its nuclear weapons program on June 26, but was not required to allow free inspections of all sites requested or to allow sampling of soil near its nuclear facilities to fully verify this information. Alongside these concessions, North Korea also refrained from further missile launches. U.S. delays in removing Pyongyang from the State Sponsors of Terror list, and serious delays to fuel deliveries, notably led North Korea to delay meeting its own commitments, with the country then in August 20008 restoring facilities at Yongbyon and barring international inspectors. This forced the U.S. to fulfil its obligations to lift the terror listing on October 11 to get Pyongyang to return to compliance.[131]

While the Bush administration had previously been described in Western assessments as "attempting to squeeze the DPRK leadership into submission or into collapse,"[132] Pyongyang's ability to press Washington to very significantly loosen economic pressure without making major concessions on its nuclear or missile programs demonstrated both the strength of its position at the time and the value of these programs to its economic security. The Bush administration's final two years in office were some of the least eventful for relations between Washington and Pyongyang, and the agreements reached would later be widely criticized as "kicking the can down the road" for failing to address and at best only stalling the issue of the country's nuclear and missile development. With the North Korean economy having partially recovered from the crisis of the 1990s, and being bolstered by booming trade with China which was by then by far the world's fastest growing economy, the relaxation of sanctions further supported this recovery.

The Iraq War ultimately served to largely paralyze the Bush administration across multiple fronts, leaving the United States poorly positioned to handle a range of foreign policy challenges, with North Korea having strengthened its position tremendously vis-a-vis the United States during those eight years as many U.S. adversaries had. Much like all major U.S. adversaries, however, from China and Russia to Iran, Syria and Libya, a change in administration in January 2009 would see the emergence of a renewed threat and mark the beginning of an entirely new phase in its relations with Washington.

Endnotes

1 'State Secretary Colin L. Powell: Interview on NBC's Meet the Press with Tim Russert,' U.S. Department of State Archive, December 29, 2002.

2 'To React to Nuclear Weapons in Kind Is DPRK's Mode of Counteraction,' *Rodong Sinmun*, January 11, 2016.

3 Bush, George W., President Delivers State of the Union Address, The White House, January 29, 2002.

4 'Bush peers into "evil" North Korea,' *CNN*, February 20, 2002.

5 Howell, Edward, *North Korea and the Global Nuclear Order: When Bad Behaviour Pays*, Oxford, Oxford University Press, 2023 (p. 131).

6 Ibid. (p. 131).

7 Armstrong, Charles, *Necessary Enemies: Anti-Americanism, Juche Ideology, and the Torturous Path to Normalization*, New York, Columbia University, Department of History, Korea Studies, Working Paper Series (p. 14).

8 Ibid. (p. 15).

9 Howell, Edward, *North Korea and the Global Nuclear Order: When Bad Behaviour Pays*, Oxford, Oxford University Press, 2023 (pp. 130–131).

10 Arkin, William M., 'Secret Plan Outlines the Unthinkable,' *Los Angeles Times*, March 10, 2002.

11 Park, Kyung Ae, *New Challenges of North Korean Foreign Policy*, London, Palgrave MacMillan, 2010 (p. 218).

12 Kim, Suk Hi, *The Survival of North Korea: Essays on Strategy, Economics and International Relations*, Jefferson, NC, McFarland, 2011 (p. 46).

Funabashi, Yoichi, *The Peninsula Question: A Chronicle of the Second Korean Nuclear Crisis,* Washington, DC, Brookings Institution Press, 2007 (p. 143).

13 Park, Kyung Ae, *New Challenges of North Korean Foreign Policy*, London, Palgrave MacMillan, 2010 (p. 218).

14 'Empire in Decline – Colonel Lawrence Wilkerson, Alexander Mercouris and Glenn Diesen,' *The Duran* (YouTube Channel), November 30, 2023.

15 Ibid.

16 Ibid.

17 Ibid.

18 Struck, Doug, 'S. Korea's Next Leader: The Indispensable Man?,' *Washington Post,* December 21, 2002 (p. A16).

Marquand, Robert, 'U.S. Bides Time on N. Korean Crisis,' *Christian Science Monitor*, January 3, 2003 (p. 7).

19 'S. Korean Says U.S. Considered Attack on North,' *Washington Post*, January 19, 2003 (p. A18).

Torchia, Christopher, 'Officials Said to Have Pondered North Korea Attack Last Month,' *Washington Times*, January 19, 2003 (p. A7).

20 'Empire in Decline – Colonel Lawrence Wilkerson, Alexander Mercouris and Glenn Diesen,' *The Duran* (YouTube Channel), November 30, 2023.

21 'North Korea: The War Game,' *The Atlantic*, July/August 2005.

22 Sokolski, Henry D., *Planning for a Peaceful Korea*, Carlisle, PA, Strategic Studies Institute, 2001 (p. 290).

23 Worldwide Intelligence Review, Hearing Before the Select Committee on Intelligence of the United States Senate, One Hundred Fourth Congress, First Session on Worldwide Intelligence Review, January 10, 1995 (p. 164).

24 'Nuclear Site in North Korea Provides Clues on Weapons,' *New York Times*, May 17, 1992.

25 Public Statements of Donald H. Rumsfeld, Secretary of Defense, 2001, Volume 1, Historical Office, Office of the Secretary of Defense, 2001 (pp. 79–80).

26 *North Korean Tactics*, Army Techniques Publication No. 7-100.2, Washington, DC, Headquarters, Department of the Army, 2020 (Chapter 7).

27 Ibid. (Chapter 7).

28 Peters, Ralph, 'Constant Conflict, Parameters,' *U.S. Army War College Quarterly*, Summer 1997 (pp. 4–14).

29 'Interview: Ashton Carter,' *Frontline*, March 3, 2003.

30 Hearing Before the Subcommittee on International Organizations of the Committee on International Relations, House of Representatives, Ninety-Fifth Congress, First Session, Part 1, June 22, 1977 (pp. 13–14).

31 Norris, Robert S. and Kristensen, Hans S., 'North Korea's Nuclear Program, 2005,' *Bulletin of Atomic Scientists*, May/June 2005 (pp. 64–67).

Schobell, Andrew and Sanford, John M., *North Korea's Military Threat: Pyongyang's Conventional Forces, Weapons of Mass Destruction, and Ballistic Missiles*, Carlisle, U.S. Army War College Strategic Studies Institute, April 2007 (p. 77).

32 Sigal, Leon, *Disarming Strangers: Nuclear Diplomacy with North Korea,* Princeton. Princeton University Press, 1998 (p. 26).

33 Hibbs, Mark, 'Isotopics Show Three North Korean Reprocessing Campaigns Since 1975,' *Nuclear Fuel*, March 1, 1993 (pp. 8–9).

34 Berry Jr., William E., 'DPRK Briefing Book: North Korea's Nuclear Program: The Clinton Administration's Response,' INSS Occasional Paper 3, *Nautilus Institute*, March 1995.

35 Worldwide Intelligence Review, Hearing Before the Select Committee on Intelligence of the United States Senate, One Hundred Fourth Congress, First Session on Worldwide Intelligence Review, January 10, 1995 (pp. 103–104).

36 'Putin says Kim Jong-il told him about North Korea's nukes back in early 2000s,' *TASS*, October 4, 2017.

37 *Washington Times,* September 27, 2002.

MacArthur, John R., *Second Front: Censorship and Propaganda in the 1991 Gulf War,* Berkeley, University of California Press, 2004 (pp. xxx, xxxi).

38 Smith, Derek D., *Deterring America: Rogue States and the Proliferation of Weapons of Mass Destruction*, Cambridge, Cambridge University Press, 2006 (p. 74).

39 Sanger, David E., 'North Korea Says It Has a Program on Nuclear Arms,' *New York Times*, October 17, 2002.

40 'State Secretary Colin L. Powell: Interview on NBC's Meet the Press with Tim Russert,' U.S. Department of State Archive, December 29, 2002.

41 Struck, Doug, 'Crisis Could Push N. Korea to Expel Nuclear Inspectors,' *Washington Post*, November 14, 2002.

42 Carter, Ashton B. and Perry, William J., 'Back to the Brink,' *Washington Post*, October 20, 2002.

43 'Interview: Ashton Carter,' *Frontline*, March 3, 2003.

44 Pritchard, Charles L., *Failed Diplomacy: The Tragic Story of How North Korea Got the Bomb,* Washington, DC, Brookings Institution Press, 2007 (p. 28).

45 Clinton, Bill, *My Life*, New York, Alfred A. Knopf, 2004 (Chapter 4).

46 Gilman, Benjamin A., 'Gilman Releases North Korea Report,' Press Release, November 3, 1999.

47 Howell, Edward, *North Korea and the Global Nuclear Order: When Bad Behaviour Pays*, Oxford, Oxford University Press, 2023 (p. 132).

48 Bolton, John R., *A Dictatorship at the Crossroads,* Speech at the Seoul Hilton, Seoul, July 31, 2003

49 'President George Bush Discusses Iraq in National Press Conference,' The White House, March 6, 2003.

50 'State Secretary Colin L. Powell: Interview on NBC's Meet the Press with Tim Russert,' U.S. Department of State Archive, December 29, 2002.

51 Albright, David, 'North Korea's Alleged Large-Scale Enrichment Plant: Yet Another Questionable Extrapolation Based on Aluminium Tubes,' *The Institute for Science and International Security*, February 23, 2007.

52 Sanger, David E. and Broad, William J., 'U.S. Had Doubts on North Korean Uranium Drive,' *New York Times,* March 1, 2007.

53 Ibid.

54 Albright, David, 'North Korea's Alleged Large-Scale Enrichment Plant: Yet Another Questionable Extrapolation Based on Aluminum Tubes,' The Institute for Science and International Security, February 23, 2007.

Sanger, David E. and Broad, William J., 'U.S. Had Doubts on North Korean Uranium Drive,' *New York Times,* March 1, 2007.

55 Harrison, Selig S., 'Did North Korea Cheat?,' *Foreign Affairs*, January/February 2005.

56 'Conclusion of non-aggression treaty between DPRK and U.S. called for,' *KCNA*, October 25, 2002.

57 van der Heide, Liesbeth, 'Cherry-Picked Intelligence. The Weapons of Mass Destruction Dispositive as a Legitimation for National Security in the Post 9/11 Age,' *Historical Social Research,* vol. 38, no. 1, 2013 (pp. 286–307).

Lee, Adrian, 'Seymour Hersh Alleges Obama Administration Lied on Syria Gas Attack,' *The Atlantic,* December 8, 2013.

58 Peterson, Scott, 'In war, some facts less factual,' *Christian Science Monitor,* September 6, 2002.

59 Sanger, David E., 'North Korea Says It Has a Program on Nuclear Arms,' *New York Times,* October 17, 2002.

60 'Conclusion of non-aggression treaty between DPRK and U.S. called for,' *KCNA*, October 25, 2002.

61 Von Hein, Matthias, 'The Iraq War: In the beginning was the lie,' *Deutsche Welle,* April 4, 2018.

'Conclusion of non-aggression treaty between DPRK and U.S. called for,' *KCNA*, October 25, 2002.

62 Von Hein, Matthias, 'The Iraq War: In the beginning was the lie,' *Deutsche Welle,* April 4, 2018.

63 Sanger, David E. and Broad, William J., 'U.S. Had Doubts on North Korean Uranium Drive,' *New York Times,* March 1, 2007.

64 Pollack, Jonathan D., 'The United States, North Korea and the end of the Agreed Framework,' *Naval War College Review*, vol. LVI, no. 3, 2003 (p. 15).

Beal, Tim, *North Korea: The Struggle Against American Power,* London, Pluto Press, 2004 (p. 214).

Harrison, Selig S., 'Did North Korea Cheat?,' *Foreign Affairs*, January/February 2005.

65 Howell, Edward, *North Korea and the Global Nuclear Order: When Bad Behaviour Pays*, Oxford, Oxford University Press, 2023 (p. 133).

66 'North Korea to Reopen Nuclear Plant Over Oil Cutoff by U.S.,' *New York Times,* December 12, 2002.

67 'Operation and Building of Nuclear Facilities to Be Resumed Immediately,' *KCNA*, December 12, 2002.

68 Ibid.

69 Sanger, David E. and Dao, James, 'North Korea Says It Regains Access To Its Plutonium,' *New York Times,* December 23, 2002.

70 Stout, David, 'Rumsfeld Says if Necessary, US Can Fight 2 Wars At Once,' *New York Times*, December 23, 2002.

71 'Statement of DPRK Government on Its Withdrawal from NPT,' *KCNA*, January 10, 2003.

72 'The DPRK delegate made speech at a meeting of the UN Disarmament Commission on April 11,' *KCNA*, April 21, 2006.

73 'US public thinks Saddam had role in 9/11,' *The Guardian,* September 7, 2003.

74 Mueller, John, *Atomic Obsession: Nuclear Alarmism from Hiroshima to Al-Qaeda,* New York, Oxford University Press, 2004 (p. 129).

75 Letter to President Clinton, Project for the New American Century, January 26, 1998 (http://www.newamericancentury.org/iraqclintonletter.htm).

76 Swansbrough, Robert, *Test by Fire: The War Presidency of George W Bush*, New York, Palgrave Macmillan, 2008 (p. 127).

77 Halper, Stefan and Clarke, Jonathan, *America Alone: The Neo-Conservatives and the Global Order*, New York, Cambridge University Press, 2004 (p. 11).

Swansbrough, Robert, *Test by Fire: The War Presidency of George W Bush*, New York, Palgrave Macmillan, 2008 (p. 128).

78 Mann, James, *Rise of the Vulcans: The History of Bush's War Cabinet*, New York, Viking, 2004 (Chapter 18).

79 'President George Bush Discusses Iraq in National Press Conference,' *The White House*, March 6, 2003.

80 Mann, James, *Rise of the Vulcans: The History of Bush's War Cabinet*, New York, Viking, 2004 (Chapter 21).

81 Presidential Comments, *CNN*, December 31, 2002.

82 'State Secretary Colin L. Powell: Interview on NBC's Meet the Press with Tim Russert,' U.S. Department of State Archive, December 29, 2002.

83 Christopher, Warren, 'Iraq Belongs on the Back Burner,' *New York Times,* December 31, 2002.

84 Mitchell, Greg, *So Wrong for So Long: How the Press, the Pundits – and the President – Failed on Iraq*, New York, Sterling Publishing, 2008 (p. 14)

85 *Rodong Sinmun*, March 28, 2003.

86 Howell, Edward, *North Korea and the Global Nuclear Order: When Bad Behaviour Pays*, Oxford, Oxford University Press, 2023 (p. 136).

87 'State Secretary Colin L. Powell: Interview on NBC's Meet the Press with Tim Russert,' U.S. Department of State Archive, December 29, 2002.

88 Hersh, Seymour M., 'The Cold Test,' *The New Yorker*, January 27, 2003 (p. 47).

89 'To Pyongyang Via Baghdad,' *The Wall Street Journal*, January 13, 2003

90 Crumplar, Robert K., *Kim Il Sung (North Korea), Another Saddam Hussein (Iraq)? Countering and Deterring Aggression in the Northern Pacific,* United States Naval War College, February 13, 1992.

Anderson, Jack and Binstein, Michael, 'North Korea: Loose Nuclear Cannon,' *Washington Post*, March 28, 1992.

91 'US: "We are seeing history unfold,"' *The Guardian*, April 10, 2003.

92 Ramesh, Randeep, 'The two faces of Rumsfeld,' *The Guardian*, May 9, 2003.

93 Bolton, John R., *A Dictatorship at the Crossroads,* Speech at the Seoul Hilton, Seoul, July 31, 2003.

94 Gordon, Michael R., 'Cheney Says Next Goal in U.S. War on Terror Is to Block Access to Arms,' *New York Times*, March 16, 2002.

95 Bush, George W., President Bush Delivers Graduation Speech at West Point, United States Military Academy, West Point, New York, June 1, 2002.

96 Drezner, Daniel W., 'North Korea Talks to Selig Harrison,' *Foreign Policy*, May 4, 2004.

97 'North Korea: Washington Flew 1,200 Spy Flights Over Country,' *Fox News*, July 25, 2004.

'North Korea Accuses U.S. of Spy Flights,' *Southern Illinoisan*, July 26, 2004.

98 Rhem, Kathleen T., 'North Korea intercepts Air Force aircraft,' *American Forces Press Service*, March 4, 2003.

99 'U.S. Repositioning Bombers Near North Korea,' *USA Today*, March 4, 2003.

100 Carpenter, Ted Galen and Bandow, Doug, *The Korean Conundrum:*

America's Troubled Relations with North and South Korea, New York, Palgrave Macmillan, 2004 (pp. 64–65).

101 Auster, Bruce B. and Whitelaw, Kevin, 'Upping the Ante for Kim Jong Il: Pentagon Plan 5030, A New Blueprint for Facing Down North Korea,' *U.S. News and World Report*, July 21, 2003.

O'Hanion, Machael E., 'North Korea Is No Iraq,' *Brookings Institute*, October 21, 2002.

Kim, Suk Hi, *The Survival of North Korea: Essays on Strategy, Economics and International Relations*, Jefferson, NC, McFarland & Co., 2011 (pp. 49–50).

Park, Kyung Ae, *New Challenges of North Korean Foreign Policy*, London, Palgrave MacMillan, 2010 (p. 218).

102 Carpenter, Ted Galen and Bandow, Doug, *The Korean Conundrum: America's Troubled Relations with North and South Korea,* New York, Palgrave Macmillan, 2004 (pp. 64–65).

Auster, Bruce and Whitelaw, Kevin, 'Upping the Ante for Kim Jong-Il,' *U.S. News & World Report,* July 21, 2003.

103 Park, Kyung Ae, *New Challenges of North Korean Foreign Policy*, London, Palgrave MacMillan, 2010 (p. 218).

104 Goodman, Peter S., 'N. Korea Moves to Activate Complex,' *Washington Post*, December 27, 2002.

105 Sanger, David E. and Schmitt, Eric, 'Satellites Said to See Activity at North Korean Nuclear Site,' *New York Times,* January 31, 2003.

106 'North Korea Restarts Plant With Ability to Fuel Arms,' *New York Times*, February 6, 2003.

107 Schobell, Andrew and Sanford, John M., *North Korea's Military Threat: Pyongyang's Conventional Forces, Weapons of Mass Destruction, and Ballistic Missiles*, Carlisle, PA, U.S. Army War College Strategic Studies Institute, April 2007 (p. 75).

The International Institute for Strategic Studies, *North Korea's Weapons Programmes: A Net Assessment*, London, Palgrave Macmillan, 2004 (p. 42).

108 Borger, Julian and Watts, Jonathan, 'North Korea Offers to Lift Nuclear Threat,' *The Guardian Weekly*, May 1–7, 2003.

109 Van Ness, Peter, 'The North Korean nuclear crisis: four-plus-two – an idea whose time has come,' in: Gurtov, Mel and Van Ness, Peter (eds.), *Confronting the Bush Doctrine: Critical views from the Asia-Pacific*, Abingdon, Routledge, 2005 (p. 251).

110 Risen, James and Johnson, David, 'Photos Give Further Sign of Violence at Prison: Dead Iraqi Detainees Lead to Questions,' *International Herald Tribune*, May 8–9, 2004 (p. 2).

111 Powers, Thomas, 'The Vanishing Case for War,' *New York Review of Books*, vol. 50, no. 19, December 4, 2003 (pp. 12–17).

Saikal, Amin, 'US Policy Has Isolated Only One Extremist Group – Its Own,' *Sydney Morning Herald*, October 31, 2003.

Dowd, Maureen, 'A Front Here, A Front There: Bush Is Scaring Up Votes,' *International Herald Tribune*, November 27, 2003.

112 Mann, James, *Rise of the Vulcans: The History of Bush's War Cabinet*, New York, Viking, 2004 (Chapter 21).

113 Woodward, Bob, *The War Within the White House: A Secret White House History 2006–2008*, New York, Simon and Schuster, 2008 (Chapter 28).

114 Nixon, Richard M., *RN: The Memoirs of Richard Nixon*, New York, Warner Books, 1978 (pp. 473–475).

115 Woodward, Bob, *The War Within the White House: A Secret White House History 2006–2008*, New York, Simon and Schuster, 2008 (Chapter 22).

116 Eberstadt, Nicholas, 'Tear Down This Tyranny,' *The Weekly Standard*, November 29, 2004.

117 Lee, Su Hoon, *Nuclear North Korea*, Seoul, Kyungnam University Press, 2012 (p. 88).

118 'DPRK Foreign Ministry Spokesman on Six-Party Talks,' *KCNA*, August 5, 2003.

119 Park, Kyung-ae, *New Challenges of North Korean Foreign Policy*, New York, Palgrave Macmillan, 2010 (p. 189).

120 Brooke, James, 'North Korea says it has atom arms; It will boycott talks on ending program; arsenal called self-defense against Bush,' *New York Times*, February 11, 2005.

121 'N.K. Plans to Unload Fuel Rods from Reactor This Month,' *Yonhap News*, April 16, 2005.

'Report: North Korea Restarted Nuclear Reactor Before International Nuclear Talks,' *Associated Press,* August 21, 2005.

122 'N. Korea Admits Building More Nuclear Bombs,' *ABC News*, June 9, 2005.

123 Greenlees, Donald and Lague, David, 'Squeeze on Banco Delta Asia hit North Korea where it hurt,' *New York Times,* January 18, 2007.

124 Solomon, Jay and King, Neil Jr., 'How U.S. Used a Bank to Punish North Korea,' *The Wall Street Journal,* April 12, 2007.

125 Bechtol Jr., Bruce E., *North Korean Military Proliferation in the Middle East and Africa,* Lexington, KY, University Press of Kentucky, 2018 (p. 88).

Spencer, Richard, 'N Korea "Tests New Missile in Iran,"' *The Telegraph*, May 17, 2007.

126 'Trigger Happy,' *CBS News*, July 31, 2008.

Rogin, Josh, 'Bush's CIA director: We determined attacking Iran was a bad idea,' *Foreign Policy*, January 19, 2012.

Hersh, Seymour M., 'The Iran Plans,' *The New Yorker*, April 9, 2006.

127 Walpole, Robert, Testimony before the Senate Governmental Affairs

Subcommittee on International Security, Proliferation, and Federal Services, February 9, 2000.

128 Gertz, Bill, 'North Korea Has More Missiles, U.S. Says,' *Washington Times*, July 13, 2006.

129 'Bush sends letter to North Korea's Kim Jong-il,' *Reuters*, December 7, 2007.

130 Onishi, Norimitsu and Wong, Edward, 'U.S. to Remove North Koreans from Terror List; Nuclear Declaration is Rewarded as Disarmament Effort Advances,' *International Herald Tribune*, June 27, 2008.

131 Choe, Sang-Hun, 'North Korea Says It Stopped Disabling Nuclear Complex,' *New York Times*, August 27, 2008.

Kessler, Glenn, 'U.S. Drops North Korea from Terrorism List,' *Washington Post*, October 12, 2008.

'N. Korea "Slowing Disablement of Nuclear Facilities,"' *Chosun Ilbo*, January 29, 2008.

Lee, Chi-dong, 'N Korea Complains About Slow Provision of Energy Aid,' *Yonhap*, June 5, 2008.

132 Lodgaard, Sverre and Maerli, Vremer, *Nuclear Proliferation and International Security*, Abingdon, Routledge, 2007 (p. 130).

CHAPTER 3

The Barack Obama Years: A New Phase of Conflict

The Obama White House and a New Global Cold War

Following a limited improvement in ties in the final years of the George W. Bush administration, U.S.-DPRK relations would deteriorate rapidly after the inauguration of Barack Obama as president in January 2009. This represented part of a much broader trend towards the Obama administration overseeing escalated tensions with adversaries with which its predecessor had either improved ties, or else had kept tensions low. Washington's stable ties with China were severely disrupted with the initiation of the Pivot to Asia initiative from 2010, under which territorial disputes in the South and East China Seas were designated core American national interests and the bulk of the U.S. Armed Forces were re-oriented towards East Asia. The following year Bush-era improvements in relations with Libya and Syria were quickly reversed as military action was taken against both. A gradual deterioration of ties with Russia, too, further escalated as the Obama administration threatened a full scale assault on its strategic partner Syria in 2013,[1] and moreso from 2014 after Washington engineered the overthrow of the Russia-friendly Ukrainian government, sparking a civil war in the country in which Moscow and NATO backed opposing sides.[2] Other examples of escalated tensions were widespread, from Pakistan and Yemen where the new president's signature drone strikes caused tremendous civilian casualties and major controversies,[3] to Turkey where Washington's perceived support for an attempted coup considerably soured the previously strong strategic partnership.[4] Under George W. Bush foreign policy and military attentions, had particularly after 2003 been very heavily focused on the three adjacent states of Iraq, Iran and

Afghanistan, leaving relations with all the aforementioned states considerably more stable.

U.S.–North Korean relations during the Obama administration's first term developed within the dual contexts of a major increase in American military interventionism abroad and a significant refocusing of attentions towards East Asia, both of which boded ill for Pyongyang's security situation. The number of drone strikes under the Obama administration were almost ten times higher than under the Bush administration,[5] with broader military campaigns targeting adversaries across a much wider range of countries and with higher intensity.[6] The rapid expansion during Obama's first year in office of a network of assets under the U.S. Military's Africa Command (AFRICOM) was one notable example, with experts observing at the end of his first term that "operations in Africa have accelerated far beyond the more limited interventions of the Bush years" – a phenomenon otherwise referred to by experts as "Obama's Scramble for Africa" pursued in parallel to the "Pivot to Asia."[7]

While outlining plans for the Asia Pivot in November 2011 President Obama referred to "a deliberate and strategic decision… [that] the United States will play a larger and long-term role in shaping this region and its future," stressing he had "directed my national security team to make our presence and mission in the Asia Pacific a top priority." He emphasized "our unique ability to project power" and efforts "to ensure that our forces can operate freely,"[8] christening the pivot with the announcement that over 2,500 U.S. Marines would be deployed in Northern Australia – a key staging ground for such power projection efforts. Over the next decade this area would come to house a growing range of key American assets, ranging from stealth fighters to expanded facilities hosting warships, and even nuclear-capable strategic bombers.[9] Within five years the number of American personnel deployed to the Pacific had increased by approximately 50 percent from 70,000 to over 100,000,[10] with a target of 60 percent of naval forces deployed to the region by 2020.[11] The president would later famously summarize the future order his administration sought to guarantee in East Asia as follows: "America should write the rules. America should call the shots. Other countries should play by the rules that America and our partners set, and not the other way around."[12]

While China was from the outset the primary target of the Pivot to Asia, handling challenges of "proliferation" was cited as the second key reason and appeared to be a thinly veiled reference to North Korea.[13] Withdrawing U.S. forces from the Iraqi quagmire in 2009 made the United States appear far more dangerous than it had in at least half a decade, and facilitated a refocusing of American assets towards the new theatre. The U.S. simultaneously began to strongly refocus on the ability to engage in conflict with major state adversaries, rather than on counterinsurgency. As its footprint abroad expanded tremendously, the country by the end of Obama's tenure maintained around 800 bases abroad and special forces deployments across 138 countries.[14]

In contrast to the relative peace seen under the three preceding administrations, Obama initiated a new Cold War on multiple fronts – from the targeting of China's tech sector to the initiation of economic warfare and proxy wars targeting Russian and Iranian interests, and the tremendous expansion of military operations in Africa to assuage growing concerns of expanding Chinese influence. With the exception of limited rapprochements with Iran and Cuba in the administration's second term, incidences of the Obama administration improving ties with states outside the Western sphere of influence were few and far between. The course of relations with North Korea would align closely with this trend.

Obama Era Pressure: Sanctions, Cyber Warfare, and the Anticipation of Collapse

North Korea had according to multiple sources sought to send a representative to President Obama's inauguration, which was interpreted at the time as indicating a desire to further improve ties, although these overtures were strongly rebuffed.[15] Reversing the reductions in tensions made in President Bush's second term, the Obama administration was quick to set out harsh terms for the normalization of relations – namely that full and unilateral nuclear disarmament was a precondition for any talks.[16] The new administration's position was characterized by Director for Asian Affairs on the Bush White House's National Security Council Victor Cha as "Hawk Engagement," which referred to its taking of a very hard line, but expending considerable efforts to portray its policies as resulting from a reasonable exhaustion of more moderate options.[17]

Less than three months after President Obama's inauguration North Korea launched the Kwangmyŏngsŏng-2 (Bright Star 2) civil communications satellite on April 5, to which the new administration responded by taking the harshest line possible on the issue. Washington claimed the launch using an Unha series rocket was a cover for the testing of intercontinental range ballistic missile technologies, emphasizing the dual uses of satellite launch technologies to argue for a denial of North Korea's rights under the Outer Space Treaty to place satellites in orbit. This mirrored the U.S. response to the 1998 launch of the Unha's predecessor, the Paektusan, despite the consensus that had emerged among Western analysts in subsequent years that these rockets were not intended to be developed into missiles.[18,i] The Obama administration pressed hard for the passage of a new resolution at the United Nations Security Council imposing additional economic sanctions, although this was blocked by China and Russia, which also prevented Western efforts to issue a strongly worded condemnation of the satellite launch.

Acting unilaterally outside the United Nations the new secretary of state, Hillary Clinton, announced plans to escalate economic warfare efforts and to consider relisting Pyongyang as a State Sponsor of Terror, while continuing to push for further resolutions at the UN Security Council to restrict North Korean trade and economic activity. This included resolutions that would allow for interdiction of its shipping.[19] Regarding trade, she clarified: "We will do everything we can to both interdict it and prevent it

i North Korean intermediate and intercontinental range missiles would use much more sophisticated engines, and while the Unha rocket's use of three stages was seen at the time as a stepping stone to developing a three-stage ICBM, no such missile would ever be deployed by the country.

and shut off their flow of money."[20] The Obama administration also appeared to be preparing to resume sanctioning third parties such as banks, which had proven damaging to the North Korean economy from 2005–2006.[21]

Pyongyang responded to American pledges to escalate economic warfare efforts with a threat to resume ballistic missile testing, a warning that it could open a uranium enrichment program, which it denied American claims of having previously begun, and with the expulsion of all remaining inspectors from the International Energy Atomic Agency (IAEA) from Yongbyon.[22] On April 20 the head of the IAEA Mohamed El Baradei announced that North Korea was assessed to have the capability to deploy nuclear weapons from missiles. "North Korea has nuclear weapons, which is a matter of fact... I don't like to accept any country as a nuclear weapon state but we have to face reality," he stated. "We need to find a solution before they go into building their nuclear power arsenal," he added, noting regarding facilities at Yongbyon that "we don't know how far they dismantled," and that North Korea could restart the facility in "a matter of months" to resume production of weaponizable plutonium.[23] Baradei concluded by confirming North Korea's claim to be a "fully fledged nuclear power."[24] Interpreted by some as an admission that North Korea's nuclearization was a *fait accompli,* the statement caused controversy among hardliners on the issue.[25]

On May 25 North Korea conducted its second detonation of a nuclear warhead, producing a yield estimated at up to 20 kilotons,[26] with state media reporting that this "helped satisfactorily settle the scientific and technological problems" related to increasing the warhead's yield.[27] Testing of ballistic missiles was subsequently accelerated to record levels with 14 launches, six of which were longer ranged classes capable of striking targets in Japan. Thus within a few months North Korea had launched as many missiles as it had throughout the preceding ten years.[28] Pyongyang's response demonstrated a new level of confidence in its ability to confront American escalation, with the rapprochement of the late Bush years having combined with a decade of slow but consistent economic recovery to strengthen its position considerably. The Obama administration again notably failed to significantly expand the scope of economic sanctions at the UN Security Council, with China and Russia insisting that sanctions remain "clearly tied to ending the DPRK program to create nuclear missiles" and not target the Korean population indiscriminately.[29] UNSC Resolution 1874 passed in May thus targeted only potential sources of financing for the country's missile and nuclear programs.

Much as had been the case under the Bill Clinton administration, policy towards North Korea under Barack Obama was heavily shaped by the perception that the state's collapse was an inevitability, with prevailing Western perceptions of the country as a one-man-state similar to Saddam Hussein's Iraq, and reports of the ailing health of Chairman Kim Jong Il, fueling predictions of a political crisis, collapse or major policy shift. This line of thinking was most prominently highlighted in a sixty-page report published by the Council on Foreign Relations foreign policy think tank in January 2009, which predicted instability and possibly state collapse on this basis.

The CFR's publications provided an effective indicator of the position of the American foreign policy establishment, which were consistently closely reflected in the policies of contemporary administrations. The *Washington Post* accordingly described the CFR's members as "the nearest thing we have to a ruling establishment in the United States," with this including almost all former CIA directors, national security advisors, UN ambassadors, Federal Reserve chairs, World Bank presidents, National Economic Council directors, the majority of state secretaries, several presidents and vice presidents, and Federal Reserve chairs, and many high ranking military commanders. The *Post* highlighted that the Council's members represented part of a foreign policy elite with shared values and worldviews, and played a major role in actively shaping policy.[30] Princeton University Professor Stephen Cohen, former advisor to President George H. W. Bush and a former CFR member, described the Council as "America's single most important non-governmental foreign policy organization," with the power to "define the accepted, legitimate, orthodox parameters of discussion.... The CFR really is what the Soviets used to call the very top-level of the Nomenklatura."[31] The influence of the CFR was widely assessed to be particularly considerable under the Obama administration, with State Secretary Clinton observing after it opened a new office in Washington in 2009 that it was responsible for informing the State Department "what we should be doing and how we should think about the future."[32]

While perceptions of a North Korean collapse as an inevitability did much to foster complacency in the United States and wider Western world, there was a far less benign aspect to the CFR's projections. The Council's paper projected that following internal instability in North Korea, the U.S. could lead a full-scale invasion and an occupying "stabilization force" of an expected 460,000 personnel. Reflecting the prevailing Western perception of North Korea as a one-man-state, the paper predicted that the death of Kim Jong Il would lead to the country's political system and military effectively falling apart, making such an invasion considerably easier.[33] This reflected a broad consensus across American think tanks, with the Brookings Institute five months later stating in the opening of its own paper that "regime change in North Korea is inevitable," and that when this occurred it would require American military intervention and a military presence in the country.[34]

Arguments for strategic patience in the face of looming instability in North Korea were bolstered by reports from mid-2009 that Chairman Kim had fallen into ill health, fueling Western projections of a coming opportunity to act against the country.[35] While this reduced the perceived urgency of action in spite of advances in North Korea's nuclear and missile programs, the Obama administration still sought to maximize pressure at minimal cost to slow the country's economic development and military modernization and to accelerate its anticipated collapse.

In parallel to the escalation of unilateral sanctions and significant expansion of the American military presence in Northeast Asia, the United States in mid-2009 attempted a major cyberattack on North Korea's nuclear program using the Stuxnet worm – the largest and costliest development in malware history. Two joint

U.S.-Israeli Stuxnet attacks were carried out in parallel against North Korea and Iran, with the worm using an unprecedented four "zero-day attacks," and in Iranian centrifuges successfully inducing excessive vibrations and distortions in the speed of the rotors causing serious damage. The *Washington Post* reported that this had forced Iran to dismantle 900–1000 centrifuges while the malware was active.[36] Efforts to insert the worm in Korea failed, however, with "North Korea's utter secrecy, as well as the extreme isolation of its communications systems" credited with having protected its nuclear infrastructure. The fact that the Yongbyon gas-graphite reactor lacked the cumbersome cascading centrifuges seen at Iranian facilities meant that even if the malware had been inserted, the damage would have been considerably less.[37] Director of America's National Security Agency Keith Alexander was among the officials to highlight the near unique resilience to Western cyberattacks that North Korea's tight security system provided, which the Stuxnet incident effectively demonstrated.[38] The Stuxnet attacks exemplified the Obama administration's focus on maximizing pressure on and disruption to adversaries at minimal cost to the United States, with the president personally ordering an intensification of cyber offensives against Iran from 2012, and subsequently against North Korea from 2014, as a prominent part of this.[39]

In August 2011 Pyongyang again made clear its openness to considering a moratorium on nuclear and missile testing. The State Department responded that "this would be welcome, but it would be insufficient," again indicating that demands from Pyongyang were too broad, and negotiating positions were too irreconcilable, for progress to be made.[40] Four months later on December 17 Chairman Kim Jong Il died of a heart attack while travelling by train. While *Voice of America* described the reaction across the European continent as "a mix of hope and watchfulness,"[41] this reflected broader optimism across the Western world that a long-awaited power struggle and destabilization of the state could ensue. With no signs of instability emerging over the following year, however, such expectations were replaced by optimistic predictions that the chairman's third son and successor, Kim Jong

Un, would reform the country along Western lines. Beyond the prevailing perceptions of the inevitability of such transformation, the fact that the new leader spent seven years studying in Switzerland was expected to ingrain in him an appreciation of the West's ideology, culture and values which could incline him to move his country in a similar direction.[42,ii]

While quickly disappointing Western expectations for a Gorbachevian reformist, as the new Workers' Party chairman Kim Jong Un quickly came to oversee a rejuvenation of the economy with a new emphasis on modernization, high end technologies and raising of living standards. Indicators ranged from the emergence of new domestically manufactured smartphones under brands such as Arirang, Jinalllae and Phurun Hanul, to considerable investments made in projects for agriculture such as fish farming[43] and floating rice fields.[44] Other notable projects ranged from scientific research facilities,[45] to new housing and infrastructure, with entertainment such as the performing arts adopting a refreshing style, as did architecture, demonstrating new levels of innovation.[46,iii]

---

ii North Korean sources emphasized continuity between the two administrations, with Head of State and President of the Presidium Kim Yong Nam, although lamenting "the biggest and the most unimaginable loss to our party and the revolution," stating that the nation would "transform the sorrow into strength and courage 1,000 times greater under the leadership of comrade Kim Jong Un." "Respected Comrade Kim Jong Un is our party, military and country's supreme leader who inherits great comrade Kim Jong Il's ideology, leadership, character, virtues, grit and courage," he added.

iii Epitomizing the spirit of this transformation was the debut of the Moranbong Band in 2013, which expert Pekka Korhonen at Finland's University of Jyväskylä referred to as "a symbol of a new era." "The band, an object of talk and admiration, became immediately extremely popular with the North Korean population. The band had style, it promised something new, had a foreign aura even when playing familiar military marches, and made music that truly inspired people. Visitors tell about people dancing in public while listening to Moranbong Band DVDs, or shops closing and streets becoming deserted when the group's concerts were broadcast on national TV," he observed. Referring its "simultaneously catchy and intricate" style, he observed that the music was working "at a more popular level." "This poetic creation is continuous. Practically all of their versions of the national hymn Aegukka are different, although there would be no ethical social realist reason for this. They simply create art," he added. (Korhonen, Pekka, 'Rock Gospels: Analyzing the Artistic Style of Moranbong Band,' *SinoNK*, March 4, 2014.)

An analysis of North Korea's political system and ideology provides a strong indication that Western predictions of collapse or westernization were ill conceived from the outset. The fact that the state had strong governing institutions, and failed to fit Western caricatures of "dictatorships" where everything rested on one supreme leader, was perhaps best demonstrated by the effectively unchanged governance in 2008 despite Chairman Kim Jong Il taking a four-month total leave of absence due to a heart attack. The predominant highly propagandized and caricatured portrayals of the state that invariably shaped Western understandings consistently limited analysts and policymakers' ability to make sound assessments. This issue was alluded to by CIA analyst John Nixon who, after working on North Korea and Iraq, noted that the American leadership consistently put their own prejudices and preconceptions above tangible intelligence, highlighting their extreme cognitive dissonance as information contradicting these preconceptions was persistently dismissed.

An issue with effective propaganda remained that when it successfully shaped a society's consensus based on false information, this invariably also influenced policymakers from that society. With Western societies strongly conditioned to see North Korea and Iraq as "evil," often based on caricaturish portrayals far removed from reality, the leaders and analysts they produced were accordingly not infrequently out of touch with reality. Nixon thus observed after several meetings in the White House and with military and intelligence officials: "I can conclude that U.S. policymakers were prisoners of what they thought they knew... countervailing intelligence be damned," and regarding their prejudices were "convinced it was right, no matter what the intelligence showed."[47] The CIA, too, "seemed completely locked into its interpretations of Kim [Jong Il]," while all evidence which contradicted their preconceived ideas being dismissed.[48]

The impact of this phenomenon on Western intelligence had previously been highlighted by former Secretary of State Madeleine Albright, who recalled that before visiting Pyongyang in 2000 her briefings on the country's leadership had been far removed from reality. Regarding Kim Jong Il, she recalled: "I went having been briefed on what kind of a weirdo he was from our own people. He was portrayed as reclusive-like with many girlfriends and watching porno movies – basically a very weird kind of person." By contrast, she recalled: "He was actually quite charming ... He was very, very well prepared, responded without notes, was not only respectful but also interested in what I had to say," and to her surprise the talks were a success.[49,iv] The former state secretary would recall 19 years later:

> I do think that what is interesting is how smart and informed Kim Jong Il was... he technically knew an awful lot of things. We were actually talking about missile limits at the time. He did not consult his experts. He really was able to talk about various aspects of the programs. And he spent a lot of time on it. It was very interesting. He also could be very gracious. I mean, it was all kinds of dinners and all kinds of things. But I think that he was determined to make some progress.... I was surprised by how technically adept and smart he was.[50]

According to Albright, the success of future diplomacy would rely heavily on whether or not American leaders would recognize how adept and capable the North Korean leadership was – in sharp contrast to what intelligence briefings had led her to believe.[51] The metanarrative, however, was near inescapable, and in the Obama years fostered a complacency that bought Pyongyang time to strengthen its position.

---

iv Documents from the U.S. National Security Archive declassified in 2020 highlighted that Albright "spoke of her astonishment over having a 'rational discussion' with him. Based on these lengthy meetings, she realized that the U.S. had until now failed to understand what type of person he really was, which was in contrast to the accepted view of him as 'strange, moody and hypersensitive.' Now, agreeing with Kim Dae Jung that their earlier assessment was wrong, Albright saw Kim Jong Il as 'practical, pragmatic, decisive, and non-ideological.' She had found him well-informed from extensive reading." (Cable, State 230629 to American Embassy Seoul, Subject: Secretary Albright's October 25 Bilateral I Seoul with Japanese FM Kono, U.S. National Security Archive, December 5, 2000.)

2013 Standoff: Escalated Hostilities Under a New North Korean Administration

On April 13, 2012, a revision of the DPRK constitution for the first time referred to the country as a "nuclear state," enshrining in the country's primary legal document the 2005 declaration of nuclear weapons possession. In January the following year official statements clarified that Pyongyang would not be open to dialogue on denuclearization, and would only disarm when other nuclear weapon states also did so, with a separate statement that month highlighting that it would respond to perceived American hostility with a nuclear test "of higher level."[52] This was followed February 12, 2013 by the country's third test detonation of a nuclear warhead, one described as "smaller and light," with significant miniaturization reportedly allowing for more efficient delivery by missile and considerable expansion of its payload.

From early 2009 a growing number of authorities, ranging from the IAEA and leading think tank analysts to the Pentagon, had reported that North Korea had sufficiently miniaturized nuclear warheads to facilitate delivery by missile. This was generally estimated to have occurred in late 2008, with this consensus forcing a major shift in Western plans for possible military action against the country.[53] The January 2013 test helped diminish remaining doubts.[v]

Other than the attempted launch of a weather satellite by Unha rocket on April 13, which state media was quick to announce had failed,[54] and a successful launch on December 12,[55] the year 2012 passed relatively without incident. The February 2013

---

v Leading U.S. expert on the North Korean nuclear and missile programs Jeffrey Lewis summarized the prevailing argument as follows in April 2013: "They've tested three nuclear devices so far. Even in the 1940s, it was possible to build working, air-deliverable nuclear weapons based on less experience than that. Missile-deliverable weapons don't necessarily take much more. In the 1960s, China conducted its fourth nuclear test by putting it on a missile and shooting it at the test site. And it's no longer the 1960s." (Lewis, Jeffrey, 'North Korea's Nuclear Arsenal: Guide for the Perplexed,' *Arms Control Wonk*, April 15, 2013.)

nuclear test a month into President Obama's second term thus represented the first major incident since the change in administration in Pyongyang. Renewed efforts by the Obama administration to significantly escalate economic warfare efforts were again constrained by China and Russia's veto power at the United Nations Security Council, with UNSC Resolution 2094 accordingly only reiterating previous resolutions, sanctioning a number of individuals linked to the nuclear program, and restricting financial transfers by North Korea diplomats. This forced the United States, the European Union, and multiple Western countries to rely on unilateral sanctions to escalate.

In the aftermath of the nuclear test U.S. and South Korean forces launched large scale Key Resolve/Foal Eagle military exercises from March 1 to April 30, which involved over 210,000 personnel. Notable American assets involved included the country's sole stealth fighter class the F-22, its most capable surface combatant the Arleigh Burke Class destroyer, and all three U.S. strategic bomber classes the B-52H, B-1B, B-2, representing a formidable display of offensive force. With the Pentagon announcing that B-52s flown over South Korea were reaffirming the U.S. "nuclear umbrella,"[56] sources in Seoul reported that assets equipped with nuclear weapons were participating in the exercises – leading to speculation that these were the B-52s or B-2s.[57] Pentagon officials highlighted that B-2 stealth bombers' nonstop mock sorties launched from Missouri demonstrated their "ability to conduct long range, precision strikes quickly and at will."[58]

A new White House–approved plan known as "the playbook" called for low altitude bomber overflights and simulated strikes among other measures, which were specifically intended to increase pressure on Pyongyang through raised military tensions and were discussed at several high-level White House meetings. The flights were deliberately carried out in broad daylight at low altitude, with one military official recalling: "We could fly it at night, but the point was for them to see it."[59] Pentagon officials "acknowledged that North Korean military officers [were] particularly agitated by bomber flights because of memories of the destruction wrought from the air during the Korean War,"[60] with

Director of National Intelligence James Clapper later recalling that North Korean officials were "especially consumed with B-52s." They found that "the United States was so threatening, particularly (again) with its B-52s" which were seen as "particularly menacing."[61] Designed to deliver nuclear payloads halfway across the world, the American use of strategic bombers for intimidation was likely to have further stimulated North Korean interest in developing an asset capable of doing the same – namely an intercontinental range ballistic missile.

Responding to the new exercises, Pyongyang on March 7 threatened to nullify the Korean War Armistice Agreement,[62] before confirming on March 13 that it had done so and could launch "merciless" retaliation.[63] In response to the passage of limited new UN Security Council sanctions on March 7, the KPA affirmed that its long-range missile arsenal would be aimed at the U.S. mainland in retaliation. Pyongyang would subsequently on March 21 single out the threat posed by the B-52s, threatening to attack American military bases in Japan and on Guam, the latter which hosted the bombers.[64] Reflecting the consensus view in the West at the time, analysts at *Defense Update* concluded: "unfortunately, the public display of all this firepower and warfighting capability appears to have failed to intimidate Pyongyang."[65]

Although the ability to strike the continental United States was not thought to be within North Korea's capabilities using ballistic missiles, ambiguity surrounding the KPA arsenal's reach led Washington to take wide ranging precautions after the March 7 announcement. On March 15 Defense Secretary Chuck Hagel announced that the U.S. would add 14 more Ground-Based Interceptor missiles to the Ground-based Midcourse Defense (GMD) anti-ballistic missile system at Fort Greely, Alaska, which represented a 47 percent increase to the arsenal.[66] These were the only American missiles capable of defending against ICBM strikes, although Pentagon reports consistently highlighted that their test record left serious questions regarding their reliability.[67] The most costly missile defense system in the world, the GMD cost an estimated $40 billion despite deploying just 44 missiles, with each new anti-ballistic missile costing over $70 million at a conservative estimate. The new missiles were expected to be deployed before the end of 2017. With the GMD's arsenal being far too small to provide a reliable defense against Chinese or Russian attacks, and having little utility beyond ICBM interceptions, an expected North Korean ICBM program had from the outset been the core rationale for its development.[vi]

At the center of uncertainty surrounding the KPA's missile reach was the Hwasong-13 ballistic missile, which had first been unveiled in Kim Il Sung Square, central Pyongyang, during a military parade on April 15, 2012. While Western sources had long claimed that North Korea's Unha series satellite launch vehicles had variants configured as ICBMs, which appeared far from viable from the outset, the Hwasong-13 was North Korea's first purpose-built ICBM, making its unveiling a major landmark. The missile's appearance had been a major surprise for Western analysts, and coincided with the first address by Kim Jong Un as chairman of the ruling Workers' Party.[68] Noticeable differences between the multiple Hwasong-13s paraded indicated that the design was still evolving and in prototype stages, which differed from the class' second appearance on July 26, 2013 when all were outwardly identical.

The Hwasong-13 was specifically cited to explain the costly expansion of the GMD anti-missile arsenal, with Defense Secretary Hagel stating on March 15, 2013 that "North Korea in particular has recently made advances in its capabilities... Specifically, North Korea announced last month that it conducted its third nuclear test, and last April displayed what appears to be a road-mobile ICBM." He also cited the successful December 12 satellite launch as an indicator of advances in ICBM-related technologies. Beyond GMD expansion, Hagel confirmed that a

---

vi In the aftermath of the 2008 financial crisis, sharp defense spending cuts in 2009 resulted in a 32-percent cut to planned missile acquisitions for the GMD, with concerns regarding North Korean missile development forcing a policy reversal four years later. As the Obama administration oversaw a raising of tensions with all major adversaries across the globe, spending on the GMD represented one of multiple examples of North Korean military advances contributing to stretching the Pentagon's increasingly insufficient funds – an issue which would become far more serious the following decade.

second TPY-2 X-band surveillance radar, the primary radar for the THAAD anti-missile system, would be deployed in Japan,[vii] where it could provide improved early warning and tracking of North Korean ICBM launches.[69] Costing approximately $200 million each, only eight of these were available for service worldwide. The systems were well optimized for cuing other missile defense systems such as the GMD on the U.S. mainland.

Further alluding to the threat posed by the Hwasong-13, Vice Chairman of the Joint Chiefs of Staff Admiral James A. Winnefeld, Jr. stated on March 15 that the ICBM had emerged as a threat "a little bit faster than we expected," indicating that despite a lack of known flight tests U.S. intelligence believed North Korea had made significant progress towards an intercontinental range strike capability.[70] U.S. intelligence appeared to have had some awareness of the Hwasong-13's development before its official unveiling, with then-Defense Secretary Robert Gates having asserted in June 2011 that North Korea was developing a road-mobile ICBM, and "now constitutes a direct threat to the United States." He stressed at the time that American forces had in the past had trouble locating road-mobile ICBMs – in contrast to the stationary satellite launch vehicles that were extremely vulnerable to targeting.[71] Further heightening concerns was the fact that the Unha-3 satellite launcher used in December 2012 had demonstrated that North Korea had mastered multi-staging of long range missiles with up to three stages. Joint Chiefs of Staff Chairman Martin Dempsey accordingly informed Congress four months later in April 2013 that the rocket's third stage "was kind of the breakthrough for the North Koreans. … now that they have that third-stage technology apparently under control, it could very well migrate to the [Hwasong-13]."[72]

The Hwasong-13 was notably never confirmed to have been test launched, and whether it was ever intended for service remains uncertain. The possibility remained that it may have been

vii The first had been deployed in Japan in 2006, which represented the first forward deployment of the system anywhere in the world, followed by a second TPY-2 deployed to Israel two years later to help counter North Korean missiles fielded by Iran and Syria.

displayed to increase American and allied concerns regarding a possible intercontinental range strike capability. The deterrence value of this ambiguous capability was attested to by then-Director of National Intelligence James Clapper, who summarized shortly after leaving office: "They achieved nuclear deterrence long ago, because we have to assume that if they do launch an ICBM at the United States, it will reach our shores and detonate. They have effectively played their nuclear hand to the hilt, for without even proving they have the relevant capability, they've capitalized on nuclear deterrence."[73,viii]

The value of an ambiguous ICBM capability was increased by the fact that North Korea's nuclear testing, its demonstrations of its missile technologies on other platforms, and the rates at which they were being improved, very significantly increased the possibility that the Hwasong-13 was somewhat operational. These factors led the Pentagon to conclude in early 2015 that although the ICBM had not been flight tested, North Korea did have the ability to mount a miniaturized nuclear warhead on it, with this conclusion publicly confirmed in April.[74] In the years leading up to North Korea's irrefutable demonstration of a fully capable intercontinental range nuclear strike capability, the Hwasong-13's contribution to the country's security was thus not insignificant. While the perception in the West that a window for preventative military action to set back North Korean weapons development was closing fueled calls for an offensive, even the slight possibility that such an offensive could end in nuclear attacks on American cities was a game changer that would strengthen voices cautioning against initiating hostilities.

North Korea's status as a "full-fledged nuclear weapons state" was signed into law on April 1, 2013,[75] with state media confirming a day later that operations would be fully resumed

---

viii The deterrence value of this ambiguity was otherwise alluded to in a later statement by Pentagon spokesman Gary Ross, who observed regarding the uncertainty surrounding North Korea's ability to miniaturize a nuclear warhead for long range missile delivery: "given the consequences of getting it wrong, it is prudent for a military planner to plan for the worst." ('North Korea's fifth nuclear test prompts U.S. calls for more sanctions,' *Reuters*, September 10, 2016.)

at Yongbyon after their partial suspension from October 2007.[76] Two days later, in response to the perceived threat to its military facilities on Guam, the Pentagon ordered the first ever deployment of a Terminal High Altitude Area Defense (THAAD) anti-missile system to the territory. This was supplemented by the deployment of two Arleigh Burke Class destroyers with the Aegis Ballistic Missile Defense System near the Korean Peninsula. These assets provided protection against medium and intermediate range ballistic missile attacks, supplementing both a Sea-Based X-band radar and the TPY-2s in Japan relied on to strengthen defenses against ICBM strikes by providing cuing data to the GMD. These assets were supplemented by South Korea and Japan's own Aegis destroyers that operated in the region in considerable numbers.

The period of the Key Resolve/Foal Eagle exercises from March 1–April 30 marked a turning point, as high tensions with Pyongyang drew attention to just how far its missile and nuclear capabilities were assessed to have advanced, which led the U.S. to take far more measures to prepare for its quickly emerging intermediate and intercontinental range strikes capabilities. Full resumption of work at Yonbgyon meanwhile allowed the KPA to more rapidly expand its nuclear arsenal. Tensions nevertheless largely abated after exercises concluded, and two months later Pyongyang and Seoul began moving to restore their deconfliction hotline and agreed to resume work at the joint Kaesong Industrial Complex, after both had been suspended by the north in response to tensions in April. China and North Korea on June 19 both called for a resumption of multilateral peace talks.[77]

To the Brink

In the aftermath of the 2013 standoff Western assessments increasingly highlighted that North Korea appeared poised to revolutionize its strategic deterrent in the near future. Adding to Western concerns, the country showed growing signs of rapidly increasing self-sufficiency to support its nuclear program. Footage in June 2013 showing a specialized flow-forming machine of the type used to make thin-walled centrifuge rotors, which was a very rare industrial asset worldwide. This had been produced domestically, and for centrifuge production used the country's Computer Numerically Controlled (CNC) machine – the development of which was considered a leading industrial achievement of the 1990s. An indigenous hot piercer mill producing preforms for the machine was also observed, with these industrial assets located at the Kanggye General Tractor Plant in a fortified underground facility.[78] Operations at Kanggye were supported by provision of advanced machine tools produced at the Huichon Ryonha General Machine Factory.[79]

While television coverage indicated an indigenous flow-forming machine had been operational at the Kusong Machine Tool Factory as early as September 2006, this much more primitive design appeared to be a prototype and lacked CNC controls needed for centrifuge manufacturing. With five North Korean researchers having been awarded a patent for a CNC Control System for an unspecified metalworking machine, with keywords suggesting it was for a flow-forming machine, the machine unveiled in June 2013 appeared highly likely to be the result of their work. Director of the Laboratory for Nuclear Security and Policy at MIT R. Scott Kemp highlighted that the equipment "appears to be state-of-the-art" and "connects nicely with another technical analyses... suggesting that the DPRK is capable of making its own maraging steel from indigenous resources," with the result being the "freeing [of] the centrifuge program from dependence on foreign supplies and technology." This was corroborated by the fact that "in the last ten years we have seen almost no reports of centrifuge-related procurements at all."[80] These advances considerably diminished Western options for crippling the North Korean nuclear program through embargoes.

As the window for action to stop North Korea's development of new longer ranged missiles narrowed, President Obama from early 2014 personally called for a stepping up of cyber and electronic attacks on the country, and on the missile program in particular, which was strongly advocated by senior Pentagon officials.[81] These attacks targeted missiles either before they reached their launch sites or as they left their launchpads, and according to intelligence sources cited by the *New York Times* were responsible for a number of failed test launches for a year from mid-2015. It was hoped that such efforts "delayed by several years the day when North Korea will be able to threaten American cities with nuclear weapons launched atop intercontinental ballistic missiles."[82] Chairman of the Joint Chiefs of Staff General Martin E. Dempsey first announced plans for disruption of enemy missile systems in 2013, referring specifically to a new emphasis on "cyberwarfare, directed energy and electronic attack." While Dempsey's policy paper did not mention North Korea by name, an accompanying map showed a KPA missile in flight towards the United States. The program appeared to gain traction from this point, with several officials and defense contractor Raytheon – a specialist in missile defense technologies – all mentioning these "left of launch" technologies with increasing frequency.

Investments in electronic sabotage were considerable and took a significant place in American military planning at the highest levels. Shortly after Chairman Dempsey's report Ashton Carter, newly appointed as secretary of defense, began calling meetings specifically focused on the possibility of disrupting North Korea's missile development. Having strongly called for an assault against the country in the 2000s to set back its nuclear and missile development, and played a central role in drafting plans for such attacks the previous decade, by the mid-2010s improvements to North Korea's strategic deterrent appeared to have forced Carter to back down from this position and to instead favor using new non-kinetic means to attack.[83] A number of sources highlighted the strong possibility that cyberattacks widely targeted the North Korean industrial base, with primary targets considered likely to include facilities such as the highly automated Pyongyang Integrated Circuit Factory, which produced a wide range of memory chips, as well as the Kusong Machine Tool Plant.[84]

From 2014 North Korea began testing ballistic missiles on an unprecedented scale, with at least sixteen short- and two medium-range ballistic missiles launched that year – a number which exceeded all launches combined during the Bush administration's eight years in office.[85] By April over half a dozen short range missile launches and two Hwasong-7 launches had already taken place. These unprecedentedly high launch rates were interpreted as a sign of a significant economic recovery, a considerable increase in the output of ballistic missiles, and a rise in the number of missile programs simultaneously being pursued. These rates would not only be sustained, but gradually increased for four years up to November 2017.

October 2014 marked the first confirmed test launch of long-range missiles from a post–Cold War new generation, namely the Pukkuksong-1, which first flew on December 21. While the success of the test was disputed, the missile demonstrated tremendous advances by local industry, as it combined an intermediate range of an estimated 2,500 kilometers with a very compact seven meter long body – less than half the approximately 15.5 meter length of the much shorter ranged Rodong-1 despite carriage of a similar sized warhead. While boasting half the size and almost double the range, the missile's most notable feature was its use of a solid rather than a liquid fuel composite.[ix] Solid fuel engines allowed missiles to be stored fully fueled, reducing launch times to a fraction of those for liquid fueled missiles, which was particularly valuable for the KPA's road-mobile arsenal. While U.S. forces had struggled profusely during the Gulf War to seek out and destroy Iraqi road-mobile Scud ballistic missiles, despite their launch times of close to an hour and in spite of the openness of the desert terrain, a transition to liquid fueled missiles would

---

ix North Korea had started testing its first solid fueled ballistic missile, the Hwasong-11, in 2006, and deploying it the following year, with this having been a derivative of the Soviet OTR-21 Tochka providing a very short range tactical strike capability. Although having a shorter engagement range than Scud-type missiles at an estimated 190km, it was only around one third the weight while carrying a similar payload, allowing it to be deployed from small six-wheeled launch vehicles. The original Soviet missile was widely reported to have been acquired through Syria, providing valuable first access to solid fueled missile engines and fuel composites. U.S. officials raised particular concerns over the new levels of precision the missile class introduced to the KPA's tactical arsenal. ('MTCR: North Korea's Missile Program,' *Wikileaks*, October 1, 2008.) (Burns, Robert, 'US Official: North Korea Has New Missile,' *Associated Press*, July 6, 2007.) ('KN-02 SRBM,' *KPA Journal*, vol. 1, no. 2, February 2010 (pp. 7–12).)

help ensure that the survivability of the North Korean strategic deterrent stayed ahead of advances in the American reconnaissance-strike complex.

Another notable feature of the Pukkuksong-1 was that it represented North Korea's first ballistic missile developed for deployment by submarine, with its first flight heralding the country's significant investments in adding a second arm to its nuclear triad, which would begin to materialize in a more viable capability in the mid-2020s. The indigenous Gorae (Whale) Class ballistic missile submarine would be used to test ejection of the missile from May 2015. Although the warship was limited by its integration of just a single missile launcher, it served as a stopgap until the program further matured, and provided a valuable testbed and training platform for the Navy until then. The ship's ability to deliver nuclear strikes meant its firepower was still far from insignificant.

The Pukkuksong-1's maiden launch marked the beginning of a new era for the North Korean ballistic missile program, moving far past the dated technologies of the Hwasong-7 and Scud-type missiles. Although the very limited capacity for launching ballistic missiles by submarine meant the Pukkuksong-1 was not thought to have been produced on a significant scale, a near identical derivative deployed from ground based transporter-erector launchers, designated Pukkuksong-2, would be successfully test launched on February 11 and May 21, 2017 before entering large-scale production. The Pukkuksong-1/2's engine was widely thought to have been used as the basis for developing a range of short-range tactical missiles which would begin to be unveiled in February 2018.

In an apparent effort to leverage the demonstrated tremendously expanded capacity for missile testing and development, which worsened America's and its allies already significant concerns regarding its rapid missile and nuclear development, Pyongyang in January 2015 offered to suspend further nuclear testing should Washington and Seoul cancel upcoming military exercises. It further reiterated its calls for dialogue, calling on Washington to "make a policy switch" and abandon its "anachronistic policy hostile towards the DPRK."[86] The Obama administration refused the proposal.

By mid-2015 there was a growing consensus among U.S. officials that North Korea already had developed a miniaturized nuclear warhead capable of being mounted on longer ranged ballistic missiles.[87] On October 7 the head of North American Aerospace Defense Command Admiral Bill Gortney stated that country "had already developed 'miniaturized' nuclear bombs that could be fitted to these rockets." "We assess that they have the capability to reach the homeland with a nuclear weapon from a rocket," he elaborated, with this clear statement by one of the most senior defense officials in the area being a major landmark in the evolution of the power balance between the two states.[88] These concerns were heightened four days later on October 11 by the appearance of a modified Hwasong-13 with a shorter but larger diameter third stage and re-entry vehicle section. The new variant was also lighter and more compact and used two rather than three stages, with the more mature design near unanimously interpreted by experts as an indication of progress towards developing a viable ICBM.[89]

Two further detonations of miniaturized nuclear warheads, North Korea's fourth and fifth, would in 2016 further shift the consensus among American analysts towards the conclusion that the country had a viable long range missile delivery capability. While working to make warheads lighter, the first test of the year on January 6 was claimed to be the first of a miniaturized thermonuclear warhead in North Korea – a more complex warhead type that used nuclear fission rather than fusion and had the potential to deliver payloads orders of magnitude more powerful.[x] This landmark achievement made the possibility of missile strikes on American territories far more dangerous.

---

x Otherwise known as hydrogen bombs, the nuclear fission process on thermonuclear bombs was similar to that occurring on the sun. Such warheads had first been detonated in the United States in November 1952, demonstrating payloads over 450 times those of the atomic bomb dropped on Nagasaki, with the greatest demonstrated detonation made by the Soviet Union nine years later, exploding with 2500 times the Nagasaki payload.

In response to North Korea's January nuclear test President Obama reiterated that the United States could "obviously destroy North Korea,"[90] while his senior diplomat on Asia, Assistant Secretary of State Daniel Russel, warned that Chairman Kim would "immediately die" if North Korea's nuclear arsenal was employed.[91] During the 55 days between the test and the imposition of sanctions by the UNSC on March 2, a record-breaking U.S.–South Korean exercise simulating a pre-emptive assault on North Korea was announced to "involve recovering key facilities that are located deep within North Korea, all the way near its northern borders." This would "include the special operations forces being deployed to border areas adjacent to China and Russia" to seal the conflict and prevent Pyongyang's neighbors from becoming involved.[92] While focusing on excluding China and Russia, exercises from 2016–2017 saw an increase in participation of personnel from Britain, France, Italy, Denmark, Australia, Canada and New Zealand, after a steady increase in non-U.S. Western involvement from 2014.[93]

On April 8 North Korea conducted a then little noticed landmark test of "a new type high-power engine of intercontinental ballistic rocket," which available evidence indicated would power its Hwasong-10 intermediate range and Hwasong-13 intercontinental range ballistic missiles.[94] Footage of the test showed a plume with a much clearer color than Scud-type engines using simple IRNFA and Kerosene propellants, indicating a more energetic propellant with revolutionary implications for the performances of its future missiles. This was one of the clearest indications that the country's missile program had reached a far more advanced stage.[95] As early as 2009 a secret telegram distributed by the office of the U.S. Secretary of State, leaked and later published by Wikileaks, highlighted concerns in Washington that the Hwasong-10's engine "represents a substantial advance in North Korea's liquid propellant technology," and "allows North Korea to build even longer range missiles – or shorter range missiles with greater payload capacity – than would be possible using Scud-type technology."[96] Seven years later the April 8 test indicated that these concerns had been well founded.

The Hwasong-10 represented both a landmark and a highly unusual stage in North Korean strategic missile development. The missile's existence was first reported in the early 2000s, albeit with a much shorter 2,500km estimated range. The relatively few applications of missiles with such ranges for the KPA, and reports of exports to and test launching in Iran from 2006, combined indicated the missile had entered production in North Korea primarily for export.[97] While South Korean estimates were that the missile entered service in the KPA around 2007,[xi] the lack of testing or of significant production, with only 30 estimated to be in service by 2016, indicated limited interest in the baseline version for domestic use.[98] The superior engine tested on April 8 appeared intended to contribute to extending this range to close to 4000km to allow a new Hwasong-10 variant to strike Guam, which was the next major milestone after the Hwasong-7 had placed Japan in range in 1993. This variant was distinguishable by its new grid fins.[99,xii]

On April 15 North Korea carried out the first confirmed test launch of the Hwasong-10. The launch and three subsequent launches over the next 16 days all ended in failure. Following revelations two years later of the Obama administration's cyber sabotage campaign aimed at North Korean missile launches, the unusual circumstances of all four failures, none of which safely left the launch site, led analysts to near unanimously attribute the

---

xi If confirmed, the successful testing of the Hwasong-10 as early as 2006, albeit outside Korea, did much to explain the extent of Western concerns regarding North Korean progress towards ICBM development from the late 2000s, which was otherwise difficult to explain if the country's industry had not yet demonstrated a viable intermediate range missile that had moved past Scud technologies.

xii Other sources asserted that Western claims of Hwasong-10 exports to Iran in the 2000s were unfounded, but were valuable to provide justification for the expansion of NATO missile defenses in Eastern Europe. The sale was raised with Russian officials on multiple occasions when they objected to these missile defense deployments, although the lack of evidence of missile testing at that stage raised serious suspicions in Moscow that the entire narrative had been fabricated, mirroring the closely coinciding Western claims of a North Korean nuclear weapons facility in Syria, which would similarly be widely considered as highly dubious. ('U.S.-Russia Joint Threat Assessment Talks – December 2009,' United States Secretary of State, 10STATE17263, February 24, 2010.)

cause to American electronic sabotage. Two simultaneous launches on June 22, however, saw both Hwasong-10s successfully leave their launch sites, although the success of their subsequent flights was disputed. Unconfirmed American reports indicated that two more launches were attempted but failed on October 15 and October 20,[100] although some sources claimed these latter tests had in fact been the country's first ever ICBM tests and launched Hwasong-13s.[101]

The June 22 test demonstrated success in extending the Hwasong-10's range by at least 40 percent using a new engine among other changes, which provided a nuclear strike range of at least 3,500km. Chairman Kim Jong Un thus proclaimed after the test regarding its implications: "We have the sure capability to attack in an overall and practical way the Americans in the Pacific operation theatre."[102] Guam Naval Base and the adjacent Andersen Air Force Base, which were at the crux of America's ability to project power in the region and vital staging grounds for a potential assault on Korea, were now within reach.

American electronic sabotage targeting the Hwasong-10's flight test program was widely interpreted as a last ditch effort by an administration increasingly short of options to stall North Korea's missile development. The *New York Times* accordingly observed: "Advocates of the sophisticated effort to remotely manipulate data inside North Korea's missile systems argue the United States has no real alternative because the effort to stop the North from learning the secrets of making nuclear weapons has already failed. The only hope now is stopping the country from developing an intercontinental missile..." It further noted regarding the president's strong personal support for disruptive attacks that "Obama ultimately pressed the Pentagon and intelligence agencies to pull out all the stops, which officials took as encouragement to reach for untested technologies."[103]

The sabotage program reportedly seriously affected Hwasong-10 launches in April and May, although countermeasures appear to have been developed which ensured that subsequent tests were successful. This led several analysts to conclude that the effort may have been highly detrimental to U.S. interests, as while its effect on the program's progress was relatively minor, it gave the KPA considerable experience in conducting missile launches under strained conditions similar to those which could be expected in wartime.[104]

Regarding the further implications of successful development of the Hwasong-10, a detailed assessment by Chinese missile experts aired by state media on April 1 highlighted that this would be a major landmark, indicating that North Korea was close to developing a viable ICBM. The experts highlighted that the country's Unha satellite launch vehicles had from 2012 already demonstrated effective stage separation technology, which was a primary technological challenge when moving from intermediate to intercontinental range missiles.[105] With the Hwasong-13 thought to use a close derivative of the Hwasong-10's engines, the path from one to the other was relatively short.

On September 9 North Korea carried out its fifth nuclear weapons test, coinciding with National Day Celebrations marking the 68th anniversary of the state's founding. Official statements subsequently clarified that the test had been of a miniaturized warhead, and confirmed the country's ability to mount nuclear warheads on ballistic missiles. Regarding the test's implications, state media subsequently reported: "The standardization of the nuclear warhead will enable the DPRK to produce at will and as many as it wants a variety of smaller, lighter and diversified nuclear warheads of higher strike power."[106] Leading American expert on the North Korean nuclear program Jeffrey Lewis at the California-based Middlebury Institute of International Studies observed: "The important thing is, that five tests in, they now have a lot of nuclear test experience. They aren't a backwards state anymore."[107]

Endnotes

1 Hersh, Seymour M., 'The Red Line and the Rat Line,' *London Review of Books,* vol. 36, no. 8, April 2014.

2 'Ukraine crisis: Transcript of leaked Nuland-Pyatt call,' *BBC News*, February 7, 2014.

Carpente, Ted Galen, 'America's Ukraine Hypocrisy,' *CATO Institute*, August 6, 2017.

Murphy, Dan, 'Amid US-Russia tussle over Ukraine, a leaked tape of Victoria Nuland,' *Christian Science Monitor*, February 6, 2014.

3 Entous, Adam, 'Obama Kept Looser Rules for Drones in Pakistan,' *The Wall Street Journal*, April 26, 2015.

Ricks, Thomas E., 'Book excerpt: Obama's drone war in Pakistan was bigger than people think,' *Foreign Policy*, May 4, 2017.

Elliott, Justin, 'Obama Administration's Drone Death Figures Don't Add Up,' *Prorepublica,* June 18, 2012.

Whitlock, Craig, 'Drone strikes killing more civilians than U.S. admits, human rights groups say,' *Washington Post,* October 22, 2013.

'Drone Strikes Reveal Uncomfortable Truth: U.S. Is Often Unsure About Who Will Die,' *New York Times*, April 23, 2015.

'The Army Chaplain Who Quit Over "Unaccountable Killing" of Obama's Secretive Drone Program,' *ABC News,* May 28, 2016.

Ackerman, Spencer, '41 men targeted but 1,147 people killed: US drone strikes – the facts on the ground,' *The Guardian*, November 24, 2014.

4 'Turkish minister says U.S. behind 2016 failed coup – Hurriyet,' *Reuters,* February 5, 2021.

'Turks Can Agree on One Thing: U.S. Was Behind Failed Coup,' *New York Times*, August 2, 2016.

5 'Obama's Cover. Drone War in Numbers: Ten Times More Strikes Than Bush,' *Bureau of Investigative Journalism,* January 17, 2017.

6 Agerholm, Harriet, 'Map shows where President Barack Obama dropped his 20,000 bombs,' *The Independent,* January 19, 2017.

Bruton, F. Brinley, 'U.S. Bombed Iraq, Syria, Pakistan, Afghanistan, Libya, Yemen, Somalia in 2016,' *NBC News,* January 9, 2017.

7 Turse, Nick, 'Obama's Scramble for Africa,' *The Nation*, July 12, 2012.

8 'Remarks by President Obama to the Australian Parliament,' *The White House Official Website*, November 17, 2011.

9 Ryan, Mick, 'The pros and cons of hosting B-52s on our shores,' *Sydney Morning Herald*, November 1, 2022.

10 'US–South Korea military drills to proceed despite North Korea's warning,' *The Guardian*, July 30, 2016.

11 'Leon Panetta: U.S. to deploy 60% of navy fleet to Pacific,' *BBC News*, June 2, 2012.

12 Obama, Barack, 'President Obama: The TPP would let America, not China, lead the way on global trade,' *The Washington Post*, May 2, 2016.

13 'Remarks by President Obama to the Australian Parliament,' Office of the Press Secretary, The White House, November 17, 2011.

14 Durden, Tyler, 'U.S. Special Forces Deployed to 70 Percent of the World in 2016,' *Ron Paul Institute for Peace and Prosperity*, February 11, 2017. Turse, Nick, 'Special Ops, Shadow Wars, and the Golden Age of the Grey Zone,' *Tom Dispatch*, January 5, 2017.

15 Kim, Hong Nack, 'U.S.–North Korea Relations under the Obama Administration: Problems and Prospects,' *North Korean Review*, vol. 6, no. 1, Spring 2010 (p. 21).

JoongAng Ilbo, January 12, 2009.

16 Kim, Hong Nack, 'U.S.–North Korea Relations under the Obama Administration: Problems and Prospects,' *North Korean Review*, vol. 6, no. 1, Spring 2010 (pp. 23–24, 28).

17 Cha, Victor D., 'Hawk Engagement and Preventive Defense on the Korean Peninsula,' *International Security*, vol. 27, no. 1, 2002 (p. 4).

Jackson, Van, *On the Brink: Trump, Kim, and the Threat of Nuclear War*, Cambridge, Cambridge University Press, 2018 (p. 69).

18 Schilling, John, 'Where's That North Korean ICBM Everyone Was Talking About?,' *38 North*, March 12, 2015.

Schiller, Markus, *Characterizing the North Korean Nuclear Missile Threat*, Santa Monica, CA, RAND Corporation, 2012.

19 *Boston Globe*, June 8, 2009.

20 Henderson, Nia-Malika, 'Clinton talks tough on N. Korea, Iran,' *Politico*, June 7, 2009.

21 Kim, Hong Nack, 'U.S.–North Korea Relations under the Obama Administration: Problems and Prospects,' *North Korean Review*, vol. 6, no. 1, Spring 2010 (p. 27).

22 *New York Times*, April 30, 2009.

23 'UN: North Korea a nuclear power,' *News 24*, April 20, 2009.

24 Moore, Malcolm, 'North Korea now "fully fledged nuclear power,"' *The Telegraph*, April 24, 2009.

25 'No Nuke Status for NK: World Should Stand Firm Against Proliferation,' *Korea Times*, April 21, 2009.

26 Charles, Deborah and Zakaria, Tabassum, 'North Korea's May nuclear test few kilotons: U.S.,' *Reuters*, June 15, 2009.

27 'KCNA Report on One More Successful Underground Nuclear Test,' *KCNA*, May 25, 2009.

28 'North Korean Missile Launches & Nuclear Tests: 1984–Present,' Missile Defense Project, Center for Strategic and International Studies (https://missilethreat.csis.org/north-korea-missile-launches-1984-present/) (accessed July 20, 2019).

29 Varner, Bill and Green, Peter S., 'UN Votes to Punish North Korea for Nuclear Test,' *Bloomberg*, June 12, 2009.

30 Harwood, Richard, 'Ruling Class Journalists,' *Washington Post,* October 30, 1993.

31 Cohen, Stephen F., 'The American Bipartisan Policy Establishment Declares Its Second Cold War vs. Russia After Years of Denying It,' *The Nation*, January 24, 2018.

32 'A Conversation with U.S. Secretary of State Hillary Rodham Clinton,' *Council on Foreign Relations*, July 15, 2009.

33 Stares, Paul B. and Wit, Joel S., *Preparing for Sudden Change in North Korea,* Council Special Report No. 42, Council on Foreign Relations Center for Preventative Action, January 2009.

34 O'Hanlon, Michael E., 'North Korea Collapse Scenarios,' *Brookings Institute*, June 9, 2009.

35 International Institute for Strategic Studies, *The Military Balance, Volume 110, Part VIII: Asia and Australasia,* 2010 (p. 380).

36 Warrick, Joby, 'Iran's Natanz nuclear facility recovered quickly from Stuxnet cyberattack,' *Washington Post*, February 16, 2011.

37 Menn, Joseph, 'Exclusive: U.S. tried Stuxnet-style campaign against North Korea but failed – sources,' *Reuters,* May 29, 2015.

38 Ibid.

39 Sanger, David E., 'Obama Order Sped Up Wave of Cyberattacks Against Iran,' *New York Times*, June 1, 2012.

40 Nuland, Victoria, Daily Press Briefing, U.S. Department of State, August 24, 2011.

41 Bryant, Lisa, 'Europe Cautious in Reaction to Kim Jong-Il's Death,' *Voice of America*, December 18, 2011.

42 '북, 사회주의 계획경제 포기 선언,' ['North Korea Abandons Socialist Planned Economy'], *Radio Free Asia,* August 8, 2012.

Cha, Victor D., 'Kim Jong Un Is No Reformer,' *Foreign Policy,* August 21, 2012.

Ascione, Ben, 'Kim Jong-un and the future of North Korean reform,' *East Asian Forum,* October 20, 2012.

43 'North Korea: Salmon farming's next superpower?,' *The Fish Site,* February 18, 2019.

44 O'Carroll, Chad, 'Floating rice plants and gardens proliferate in Pyongyang: photos,' *NK News,* June 28, 2017.

45 Williams, Martyn, 'Can Science and Technology Be a Silver Bullet for the North Korean Economy?,' *38 North*, January 8, 2020.

46 Makinen, Julie, 'North Korea is building something other than nukes: architecture with some zing,' *Los Angeles Times*, May 20, 2016.

47 Nixon, John, *Debriefing the President: The Interrogation of Saddam Hussein*, London, Bantam Press, 2016 (pp. 204–205, 220).

48 Ibid.

49 'Nuclear Nightmare: Understanding North Korea,' *Discovery Times,* aired August 6, 2003 (00:35:50–00:37:42).

Gender in Mediation: An Exercise for Trainers, CSS Mediation Resources, ETH Zurich Center for Security Studies and Swisspeace, 2015 (p. 59).

50 'Transcript: Securing Tomorrow with Madeleine Albright,' *Washington Post,* May 31, 2018.

51 Ibid.

52 'N. Korea Ready to Conduct Nuke Test if Leadership Makes Decision: Defense Ministry,' *Yonhap*, January 24, 2013.

53 Parry, Richard Lloyd, 'N. Korea is Armed for Nuclear War,' *USAF Counterproliferation Center CPC Outreach Journal*, no. 706, April 24, 2009.

Parry, Richard Lloyd, 'North Korea is fully fledged nuclear power, experts agree,' *The Times*, April 24, 2009 (p. 35).

54 *KCNA*, April 13, 2013.

55 'North Korean satellite "orbiting normally" after rocket launch,' *The Guardian*, December 13, 2012.

56 Choe, Sang-Hun, 'North Korea Threatens U.S. Military Bases in the Pacific,' *New York Times,* March 21, 2013.

57 'U.S. nukes to remain in South,' *JoongAng Ilbo,* March 12, 2013.

58 'U.S. B-2 bombers conduct extended deterrence mission to the Republic of Korea,' *United States Air Force Global Strike Command Official Website,* March 28, 2013.

59 Solomon, Jay and Barnes, Julian E. and Gale, Alastair, 'North Korea warned,' *The Wall Street Journal*, March 29, 2013.

60 Barnes, Julian E., 'U.S. pledges further show of force in Korea,' *The Wall Street Journal*, March 29, 2013.

61 Clapper, James R., *Facts and Fears: Hard Truths from a Life in Intelligence,* New York, Viking, 2018 (Chapter 9).

62 'Second Korean War Is Unavoidable: DPRK FM Spokesman', *KCNA*, March 7, 2013.

63 Lim, Chang-Won, 'North Korea confirms end of war armistice,' *AFP,* March 15, 2013.

64 Choe, Sang-Hun, 'North Korea Threatens U.S. Military Bases in the Pacific,' *New York Times,* March 21, 2013.

65 Dudley, Richard, 'US Reinforcing Pacific Defenses to Counter North Korean Threats,' *Defense Update*, April 6, 2013.

66 'Missile Defense Announcement as Delivered by Secretary of Defense Chuck Hagel,' *U.S. Department of Defense,* March 15, 2013.

67 Hitchens, Theresa, 'No US missile defense system proven capable against "realistic" ICBM threats: Study,' *Breaking Defense*, February 22, 2022.

'GMD: Frequently Asked Questions,' Center For Arms Control and Non-Proliferation (https://armscontrolcenter.org/issues/missile-defense/gmd-frequently-asked-questions/).

Grego, Laura, 'What You Should Know about the Upcoming GMD Missile Defense Test,' *Union of Concerned Scientists,* May 29, 2017.

68 'What we can learn from North Korean military parades,' *CNN,* April 14, 2017.

69 'Missile Defense Announcement as Delivered by Secretary of Defense Chuck Hagel,' *U.S. Department of Defense,* March 15, 2013.

70 'Announcement shift to Asia,' *C-Span,* March 15, 2013.

71 Barry, John, 'The Defense Secretary's Exit Interview,' *The Daily Beast,* June 21, 2011.

72 National Defense Authorization Budget Request From the Department of Defense, House Hearing, Oversight of Previously Authorized Programs Before The Committee on Armed Services House of Representatives, One Hundred Thirteenth Congress, First Session, April 11, 2013.

73 Clapper, James R., *Facts and Fears: Hard Truths from a Life in Intelligence,* New York, Viking, 2018 (Chapter 2).

74 Mehta, Aaron, 'US: N. Korean Nuclear ICBM Achievable,' *Defense News,* April 8, 2015.

75 'Law on Consolidating Position of Nuclear Weapons State,' *KCNA,* April 1, 2013.

76 'DPRK to Adjust Uses of Existing Nuclear Facilities,' *KCNA,* April 1, 2013.

77 'North Korea, China wants to resume nuclear talks,' *CNN,* June 19, 2023.

78 Kemp, R. Scott, 'Is This Where North Korea Makes its Centrifuges?,' *Arms Control Wonk,* June 24, 2013.

79 Lewis, Jeffrey, 'North Korea Machine Tool Sites,' *Arms Control Wonk,* September 4, 2013.

80 Kemp, R. Scott, 'Is This Where North Korea Makes its Centrifuges?,' *Arms Control Wonk,* June 24, 2013.

81 Perry, William J., at *38 North* Press Briefing, The US-Korea Institute, Washington, DC, January 9, 2017.

Sanger, David E. and Broad, William J., 'Trump Inherits a Secret Cyberwar Against North Korean Missiles,' *New York Times,* March 4, 2017.

82 Perry, William J., at *38 North* Press Briefing, The US-Korea Institute, Washington, DC, January 9, 2017.

Sanger, David E. and Broad, William J., 'Trump Inherits a Secret Cyberwar Against North Korean Missiles,' *New York Times,* March 4, 2017.

83 Carter, Ashton and Perry, William J., 'Back to the Brink,' *Washington Post,* October 20, 2002.

84 Lewis, Jeffrey, 'Identifying DPRK Machine Plants,' *Arms Control Wonk,* January 17, 2019.

'Pyongyang Integrated Circuit Factory,' *KCNA Watch*, November 5, 1999.

85 'North Korean Missile Launches & Nuclear Tests: 1984–Present,' Missile Defense Project, Center for Strategic and International Studies (https://missilethreat.csis.org/north-korea-missile-launches-1984-present/) (accessed July 20, 2019).

86 'KCNA Report,' *KCNA*, January 10, 2015.

87 Jackson, Van, *On the Brink: Trump, Kim, and the Threat of Nuclear War*, Cambridge, Cambridge University Press, 2018 (p. 70).

88 'Protecting the Homeland: Featuring ADM William Gortney,' Brent Scowcroft Center, Atlantic Council, October 7, 2015.

89 Schilling, John and Lewis, Jeffrey and Schmerler, David, 'A New ICBM for North Korea,' *38 North*, December 22, 2015.

90 Blair, David, '"We could destroy you," Obama warns "erratic" North Korean leader,' *Telegraph*, April 26, 2016.

91 'N. Korea lambasts Russel for his "immediately die" comment,' *Yonhap*, October 15, 2016.

92 Yoon, Min-sik, 'Drills to map out endgame scenario for Pyongyang,' *The Korea Herald*, February 18, 2016.

93 Engman, Mats, 'U.S.-ROK Military Exercises: Provocation or Possibility?,' *Institute For Security and Development Policy*, March 2018 (p. 8).

94 'Kim Jong Un Guides Ground Jet Test of New-type High-Power Engine of Inter-continental Ballistic Rocket,' *KCNA*, April 9, 2016.

95 Lewis, Jeffrey, 'New DPRK ICBM Engine,' *Arms Control Wonk*, April 9, 2016.

96 'Missile Technology Control Regime: North Korea's Missile Program,' Telegram From the Secretary of State, October 6, 2009.

97 Bechtol Jr., Bruce E., *North Korean Military Proliferation in the Middle East and Africa*, Lexington, KY, University Press of Kentucky, 2018 (p. 88).

Spencer, Richard, 'N Korea "Tests New Missile in Iran,"' *The Telegraph*, May 17, 2007.

98 Kim, Jack, 'North Korea leader says missile launch shows ability to attack U.S. in Pacific,' *Reuters*, June 23, 2016.

99 Bechtol Jr., Bruce E., *North Korean Military Proliferation in the Middle East and Africa*, Lexington, KY, University Press of Kentucky, 2018 (p. 21).

100 'N. Korea's launch of Musudan missile ends in failure again: military,' *Yonhap*, October 20, 2016.

'US military detects "failed ballistic missile launch" in North Korea after state media vows revenge for "hostile acts,"' *The Independent*, October 15, 2016.

101 Fifield, Anna, 'Did North Korea just test missiles capable of hitting the U.S.? Maybe,' *Washington Post*, October 26, 2016.

102 Kim, Jack, 'North Korea leader says missile launch shows ability to attack U.S. in Pacific,' *Reuters*, June 23, 2016.

103 Sanger, David E. and Broad, William J., 'Trump Inherits a Secret Cyberwar Against North Korean Missiles,' *New York Times,* March 4, 2017.

104 Jackson, Van, *On the Brink: Trump, Kim, and the Threat of Nuclear War,* Cambridge, Cambridge University Press, 2018 (pp. 77–78).

105 '朝鲜成功研发新型洲际导弹KN-14？美媒 — 朝鲜成功研发针对美国本土的新型洲际弹道导弹' ['North Korea successfully developed a new ICBM KN-14? US Media – North Korea successfully developed a new intercontinental ballistic missile targeting the United States'], *CCTV 4,* aired April 1, 2016 (http://tv.people.com.cn/n1/2016/0401/c67816-28245618.html).

106 Pearson, James, 'North Korea's bomb is more powerful, but worry is miniaturisation,' *Reuters*, September 9, 2016.

107 'North Korea's fifth nuclear test prompts U.S. calls for more sanctions,' *Reuters*, September 10, 2016.

CHAPTER 4

The Obama Administration on the Offensive

How North Korea Deterred an Obama Era Assault

North Korean weapons tests demonstrated that the country was by 2016 on the cusp of developing a viable intercontinental range thermonuclear strike capability, while it was increasingly recognized from June that American electronic sabotage could only go so far. Facing a highly unfavorable power trajectory, and seeking to prevent Pyongyang from crossing further milestones in its weapons programs, the Obama White House reportedly seriously considered launching an assault to target the country's nuclear facilities. Citing informed sources, the *New York Times* would later report that the president was personally eager to strike not only nuclear weapons sites, but also to attack and eliminate the North Korean leadership.[1]

The perceived need for decisive military action, intended not only to destroy North Korea's nuclear program, but also kill the political leadership with the intention of destabilizing and destroying the state itself, increasingly in 2016 appeared to reflect the consensus view in the U.S. foreign policy establishment. The tone of administration officials towards North Korea that year became highly reminiscent of that of Bush administration officials towards Iraq in 2002, and demonstrated a degree of hostile intent towards Pyongyang unprecedented since the Korean War.

In September 2016 Chairman of the Joint Chiefs of Staff Admiral Mike Mullen advocated attacks on missile launch pads should North Korea appear to be preparing for an ICBM test, proposing Washington go so far as to launch a war should the country further its missile testing efforts as it was expected to do in the following months.[2] In late October the president of the

Center for Strategic and International Studies and former deputy secretary of defense under President Bill Clinton, John Hamre, observed: "I've been at meetings with senior officials who say we need to change policy to formally embrace regime change."[3] Secretary of State John Kerry, in his speech at the U.S. Naval Academy the following month, implied that the United States may need to launch military action to destroy the North Korean state should it continue to develop its strategic deterrent.[4] Commander of U.S. Forces in Korea General Walter Sharp similarly stated on December 1 that should North Korea so much as place a single ICBM on a launchpad, the U.S. should launch an attack.[5]

The most significant indicator of the consensus within the foreign policy establishment was the Council on Foreign Relations' publication of its most prominent paper of the year in September titled "A Sharper Choice on North Korea," the contents of which closely mirrored the Obama White House's position on the issue. The paper not only highlighted the possibility of launching attacks to prevent North Korea from further enhancing its nuclear and missile deterrents, much as the president was pushing for,[6] but it also indicated a strong preference for the destruction of the North Korean state and the forceful integration of its territory into South Korea, and advocated pledging benefits to China should it allow this to be realized.[7]

In an apparent attempt to provide justification for a U.S.-led military assault aiming to take over and dismantle North Korea, CFR president Richard N. Hass in January 2017 published the article "World Order 2.0" in the Council's journal *Foreign Affairs.* "The rules, policies and institutions that have guided the world since World War II, have run their course. Respect for sovereignty alone cannot uphold order," he stated, advocating moves "to amend the concept of self-determination away from its inherent unilateralism on the part of the entity seeking a state of its own and replace it with the notion that statehood is something to be granted rather that asserted." Under World Order 2.0 Hass advocated that states accused of humanitarian abuses could have their rights to see their borders and peace respected stripped from them and foreign military intervention legitimized.[8] The article was captioned by a picture of the Chairman Kim Jong Un and other figures in the North Korean leadership, leaving little doubt as to the target in mind.

Regarding the transformation in world order Hass was advocating which, on the basis of predominant Western portrayals and perceptions of North Korea would justify an American invasion, he wrote:

> Necessity may also lead to reducing or even eliminating sovereignty when a government, whether from a lack of capacity or conscious policy, is unable to provide for the basic needs of its citizens... Our notion of sovereignty must therefore be conditional, even contractual, rather than absolute. If a state fails to live up to its side of the bargain... then it forfeits the normal benefits of sovereignty and opens itself up to attack, removal or occupation. The diplomatic challenge for this era is to gain widespread support for principles of state conduct and a procedure for determining remedies when these principles are violated.[9]

While CFR publications were alone one of the most reliable indicators of the consensus in the American foreign policy establishment, another was the tone set by national media outlets regarding the possibility of war, which from late 2016 came to closely mirror that seen from 2002 in the lead up to the invasion of Iraq.[10] The strong parallels were effectively summarized as follows by Defense & Strategy Fellow at the Center for Strategic Studies Van Jackson, a former policy adviser at the Office of the Secretary of Defense and group chair of the U.S.–ROK Extended Deterrence Policy Committee:

> national media outlets and commentators started regularly churning out stories with headlines such as "What Would Happen in Minutes and Hours after North Korea Nuked the United States?," "Pre-empting a North Korean ICBM Test," "What the U.S. Would

> Use to Strike North Korea," and "Should Washington Strike North Korea's Dangerous ICBMs Before It's Too Late?" Commentaries strongly opposed to attacking North Korea were forced to focus primarily on the question of military strikes rather than some non-violent alternative... Not only had the North Korea policy landscape developed a hawkish tilt; the terms of debate about North Korea policy had shifted dramatically into the military realm. This was the prevailing state of mind among Washington policy elites as Trump entered the White House.[11]

President Obama in 2016 appeared far closer to authorizing an attack on North Korea than his predecessor George W. Bush ever had, but was reportedly deterred by two primary factors. Neither were related to the fact that an attack would have represented a violation of international laws against crimes of aggression, but rather to the practical difficulties of attacking what was by far the best prepared target the U.S. would have faced since the Second World War. The first factor was that North Korea's retaliatory capabilities were highly considerable, ranging from Hwasong-10 missiles aimed at Guam to Pukkuksong and Hwasong-7 missiles aimed at U.S. bases across Japan, and the world's largest artillery force holding much of South Korea within reach. These was paired with the country's massive conventional forces that had made an indelible impression on the U.S., as well as a WMD capability suspected to include assets ranging from VX nerve gas to nuclear warheads and possibly even biological weapons.

The second factor was that the Pentagon had informed the president that options for setting back the North Korean nuclear and missile programs with air strikes were effectively non-existent. The country was by this time estimated to have dozens of nuclear warheads, which alongside the KPA's highly mobile delivery systems were stored deep underground in facilities which the U.S. could not locate or easily neutralize from the air. The Pentagon had concluded on this basis that nothing short of a full-scale ground invasion could disarm North Korea of its nuclear deterrent. As journalist Bob Woodward observed at the time: "The Pentagon reported that the only way 'to locate and destroy – with complete certainty – all components of North Korea's nuclear program' was through a ground invasion… A ground invasion would trigger a North Korean response, likely with a nuclear weapon."[12] Even in a conventional war American casualties were expected to reach hundreds of thousands within weeks,[13] and attempting full scale invasion or provoking KPA use of weapons of mass destruction would only increase these losses.

Much as had been the case when the Obama administration launched the failed Stuxnet attack on North Korea, a key facilitator of the country's security was its intelligence and internal security apparatus, with its effectiveness in limiting U.S. and Western intelligence collection having been a central factor shifting the White House's calculus. As observed by CIA director under the Clinton administration Robert Gates, North Korea was a unique "black hole" for American intelligence considered "without parallel the toughest intelligence target in the world" – an assessment widely shared.[14,i] Victor Cha would in assessments spanning over a quarter of a century similarly refer to the country or aspects of its policymaking as "the blackest of black boxes" or "about as black a box as you can imagine," with reliable intelligence collection near impossible.[15] In this regard, while Western intelligence agencies had gained freer rein across the majority of the world since 1950s, little had changed with regard to North Korea since the outset of the Korean War, with journalist Tim Weiner concluding in his award winning detailed history of the CIA: "the inability to penetrate North Korea remains the longest-running intelligence failure in the CIA's history."[16,ii] As a result the locations of the

---

i Director of the Laboratory for Nuclear Security and Policy at MIT R. Scott Kemp otherwise observed: "There are pretty severe limits on traditional intelligence-gathering. Spy agencies frequently disagree about what's happening in the country, and rarely can they ever say anything conclusive. North Korea is simply too closed and too disconnected to go snooping around in the usual manner." (Kemp, R. Scott, 'Is This Where North Korea Makes its Centrifuges?,' *Arms Control Wonk*, June 24, 2013.)

ii A notable indicator of this was how frequently the U.S. Strategic Command had in the preceding months misidentified missile classes launched by

DPRK leadership and its nuclear and missile arsenals were unknown, which made arranging an effective strike nearly impossible. This, and the country's wide ranging and massive options for retaliation, were thus key to preventing war.

Evaluating Strategic Patience: Obama's Unseen War on North Korea

Aside from increased missile defense deployments, the imposition of increasingly harsh economic sanctions remained at the core of the Obama administration's approach to North Korea as part of its effort to force the country to make unilateral concessions on its nuclear program.[17] As one former assistant secretary of state summarized: "the Obama administration was beginning to move in th[e] direction" where "if you can create in the leadership's minds the fear that they are putting their country on the verge of extinction, the rational decision will be to realize this."[18] Officials on the Obama administration's National Security Council referred to this policy as one aiming to instigate "evolution and revolution in North Korea," forcing the state to adopt a lasting change in its foreign policy and stance on nuclear development in response to deteriorating economic conditions.[19]

The Obama administration's policy towards North Korea, which came to be known as Strategic Patience, would be widely criticized throughout its eight year tenure as insufficiently proactive, with concerns raised by a number of officials within the administration. Director of National Intelligence (DNI) James Clapper, for one, recalled:

> There is an unwritten, almost sacred writ of the intelligence profession that we in intelligence should avoid

North Korea, an example being in September 2016 when three missiles launched were identified as Hwasong-7s, then as Hwasong-10s, before footage released by state media confirmed they were Hwasong-9s – an extended range derivative of the Scud design. Both reports were missile classes entirely different both from each other and from the class actually tested. ('Did North Korea just test missiles capable of hitting the U.S.? Maybe,' *Washington Post*, October 26, 2016.)

> engaging in policy formation or execution. We support policy makers by providing them timely, accurate, relevant, even anticipatory intelligence, but we don't participate in making the policy sausage. Our objective typically is to reduce uncertainty for decision makers as much as possible, whether they're in the Oval Office, at the negotiating table, or on the battlefield. As DNI, I was careful not to advocate for specific policies in National Security Council meetings. However, Korea was one issue on which I let President Obama know – privately – that I thought his policy rationale of not discussing anything else until North Korea agreed to end its nuclear capacity and ambitions was flawed.[20]

Despite East Asia having been identified as a leading priority from the administration's first months in office, with the Pivot to Asia accordingly otherwise known as the Obama Doctrine, there was a significant deficit in expertise and interest in the region which further worsened in the administration's second term. While State Secretary Hillary Clinton, Assistant State Secretary for East Asian and Pacific Affairs Kurt Campbell, and National Security Advisor Tom Donilon had all been committed to the Pivot to Asia, all three had left the administration by late 2013, with their successors showing far less interest in the region. The new state secretary John Kerry, for example, when advised to make his first trip in office to the Asia-Pacific as Secretary Clinton had, quickly ruled it out – reflecting his interest in prioritizing the pursuit of an Israeli-Palestinian peace deal. Under new National Security Advisor Susan Rice the National Security Council faced similar issues, with its most time-consuming cases almost all occurring in the Middle East far from where the most serious and consequential challenges to American power were being issued.[21] The outbreak of war in Ukraine from February 2014 further exacerbated the issue. Where the Bush administration had been lambasted for invading Iraq before fully dealing with Al Qaeda or stabilizing Afghanistan, under the Obama administration

Washington increasingly appeared to be fighting every country outside its sphere of influence at once.

Exacerbating the issue was the fact that in spite of the very smooth leadership transition in Pyongyang from December 2011, which disappointed widespread Western predictions of instability, President Obama continued to hold a strong personal belief in the inevitability of a North Korea collapse from within. A notable indicator was his statement as late as January 22, 2015 that: "Over time you will see a regime like this collapse. We will keep on ratcheting the pressure, but part of what's happening is that the Internet, over time, is going to be penetrating this country. And it is very hard to sustain that kind of brutal authoritarian regime in this modern world. Information ends up seeping in over time and bringing about change, and that's something that we are constantly looking for ways to accelerate."[22] DPRK analysts referred to this as Obama's "coming out as a North Korea collapsist," which was an idea that had been increasingly discredited as the world moved further past the post–Cold War era.[23] Army Lieutenant General H. R. McMaster would years later summarize that "the administration assumed that the Kim regime was… an impossible state that would ultimately collapse due to its brutality, corruption, and dysfunction."[24] This was likely a major contributor to the complacency the administration showed on the issue at least until its final year in office.

Despite criticisms of the administration's position on North Korea, often as having been a "do-nothing policy" which "ignored" the country's weapons programs,[25] belying Strategic Patience President Obama had overseen an escalation of efforts to target the country which were in many respects revolutionary. This was part of a broader revolution in how the United States worked to undermine its adversaries across multiple fronts which proved highly effective. Where the Bush administration had waged war on the governments of Afghanistan and Iraq with massive troop deployments, followed by long and occupations costing trillions of dollars and incurring extensive casualties, its successor made effective use of both state and non-state proxies and a range of emerging technologies to achieve similar objectives at a much lower cost in blood and treasure. This proved highly effective in Libya and Syria, in the latter case ending government control over the majority of the country while avoiding the need to engage its large conventional forces, air defenses, ballistic missiles and chemical weapons which, while they would have challenged a Western invasion force, were of limited value facing a Western-sponsored insurgency.[26] Against Russia, the engineering of the overthrow of the Ukrainian government through protests followed by a coup in February 2014 facilitated the turning of Ukraine's vast Soviet-built arsenals against its neighbor. This almost overnight placed the Soviet industrial and agricultural heartland under Western influence at negligible cost, and paved the way to a full-scale war eight years later forcing Russia to expend tens of thousands of lives and billions of dollars to try to reverse these gains. Similar very low-cost approaches were taken to tackling adversaries across the world, with Obama overseeing a greater expansion of Washington and its allies' global sphere of influence than any president other than Truman or H. W. Bush (who oversaw the fall of the Axis and Warsaw Pact respectively), and far more quietly and less expensively than either of them.

An integral part to the global offensives the Obama administration oversaw was a significant expansion of state collaboration with tech giants at the heart of shaping changes in the global information space, which provided a major edge in the weaponization of information against multiple targets ranging from Hong Kong and Ukraine to Syria and Iran. As summarized by a prominent 2015 paper on information warfare from the NATO Cooperative Cyber Defense Center of Excellence: "information can be used to disorganize governance, organize anti-government protests, delude adversaries, influence public opinion, and reduce an opponent's will to resist." This, it observed, could be pursued alongside other forms of warfare, perhaps preceding a ground invasion, but could equally prove effective on its own.[27] This began to materialize well within the administration's first year, when U.S. social media giants played a pivotal role in fueling anti-government sentiments in Iran in 2009 and in organizing protests over the disputed outcome of the country's presidential election. Twitter notably delayed its scheduled maintenance to remain active for the specific purpose of helping to facilitate protests, and made this decision upon the advice of prominent State Department foreign policy advisor and leading CFR member Jared Cohen – who was also the director of Google Ideas.[28]

Gaining a reputation as "director of regime change," Cohen played a central role in the escalation of information offensives. He was among multiple influential figures to strongly advocate leveraging dominance of the global information space, particularly through social media, to topple adversary governments and propagate Western ideology, social values and political norms globally. Cohen was notably in the Middle East in early 2011 spearheading ideologically-driven Google Ideas projects targeting U.S. adversaries, which emphasized engaging local communities and engineering "social change," weeks before major social unrest erupted.

Wikileaks founder Julian Assange, who interviewed Cohen at length and published an extensive analysis of Google's geopolitical role, observed: "Cohen's directorate appeared to cross over from public relations and 'corporate responsibility' work into active corporate intervention in foreign affairs at a level that is normally reserved for states... he was trying to plant his fingerprints on some of the major historical events in the contemporary Middle East." Under Cohen: "Google's geopolitical aspirations are firmly enmeshed within the foreign-policy agenda of the world's largest superpower. Its influence on the choices and behaviour of the totality of individual human beings translates to real power to influence the course of history." Assange compared Google's relationship with and role in U.S. foreign policy activities to that of the private security contractor firm Blackwater/ Xe Services/Academi, with both having revolving doors with the public sector and employing unique capabilities to further U.S. interests. Google's power was such that, according to Assange's 2014 assessment, it would soon be able to "interpose itself, and hence the United States government, between the communications of every human being not in China" – a very major asset for any social engineering effort.[29]

Similarly, belying its lack of focus on North Korea, the Obama administration proved characteristically innovative in key aspects of its approach to undermining the country, with its signature focus on information warfare also manifesting prominently. At the end of the administration's first year the Council on Foreign Relations published a paper identifying and strongly advocating the use of information warfare as the most effective medium for toppling the North Korean state, including funding of radio broadcasts and documentaries targeting the population with pro-Western narratives on political and historical issues. Infiltration of Western popular media to positively shape North Koreans' perceptions of the Western world was also called for. The paper advocated policies to "help create an environment in which unauthorized information spread faster and more easily," concluding: "the United States should be cultivating a political opposition and alternative elite that could one day replace the fallen Kim regime."[30] In parallel to similar campaigns targeting the populations of adversary states across much of the rest of the world, the Obama administration would pursue a policy towards North Korea closely in line with these recommendations. Ashton Carter, who was from 2013 appointed defense secretary by Obama, had been at the center of creating such strategies for the administration.[31]

The use of media to target the populations of adversary states for subversive purposes would gain growing attention under the Obama administration, primarily due to Western allegations of nefarious intentions behind the growing influence of Russian media. As noted by Kier Giles, author of NATO's Handbook of Russian Information Warfare for the NATO Defense College, Western states were mistaken in "treating these Russian propaganda outlets as media rather than as an arm of an adversary government which is seeking to subvert our societies."[32] Moscow was otherwise alleged to have used obscurantist means to promote Russophilian narratives and undermine faith in the institutions, political systems and ideologies of the targeted Western countries with the end goal of subversion and the furthering of its interests.[33] These allegations notably very closely mirrored North Korean allegations of the Western information warfare efforts against its population, which was referred to as a program of "tenacious ideological and cultural infiltration" and in similar terms.[34] Information efforts targeting the North Korean population were notably largely financed as part of U.S. defense spending, and were referred to by Germany's *Deutsche Welle* as "playing catch-up to Russia" in the field of information warfare, and intended to "improve the image of the U.S. and South Korea for North Koreans" and "tell North Korean citizens the truth about Kim Jong Un's repressive regime."[35] Efforts to undermine faith in the state and its leaders and institutions and create positive affinities with the adversary state mirrored what the West alleged Russian media had done.[iii] Where Russia's relatively peripheral position in the global information space limited the threat any such efforts could pose to the West, however, the Western world's overwhelming information dominance represented an imminent threat to North Korea and other targets, and consistently proved to be one of the Western Bloc's most potent tools to destabilize its adversaries and reshape their societies in line with its interests.

A comprehensive 2012 study of media in North Korea and the influences of Western media on the population was authored by the associate director of the research consultancy Intermedia Nat Kretchun, and the Korea projects coordinator at the EastWest Coalition NGO Jane Kim, and emphasized America's role in reshaping North Korea through information warfare. The paper stressed the long-term nature of such a campaign, highlighting

---

iii The importance attributed to influencing an adversary population's political narratives would only increase in the 2020s, an example being the statement by French Army General Pierre Schill in June 2024 that conflict with Russia had highlighted "the need to control information to influence both national and international public opinion" to be of "vital importance." This had implications not only for civilian populations, but also due to the dangers of dissemination of information by adversaries within the ranks of one's armed forces, with Schill stressing: "The army plays a crucial role in the information domain . . . Without the capacity to convince and to counter adverse influence, any military engagement can fail." (Ruitenberg, Rudy, 'French Army head Schill talks force modernization, Ukraine war lessons,' *Defense News*, June 16, 2024.)

the importance of Western NGOs actively working to infiltrate media into the country, and alluding to their creating "significant pushback against the regime from the ground up" and "laying the ground for a more open North Korea" as long term objectives. It also emphasized the benefits of using popular media such as soap operas over other forms of media, and consistently equated progress and positive developments with the emergence among the population of positive attitudes towards America and South Korea and negative attitudes towards their own government and political system.[36] Examples of such efforts worldwide showed that a public so inclined could weaken and eventually topple their state, removing the need for a Western invasion, and in the case that an invasion did take place would show far lower levels of resistance. The shifting of public consensus could potentially also influence future generations of leaders to maintain worldviews and conduct policies that were far more favorable to Western interests.

The North Korea Strategy Center was among the Western NGOs with a central role in efforts to reshape DPRK society, and had the officially stated goal of achieving the state's overthrow. It invested heavily in the smuggling of flash drives into the country for dissemination, with content ranging from an encyclopedia co-developed by the Wikimedia Foundation promoting Western-favored political narratives, to popular media pictures such as *Friends*, *Superbad* and *Sex and the City*. To select content for dissemination, one of the means used by the Strategy Center to ascertain its psychological impacts was screening it to North Korean defectors abroad. One report highlighted, as an example, regarding one North Korean viewer of *Superbad* at such a screening:

> She would later explain to me that she "had never seen a movie on that scale of filthiness before," and she doesn't hide her reaction; she spends most of the 113-minute barrage of adolescent sexual angst and dick jokes covering her face with the backs of her hands, as if to cool off her burning cheeks.... [she] starts by listing the most astonishing elements from a North Korean perspective: the frank sex talk, constant genitalia

> references, underage drinking, cops crashing their car, teenage McLovin shooting a gun. All would be seen as indescribably alien, she says. "Even watching it now, I find it vulgar and shocking," she says. "If I were still in North Korea, it would blow my mind."[37]

Although meeting with reactions of aversion and distaste, this shock factor was regarded as key to Western efforts to force societal change, with its effectiveness having been highlighted by psychological warfare experts in the U.S. military for decades. An example was a highly influential 1997 paper by Major Ralph Peters referring to "a deluge of information telling him [the non-Westerner – the target], exaggeratedly and dishonestly, how well the West lives.... America's irresponsible fantasies of itself; [which] he sees a devilishly enchanting, bluntly sexual, terrifying world from which he is excluded." Western popular media "that feature extreme violence and to-the-victors-the-spoils sex – are our most popular cultural weapon, bought or bootlegged nearly everywhere," Peters summarized, with such content featuring predominantly in Western efforts to reshape North Korea's culture, values and information space.[38]

The North Korea Strategy Center was one of multiple NGOs involved in the tremendous escalation of information offensives during the Obama years with the stated aim of reshaping its political culture to stimulate dissent,[39] much as Western NGOs had played key roles in doing across multiple targets from Syria and Belarus to Hong Kong and Thailand. Indeed, the New York–based Human Rights Foundation had a specific "Disrupt North Korea" program for pursuing "initiatives that disrupt the North Korean regime" through information offensives,[40] one of which involved sending 10,000 copies of the film *The Interview* (see below) into the country by balloon.[41] Other NGOs would use balloons to fly pornographic materials into North Korea, including photoshopped leaflets showing the First Lady Ri Sol Ju, formerly a much celebrated singer and national icon, performing sexual acts on South Korean politicians. Campaign organizers stated that they received considerable funding for such activities from the U.S., and were paid about 1.5 million won ($1,234) per balloon. More radical elements would in 2020 suggest "filling the balloons bound for North Korea with dollar bills smeared with stuff that COVID-19 patients had breathed on."[42]

Other prominent NGOs participating in these offensives included North Korean Intellectuals Solidarity and the Fighters for a Free North Korea, both of which strongly advocated forced regime change and worked closely with Western intelligence organizations. These efforts were complemented by Western states' funding of increased radio broadcasts into the country, among them Radio Free Chosun, North Korea Reform Radio, Free North Korea Radio, the North Korea Development Institute and Save North Korea, all of which were directly financed by the U.S. Congress through the National Endowment for Democracy,[43] which had had very close ties with the CIA since its foundation.[44] Other notable broadcasters included the state-funded Voice of America[45] and the BBC.[46,iv]

Targeting North Korea Abroad

While the Obama administration oversaw a significant escalation of efforts to reshape the values and the information space within North Korea, internationally the global reach and near ubiquitous international use of tech giants such as Google and Facebook was also leveraged extensively both to promote content and narratives favoring Western interests, and to limit or

---

iv North Korea was notably one of multiple Western adversaries which would see information offensives targeting its population escalate considerably under Obama. Descriptions of the targeting of Russia or other adversaries could often word for word also be used to describe the parallel efforts against North Korea, an example being former director of security at Senate Intelligence Committee Paul Joyal's 2016 emphasis on: "the strategic approach of focusing our resources on delegitimizing the regime itself. Which was an essential part of what we did during the Cold War. And that includes heavy use of covert action. Its more than just a public event." Other experts such as Kier Giles consistently highlighted the importance of projecting Western media into Russia to reach its population, much as was being done to North Korea, China, Iran and a wide range of more minor targets. ('Continuity and Innovation in Russia's Way of War,' *CSIS* (YouTube Channel), May 11, 2016.)

censor content seen to be detrimental to these interests. A notable example was Google's confirmation in 2019 that Russian state media outlets, which had gained fast growing readerships and followings internationally over the preceding decade, would be de-ranked worldwide on Google Search.[47] While this ensured a stronger position for media outlets promoting messages favorable to Western interests, which were consistently detrimental to those of North Korea, the limited content available from the DPRK was also consistently targeted. An example was the consistent blanket banning and content purges targeting YouTube channels deemed pro–North Korean, which shared often apolitical media from the country ranging from historical documentaries to popular music – with Chosun TV, KCTV, StimmeKoreas, Tonpomail, and Uriminzokkiri being among the targeted channels.[48] These preceded similar blanket bans on Russian state media that began from late 2021 to early 2022,[49] and mirrored similar blanket bans on channels from other Western adversaries such as Syria[50] and Iran,[51] and even non-state news channels whose coverage was deemed unfavorable from regions ranging from Eastern Ukraine[52] to India.[53] Such targeting of media covering North Korea that challenged challenging Western paradigms for viewing the country was thus part of a much broader global trend, and would continue into the 2020s.[54]

Similar bans on media outlets from adversary states were widely implemented by other tech giants such as Facebook,[55] with Twitter consistently banning information sources associated with Western adversaries such as Russia, China,[56] and Cuba,[57] including the accounts of leaders such as Cuban First Secretary Raoul Castro[58] and Iranian Supreme Leader Ali Khamenei.[59] American tech giants' global reach and emergence as international utilities provided Washington with a unique means of doing so for audiences across the world. Thus parallel efforts were made both to push certain kinds of media into North Korea, while also blocking North Korean content from the populations of the wider world using the global reach of U.S. tech giants, mirroring similar efforts being made against adversaries across the world.[v]

The Obama administration oversaw a significant escalation of efforts to reshape global perceptions of North Korea. During the George W. Bush years narratives had centered around the testimony of defector Shin Dong Hyuk, whose allegations of severe human rights abuses, although totally unevidenced, were widely reported as fact by the Western press, activists, political figures and NGOs. Shin's life story, *Escape from Camp 14: One Man's Remarkable Journey from North Korea to Freedom in the West*, was used as the primary basis for Western human rights organizations' reports on the country, and subsequently served as pretext for further Western economic sanctions. It was said to have "shifted the global discourse about North Korea,"[60] with a Western-led United Nations commission in 2014 basing its report and positions almost exclusively on it.[vi] The *New York Times* correspondent in Seoul, Choe Sung Hun, highlighted growing suspicions surrounding Shin's testimony and later concluded: "Shin lied to me and so many others." Outspoken critic and expert on North Korea Andrei Lankov similarly acknowledged that Shin had been pressured by

---

v Censorship efforts extended far beyond tech giants alone, with a prominent 2011 article written for the German Institute of Global Area Studies by researchers David Shim and Dirk Nabers highlighting that positive images of North Korea were tightly and effectively censored in Western press. "Images of North Korea showing its military "strength" and internal "weakness" are highlighted as idiosyncratic aspects to emphasize its Otherness. The use of images marks North Korea in particular ways, which separate "them" from "us"... A good example of what is made almost invisible in Western representations of North Korea is smiling or joyful ordinary North Korean people," they concluded. (Shim, David and Nabers, Dirk, *North Korea and the Politics of Visual Representation*, German Institute of Global and Area Studies, April 2011).

vi Translated into 27 languages, the testimony was retold several times in movies and documentary films. Bestselling military fiction writer James Barrington, for example, had the lead character in his 2007 novel *Foxbat* observe of Camp 22, which according to Shin had been an even more horrific counterpart to Camp 14: "The North Koreans have pulled off a difficult trick: They've managed to make the Nazis' concentration camps look relatively humane," with the author clarifying in an endnote that these fictional portrayals reflected the actual reality in the country. (Barrington, James, *Foxbat*, London, Macmillan, 2007 (Chapter 19).)

anti-Pyongyang groups to tell his story as he had, with the hype surrounding him for years preventing an objective analysis.[61] Other lower profile North Korean defectors notably referred to Shin's testimony as "complete lies."[62]

It was only years later in 2015 that the author of *Escape from Camp 14,* Blaine Harden, revealed that much of it had been fabricated, emphasizing that "Shin was the only source of information about his early life" which allowed his account to be altered freely in the knowledge that it would be accepted without corroboration or evidence.[63] Shin later admitted to the fabrication.[64] Nevertheless, as highlighted in an assessment of North Korean defector testimonies in the *International Journal of Communication Ethics*: "the discrediting of Shin did little to dampen the enthusiasm for celebrity defectors and their stories," with his testimony being far from the last to significantly shape policy and shift public opinion before being proven false.[65] What the DPRK's adversaries needed was not necessarily a verifiable story, but rather an emotional and horrifying one which could be used to vilify the country before the world and serve to legitimize the West's hostile actions. Shin's testimony filled this role perfectly, and there was no need for it to be even remotely true to do so, with a significant indication being that Western sanctions and UN reports made on the basis of his allegations were not reviewed.[66]

Within months of Shin's discrediting a new high profile defector, Park Yeonmi, emerged with considerable support and U.S. government funding to propagate new atrocity stories, which to an even greater extent than Shin's were consistently quickly exposed as fabrications. Park was supported and trained by the Teach North Korean Refugees Global Education Center, which was founded by International Director of the Atlas Network NGO Casey Lartigue, with this NGO in turn funded by the U.S. State Department and the U.S. Congress.[vii] Speaking to the writer, Lartigue would make

---

vii When meeting the writer in person, Lartigue emphasized that he and his associates had the goal of nothing less than the total destruction of the North Korean state, the remaking of its society and punishment of its leadership. "If you met Kim Jong Un, what would you say to him?" he asked. Answering his own question, he said: "I would have nothing to say to him,

clear that Yeonmi's testimonies were his organization's prime achievement and his personal "claim to fame" – in his words. At her debut speech at the One Young World Summit in Dublin in October 2014 Park dressed in highly presentable pink traditional clothing, conspicuously wiped her eyes and held her hand to her mouth with long pauses which gave her words much added dramatic effect, and stated falsehood after falsehood which were consistently widely publicized by the Western press. The video went viral, quickly gaining over 80 million views.

Following her debut, Park embarked on an international promotional tour that included radio and television appearances around the world, and subsequently appeared on a panel at the State Department on Human Rights Day to present her claims. Her memoir, *In Order To Live: A North Korean Girl's Journey to Freedom*, was written by veteran ghostwriter Maryanne Vollers who had famously written Hillary Clinton's own books. It received very strong promotion and endorsements and sold over 100,000 copies. As noted by the *Washington Post*: "Park has become a multiplatform star in America... Her tales of the gothic punishments that await dissidents are widely shared on YouTube, where videos with titles such as 'THIS is a Crime in North Korea!?' can earn more than 10 million views."[67] Her verifiably false claims quickly became too numerous to list, but some examples are given below: "North Korea is an unimaginable country. There is only one channel on tv. There is also no internet." North Koreans had never heard of Africa, there was no word for "love" in North Korea,[68] there was virtually no word for "I."[69] "When I was nine years old I saw my friend's mother publicly executed. Her crime – watching a Hollywood movie."[70] North Koreans lived off "eating

---

there's nothing one can say to these kinds of people, their only job is killing Koreans, and the only way to help North Koreans is to bring them down." He showed the writer photos of himself alongside Park, whose work he expressed considerable pride in and to whom he said his organization had provided tremendous support, alongside other defectors, to speak against the country. To one familiar with North Korea, Lartigue gave the impression of being an extremist who firmly believed that those who rejected the West's hegemony, values and ideology needed to be destroyed. His group's work and funding were vital facilitators of Park's rise to international fame.

grasshoppers, dragonflies, a lot of insects, tree bark, plants, flowers."[71] North Koreans saw "piles of human bodies" every spring dead from malnutrition, "and you see children, just rats eating human eyes, first, and then children catching these rats and they eat them and they somehow die from – I don't know what it is. Then rats eat the children back. So this cycle of us eating rats and they eat us back is going to continue and continue."[72]

Park had by the early 2020s gained 600,000 subscribers on her YouTube channel *Voice of North Korea,* publishing new videos several times a week making consistently ludicrous claims and frequently predicting the country's imminent collapse.[73] Examples from the first half of 2021 alone include: Kim Jong Un's sister and many North Korean children being frequent consumers of crystal meth;[74] disabled people[75] and AIDS patients being executed or experimented on with chemical weapons;[76] women being sold by the government as sex slaves to China;[77] Kim Jong Un being secretly gay;[78] Kim Jong Un having several mistresses[79] and female sex slaves;[80] among hundreds of others.[viii] The extreme nature of Park's claims and the unprecedented publicity they gained were hallmarks of escalated atrocity fabrication efforts seen under the Obama administration, and much like Shin had met with President Bush and seen his narrative strongly promoted, Park met with State Secretary Clinton and saw her narratives propagated much more effectively.[ix]

Beyond defector testimonies, during the Obama years the propagation of fabricated information vilifying North Korea both by state media and by non-state outlets with close ties to the state

viii While the debunking of Park's claims and narratives gained growing publicity in the early 2020s, as reflected in the changing contents of her Wikipedia page, during the Obama years her narratives played a central role in shaping Western and global thought on North Korea as part of a broader escalation of information warfare campaigns. Inconsistencies in her stories spanning back to 2014 began to be highlighted only after she began in the 2020s to side openly with American right on domestic political issues and to criticize the Democratic Party establishment.

ix For the writer's much more comprehensive detailing of the use of fabricated information to vilify North Korea, see Abrams, A. B., *Atrocity Fabrication and its Consequences: How Fake News Shapes World Order*, Atlanta, Clarity Press, 2023 (Chapters 2 and 7).

were considerable. One notable example was the U.S. government-funded Radio Free Asia (RFA), established with the stated purpose of "advancing the goals of U.S. foreign policy,"[81] and referred to by the *New York Times* as a "CIA broadcasting venture" for its close ties to U.S. intelligence.[82] Playing a central role in shaping global perceptions of Chairman Kim Jong Un during his early years in office, one of RFA's most widely circulated stories alleged he had "fed his uncle to dogs"[83] – a story widely re-reported in Western news outlets which proved to be entirely false.[84] The outlet's portrayals cast the state not only as brutal, but also as ludicrous, an example being the report two months later that a new law required all North Korean men to copy Chairman Kim's exact haircut[85] – which was similarly widely re-reported as fact without evidence or corroboration,[86] and later proved to be entirely false.[87]

Western journalists widely attested to the lack of standards when writing negative stories on North Korea, with Max Fisher from the *Washington Post* observing that "almost any story is treated as broadly credible, no matter how outlandish or thinly sourced."[88] Isaac Stone-Fish wrote in *Foreign Policy* that: "as an American journalist you can write almost anything you want about North Korea and people will just accept it," admitting to having done so himself when inventing a story of a severe North Korean drug epidemic, which was accepted without evidence and later proved to be entirely false.[89] A study published in the *International Journal of Communication Ethics* by Richard Murray observed accordingly: "North Korea's isolation has resulted in an 'anything goes' approach to reporting on the nation that would not be acceptable in covering any other country"[90] – a conclusion widely reached in other Western assessments.[91] The extremity of these narratives and the scale on which they were published reached entirely new levels in the Obama years, including frequent reports of executions of high profile North Koreans from leading pop singers to generals – with these consistently followed by their debunking as those reported dead reappeared on camera.[92]

As was the case for a range of American adversaries, the shaping of the global information space to vilify North Korea was closely coordinated with military and diplomatic efforts to place pressure on and isolate the country. Notable insight into this process would be provided by U.S. Navy Commander Guy Snodgrass, Pentagon Communications Director under the Trump administration's first Defense Secretary Jamies Mattis, who recalled being ordered by Mattis in early 2018: "I need you to get with Stephen Miller. I saw him recently at the White House. He's got some good ideas for language we can use for North Korea." Commander Snodgrass referred to Miller, who then served as Senior Advisor to the President and White House Director of Speechwriting, as "a far-right ideologue," highlighting that "he had a reputation for being a provocateur," although the new rhetoric he proposed putting forward was far from out of line with that seen in previous decades.[93]

Miller stressed at the subsequent meeting: "We must counter North Korean rhetoric. This is a repressive regime that murders innocents... we must highlight the depravity of the regime," with Snodgrass recalling that "he was comfortable including tougher language with the understanding that we wanted to maintain the "maximum pressure campaign." "We need public and international support for our maximum pressure campaign as we attempt to reach the 'international left' – portray [the North Koreans] as racist, anti-women, anti-gay, ethnocentric fascists. This is a country with prison and labor camps, that uses public execution, and with a dictator who murdered his brother in an international airport." "It wasn't lost on me," Snodgrass concluded, "that we were developing a coordinated message that would soon become the official stance of the United States of America."[94]

Significant insight into the role of the U.S. government in shaping the creation of content related to North Korea was provided by the hack of Sony Pictures in 2015. This revealed that the film *The Interview*, the story of American agents' mission to assassinate Kim Jong Un, had seen its production specifically requested by the Democratic Party and the defense establishment and its content tailored to their requirements.[95] The film's director, Seth Rogen, himself highlighted the role of government officials as consultants for the film, stressing he was "convinced [they] are in the C.I.A."[96] The State Department remained in close communication with Sony Entertainment chief executive Michael Lynton to shape the film's content, informing him of its significant potential political impacts in North Korea.[97] An example was its emphasis on including a gory execution of Chairman Kim, which Pentagon-linked experts believed the country's population "needed to see" to help achieve the political change Washington was seeking to stimulate.[98]

Executive board member of the Korea Policy Institute Professor Christine Hong observed regarding the intentions behind the production of *The Interview*:

> If you actually look at what the Sony executives did, they consulted very closely with the State Department, which actually gave the executives a green light with regard to the death scene. And they also consulted with a RAND North Korea watcher, a man named Bruce Bennett, who basically has espoused in thesis that the way to bring down the North Korean government is to assassinate the leadership. And he actually stated, in consulting with Sony about this film, that this film, in terms of the South Korean market, as well as its infiltration by defector balloon-dropping organizations into North Korea, could possibly get the wheels of a kind of regime change plot into motion. So, in this instance, fiction and reality have a sort of mirroring relationship to each other.[99]

North Korea was itself notably accused of launching the hack, having protested the film's crude and at times vulgar depictions of the country and gory killing of its leader. The production was widely accused, even by the country's Western critics, of having strong racist and bigoted depictions of East Asian peoples – particularly women.[100] Contributor to *The Nation* and *The National Interest* and expert on U.S.-DPRK relations Tim Shorrock observed: "The film used every racist image and trope that [director] Rogen could dream up, from the sing-songy caricatures of Asian speech that were a film staple in the 1940s and '50s, to the concept that Koreans are either robotic slaves (like Kim's security guards) or sex-starved submissives who crave American men."[101] President Obama warned of a proportional response to the alleged hacking, and a large scale cyberattack on North Korean internet servers shortly afterwards was speculated to have been carried out by the U.S.[102] This was followed by additional economic sanctions against the Pyongyang.[x]

While the hacking of Sony revealed the extent of the state and party's collaboration with Hollywood, it appeared to be far from an isolated case. The Obama years saw a surge in the number of productions casting North Korea as an imminent threat to the American people, ranging from the videogame Homefront to the films Red Dawn and Olympus Has Fallen, which all depicted North Korean soldiers on American soil attempting to destroy or conquer the United States.

In parallel to the expansion of cooperation with tech giants and film producers, the Obama administration also increased cooperation with non-state groups, many of them highly radical, which could go where the Pentagon could not in taking to the offensive against Western Bloc adversaries. Examples abroad ranged from the Mujahideen-e Khalq terror group in Iran,[103] to the far-right Azov Battalion and similar groups in Ukraine,[104] and a wide range of Al Qaeda affiliates in Libya,[105] among many others extremist groups operating from China to East Africa. Although

x Experts widely raised significant questions regarding Pyongyang's culpability. Senior vice president at the leading American cybersecurity firm Norse Corp Kurt Stammburger, for one, informed law enforcement: "We can't find any indication that North Korea either ordered, masterminded or even funded this attack… Nobody has been able to find a credible connection to the North Korean government." Data instead pointed to a former Sony employee with insider knowledge of the company. Shlomo Argamon, chief scientist at cybersecurity consulting firm Taia Global, similarly found a complete lack of signs that North Korea was responsible, stating: "There's certainly reason to doubt the total attribution of this to North Korea." A number of other experts, including hackers and security researchers, reached very similar conclusions. ('Sony insider – not North Korea – likely involved in hack, experts say,' *Los Angeles Times*, December 30, 2015.) ('Former Anonymous hacker doubts North Korea behind Sony attack,' *CBS News*, December 18, 2014.) ('The Evidence That North Korea Hacked Sony Is Flimsy,' *Wired*, December 17, 2014.)

opportunities for such cooperation were more limited in North Korea's case, a notable example was the Cheollima Civil Defense group, which although formally founded two months after Obama left office, had seen the groundwork for its organization, operations and close coordination with U.S. intelligence laid in the preceding years. Devoted to the forced destruction of the North Korean state, the group maintained close ties to the CIA, with whom its leadership held regular meetings, and would make headlines with a major paramilitary operation on February 27, 2019 attacking the North Korean embassy in Madrid.

Leading the Cheollima Civil Defense group attack was Adrian Hong, President of Joseon Institute and founder of the anti-Pyongyang organizations Liberty in North Korea and Pegasus Strategies, which were playing leading roles in information warfare efforts against the state. Former U.S. Marine and intelligence specialist in the Iraq War Christopher Ahn was another notable confirmed participant. A Spanish investigation in the aftermath of the attack found at least two of the perpetrators had direct links to the CIA, with the *Financial Times* being among the sources to highlight that the CIA maintained close ties with such anti-Pyongyang NGOs.[106] Spanish officials were reported to have "solid proof" that Hong had met with CIA officials including photographs and communication records,[107] with the Seoul-based conservative paper *Chosun Ilbo,* known for its close contacts with South Korean intelligence, attesting to Hong's close ties to the CIA.[108] Hong reportedly had at least one meeting in Washington at the Office of the Director of National Intelligence in 2018.[109]

Carrying imitation guns and balaclavas, and armed with mace spray, crowbars, metal handcuffs and other restraints, the assailants penetrated the embassy, tied up up North Korean diplomats and their families, seized computers holding highly sensitive information, and threatened the commercial attaché with beatings in an attempt to force his defection.[110] This fit into a broader pattern of Cheollima Civil Defense playing central roles in defector extraction operations targeting prominent North Koreans across the world. Computers, encryption equipment and other systems taken by the attackers were assessed to represent a "treasure trove" of information to Western intelligence services,[111] with such forced physical entry considered the most effective means to gain access to encrypted state communications between Pyongyang and its embassies across the world.[112] Spanish investigations would in 2021 provide significant evidence of violence having been used in the operation.[113] Although the operation was cut short after the wife of one of the embassy staff escaped by jumping from an upper floor window, allowing her to alert police, the assailants were able to escape with the government materials, which were then handed over to American intelligence.

Access to private information on the former North Korean ambassador to Spain, Kim Hyok Chol, who was playing a central role in ongoing negotiations with the United States, was speculated to be the reason why the Madrid embassy had been chosen preceding a key summit meeting in Hanoi five days later. In parallel to intelligence collection and the attempt to force a defection, the assailants pulled down photos of Kim Il Sung and Kim Jong Il, smashing them on the floor and filming this, with the intention of using this footage in later propaganda to be broadcast into North Korea. The Spanish National Intelligence Center concluded that the means by which the embassy was attacked resembled the "method of work" of the American intelligence services – citing the "perfectly coordinated" military precision of the operation. The attackers were "professionals, and were responsible for lowering the power, dimming the street lights on the road in front of the embassy and neutralizing other security systems around the building without raising an alarm."[114] While the involvement of U.S. intelligence was widely suspected, Spanish government sources admitted that proving this in court would be extremely difficult.[115]

The Obama administration oversaw the escalation of tensions and creation of a much more comprehensive set of means for attacking North Korea, mirroring its approach to American adversaries across the world. Cyber warfare, multiple kinds of sophisticated information warfare and narrative shaping, and partnerships with and support for radical groups serving as effective proxies, were all effective hallmarks of the administration's policies, with much more intensive non-kinetic global warfare being a primary legacy of his era.

Endnotes

1 Sanger, David E. and Broad, William J., 'Trump Inherits a Secret Cyberwar Against North Korean Missiles,' *New York Times,* March 4, 2017.

2 Lee, Yon-soo, 'Ex-U.S. Military Chief Suggests Pre-emptive Strike on North Korea,' *Chosun Ilbo*, September 19, 2016.

3 Shorrock, Tim, 'Hillary's Hawks Are Threatening Escalation Against North Korea,' *The Nation,* October 26, 2016.

4 Jackson, Van, *On the Brink: Trump, Kim, and the Threat of Nuclear War,* Cambridge, Cambridge University Press, 2018 (p. 93).

5 Sisk, Richard, 'Former US General Calls for Pre-emptive Strike on North Korea,' *Defense Tech,* December 1, 2016.

6 Mullen, Mike and Nunn, Sam and Mount, Adam, *A Sharper Choice on North Korea: Engaging China for a Stable Northeast Asia*, Council on Foreign Relations, Independent Task Force Report No. 74, September 2016 (p. 11).

7 Ibid. (pp. 7, 31, 46).

8 Hass, Richard N., 'World Order 2.0: The Case for Sovereign Obligation,' *Foreign Affairs,* January/February 2017.

9 Ibid.

10 Hayes, Danny and Guardino, Matt, 'Whose Views Made the News? Media Coverage and the March to War in Iraq,' *Political Commission,* vol. 27, no. 1, 2010 (pp. 59–87).

McSmith, Andy, 'Iraq and the Rupert Murdoch connection: The media mogul's network of pro-war campaigners,' *The Independent,* July 7, 2016.

11 Jackson, Van, *On the Brink: Trump, Kim, and the Threat of Nuclear War,* Cambridge, Cambridge University Press, 2018 (p. 93).

12 Johnson, Jesse, 'Obama weighed pre-emptive strike against North Korea after fifth nuclear blast and missile tests near Japan in 2016, Woodward book claims,' *Japan Times,* September 12, 2018.

'Obama mulled preemptive attack on N. Korea: book,' *Yonhap,* September 12, 2018.

13 'North Korea: The War Game,' *The Atlantic*, August 15, 2005.

14 Litwak, Roberto, *Rogue States and U.S. Foreign Policy: Containment After the Cold War*, Washington, DC, Woodrow Wilson Center Press, 2000 (p. 223).

15 Cha, Victor D., 'The Rationale for "Enhanced" Engagement of North Korea: After the Perry Policy Review,' *Asian Survey*, vol. 39, no. 6, 1999 (p. 847).

'Do Sanctions Really Work on North Korea? The Impossible State Live!,' *Center for Strategic and International Studies* (YouTube Channel), March 8, 2023.

16 Weiner, Tim, *Legacy of Ashes: The History of the CIA*, New York, Anchor Books, 2008 (Chapter 6).

17 Howell, Edward, *North Korea and the Global Nuclear Order: When Bad Behaviour Pays*, Oxford, Oxford University Press, 2023 (p. 183).

18 Ibid. (p. 183).

19 Ibid. (p. 184).

20 Clapper, James R., *Facts and Fears: Hard Truths from a Life in Intelligence*, New York, Viking, 2018 (Chapter 2).

21 Rachman, Gideon, *Easternisation: War and Peace in the Asian Century*, New York, Vintage, 2017 (pp. 77–78).

Washington Post, January 18, 2009.

22 Foster-Carter, Aidan, 'Obama Comes Out as a North Korea Collapsist,' *The Diplomat*, January 20, 2015.

23 Ibid.

24 McMaster, H. R., *Battlegrounds: The Fight to Defend the Free World,* New York, Harper, 2020 (Chapter 11).

25 Pompeo, Mike, *Never Give an Inch: Fighting for the America I Love*, Northampton, MA, Broadside Books, 2023 (Chapter 8).

26 'Prospects for Syrian No-fly Zone Assessed at USIP,' *United States Institute of Peace*, May 30, 2013.

Kaplan, Fred, 'Assad's Situation,' *Slate*, April 15, 2003.

Gordon, Philip H., 'After Iraq: Is Syria Next?,' *Brookings Institute,* April 25, 2003.

27 Geers, Kenneth, *Cyber War in Perspective: Russian Aggression against Ukraine*, Tallinn, NATO CCD COE Publications, 2015 (Chapter 10).

28 MacAskill, Ewen, 'US confirms it asked Twitter to stay open to help Iran protesters,' *The Guardian,* June 17, 2019.

29 Schmidt, Eric and Cohen, Jared, 'The Digital Disruption, Connectivity and the Diffusion of Power,' *Foreign Affairs*, November/December 2010.

Assange, Julian, *When Google Met Wikileaks*, New York, OR Books, 2014 (pp. 22, 45, 46, 55).

30 Lankov, Andrei, 'Changing North Korea: An Information Campaign Can Beat the Regime,' *Foreign Affairs,* vol. 88, no. 6, November/December 2009 (pp. 95–105).

31 'The Korean Nuclear Crisis: Preventing the truly dangerous spread of weapons of mass destruction,' *Harvard Magazine*, September-October 2003.

32 'Continuity and Innovation in Russia's Way of War,' *CSIS* (YouTube Channel), May 11, 2016.

33 Richter, Monika L., 'The Kremlin's Platform for "Useful Idiots" in the West: An Overview of RT's Editorial Strategy and Evidence of Impact,' *European Values: Protecting Freedom,* September 18, 2019.

'America's exposure to Russian information warfare,' *Financial Times,* December 19, 2018.

Putin's Asymmetric Assault on Democracy in Russia and Europe: Implications for U.S. National Security, A Minority Staff Report Prepared for the Use of the Committee on Foreign Relations, United States Senate, One Hundred and Fifteenth Congress, Second Session, January 10, 2018.

34 'Respected Comrade Kim Jong Un Sends Letter of Congratulations to Trustworthy Young People,' *KCNA*, August 29, 2021.

35 Ryall, Julian, 'US invests millions to expose regime to North Koreans,' *Deutsche Welle*, January 16, 2023.

36 Kretchun, Nat and Kim, Jane, *A Quiet Opening: North Koreans in a Changing Media Environment*, Washington, DC, Intermedia, May 2012.

37 Greenburg, Andy, 'The Plot to Free North Korea with Smuggled Episodes of "Friends,"' *Wired*, March 1, 2015.

38 Peters, Ralph, 'Constant Conflict, Parameters,' *U.S. Army War College Quarterly*, Summer 1997 (pp. 4–14).

39 *Flash Drives for Freedom,* accessed August 2, 2017 (https://flashdrivesforfreedom.org).

40 'Disrupt North Korea,' Politics/Causes, *Human Rights Foundation*, June 21, 2017.

41 Bond, Paul, 'Largest Balloon Drop of "The Interview" Underway Over North Korea,' *Hollywood Reporter,* April 15, 2020.

42 'Defector groups get paid to launch propaganda balloons, former N. Korean soldier says,' *Hankyoreh*, June 15, 2020.

Asmolov, Konstantin, 'North Korea: What Is and What Should Never Be,' *Valdai*, June 19, 2020.

43 Chun, Susan, 'Radio gives hope to North and South Koreans,' *CNN*, February 27, 2008.

44 Blum, William, *Rogue State: A Guide to the World's Only Superpower,* London, Zed Books, 2006 (Chapter 19).

45 VOA Broadcasting in Korean, Voice of Asia Public Relations, accessed August 3, 2019 (https://www.insidevoa.com/p/6438.html).

46 Williams, Martyn, 'The BBC Launches Korean Language News: A New Option for North Korean Radio Listeners,' *38 North*, September 26, 2017.

47 Sabur, Rozina, 'Google to "de-rank" stories from Russia Today and Sputnik,' *The Telegraph,* November 21, 2017.

'Twitter Suspends Russian Embassy in Syria's Account,' *Moscow Times,* July 31, 2019.

48 Solon, Olivia, 'YouTube shuts down North Korean propaganda channels,' *The Guardian,* September 9, 2017.

Macdonald, Hamish, 'YouTube continues to terminate North Korea–related channels,' *NK News,* September 8, 2017.

Fifield, Anna, 'YouTube has shut down more North Korean channels – and researchers are livid,' *Washington Post,* September 14, 2017.

49 'YouTube again blocks German-language RT channel,' *Deutsche Welle*, December 16, 2021.

50 'YouTube shuts down pro-Syrian government channels,' *Al Jazeera,* September 10, 2018.

'YouTube Offers Cryptic Explanation on Shutdown of Syrian Government Accounts,' *Sputnik News*, September 12, 2018.

51 'YouTube Censors Iranian Press, HispanTV, Press TV Targeted,' *Telesur,* April 19, 2019.

'Google "disables" Press TV's YouTube account,' *Islamic Republic News Agency,* April 19, 2019.

52 '"We got a complaint": YouTube deletes channels focusing on Crimea & eastern Ukraine, cites "terms of use" violation,' *RT*, May 20, 2020.

53 'YouTube blocks WION for reporting Russian statement,' *WION*, March 26, 2022.

54 Zwirko, Colin, 'Twitter abruptly restricts North Korean state media's @coldnoodlefan account,' *NK News*, August 12, 2020.

O'Carroll, Chad, 'YouTube deletes North Korean state media channel featuring vlogger Un A,' *NK News*, December 11, 2020.

55 'Facebook bans Press TV page AGAIN as Iranian outlet decries move as "censorship" & "attack on free speech,"' *RT*, March 27, 2021.

56 'British scholar tells the truth about deleted social media accounts related to Hong Kong issues,' *CTGN,* September 18, 2019.

57 'Twitter blocks accounts of Raúl Castro and Cuban state-run media outlets,' *The Guardian*, September 12, 2019.

Sweeney, Steve, 'Cuban journalists condemn Twitter's mass blocking of their accounts,' *Morning Star,* September 12, 2019.

58 Marsh, Sarah, 'Twitter blocks accounts of Raúl Castro and Cuban state-run media,' *Reuters,* September 12, 2019.

59 'Twitter suspends Iran Leader's accounts,' *Press TV,* March 31, 2020.

60 'Shin Dong-hyuk,' Dalhousie University, Academics, Convocation, Ceremonies, Honorary Degree Recipients, Honorary Degree 2014.

61 Lankov, Andrei, 'After the Shin Dong-hyuk affair: Separating fact, fiction,' *NK News,* February 3, 2015.

62 '그는 처음부터 18호 수용소에서 살았다' ['He Lived in Camp 18 From the Beginning'], *Hankyoreh*, April 1, 2016.

63 Harden, Blaine, *Escape from Camp 14: One Man's Remarkable Odyssey from North Korea to Freedom in the West*, New York, Viking, 2012 (p. 46).

64 Fifield, Anna, 'Prominent N. Korean defector Shin Dong-hyuk admits parts of story are inaccurate,' *Washington Post*, January 17, 2015.

65 Murray, Richard, 'Reporting on the impossible: The use of defectors in covering North Korea,' *The International Journal of Communication Ethics*, vol. 14, no. 4, 2017 (pp. 17–24).

66 Dorell, Oren, 'U.S. puts N. K. leader Kim Jong Un on sanctions list for human rights abuses,' *USA Today*, July 6, 2016.

67 Sommer, Will, 'A North Korean defector captivated U.S. media. Some question her story,' *Washington Post*, July 16, 2023.

68 'There's no word for love in North Korea,' Yeonmi Park at Google Zeitgeist, May 2016.

69 Interview with Yeonmi Park in: 'Tyranny, Slavery and Columbia U,' *The Jordan B. Peterson Podcast*, Season 4, Episode, 26, May 31, 2021.

70 Jolley, Mary Ann, 'The Strange Tale of Yeonmi Park,' *The Diplomat*, December 10, 2014.

71 Ibid.

Interview with Yeonmi Park in: 'Tyranny, Slavery and Columbia U,' *The Jordan B. Peterson Podcast*, Season 4, Episode, 26, May 31, 2021.

72 Interview with Yeonmi Park in: 'Tyranny, Slavery and Columbia U,' *The Jordan B. Peterson Podcast*, Season 4, Episode, 26, May 31, 2021.

73 'How Covid-19 is Destroying the North Korean Regime,' *Voice of North Korea by Yeonmi Park* (YouTube Channel), June 1, 2021.

'Uprising inside North Korea,' *Voice of North Korea by Yeonmi Park* (YouTube Channel), April 28, 2021.

'Is the North Korean Regime Collapsing,' *Voice of North Korea by Yeonmi Park* (YouTube Channel), May 27, 2021.

'The End of Kim Jong-un,' *Voice of North Korea by Yeonmi Park* (YouTube Channel), January 31, 2021.

'Coup in North Korea,' *Voice of North Korea by Yeonmi Park*, (YouTube Channel), March 1, 2021.

'Breaking News: Massive Uprising in Musan, North Korea,' *Voice of North Korea by Yeonmi Park* (YouTube Channel), March 9, 2021.

'Is Kim Jong-Un about to be replaced,' *Voice of North Korea by Yeonmi Park* (YouTube Channel), June 17, 2021.

'The Deadly New Virus Spreading in North Korea Might Bring Down the Regime,' *Voice of North Korea by Yeonmi Park* (YouTube Channel), May 3, 2021.

74 'Shocking Secret of Kim Yo-jeong,' *Voice of North Korea by Yeonmi Park* (YouTube Channel), July 7, 2021.

75 'What Happens If you become disabled in North Korea?,' *Voice of North Korea by Yeonmi Park* (YouTube Channel), January 14, 2021.

76 'The Deadly New Virus Spreading in North Korea Might Bring Down the Regime,' *Voice of North Korea by Yeonmi Park* (YouTube Channel), May 3, 2021.

77 'How Much Does North Korean Regime Earn Selling Their Women to China,' *Voice of North Korea by Yeonmi Park* (YouTube Channel), February 21, 2021.

78 'Is Kim Jong-Un Gay?,' *Voice of North Korea by Yeonmi Park* (YouTube Channel), February 26, 2021.

79 'Will Kim Jong Un's Mistress Take Over North Korea?,' *Voice of North Korea by Yeonmi Park* (YouTube Channel), March 15, 2021.

80 'The True Dark Side of North Korea Pleasure Squad,' *Voice of North Korea by Yeonmi Park* (YouTube Channel), April 19, 2021.

'North Korea's Secret 'Pleasure Squad' Parties,' *Voice of North Korea by Yeonmi Park* (YouTube Channel), December 17, 2021.

'Exclusive: New Photos of Kim Jong Un's Pleasure Squad,' *Voice of North Korea by Yeonmi Park* (YouTube Channel), December 23, 2020.

81 Radio Free Asia, 'About,' Broadcasting Board of Governors, n.d., accessed June 5, 2016.

Sosin, Gene, *Sparks of Liberty: An insider's memoir of Radio Liberty*, University Park, PA, Pennsylvania State University Press, 1999 (p. 257).

Welch, David, *Propaganda, Power and Persuasion from World War I to Wikileaks*, London/New York, I. B. Tauris, 2014.

82 'Worldwide Propaganda Network Built by the C.I.A.,' *New York Times*, December 26, 1977.

83 Dier, Arden, 'Report: Kim Jong Un fed uncle alive to 120 starved dogs,' *USA Today*, January 3, 2014.

84 Kaiman, Jonathan, 'Story about Kim Jong-un's uncle being fed to dogs originated with satirist,' *The Guardian*, January 6, 2014.

85 'North Korean University Students Copy Kim Jong Un's Hairstyle,' *Radio Free Asia*, March 25, 2014.

86 'North Korea: Students required to get Kim Jong-un haircut,' *BBC News*, March 26, 2014.

87 Asmolov, Konstantin, 'How the Radio Free Asia released the whole set of baloney,' *New Eastern Outlook*, November 26, 2016.

Macdonald, Hamish, 'Why men's Kim Jong Un hairstyle requirement is unlikely true,' *NK News*, March 26, 2014.

88 Fisher, Max, 'No, Kim Jong Un probably didn't feed his uncle to 120 hungry dogs,' *Washington Post*, January 3, 2014.

89 Stone Fish, Isaac, 'The Black Hole of North Korea,' *New York Times*, August 8, 2011.

90 Murray, Richard, 'Reporting on the impossible: The use of defectors in covering North Korea,' *The International Journal of Communication Ethics*, vol. 14, no. 4, 2017 (pp. 17–24).

91 O'Carroll, Chad, 'North Korea's invisible phone, killer dogs and other such stories – why the world is transfixed,' *The Telegraph*, January 6, 2014.

Taylor, Adam, 'Why You Shouldn't Necessarily Trust Those Reports of Kim Jong- un Executing His Ex-Girlfriend,' *Business Insider*, August 29, 2013.

92 'Former North Korean general believed executed turns up alive,' *Fox News*, May 10, 2016.

Hancocks, Paula, 'North Korean leader ordered aunt to be poisoned, defector says,' *CNN,* May 12, 2015.

Hotham, Oliver, 'Kim Jong Un's aunt, once reported killed, makes first appearance in six years,' *NK News,* January 25, 2020.

'Kim Jong Un's Ex-Lover Hyon Song-Wol "Executed By North Korean Firing Squad After Making Sex Tape,"' *Huffington Post*, August 23, 2018.

93 Snodgrass, Guy M., *Holding the Line: Inside Trump's Pentagon with Secretary Mattis*, New York, Sentinel, 2019 (Chapters 8, 16).

94 Ibid. (Chapter 16).

95 '"The Interview" Belittles North Korea, But is Film's Backstory and U.S. Policy the Real Farce?,' *Democracy Now,* December 22, 2014.

Thielman, Sam, 'WikiLeaks republishes all Sony hacking scandal documents,' *The Guardian,* April 17, 2015.

'Sony,' *Wikileaks,* April 16, 2015.

96 Itzkoff, Dave, 'James Franco and Seth Rogen Talk About "The Interview,"' *New York Times,* December 16, 2016.

97 Hornaday, Ann, 'Sony, "The Interview," and the unspoken truth: All movies are political,' *Washington Post,* December 18, 2014.

98 De Moraes, Lisa, '"The Interview" Release Would Have Damaged Kim Jong Un Internally, Says Rand Expert Who Saw Movie at Sony's Request,' *Yahoo News*, December 19, 2014.

99 '"The Interview" Belittles North Korea, But is Film's Backstory and U.S. Policy the Real Farce?,' *Democracy Now,* December 22, 2014.

100 Builder, Maxine, 'The Real Problem With "The Interview" Is Its Racism, Not Its Satire,' *Medium,* December 18, 2014.

Kim, Ji-Sun (Grace), '"The Interview": No Laughing Matter,' *Huffington Post,* January 8, 2015.

101 Shorrock, Tim, 'How Sony, Obama, Seth Rogen and CIA secretly planned to force regime change in North Korea,' *The Grey Zone,* September 5, 2017.

102 'North Korean Internet Collapses After Obama's Warning,' *Time,* December 22, 2014.

103 Fisher, Max, 'Blowback: In Aiding Iranian Terrorists, the U.S. Repeats a Dangerous Mistake,' *The Atlantic*, April 6, 2012.

104 Carden, James, 'Congress Has Removed a Ban on Funding Neo-Nazis From Its Year-End Spending Bill,' *The Nation*, January 14, 2016.

'Analysis: U.S. Cozies Up to Kiev Government Including Far Right,' *ABC News*, March 30, 2014.

Edgar, David, 'What did happen?,' *London Review of Books*, vol. 38, no. 2, January 21, 2016.

Greenwald, Glenn, 'Clapper Calls for Arming Ukrainian Forces: Who Would That Actually Empower?,' *The Intercept*, February 27, 2015.

105 Kuperman, Alan J., 'America's Little-Known Mission to Support Al Qaeda's Role in Libya,' *The National Interest,* August 13, 2019.

Greenhill, Sam, 'Flying proudly over the birthplace of Libya's revolution, the flag of Al Qaeda,' *Daily Mail,* November 2, 2011.

'Libya: Wake-Up Call to Misrata's Leaders: Torture, Killings May Amount to Crimes against Humanity,' *Human Rights Watch*, April 8, 2012.

106 'A tale of daring, violence and intrigue from a North Korea embassy,' *Financial Times*, March 29, 2019.

107 Shorrock, Tim, 'Did the CIA Orchestrate an Attack on the North Korean Embassy in Spain?,' *Foreign Policy,* May 2, 2019.

108 Cho, Yi Jun, 'Who Is Anti-N.Korean Guerrilla Leader?,' *Chosun Ilbo,* April 4, 2019.

109 Taylor, Adam and Kim, Min Joo, 'The covert group that carried out a brazen raid on a North Korean embassy now fears exposure,' *Washington Post*, March 28, 2019.

110 Shorrock, Tim, 'Did the CIA Orchestrate an Attack on the North Korean Embassy in Spain?,' *Foreign Policy,* May 2, 2019.

111 Hudson, John, 'A shadowy group trying to overthrow Kim Jong Un allegedly raided a North Korean embassy in broad daylight,' *Washington Post*, March 15, 2019.

112 Dilanian, Ken and De Luce, Dan and Lederman, Josh, 'FBI has data stolen from North Korea embassy by anti-regime group,' *NBC News*, March 29, 2019.

113 O'Carroll, Chad, 'Spanish evidence claims Free Joseon used violence, weapons during embassy breach,' *NK News,* June 14, 2021.

114 Ryall, Julian and Badcock, James, 'Was North Korea's vital "transformation computer" taken in raid on Madrid embassy?,' *The Telegraph*, March 26, 2019.

Dolz, Patricia Ortega, 'Spain investigates alleged attack on North Korean embassy in Madrid,' *El País,* February 27, 2019.

115 González, Miguel and Dolz, Patricia Ortega, 'CIA implicated in attack on North Korean embassy in Madrid,' *El País*, March 13, 2019.

CHAPTER 5

Fire and Fury: The Military Standoff That Ended an Era

Escalated Economic Warfare and Pressuring China

The final three years of the Barack Obama administration saw North Korea significantly escalate the testing of technologies for its ballistic missile deterrent, with at least 52 launches taking place demonstrating major improvements across multiple performance areas, from range and efficiency to launch times, precision and reliability.[1] The development of a miniaturized thermonuclear warhead, paired with the successful demonstration of the Hwasong-10's capabilities, also placed the country well on course to relatively swiftly begin flight testing an ICBM able to strike the U.S. mainland.[2] There was also growing pessimism in the West regarding the possibility of achieving a turnaround through use of economic sanctions. This emerging consensus was highlighted by *Reuters'* citing of University of Tokyo professor Tadashi Kimiya on September 10, 2016, who stated: "Sanctions have already been imposed on almost everything possible, so the policy is at an impasse. In reality, the means by which the United States, South Korea and Japan can put pressure on North Korea have reached their limits."[3]

In the final months of the Obama administration the possibility of placing pressure on China to in turn pressurize its neighbor rapidly gained considerable traction. On September 7, 2016 the Council on Foreign Relations published the prominent paper "A Sharper Choice on North Korea: Engaging China for a Stable Northeast Asia," which in its opening paragraph directly blamed Beijing for North Korea's expanding nuclear and missile capabilities due to its failure to more actively support Western efforts. It thus advocated "a major diplomatic effort to elevate the issue to the top of the U.S.-China bilateral relationship." The CFR paper notably further called for raising a threat of military action against North Korea, and thus threatening to start a major war on China's border, if Beijing failed to comply.[4] This approach had already had some successes, with a key achievement of the Obama administration in its final year being its breakthrough in pressing Beijing and Moscow to approve a tremendous expansion of the scope of the sanctions regime imposed through the UN Security Council from March 2016 (see below).

On September 9, 2016, two days after the CFR paper's publication, and hours after North Korea fifth nuclear test, Defense Secretary Ashton Carter advocated a strategy that mirrored the paper's approach, emphasizing: "China has and shares an important responsibility for this development and has an important responsibility to reverse it... it's important that it [China] use its location, its history and its influence to further the denuclearization of the Korean peninsula."[5] This approach was strongly endorsed by other prominent figures in Washington, with State Secretary John Kerry advocating a similar course of action three days before he left office.[6] Despite significant disruptions in the transition between the Obama and Trump administrations, the latter would largely continue its predecessor's strategy of attempting to leverage Sino-U.S. interdependence to press Beijing to pressurize Pyongyang.

In his annual New Year's address, which in January 2017 focused primarily on economic programs, Chairman Kim Jong Un lauded the first test of a thermonuclear warhead and announced that his country was "entering the final stage of preparation for the test launch of an intercontinental ballistic missile," which would "remarkably raise the strategic position of the DPRK."[7] President-elect Donald Trump responded the following day on Twitter: "North Korea just stated that it is in the final stages of developing a nuclear weapon capable of reaching parts of the U.S. It won't happen!"[8] His second tweet later that day lamented: "China has been taking out massive amounts of money & wealth from the U.S. in totally one-sided trade, but won't help with North Korea. Nice!"[9] Trump administration officials on multiple occasions indicated that the terms of future trade Sino-U.S. agreements would be significantly influenced by the extent of Chinese cooperation on North Korea,[10] with hopes widely expressed in the West that pressing Beijing to better enforce UN Security Council sanctions could force the DPRK's economy into crisis.[11]

While pressuring China yielded gains at the UN, the approach had serious unforeseen limitations primarily because, while the Western sources continued to portray North Korea's missile and nuclear programs as unacceptable to the world, the only serious opposition to it came from the Western world, Japan and to lesser extents South Korea and Israel. China, like the majority of the international community, was interested not in sanctions enforcement per se but rather in providing the illusion of enforcement to placate Western demands, with Western sources' ability to confirm or deny enforcement along the highly porous border with North Korea being highly limited. While China did not present the CIA and other Western intelligence agencies with the "intelligence black hole" that North Korea did, it still retained one of the world's most challenging security systems for them to operate in,[12] with reports of extensive tunnel networks for underground smuggling further limiting Western options to quantify cross-border trade.[13] Experts described Sino–North Korean trade as occurring through "remarkably robust networks that can support cross-border trade in adverse conditions," with traders highly adept at evading restrictions particularly if Chinese authorities turned a blind eye.[14]

Across the remainder of the non-Western world, it was the fear of Western reprimand and secondary sanctions, rather than a genuine will to act against North Korea, which motivated states to comply with the sanctions regime. As a result, so long as information on trading relations could be concealed from the West, these relations were maintained. Indeed, Western officials and analysts had for years lamented the majority of UN member states' reluctance to turn in reports on sanctions implementation, which by 2016 stood at just 20 percent, almost all of them from the Western world. Non-Western member states also consistently refrained from targeting North Korean shipping for inspections and seizures as obliged by the sanctions regime.[15] From Namibia, Ethiopia, Angola, Senegal and Uganda to Sri Lanka, India, Thailand and

Algeria, across the world even those non-Western states expressing willingness to comply with Western-led economic warfare efforts consistently in practice refrained from doing so, with China's own policies reflecting its alignment with this broad international consensus.[16] This led Western experts on the sanctions regime to liken enforcement to "a game of 'whack-a-mole,'"[17] in which the U.S., European Union and individual European states were consistently forced to issue threats against countries across the world found not to be enforcing sanctions, as almost none seemed genuinely incentivized to comply.

A second notable cause for the failure of efforts to pressure North Korea through China was a general misunderstanding in the West of the nature of the relationship between Pyongyang and Beijing. Western assessments were consistently strongly shaped by perceptions of the former as a client of the latter, similar to the relationships the Philippines, Japan and South Korea had with the United States, or the Warsaw Pact states with the Soviet Union. While the U.S. maintained very extensive influence over the foreign and security policymaking of clients across the world, China's relations with its neighbors were premised on a wholly different model, which was reflected in the repeated statements by Beijing that it did not seek hegemony or a compromising of the sovereignty of others.[18] The fact that North Korea, despite being heavily dependent on Chinese trade, remained fiercely independent in its governance, bore strong testament to this, as did numerous other examples both historical and current of Chinese relationships with small states.[19,i]

---

i *Foreign Policy* magazine went as far as to suggest in 2017 that the Korean crisis could be solved by a permanent presence of tens of thousands of Chinese military personnel in North Korea. While mirroring American personnel deployments in over 200 countries at the time, including close to 30,000 in South Korea, this was wholly at odds with the nature of Sino–North Korean ties. In sharp contrast to the Western world, incidences of permanent overseas military presences have been negligible in the 5,000-year histories of both nations, with Chinese forces having left North Korea in 1958 after the state's post-war reconstruction was complete. (Frye, Alton, 'China Should Send 30,000 Troops Into North Korea,' *Foreign Policy,* November 28, 2017.)

As observed by Defense & Strategy Fellow at the Center for Strategic Studies Van Jackson: "A blanket error of U.S. policymakers since the 1960s has been the incorrect assumption that the Chinese or the Soviets might control North Korea, when the reality was always that no outside power could."[20] Reflecting the consensus view in the Western world, President Trump similarly alluded to a belief in a neo-colonial Sino–North Korean relationship on multiple occasions, stating when on campaign in 2016 that "China has control – absolute control – over North Korea."[21]

Much as had been the case in Obama's final year, and as advocated in the CFR paper, at the core of Trump administration efforts to pressure China was the raising of the possibility of military action against its neighbor. Having tweeted on March 31 that "the meeting with China next week will be a very difficult one," Trump warned three days later on April 3: "China has great influence over North Korea. And China will either decide to help us with North Korea or they won't... If they do, that will be very good for China, and if they don't, it won't be good for anyone... if China is not going to solve North Korea, we will. That is all I am telling you."[22] This was widely seen to imply that Beijing was being presented with a choice between providing greater support with sanctions or forcing Washington to take military action.

Following months of speculation that President Trump could make a breakthrough on North Korea in his first meeting with his Chinese counterpart Xi Jinping, who visited Mar-a-Lago on April 6–7, Trump proceeded to send a strong signal as the two dined on the second evening. During dinner the U.S. Navy launched 59 cruise missiles in a major strike on military sites in Syria, a close economic and security partner of both China and North Korea, with Trump reportedly leaning over to Xi mid-meal to inform him of the attack.[23] This was particularly significant since Beijing had consistently blocked Western efforts either to sanction Damascus though the UN Security Council, or to authorize military action against it, which made the unprovoked attack entirely illegal and Trump's statement highly provocative. The attack demonstrated Washington's readiness sidestep the Security Council and launch attacks in direct and brazen violation of international law, and to do so in a conflict with far lower stakes for U.S. security interests than that in Korea. The implications of this for the Korean conflict were highly significant.

In the aftermath of the meeting President Trump appeared to have been persuaded that Sino-DPRK relations were far more complex than he had believed, and that options for pressuring China on the issue were thus limited. "After listening for 10 minutes, I realized it's not so easy," the president told the *Wall Street Journal* on April 12. "I felt pretty strongly that they had a tremendous power [over] North Korea. ... But it's not what you would think," he recalled. Trump nevertheless confirmed that he had offered China better terms on a trade deal then under discussion in exchange for help on the issue.[24]

Policy Shift Under the Trump Administration

Shortly before leaving office, President Obama had advised his successor that North Korea would represent his administration's toughest foreign policy challenge.[25] Obama and his administration would be sharply criticized by Trump for their failure, alongside the preceding Bush and Clinton administrations, to stall North Korea's nuclear and missile programs,[26] with similar criticisms leveled by several prominent analysts,[27] and by a number of officials such as National Security Advisor H. R. McMaster.[28] The fact that North Korea would within little over half a year cross Washington's red line for its deterrence program, namely with the attainment of an intercontinental range nuclear delivery capability, showed that the new administration had from the outset had very little room to maneuver on the issue.

By the end of President Obama's second term it was increasingly clear that a consensus had emerged on the need for a major policy shift, and that more radical policies including military options either to set back nuclear and missile development, or else to totally dismantle the state, needed to be seriously considered. Much as the preceding George W. Bush administration's "anything but Clinton" policy outlook had led to major changes at the beginning of its first term, however, so too did the Trump administration initially appear willing to make major changes to foreign policy. The most notable indicator was the new president's withdrawal from the Trans-Pacific Partnership trade agreement within 48 hours in office, which had been one of Obama's most central policy focuses and a fundamental cornerstone of the Pivot to Asia initiative and the economic containment of China. On North Korea, too, where Trump's rival for the presidency, Democratic Party nominee Hillary Clinton, was surrounded by much of the same foreign policy establishment as Obama, a number of whom were even more vocal in advocating a military assault, a change in administration that was far from smooth allowed much of the consensus and momentum for such action to dissipate.

Having been set to become one of the most influential figures on Clinton's foreign policy team, former undersecretary of state Wendy Sherman had openly advocated efforts to topple the North Korean state,[29] with other figures associated with the candidate advocating similarly hard lines.[30] Retired Admiral James Stavridis, a leading Clinton advisor, also advocated escalating cyber warfare and, if necessary, a kinetic assault to set back North Korea's nuclear and missile development.[31] Clinton had herself promised harsher sanctions,[32] sustainment of high preconditions for negotiations,[33] and greater state sponsored publicity for alleged DPRK human rights abuses.[34] Her leading rival for party nomination Bernie Sanders had had a similarly long history of supporting military interventions abroad, from the assault on Yugoslavia to the Iraq Liberation Act. Unlike Clinton or Trump, he had singled out North Korea as the greatest threat to the United States to advocate maximum pressure on the country.[35]

Donald Trump by contrast expressed a willingness to personally negotiate with and even a degree of praise for the North Korean leadership,[36] including readiness to share "a burger on a conference table" with Chairman Kim,[37] and to receive him at the White House.[38] Trump consistently strongly criticized his predecessors' history of military interventionism, pledging to pull American forces out of Afghanistan and South Korea as part of a broader policy shift.[39] While these stances were slammed as isolationism by allies in Europe,[40] and by the Democratic Party establishment,[41] and were highly contrary to those of the U.S. foreign policy establishment,[42] they were important to much of the new president's support base.[43]

As president, Trump quickly came into conflict with the foreign policy establishment, with clashes with the CIA and the wider intelligence community surfacing repeatedly.[44] These institutions as a result increasingly conducted foreign policy independently of the presidency,[45] with direct contradictions with the military,[46] the State Department,[47] and the intelligence services,[48] all arising frequently, as did clashes within the White House as the vice president and national security advisor opposed Trump's policies.[49]

As observed by intelligence & judiciary committees GOP counsel Steve Castor, commenting on the case of President Trump's conflict with the intelligence community over aid to Ukraine: "a lot of the inner agency officials, I think, became very sad that the president didn't revere their policy-making apparatus... I think the president is skeptical of the inter-agency bureaucracy."[50] The intelligence community and foreign policy establishment were consistently strongly supported by states across the remainder of the Western world in opposing Trump's foreign policy shifts. Beyond Ukraine, a notable example was European states' strong lobbying of Washington not to withdraw forces from Syria, and their preparations to themselves take over the occupation should this fail.[51] The Pentagon openly defied the White House's orders to withdraw, with extensive measures taken to conceal this from the president and ensure that the figures he saw for the number of personnel in the country did not reflect the real size of the forces present.[52]

Two notable incidents in the Trump administration's first five months in office played central roles in shaping discourse related to North Korea away from the initially stated intention for rapprochement. The first was the assassination of Chairman Kim Jong Un's half-brother Kim Jong Nam 24 days after Trump's inauguration on February 13, 2017. This took place at Kuala Lumpur International Airport, Malaysia, in an operation which saw women of Indonesian and Vietnamese origin reportedly use VX nerve agent. Within hours South Korea's ruling party had stated with certainty that Pyongyang was responsible, terming it a "naked example of Kim Jong Un's reign of terror,"[53] with Western sources being quick to follow. Although no investigation had taken place, Western influence over the global information space was such that North Korean culpability was for all intents and purposes made fact in the eyes of the world – regardless of what the Malaysian investigators would themselves conclude. Western media focused overwhelmingly on what Western and South Korean sources had to say and effectively ignored the local investigation, which quickly cleared staff at the North Korean embassy of all suspicion. The investigation did not state that North Korea was the perpetrator,[54] and claims of Pyongyang's culpability were later dismissed as pure speculation by the Malaysian prime minister.[55]

There were considerable incentives for multiple parties to have organized Kim Jong Nam's assassination, which coincided with the Trump administration's review of policy towards North Korea that was expected to lead to a much more conciliatory line than that favored by the foreign policy and the intelligence communities. This fueled speculation of U.S. involvement, with prominent analysts concluding that the assassination was key to setting a more negative tone for the administration's position towards Pyongyang.[56] With Malaysia having had a large North Korean diaspora and being a key trading partner at a time of mounting Western economic pressure, the incident also provided an optimal means of souring relations and thus furthering Pyongyang's isolation. Kim Jong Nam was subsequently revealed to have been working as a CIA informant,[57] although as he had regularly stayed at the North Korean embassy, killing him so publicly, and doing so at a time of possible détente with the U.S., appeared unlikely. The only way North Korean culpability made sense was if it was intended as a very public show of force to demonstrate the international reach of its operatives deploying WMD.

The second incident setting the tone for relations was the release of American student Otto Warmbier to U.S. custody on June 13, 2017, 17 months after his arrest for violation of and theft from a restricted government area in Pyongyang. Having fallen into a coma, Warmbier was hospitalized as soon as he returned to the United States and died six days later.[58] His parents alleged that their son's passing was the result of torture in North Korea, which was widely re-reported across Western media but sharply contradicted the assessments of coroners in the United States. Warmbier's father, for example, had made an emotionally charged statement that: "His bottom teeth look like they had taken a pair of pliers and rearranged them," directly contradicting the subsequent assessment of Hamilton County Coroner's Office, which examined his body, that: "the teeth are natural and in good repair." Addressing the statements by Warmbier's parents, which were widely re-reported by a number of media outlets, Coroner Dr. Lakshmi Kode Sammarco stated: "I felt very comfortable that there wasn't any evidence of trauma. We were surprised at the [parents'] statement." She said her team, which included a forensic dentist, thoroughly evaluated and assessed various scans of his body.[59] Warmbier's parents declined to comment on the Coroner's report, and notably refused to allow an autopsy which could determine the cause of their son's death, before subsequently seeking half a billion dollars in compensation through American courts.[60] Forensic scientists were highly critical of the unusual and unexpected decision not to perform an autopsy.[61] In line with predominant Western metanarratives surrounding North Korea, however, the narrative of death by torture pervaded, personalizing the conflict with the story of unusually cruel treatment of an American youth.[ii]

With the deaths of Kim Jong Nam and Otto Warmbier having considerably influenced U.S. public sentiments, a policy shift on

---

ii Brain tissue damage from suffocation, reports of hypoxia, and a total lack of trauma or injury on the rest of the body, were consistent with an attempted suicide by hanging, which a number of analysts speculated was the likely cause. A blood clot, pneumonia, sepsis, kidney failure, and sleeping pills were also cited as potential causes and could have stopped Warmbier from breathing if he had botulism and was paralyzed from it. Warmbier reportedly had had a neurological injury "for 15 months or so" according to U.S. sources, indicating he may have been in poor health before entering Korean custody. (Basu, Zachary, 'What we're reading: What happened to Otto Warmbier in North Korea,' *Axios*, July 25, 2018.) (Fox, Maggie, 'What killed Otto Warmbier?,' *NBC News*, June 20, 2017.)

North Korea was politically unviable. With rapprochement ruled out, the Trump administration in its first six months in office appeared to be rapidly running out of options reach a favorable conclusion to the escalating conflict with North Korea, with the country's economy remaining stable under unprecedented sanctions while its policymakers continued to appear unphased by military threats and diplomatic pressure.

"Changing the Entire Structure of the World": North Korea Completes its Missile Deterrent

Following the successful testing of the aforementioned Pukkuksong-2 solid fueled medium range ballistic missile on February 11 and May 21, more advanced successors to the intermediate range Hwasong-10 and intercontinental range Hwasong-13 were quickly unveiled and tested. Facilitating these advances was the landmark ground test of a much improved new liquid propellant rocket engine on the morning of March 18, named the March 18 Revolution engine, which state media described as an "unforgettable day for the DPRK's rocket development history" and a milestone in the history of the country's defense industry. The highly auspicious nature of the test would become increasingly clear over the next nine months, with the new engine boasting a much higher thrust compared to previous models, leading to its variants being used to power the three major new strategic missile classes unveiled and launched during that time.[62] The test's importance was reflected in the particularly widespread coverage its five year anniversary would gain in March 2022.[63] American missile expert Jeffrey Lewis would summarize that the new engine "represents a new era in which North Korea has progressed from copying Soviet engines to designing its own engines for a new generation of more capable missiles."[64]

Directly succeeding the Hwasong-10, the first missile using the next generation March 18 engine was the intermediate range Hwasong-12, which saw three failed test flights on April 4, 15 and 28, before a highly successful test on May 14 and two more on August 29 and September 15. Dubbed "Guam Killer" by analysts, the missile revolutionized North Korean strike capabilities against American facilities on the island territory. Some sources estimated the missile had a 6,000 kilometer range, which would allow it to strike targets on Wake Island and Alaska, although more conservative estimates placed its range at 4,000–4,500 kilometers. Much as the successful testing of the intermediate range Hwasong-10 had raised considerable concern in the West due to the relatively small size of the technological leap needed to perfect the Hwasong-13 ICBM, so too was the Hwasong-12 seen as a stepping stone to a more capable ICBM class. As summarized by Jeffrey Lewis: "it became clear that this was an entirely new missile, with a new engine and improved design characteristics... it displayed all the technologies necessary to build a missile that can strike the United States." "If we wish to understand North Korea's ICBM program, we must start with the Hwasong-12," Lewis noted, adding that its capabilities "signaled that North Korea's missile program has entered a new phase with far more capable missiles."[65]

On July 4 North Korea conducted the first confirmed launch of an intercontinental range ballistic missile. This landmark test was met with particularly harsh rhetorical responses from across the Western world, while sparking mass celebrations in the DPRK itself.[iii] Designated Hwasong-14, the missile's introduction represented a profound and irrevocable shift in the balance of power between North Korea and the United States in their 70 year long

---

iii Having been in Pyongyang at the time of the launch, the writer witnessed the streets of the city center flooded with thousands of men in suits and women in traditional dress dancing and singing, with part of the elated crowd moving towards Kim Il Sung Square where an announcement by Workers' Party officials regarding the significance of the landmark missile test was made. As the writer's specialization in East Asian security affairs was known, he was repeatedly questioned regarding what the successful test of the Hwasong-14 meant for the country. While people showed a great deal of pride in their missile program, there was genuine concern that the new U.S. administration would launch a military attack. Initially, thinking based on the description that the missile tested was an enhanced Hwasong-13 – the only North Korea ICBM known before that day – the writer assured them that the new missile meant mutual vulnerability with the United States mainland had been achieved, and that this would very likely take American military options off the table to guarantee their future security.

conflict, and with an estimated 10,000 kilometer range it could engage targets across approximately half of the American mainland. In contrast to the Hwasong-13 ICBM, which in the five years since it was first displayed was never confirmed to have been flight tested, the Hwasong-14's existence was only disclosed on the day of its first test launch. Mirroring Hwasong-13's significant commonalities in engine and other technologies with the Hwasong-10, the new ICBM had similar commonalities with the Hwasong-12.

Where the United States had from 1950 demonstrated the ability to firebomb Korean cities from end to end with nuclear-capable strategic bombers, the introduction of genuine mutual vulnerability between the population centers of the U.S. and DPRK ensured that American cities would be firmly in the line of fire for nuclear strikes if a similar mass targeting of Korean civilians reoccurred. While the Soviet Union and China had previously gained intercontinental range nuclear strike capabilities, the former in 1949 using bombers and ten years later with the R-7 ICBM, and the latter in 1981 with the DF-5 ICBM, 2017 represented the first time a medium or small state gained the power to effectively deter a superpower at such a peer level without relying on the nuclear umbrella of a superpower sponsor. This historically unprecedented achievement was later referred to by Vice Chairman of the Joint Chiefs of Staff and former Commander of the U.S. Strategic Command John Hyten as having "changed the entire structure of the world."[66]

The Hwasong-14 saw a second flight test on July 28, and again demonstrated the range required to deliver nuclear strikes across much of North America. Eleven days later on August 8 the *Washington Post* published part of a leaked Defense Intelligence Agency assessment confirming this capability, estimating that North Korea fielded approximately 60 nuclear warheads and was capable of miniaturizing them sufficiently for mounting on an ICBM.[67] U.S. intelligence specifically confirmed to the press that North Korea was thought to have developed a viable re-entry vehicle for its ICBMs, which was one of the greatest challenges common to both intermediate and intercontinental range missile development due to the immense temperatures endured when re-entering the atmosphere at extreme speeds.[68] Confidence in North Korea's development of re-entry vehicles had been increased by the release of images in 2016 showing a static test of an ablative carbon-composite tip for such a vehicle, in which a rocket engine simulated the heat of the re-entry environment. The Chemical Materials Institute in Hamhung, which produced carbon composite components, was thought to be responsible. Modern advances in materials science such as carbon-composite materials made reentry vehicles much easier to develop than in the Cold War era, when the Chinese, Soviets and Americans had all struggled to do so. Confirmation that U.S. intelligence believed North Korea had demonstrated the capability to deliver nuclear retaliation against much of the American mainland was widely considered by analysts to be a major turning point in the decades-long conflict.

North Korea's mounting technological successes over a very short period, and with a relatively small defense budget, totally contradicted the prevailing Western metanarrative of a state that was inept, insane, backward and among the world's most corrupt. Western sources accordingly widely attempted to rationalize the new developments with extensive speculation attributing the advances to external support – whether from Russia, Ukraine or China. The London-based International Institute for Strategic Studies, for example, on August 14 published a report stating with a high degree of certainty that new high performance missile engines had been smuggled from Ukraine or Russia, although this was quickly dismissed by American intelligence officials.[69] "We have intelligence to suggest that North Korea is not reliant on imports of engines," one official told *Reuters*, adding: "Instead, we judge they have the ability to produce the engines themselves."[70]

Four years prior in 2013, widespread Western portrayals of North Korea's missile program as running on smuggled parts and illicit transfers from communist or former communist states were seriously undermined by South Korean Defense Ministry reports on the country's satellite launch vehicles after their recovery. The vehicles were found to have been produced almost entirely domestically and had no sensitive foreign components or technologies. The South Korean Agency for Defense Development observed:

"The foreign parts would have been easy to buy, even by someone who was traveling," and included DC converters, temperature sensors and a number of other electronic devices for everyday use that did not fall under the UN sanctions regime. Local media concluded at the time: "it appears unlikely that North Korea smuggled in these parts, as was suggested by certain groups."[71] The indications this had for the diversity and sophistication of the North Korean industrial base were wholly at odds with prevailing Western worldviews and portrayals of the country, leading to significant signs of cognitive dissonance among a large number of analysts as such findings were consistently overlooked. The IISS report on missiles using smuggled engines was a case in point.[iv]

Much like the technologies and components in the missiles themselves, North Korea's advanced hypergolic liquid rocket propellants were widely claimed by Western sources to have been imported from Russia or China. This, too, was debunked by a number of studies as well as by U.S. intelligence. A study by the James Martin Center for Non-Proliferation Studies at Middlebury College was particularly detailed in its findings, which showed that North Korea had developed highly secure supply chains for its missile program.[72] The study showed that even the fuel used by missiles, known as unsymmetrical dimethylhydrazine (UMDH), was synthesized in a known chemical plant in the country using technologies which also had applications in synthetic textile manufacturing.[73] Thus even a complete oil embargo, which the United States and its European allies were strongly pushing to be imposed through the UN Security Council, would be limited in its ability to force an end to missile testing.[74]

Director of the James Martin Center's East Asia Nonproliferation Program Jeffrey Lewis noted following the

---

iv The means by which Western assessments sought to justify the significant contradictions between demonstrated advances by North Korea's defense sector and prevailing Western portrayals of the country were notably far from unusual. Another notable example was the strong tendency for almost any major technological advances seen in China to be widely attributed by Western sources to industrial espionage. This continued despite the Chinese technologies being referred to by the late 2010s in many cases having no Western equivalents.

publication of findings that predominant Western depictions of North Korea sharply contrasted with its technological achievements, of which the missile program was a prime example. "If you watch them in satellite photos and read their technical publications, it looks like a totally different country... We're in full-scale denial about North Korea's capabilities," he concluded.[75] Leading American expert on the missile program Ankit Panda observed to much the same effect: "With everything we've seen out of North Korea this year, we should both stop being surprised when they demonstrate increasingly more impressive capabilities and also stop underestimating the extent of their knowhow. In the end, *Juche*, the ideology of self-reliance at the core of the North Korean project since the founding of country, is there for more than just show."[76]

War Preparations and Intimidation Under Trump

Following the publication on August 8 of a leaked Defense Intelligence Agency assessment confirming the intelligence community's belief in a North Korean nuclear ICBM capability, President Trump that day warned: "North Korea best not make any more threats to the United States. They will be met with fire and fury like the world has never seen."[77] "Fire and Fury" was the term President Harry Truman had used to describe mass firebombing and nuclear attacks on Japanese population centers, which remain the deadliest in human history. With the very similar firebombing of population centers across Korea that began five years later being deeply ingrained in North Korean historical memory, President Trump, whether intentionally or not, was evoking the incidents that had been at the heart of Pyongyang's rationale for developing a deterrent capability to begin with. Nevertheless, his statement fell short of an indication of intent to attack. Coming eleven days after the second Hwasong-14 launch it appeared to be an effort to limit the public relations fallout from his administration's apparent failure to stop Pyongyang's missile development through "tough talk" – a strategy the president used throughout his term.

Pyongyang responded to Trump's statement in kind, and brandishing the newly demonstrated capabilities of the Hwasong-12 it within hours warned that it was considering a strike to create "an enveloping fire" around Guam. Korean People's Army General Kim Rak Gyom responded that: "Sound dialogue is not possible with such a guy bereft of reason and only absolute force can work on him."[78] Further brandishing its newly demonstrated ICBM capabilities in ways that had not been possible beforehand, the KPA Strategic Force issued the following statement:

> Will only the U.S. have the option called "preventive war" as is claimed by it? It is a daydream for the U.S. to think that its mainland is an invulnerable Heavenly Kingdom. The U.S. should clearly face up to the fact that the ballistic rockets of the Strategic Force of the KPA are now on constant standby, facing the Pacific Ocean and pay deep attention to their azimuth angle for launch.[79,v]

Twenty days after Trump's threat, the United States National Nuclear Security Administration announced a flight test of a new tactical nuclear weapon, the B61-12 gravity bomb, which was expected to raise particularly high concerns in North Korea. These variable yield precision guided warheads were expected to be used to neutralize North Korea's large ground forces and underground fortifications in the event of war, and represented precisely the kind of American nuclear assets most dangerous to the country's security.[80] The bombs' high precision, and their ability to be primed to detonate with yields as low as 300 tons, made them highly "usable" on the battlefield in ways that nuclear warheads

---

v Director for nonproliferation policy at the Arms Control Association Kelsey Davenport assessed these statements as follows: "I think North Korea has typically responded to threats with threats, to provocations with provocations. In part, North Korea is responding to the dangerous and bellicose rhetoric of President Trump." She observed that Pyongyang was nevertheless "keeping the door open for negotiations, if the United States rolls back its more hostile posturing and rhetoric." (Boghani, Priyanka, 'The U.S. and North Korea On The Brink: A Timeline,' *PBS*, February 28, 2019.)

of the Korean War era had not remotely been, with accuracy improved considerably compared to prior B61 variants. Weighing just 320 kilograms, they were deployable from even America's lightest single engine fighter the F-16, while a B-2 stealth bomber could drop up to sixteen per sortie. The need to deter possible use of American tactical nuclear weapons to nullify North Korea's conventional forces was widely assessed to be a primary factor that had stimulated its pursuit of a nuclear deterrent.

Five days after the announcement of a B61-12 test, KCNA on September 2 announced the completion of a new variable yield thermonuclear warhead: "The H-bomb, the explosive power of which is adjustable from tens to hundreds of kilotons, is a multi-functional thermonuclear nuke with great destructive power which can be detonated even at high altitudes for super-powerful EMP attack according to strategic goals."[81] Photos of Chairman Kim inspecting the new warhead were released at the time, with the leader personally elaborating: "All components of the H-bomb were homemade and all the processes ... were put on the Juche basis, thus enabling the country to produce powerful nuclear weapons as many as it wants."[82] In the aftermath of two successful Hwasong-14 tests, the warhead was announced to be sufficiently miniaturized for intercontinental range launches.

The new "two-stage thermonuclear weapon" was detonated hours later in the early morning of September 3,[83] and while Western sources had in the preceding hours widely expressed skepticism regarding the new bomb, they proved significantly more widely accepting of North Korean claims after this nuclear test than they had following previous tests.[84] Director of proliferation and nuclear policy at the Royal United Services Institute Tom Plant, for one, observed: "The North Koreans do bluff sometimes, but when they make a concrete claim about their nuclear programme, more often than not it turns out to be true... I think the balance is in favour of it being a thermonuclear bomb rather than a conventional atom bomb."[85] The head of U.S. Strategic Command John E. Hyten stated 12 days after the test that he assumed the same,[86] with a later CFR assessment concluding that the test "gives credence to North Korea's claims of having developed a hydrogen bomb."[87] Re-assessments of test data in 2019 were seen to more strongly support this conclusion, with the warhead's yield considered likely to exceed 200 kilotons –approximately 14 times the payload of the warhead used against Hiroshima.[88]

The nuclear test was followed by the year's third successful Hwasong-12 test launch on September 15, after which North Korea began a self-imposed moratorium on further missile or nuclear testing. This moratorium was widely interpreted as being intended to signal Pyongyang's readiness to begin dialogue, and was followed by a statement by U.S. Special Representative for North Korea Policy Joe Yun confirming that continuing this pause on launches would signal its seriousness about negotiating.[89] The September 15 launch was interpreted by a number of Western analysts as having been conducted to minimize provocation and signal Pyongyang's readiness to open dialogue, with the missile targeted far to the north of Guam where it landed far from any potential targets, meaning Pyongyang did not follow through on earlier pledges to fire into the sea near American bases there.[90] The beginning of the moratorium followed remarks by Chairman Kim Jong Un a month prior on August 14 which were widely seen as conciliatory both by U.S. analysts and by members of the Trump administration.[91]

Four days after the test launch President Trump addressed the United Nations General Assembly on September 19 and stated: "the United States has great strength and patience, but if it is forced to defend itself or its allies, we will have no choice but to totally destroy North Korea. Rocket Man [Chairman Kim] is on a suicide mission for himself and for his regime. The United States is ready, willing and able, but hopefully this will not be necessary." Trump's statement appeared to be intended more as a show of strength and resolve than as a sign the U.S. actually had a plan to roll back advances in North Korea's weapons programs with military action.[vi] Similar statements by the president

vi To place President Trump's statement in perspective, President Obama previously warned that the U.S. could "destroy North Korea with our arsenals" in April 2016. While Trump had warned Pyongyang of the consequences of an attack on America or its allies – a moot point since

over the past month, while using extremely bellicose language, consistently threatened only retaliation to a hypothetical DPRK attack rather than indicating an intent to initiate hostilities.[92] Thus while of the president's critics depicted his UN statement as a threat of genocide, the threat of genocidal retaliation against a prior act of war still fell far short of professing hostile intent.[93] The statement was nevertheless credited with blunting what was widely seen as an opening for diplomacy, following speculation that delegations from the two countries could use sidelines of the General Assembly for informal meetings.[94,vii]

Chairman Kim was quick to deride President Trump as "mentally deranged" and "a rogue and a gangster fond of playing with fire," vowing to make him "pay dearly for his speech calling for totally destroying the DPRK."[95] Speaking at the UN four days later, Foreign Minister Ri Yong Ho stressed that Pyongyang's "ultimate goal is to establish the balance of power with the U.S.," highlighting the U.S. president's rhetoric to stress that the country's "national nuclear force is, to all intents and purposes, a war

---

the likelihood of Pyongyang itself initiating hostilities was negligible – Obama's threat made no mention of a Korean attack as a precondition for it to "destroy" the country. Rather, his threat appeared to be a reiteration of the option for massive assault to end the state's existence, which was at the time under consideration in the White House. Calls by a wide range of figures, from Ashton Carter to Philip Zelikow, for unprovoked preventative attacks on the country since the early 1990s were similarly far more provocative than Trump's threat of retaliation. (Blair, David, '"We could destroy you," Obama warns "erratic" North Korean leader,' *The Telegraph*, April 26, 2016.)

vii This was hardly the only time President Trump used extremely bellicose rhetoric in a purely hypothetical context to cover for a far more nuanced and at times conciliatory policy. In July 2019, for example, he stated regarding the war in Afghanistan: "if I wanted to win that war, Afghanistan would be wiped off the face of the earth. It would be gone. It would be over in – literally, in 10 days. And I don't want to do – I don't want to go that route." Such rhetoric gave cover to his subsequent moves to draw down the U.S. military presence and deescalate the war in coordination with Pakistan, effectively pre-empting critics who might claim that he was weak on defense. With Washington by September increasingly restricted in its options, and already applying maximum pressure against the DPRK, the bombast of Trump's UN address could effectively cover America's inability to respond effectively. (Shalizi, Hamid, 'Kabul seeks clarification on Trump talk of wiping out Afghanistan,' *Reuters*, July 23, 2019.)

deterrent for putting an end to nuclear threat of the U.S. and for preventing its military invasion."[96] The Foreign Ministry subsequently threatened to shoot down American bombers, which were carrying out frequent mock sorties near its airspace, with ambiguity regarding how far the North Koreans were willing to go used to put pressure on their adversaries. In the eyes of the Pentagon leadership, well aware of the KPA's Cold War era history of attacks on its ships and aircraft operating in or near its territory, there were concerns that the state's new long-range missile deterrent had the potential to embolden it to pursue a more active defense of its airspace.

Both the foreign policy establishment and lawmakers in Washington appeared divided over the course of action after the July Hwasong-14 tests, and moreso after the September nuclear test, with a number of outspoken voices advocating a limited "bloody nose" strike which they believed would not be met with a nuclear response.[97] Arguments for such a strike were undermined, however, when the Office of the Chairman of the Joint Chiefs of Staff made clear in October that North Korea's nuclear program could not be totally neutralized with anything short of a full ground invasion, meaning U.S. objectives could only be obtained militarily through full scale war which would guarantee a full nuclear response.[98] This growing consensus was later summarized as follows by Former Director of National Intelligence Admiral Dennis Blair:

> With all the tunnels they have, with all of the difficulties of intelligence in that country, I don't think an American–South Korean strike would have a high probability of taking out all of their nuclear capability and then you've left them with not only with nuclear capability but also an aggrieved sense of it... a lot of this talk about you know, sneak up on them and give them a bloody nose, be unpredictable, I think is not correct for dealing with a country like North Korea.[99]

Although evaluations of the consequences of an attack had by the middle of the year shifted the prevailing discourse, mirroring the events of 1993–94, 2001–2003 and 2016, reports of U.S. preparations for war in major American news outlets still pervaded. Many of these were later debunked as false. The extent to which Washington was posturing in subsequent months, hoping to intimidate Pyongyang into conceding, remains uncertain. CIA Director Mike Pompeo, Defense Secretary James Mattis, Vice President Mike Pence, National Security Advisor H. R. McMaster and Ambassador to South Korea Harry Harris, and much of the National Security Council had all reportedly continued to advocate military action, while there was a strong demand across the Western world for a harsh response. It was subsequently reported that an evacuation operation was being planned to remove American civilians from South Korea, that U.S. Navy surface ships were given "warning orders" to program North Korean targets into their guidance systems,[100] and that nuclear-capable bombers in the Pacific being placed on 24-hour alert – a state of readiness unheard of since the Cold War.[101]

On October 17 it was reported that a U.S. Navy Ohio Class nuclear submarine carrying over 60 SEALs special operations personnel had docked in South Korea. With their reputation burnished by the assassination of Osama Bin Laden six years prior, these units were tasked with infiltrating North Korea and assassinating its leadership in the event of war.[102] Operations Plan 5015 would see U.S. and South Korean units cooperate closely on such assassinations,[103] although with efforts to infiltrate hostile forces into North Korea having a long history of tremendous failure widely equated with suicide missions,[104] experts raised serious questions regarding the possibility such missions had of success.[105] The following day it was reported that the U.S. Air Force redeployed 816,393 bombs (1.5 million pounds of munitions) to Andersen Air Force Base on Guam – the base from which American strategic bombers would be deployed to strike North Korea in the event of war and a supply hub for any air campaign in the Pacific.[106]

Five days later on October 23 the nuclear powered U.S. Navy Nimitz Class supercarrier the *USS Theodore Roosevelt* entered the

Western Pacific with a full strike group, bringing the number of strike groups in the region to three. The *Roosevelt's* deployment marked the first time since 2007 that three 100,000-ton supercarriers were deployed for a joint operation, with the groups between them able to deploy approximately 190 F-18E/F fighters and E/A-18G attack jets as well as a range of supporting assets and massive missile defense and cruise missile arsenals. From November 11 the three strike groups carried out joint four-day exercises near the Korean Peninsula to demonstrate the Navy's "unique capability to operate multiple carrier strike groups as a coordinated strike force effort," and were joined on November 12 by a Japanese Izumo Class carrier and two destroyers.[107] The carrier groups then linked up with seven South Korean warships including two destroyers. The ability to deploy such tremendous quantities of firepower across the ocean to North Korea's doorstep was among the notable indicators of the tremendous asymmetry between the global superpower and the small garrison state, which had changed only from mid-2017 as ICBMs gave the KPA a similarly long reach.

On November 16 the U.S. Strategic Command published a statement on Twitter with an ominous nuclear threat that played on Pyongyang's longstanding concerns. The statement claimed that the U.S. retained secret nuclear weapons silos in South Korea, which Pyongyang had long suspected. Not only had international inspectors never verified their withdrawal from the country, but declassified documents in 2004 confirmed American nuclear weapons had remained in Korea for at least seven years after Washington and Seoul claimed they had been withdrawn, providing some grounds for prevailing concern.[108] The Strategic Command further claimed that B-1B bombers, which were supposedly denuclearized after the Cold War, retained the ability to deploy nuclear warheads. These bombers had in the preceding months very frequently launched mock bombing runs near North Korea.[109] Whether this statement was intended to play on Pyongyang's fears, or whether there was any truth to its assertions, remained uncertain.

Further heightening tensions, it was revealed on September 20 that an unusually high-profile inspection of U.S. logistics and evacuation preparations in South Korea had been made, with senior officials visiting especially to oversee this.[110] Such a non-combatant evacuation operation would be standard procedure preceding an attack on North Korea – and was thus met with considerable apprehension in both Pyongyang and Seoul. The following day American civilians in South Korea widely received messages instructing them to evacuate immediately, which U.S. Forces Korea subsequently denied having sent out.[111]

With Pyongyang having maintained a missile testing moratorium from September 15, and otherwise indicated a more conciliatory position to pave the way for dialogue, Washington appeared to have taken this as a sign of weakness and a cue to escalate. President Trump accordingly said these concessions were a sign that Chairman Kim "is starting to respect us,"[112] with the U.S. further increasing military and economic pressure potentially hoping for the beginnings of a capitulation by Pyongyang. With the moratorium not reciprocated, and Joe Yun subsequently dismissed, the lesson for North Korea was clear: any departure from its long-maintained position of responding to American pressure with reciprocal pressure would only embolden its adversary.

The escalation of U.S.-led military exercises near North Korean territory in November, which simulated an assault on the country, alongside continued calls in the West for military action, added urgency for Pyongyang to reiterate the U.S. mainland's vulnerability. This was only worsened by the announcement on November 24 that the U.S. and South Korea would launch Vigilant Ace military drills from December 5, which would see a vast array of assets deployed to simulate a mass offensive against North Korea.[113] Drills were massive in scale, involving tens of thousands of personnel along with the largest air contingent in the history of the two countries' exercises at over 270 aircraft including B-1B bombers, EA-18G electronic attack jets, F-15 and F-22 fighters, and special forces "decapitation units." Pyongyang protested the exercises as "a grave military provocation that could lead to a nuclear war," and accordingly ended its strategic weapons testing moratorium four days later on November 28 with the landmark successful launch of an even longer ranged ICBM than the Hwasong-14 – the Hwasong-15.

Facing prevailing calls in the United States for military action before the North Korean arsenal could further mature, the testing of a second ICBM class provided an effective response which would seriously dissuade such action. The missile demonstrated a 13,000 kilometer range allowing it to strike the entire American mainland including Washington, D.C. and New York City.[114] The visibly blunter nose on its re-entry vehicle relative to that of the Hwasong-14 appeared intended to accommodate a larger payload,[viii] and it was speculated by some sources to carry multiple re-entry vehicles allowing each to deliver more than one thermonuclear warhead.[115] This much larger capacity also dispelled any remaining doubts regarding whether warheads had been sufficiently miniaturized for ICBM launches. Summarizing the emerging consensus which the Hwasong-15 launch helped strengthen, expert Jeffrey Lewis concluded immediately after the test: "We don't have to like it, but we're going to have to learn to live with North Korea's ability to target the United States with nuclear weapons."[116] The ICBM launch appeared to mark the beginning of the end of the crisis, taking American military options more decisively off the table and stimulating a major policy shift in Washington which began to materialize early the following year.[ix]

---

viii North Korean references to the missile as carrying a "super-large heavy warhead" indicated that the Hwasong-15 may have been intended to carry a larger warhead than that deployed on the Hwasong-14, with the smaller ICBM presumably using the same warhead type as the closely related Hwasong-12.

ix Tensions surrounding Vigilant Ace nevertheless continued to grow, with the DPRK Foreign Ministry stating on December 2, two days before the exercises commenced, that President Trump was "begging for a nuclear war" through an "extremely dangerous nuclear gamble on the Korean Peninsula." White House National Security Adviser H.R. McMaster stated later that day at the Reagan National Defense Forum that the chances for war on the peninsula were "increasing every day." (Lee, Taehoon and Sterling, Joe, 'North Korea: Trump is "begging for nuclear war,"' *CNN*, December 2, 2017.) (Luncheon with National Security Advisor Lt. General H.R. McMaster, Reagan National Defense Forum, December 2, 2017.)

North Korea's Neighbors Intervene

A major landmark in the Trump administration's escalating rhetoric on North Korea came on November 29, when Ambassador to the United Nations Nikki Haley, speaking at the Security Council, classified the testing of the Hwasong-15 as an "act of aggression," and strongly indicated that Washington could launch a war if missile testing continued.[117] "If war does come, it will be because of continued acts of aggression like we witnessed yesterday," she stated, with the equation of missile testing with "aggression" being highly unusual, as similar testing was conducted by multiple countries across the world from France and the U.S. itself to India and Israel. "If war comes, make no mistake, the North Korean regime will be utterly destroyed," she added.[118] While President Trump and other officials threatened use of force, from "fire and fury" to actions "to totally destroy North Korea," it was consistently a threat of response should the country attack first. Ambassador Haley's rhetoric stood out, however, for threatening war and "utter destruction" should the country only continue to develop its weapons programs, with no condition of actual North Korean provocations or aggression needed, since she deemed weapons testing itself to be an act of aggression. The ambassador's position, if taken by the administration, represented an extreme and imminent threat to North Korean and broader regional security.[x]

x Haley's rhetoric had previously stood out from that of other administration officials as particularly aggressive, most notably with her reference on September 4 to North Korea's sixth nuclear test as grounds for military action, stating that Chairman Kim's "abusive use of missiles and his nuclear threats show that he is begging for war." "Our country's patience is not unlimited," she added at the time, indicating military action would be taken if weapons testing continued. The ambassador's statements appeared not to have reflected the administration's general stance, however, with then-CIA Director Mike Pompeo's memoir highlighting that she was widely regarded as a loose cannon who consistently failed to follow protocol, was second only to John Bolton in frequently undermining the administration, and that "Haley and her team hated [Rex] Tillerson" who ran the state department at the time. (Remarks at an Emergency UN Security Council Briefing on North Korea, United States Mission to the United Nations, September 4, 2017.) (Pompeo, Mike, *Never Give an Inch: Fighting for the America I Love,* Northampton, MA, Broadside Books, 2023 (Chapter 4).)

Pyongyang's moratorium on missile testing and calls for negotiation, having been brazenly ignored through the announcement of the Vigilant Ace drills, appeared to have the effect of winning it considerably more international sympathy. The Hwasong-15 launch was accordingly more widely understood both as having been easily preventable by Washington, and as a response to provocation by a country seeking peace rather than as a provocative act. Russia and China in particular, through statements from their foreign ministries and the Russian presidency, showed considerably greater solidarity with Pyongyang as the party seeking deescalation. This sympathy with Pyongyang's position appeared to have only been further increased in the aftermath of Nikki Haley's November 29 statement, with Russian Foreign Minister Sergei Lavrov slamming her threat as "a really bloodthirsty tirade," stressing that "if someone really wants to use force to, as the U.S. representative to the United Nations put it, destroy North Korea ...then I think that is playing with fire and a big mistake." Lavrov pledged that Russia would "do our utmost" to prevent the U.S. from starting a war.[119]

At the center of efforts to diffuse the crisis, China and Russia had long strongly advocated a "freeze for freeze" agreement at the Security Council under which North Korea would cease strategic weapons testing while the U.S. correspondingly ceased major military exercises near DPRK territory. American representatives had made clear, however, that anything less than a unilateral standing down by Pyongyang was unacceptable, with Ambassador Haley referring to propositions for mutual concessions as "insulting," on the basis that North Korea as a "rogue regime" could not be held to the same standards.[120] It would take a further strengthening of the North Korean nuclear deterrent, moving Washington's military options further off the table, as well as a further demonstration of resilience to economic warfare efforts, before the U.S. would make an unspoken acquiescence to such an agreement in 2018.

In August Russia had increased deployments of advanced long-range air defense assets near the North Korean border, providing radar and missile coverage across the country's territory. The Russian Foreign Ministry's acknowledgement that North

Korean missile tests did not threaten Russia's security,[xi] and the Defense Ministry's stated readiness to shoot down any missiles fired over North Korean territory, led these deployments to be interpreted by a number of analysts as steps by Russia to protect its neighbor from possible U.S.-led strikes.[121] Shortly after the expansion of air defense deployments, Senior Fellow at the Russian Academy of Sciences Center for Korean Studies Evgeny Kim was among those to observe that while the chances of North Korea starting a war were negligible, an American missile attack was plausible, and in such a case "of course, our [Russian] air defense systems could intercept them."[122]

Moscow and Pyongyang had signed an agreement on air defense cooperation in early 2015,[123] raising the significant possibility that their assets could be integrated as part of a single network. This could allow Russian air defense systems to provide targeting data to their North Korean counterparts, limiting the effectiveness of Western jamming, much as Russia had done to bolster Syrian missile defenses. Alongside ground-based systems, Russia had from December 2015 deployed a MiG-31BM interceptor regiment at Tsentralnaya Uglovaya Air Force Base 160 kilometers from the Korean border. These carried far larger radars than any other combat jets in the world and were well optimized both to providing air defenses with targeting data on enemy missiles, and to shooting down missiles at long ranges themselves.[124]

---

xi Reflecting what appeared to be the consensus in Moscow regarding North Korea's nuclear weapons and missile programs and their implications for regional security, prominent Russian nuclear weapons expert Vladimir Khrustalev observed: "Russia and China are not directly threatened by these [KPA] missiles. Like any other means of nuclear deterrence, they threaten those who would attack the owner of nuclear weapons. It is obvious that it makes no sense for the DPRK to 'go crazy' and press the red button for no reason... In this case, any scenario of attack on the DPRK makes no sense because the attacker would pay a price that would scare away anyone considering such attempts. In fact, it is a reproduction of the model, which was between the Soviet Union and the United States and which now exists between India and Pakistan." On this basis, he observed, North Korea's development of nuclear weapons was strongly opposed by those with offensive designs against the country. ('North Korea Reached "Point of No Return" in Obtaining Nuclear Technology,' *Sputnik News*, September 9, 2016.)

Just hours after reports emerged of Russia's expanded air defense deployment, the Chinese *Global Times* paper affiliated with the ruling Communist Party published an article warning that if America attacked North Korea, China would intervene to support Pyongyang. Beijing would otherwise "remain neutral" if North Korea initiated a conflict with the United States. This provided clarification regarding the state of the treaty alliance between the two states,[xii] with an almost total lack of signs of security cooperation having previously long raised questions regarding the validity of Chinese security guarantees.[125] Claims in the West that China would not honor treaty commitments had for years been central to many arguments for an attack on North Korea.[126] The Chinese People's Liberation Army that month deployed its own long range air defense systems near the Korean border, and in early September held nighttime drills intended to prepare for surprise attacks by hostile forces. Much like their Russian counterparts, Chinese systems such as the HQ-9B could engage targets far across the border, and were highly mobile allowing them to be quickly redeployed to operate from North Korean soil in the event of war.

Any American assault on North Korea would strongly prioritize rapid targeting of its ballistic missiles to limit the country's capacity for retaliation. The combination of KPA missiles' road mobility, shorter launch times, use of concealed and hardened underground highways and bases, and the state's tight security against enemy intelligence gathering, made such targeting particularly difficult. In parallel to signs of significant air defense modernization within North Korea, the significant possibility of Chinese and Russian intervention to intercept incoming American strikes could buy considerable time for the KPA to launch retaliatory strikes. Thus, even their limited intervention using air defense systems could contribute very considerably to North Korean deterrence capabilities, and was highly plausible as a defensive

---

xii The Treaty of Friendship, Co-operation and Mutual Assistance between the People's Republic of China and the Democratic People's Republic of Korea was first signed in July 1961, and was subsequently extended twice leaving it still in effect in 2017.

measure carrying minimal risks of escalated conflict with the United States.

In late July and early August the Chinese People's Liberation Army Navy held exercises in the Yellow Sea near the Korean coast. These were widely interpreted by analysts as shows of force aimed at the United States, with further naval drills launched near Korea in September, which particularly focused on testing Chinese warships' air defense capabilities. Chinese naval expert Li Jie reported that the drills showed that "China is prepared and able to stop any power that threatens stability in the region" and were intended to warn the United States against staging an attack on North Korea. With Washington remaining highly unpredictable, he noted, "China can only rely on more drills to raise its military capability amid an unstable situation."[127] In December Russian forces staged a show of force with the deployment of large numbers of Naval Infantry for live fire exercises little over 100 kilometers from the Korean border,[128] followed by further nearby live fire exercises by Russian air units later that month.[129]

U.S. government projections of the possible outcomes of various plans for military assaults on North Korea in 2017 were very frequently criticized as being overly optimistic, with one of the most significant outstanding shortcomings being that they totally ignored the possibility of even a limited Chinese or Russian military intervention.[130] This made Beijing and Moscow's demonstration of readiness to intervene particularly important as a means of shifting the American calculus. With DPRK air defense modernization and the building of intermediate and intercontinental range arsenals still in their early stages, the provision of Russian and Chinese support was invaluable until these capabilities could be further expanded in subsequent years to better ensure U.S. military options remained fully off the table.

Economic Sanctions at the United Nations: Gaining Beijing and Moscow's Cooperation

In parallel to the escalated sanctioning of Chinese firms and banks doing business with North Korea, and an increase in pressure on Beijing to better enforce existing UNSC sanctions, the Obama administration had in its final year made it increasingly clear that it was taking military options seriously. Mirroring the specific advice put forward in the CFR's September paper *A Sharper Choice on North Korea,* this was seen to place Washington in a strong position to demand greater Chinese and Russian support with sanctions. This had allowed the administration to achieve a watershed success on March 2, 2016 with the adoption of Security Council Resolution 2270 in response to North Korea's fourth nuclear test, which for the first time targeted its economy as a whole rather than the nuclear and missile programs specifically.[xiii] This included exports such as rare earths, iron and gold, as well as financial transactions, aviation and shipping, and banning joint ventures, ownership interest and establishment of relations with DPRK banks. Travel bans and asset freezes further targeted individuals including those involved in the scientific, mining, shipping, space exploration, trading and financial sectors. Specific further targeting of the tech sector included banning teaching North Koreans "advanced physics, advanced computer simulation and related computer sciences, geospatial navigation, nuclear engineering, aerospace engineering, aeronautical engineering and related disciplines."

The Obama administration's success in escalating sanctions through the UNSC was replicated on November 30 with the passage of UNSC Resolution 2321, which placed greater restrictions on scientific or technical cooperation and called on all UN Member States to reduce the number of staff at North Korean diplomatic

xiii Unilateral Western sanctions had targeted the wider North Korean economy for decades, and the new UNSC resolution was accompanied by an escalation in unilateral sanctions by the United States, the European Union and other Western parties as well as Japan. While sanctions had already been comprehensive, they began to target almost anything which could be sanctioned in an attempt to cripple the DPRK economy. The United States Treasury Department notably used the Patriot Act Title III: Anti-Money Laundering to Prevent Terrorism to pass particularly harsh restrictions on the DPRK's access to the international financial system – despite Pyongyang not being designated a State Sponsor of Terror at the time. ('Treasury Takes Actions to Further Restrict North Korea's Access to the U.S. Financial System,' *U.S. Department of the Treasury* (press release), June 1, 2016.)

missions. It further expanded the arms embargo to target dual-use goods, seriously restricted Pyongyang's ability to operate international cargo ships, and restricted key exports of coal, copper, nickel, silver, zinc as well as statues and transport vessels. Although far less harsh than the restrictions initially pushed for by Western states, a CFR assessment summarized that "on paper, UNSC 2321 essentially calls upon member states to place North Korea under economic quarantine unless it reverses course on nuclear development."[131] The fact that the resolution responded to the DPRK's September 9 nuclear test, but took an unprecedented 82 days to adopt, was interpreted to reflect the contentious negotiations at the Security Council to secure its passage, with Resolution 2270 having taken two months to pass apparently for similar reasons.

The passage of Resolution 2321 took place in the context of a surge in the U.S. military presence around Korea and the initiation of particularly provocative exercises simulating offensives against the north, with U.S. forces from October 10–16 leading the Invincible Spirit exercises which had an unprecedented focus on simulating attacking DPRK nuclear facilities. Also simulated were attacks on missile facilities, the killing of the North Korean leadership, and perhaps most provocatively, the razing of large parts of the capital, Pyongyang.[132] Simultaneous U.S.–South Korean exercises from 3–26 October, also involving New Zealand and NATO forces, had further simulated air operations against the country.[133] As had been highlighted in the CFR September paper, the presentation of military action as an alternative to sanctions appeared to have been key to Western efforts to gain China's cooperation with the sanctions regime, with the Invincible Spirit exercises launched in the midst of negotiations on Resolution 2321.

The view in the West of economic warfare as an alternative to military action had a long history, with predictions of successful economic coercion having consistently provided a primary argument against using force. As early as the 1920s U.S. President Woodrow Wilson had observed of embargoes: "Apply this economic, peaceful, silent, deadly remedy and there will be no need for force."[134] A century later a paper in the CFR journal *Foreign Affairs* referred to America's "ability to use dollars as an alternative to military force,"[135] with a separate paper from the journal characterizing sanctions as measures which "fill the void between empty diplomatic declarations and deadly military interventions."[136] Shortly before becoming president of CFR, Richard Hass had in 1998 observed that "sanctions provide a visible and less expensive alternative to military intervention and to doing nothing," stressing "their growing importance for U.S. foreign policy."[137] Thus the less the U.S. and Western world believed their objectives in Korea could credibly be achieved through sanctions, the more seriously they were to consider using military force, with this being critical between 1992 and the late 2010s when Pyongyang had neither a superpower protector nor a fully mature deterrent capability.

Deputy Assistant to the President For National Security Affairs Anthony Roggerio was among multiple figures to attest to the continuity between the Obama and Trump administrations in their approaches to targeting Pyongyang through Beijing, stressing that this was maintained "under a Democratic president and a Republican president, two people who could not be more opposite than each other."[138] With North Korea's successful testing of Hwasong-14 ICBMs in June adding significant further urgency to American efforts to impose pressure, President Trump tweeted hours after the second launch on July 28, in what was widely interpreted as an allusion to Beijing's continued resistance to supporting further UNSC resolutions: "I am very disappointed in China. Our foolish past leaders have allowed them to make hundreds of billions of dollars a year in trade, yet they do NOTHING for us with North Korea, just talk… We will no longer allow this to continue. China could easily solve this problem!"[139]

While leading experts on Korean security observed that 2017 "contained more than a dozen moments when the North Koreans might have interpreted that action was underway for a sudden, all-out attack,"[140] this appeared to have been as much a show of force aimed at pressing Pyongyang's neighbors to take action as it was at the country itself. The Trump administration was thus able to pass resolutions 2371, 2375 and 2397 through the Security Council in August, September and December respectively, and despite significant successes by the Chinese and Russian delegations to lessen their severity during negotiations, they were still unprecedented in their indiscriminate targeting of the North Korean economy. Amid ongoing efforts to maximize pressure during negotiations on Resolution 2397, which would pass ten days later, the Assistant to the President for National Security Affairs Lieutenant General H. R. McMaster stated on December 12 that while sanctions resolutions were encouraging, "it is time to do much more." He stressed that military action was still a very real possibility unless "all nations" were to "move beyond UN resolutions" to take unspecified further moves against Pyongyang.[141]

One of the most significant restrictions was a cap on North Korean oil imports at just 500,000 barrels (59,172 metric tons) per year. To place the implications for the country's economy in perspective, oil imports in 1991 had been 3.8 million metric tons – or 64 times greater than the limit the Western-drafted sanctions were imposing.[142] While industry was beginning to recover from the crisis of the 1990s, new sanctions appeared to be intended to almost completely deindustrialize the country, including its oil-intensive agriculture sector. Oil consumption per capita under the latest resolution would make North Korea one of the very lowest consumers in the world, with gross consumption among the world's twelve lowest, below that of sparsely populated deindustrialized island nations such as the Solomon Islands and St Vincent and the Grenadine with populations of well under 1 million. For an industrial and resource-scarce country of over 24 million this was effectively a death sentence unless the embargo could be violated.[143] All natural gas imports were also banned, while over 90 percent of exports were blocked including textiles, food, machinery and coal, with further prohibitions put in place on joint ventures with DPRK firms. UN sanctions thus covered all major sectors of the North Korean economy other than tourism, and were paired with much wider ranging unilateral Western secondary sanctions regimes. As one European official told the writer in 2017: "they are sending North Korea into a black hole."

While the Korean People's Army was sufficiently capable even in the 1990s to incline the West to favor sanctions, there was a delicate balance between the perceived urgency in Western capitals of forcing change in Pyongyang, the potency of North Korean military capabilities, and the extent to which there were prospects that sanctions could provide a non-military means of achieving Western objectives. In the 1990s, for example, although confidence in the U.S. Armed Forces had swelled after Operation Desert Storm, a primary factor leading Washington to avoid military options was North Korea's economic decline, which increased Western confidence that economic warfare would be sufficient to force a total collapse of the country. By the mid-2020s, by contrast, North Korean military capabilities had grown to the extent that even with negligible hope of achieving its objectives through sanctions, the West could no longer seriously consider military options. In 2016–2017, however, not only was stopping Pyongyang's nuclear and missile programs a primary and particularly urgent U.S. foreign policy priority, but the KPA's capabilities were insufficient to fully deter military action, which made increasing Western hopes of achieving their objectives through sanctions critical to preventing war.

Aside from offering the United States an alternative to military action for escalating pressure, Beijing and Moscow's allowing for the passage of sanctions also reduced risks of a breakdown in cooperation with Washington on nuclear non-proliferation. While Beijing consistently blocked Western efforts to sanction adversaries across the world through the Security Council, from Zimbabwe and Sudan to Syria and Myanmar, it allowed sanctions to pass against Iran and North Korea from the 2000s as both showed signs of developing nuclear weapons. Being seen to endorse or facilitate such efforts would have otherwise broken great powers' understanding on nuclear proliferation that had remained in place since the Cuban Missile Crisis, under which the U.S. had played a key role in cutting short South Korea and Taiwan's own nuclear programs that had threatened Chinese security.[144] Openly allowing North Korea to develop nuclear weapons without reprimand would pave the way to the United States allowing, or even assisting, Japan, South Korea, Australia or Taiwan to do the same, increasing the danger of nuclear war for all parties.[145] China had to approve sanctions not due to any particular objections to its neighbor developing a nuclear deterrent per se, which it as well as Russia repeatedly indicated did not threaten it, but rather due to the potential consequences of openly condoning nuclear proliferation.

North Korea's Economic Show of Force

The imposition of five rounds of unprecedentedly extreme economic sanctions broadly and severely targeting the North Korean economy at the Security Council in 2016 and 2017 provided the Western world with significant grounds for confidence in their ability to force Pyongyang into submission. Western economic sanctions had since the end of the Cold War demonstrated the capability to devastate targeted economies, particularly when Western-drafted resolutions could be imposed through the Security Council. As observed in *Foreign Affairs* in 1999, sanctions "may have contributed to more deaths during the post–Cold War era than all weapons of mass destruction throughout history."[146] Sanctions against Iraq that decade, for example, were credited at a conservative estimate with causing 40,000 deaths annually of children under the age of 5 and 50,000 annually among older Iraqis,[147] and it was estimated that 500,000 died as a direct result from 1991–1995 alone when they were at the height of their effectiveness.[148] While the effects of the sanctions regime was particularly severe in Iraq, due primarily to the devastation of critical infrastructure by Western bombardment months after the regime was imposed, they proved effective in stimulating economic crisis, runaway inflation and major declines in living standards across the world, with notable examples in the 2010s including Iran, Syria and Venezuela.[149]

In contrast to other targets, Western sources consistently reported on the state of North Korea's economy with surprise, with *Reuters* having reported in late 2016 that "the price of rice, corn, pork, petrol and diesel remained relatively stable over the past year, demonstrating resilience to domestic and outside events." It highlighted that this would help strengthen the government's stability in power, citing growing production of consumer goods "from toothpaste to perfume" as a possible contributor to stabilizing the value of the North Korean won.[150] Where Iran, Russia, and others had seen their currency situations rapidly deteriorate in the face of far less stringent Western sanctions regimes, the contrasting stability of won to dollar exchange rates was "a bit of a mystery to everyone," as noted by University of California expert on the North Korean economy Stephan Haggard.[151] Citing "easily traceable macro-economic indicators" such as exchange rates and prices of staple foods, expert Andrei Lankov observed that reports "do not indicate any deterioration in the economic situation.... it is still remarkable that the sanctions regime has failed to produce any noticeable impact on any major economic indicators."[152] Strongly advocating further escalated sanctions to force an economic crisis, a Council on Foreign Relations report in September highlighted that "the increasing complexity of its economy affords North Korea greater ability to resist and circumvent the international sanctions regime."[153]

As sanctions tightened in 2017 Western surprise at North Korea's economic resilience only grew. Citing South Korean official figures, *Reuters* observed in July that economic growth rates were "at [a] 17-year high despite sanctions" at 3.9 percent.[154] *USA Today* reported four months later that North Korea's economy was "beating sanctions" and "kept humming despite ever-tighter sanctions," stressing "no shortage of imported goods or of foreign currency needed to buy them." "North Korea's economy has proven resilient and seems to have fended off the suffering President Trump has sought to halt the country's nuclear program," it summarized.[155] By the end of 2017 the economy was continuing to grow, and both exchange rates and prices for most basic goods remained stable.[156]

Despite optimistic projections in the West that sanctions would have delayed effects, and that North Korean living standards would start to suffer more drastically in 2018, such hopes were never realized.[157] As summarized in the title of an *Associated Press* report in November 2018, titled: "North Korea's Stable Exchange Rates Confound Economists," the country's ability to withstand a historically unprecedented economic warfare campaign raised serious concerns. "It's a question that nags at North Korea economy watchers: How has the country been able to maintain stable exchange rates – and avert hyper-inflation – despite intense sanctions, political tensions and a swelling trade imbalance?," the report noted, with such perplexion widely expressed by Western analysts.[158]

Former South Korean Minister of Unification Lee Jong Seok was among the prominent sources to observe that his government's official estimates of North Korean growth rates, although still far higher than Western assessments had expected, were "unrealistic and unbelievable." He cited among, other indicators, massive construction projects across the country and the proliferation of automobiles as indicators of far higher growth rates.[159] A December 2019 report by the South Korean Sejong Institute think tank was among several to highlight North Korea's strong economic performance, observing its construction boom, surge in production of consumer goods, and exchange rate and price stability, with performance expected only to further improve in the following years.[160] Visits to shopping centers, outdoor markets and convenience stores from 2016–2019 showed the range domestically produced consumer goods was indeed growing fast. Other signs of increased economic dynamism included the emergence of new domestic smartphones brands such as Arirang, Jinalllae and Phurun Hanul, the completion of significant agriculture projects such as fish farming and floating rice fields, and the completion of new scientific research facilities, new modern housing, and infrastructure projects.

A key factor in the North Korean economy's resilience was not only a far lower reliance on imports than other Western targets, but also a low reliance on exports for growth and heavy reliance on domestic consumption. As observed by leading economist with the Pyongyang-based Academy of Social Sciences Economic Institute Ri Ki Song: "Our economy is not an economy that relies on exports... Due to the sanctions, we are not making a lot of trade or financial dealings with other countries, so there will be not so many changes in the exchange rates."[161] Increased investment in domestic production, ranging from catfish and goat farming to multiple hydroelectric dams, increasingly efficient food production, and greater production of quality consumer goods from tablet computers to violins, were important contributors. Senior researcher and North Korea expert at the Niigata-based Economic Research Institute for Northeast Asia Mitsuhiro Mimura, who had visited the country over 45 times, was among a number of analysts to stress the importance of this.[162] The fact that private firms and consumer markets saw very few taxes imposed, and often none at all, reportedly contributed significantly to their success.

North Korea's demonstration of immense economic resilience served as a major show of force highly complementary to its newly demonstrated military capabilities, showing that Western options for quashing the country either economically or militarily had been made increasingly unviable, and thus forcing the U.S. to accept the need for a negotiated settlement. Much as devastation wrought by Western firepower against non-Western cities across the world served as a warning to those who considered stepping out of line, from Tokyo and Nagasaki to Belgrade and Fallujah, so too did the devastation caused by sanctions serve as a complementary deterrent that similarly helped keep the international community's policies aligned with Western interests. This made the inability of economic warfare efforts to induce crisis in North Korea's case a particularly hard felt blow to Western Bloc interests, which would go far from unnoticed elsewhere in the non-Western world.

Restoring Stability in Northeast Asia: The North Korean Nuclear Deterrent and a New Regional Order

Despite North Korea having had an ambiguous nuclear weapons capability since the early 1990s, and by the end of the Obama administration having a possible very limited nuclear ICBM capability, it would take until a year into the Trump administration and the demonstration of significant further capability advances for an American consensus to solidify against a decision to attack. The stronger the deterrent demonstrated, the stronger the arguments in Washington against military action became, particularly if this showed a capability to engage targets on the American mainland itself.

One of the most significant signs of a shift among Trump administration officials, and of growing contentions between them over the possibility of military action, emerged exactly two weeks after the Hwasong-15 test launch demonstrated an expanded reach for KPA nuclear strikes. Heralding a major policy shift which would fully materialize the following year, Secretary of State Rex Tillerson on December 12 made an unprecedented call for dialogue, stating at an Atlantic Council event:

> We're ready to talk any time North Korea would like to talk. We are ready to have the first meeting without precondition. We can talk about the weather if you want. Talk about whether it's going to be a square table or a round table, if that's what you are excited about. But can we at least sit down and see each other face to face, and then we can begin to lay out a map, a road map of what we might be willing to work towards. But can we at least sit down and see each other face to face.

Further clarifying the implications of his statement, and implicitly criticizing his and the preceding administrations' extensive preconditions for talks, Tillerson stated: "It's not realistic to say we're only going to talk if you come to the table ready to give up your program. They have too much invested in it."[163] While the consensus among analysts and those officials with some expertise in North Korea was almost unanimous that a strike would be met with significant retaliation, many in the Trump administration had shown signs they believed otherwise,[164] which may have thus led Secretary Tillerson, long seen as a voice of reason, to urgently seek to reduce tensions.[165] So long as negotiations were underway, military options were less likely to be taken, with Tillerson's actions thus having the potential to reduce the serious possibility of war.

The White House notably countermanded Tillerson's statement within 24 hours, asserting that "the administration is united in insisting that any negotiations with North Korea must wait until the regime fundamentally improves its behavior... clearly right now is not the time."[166] This was far from unprecedented, and amid unconfirmed reports in September that the state secretary was seeking to begin talks with Pyongyang, President Trump had implicitly confirmed this by undercutting it, tweeting on October 1: "I told Rex Tillerson, our wonderful Secretary of State, that he is wasting his time trying to negotiate with Little Rocket Man. Save your energy Rex, we'll do what has to be done!"[167] With Pyongyang's recent moratorium on nuclear and missile testing and conciliatory statements notably met only with further pressure and threats, it appeared that Washington had left no clear path to negotiations other than through a full capitulation. Tillerson appeared ahead of the curve among administration officials in recognizing that with Pyongyang having shown considerable resilience to sanctions and demonstrated a viable intercontinental range nuclear deterrent, Washington would sooner or later be forced to the table without preconditions once it came to terms with these new realities.

While North Korea demonstrated the capability to deliver thermonuclear warheads to the United States mainland increasingly convincingly from July 4, the Western world remained incredulous to this reality for some time. Leading American authority on nuclear proliferation Jeffrey Lewis observed to this effect: "There is no reason to think that the North Koreans aren't making the same progress after so many successful nuclear explosions... it seems to me a lot of people are insisting on impossible levels of proof because they simply don't want to accept what should be pretty obvious."[168] As late as July 28 the *New York Times* reported that it would take approximately a year for North Korea develop a viable ICBM delivery capability.[169] Less than two weeks later, however, the leaking of a Defense Intelligence Agency assessment confirmed that this had already been achieved.[170] Further confirmation of this reality, and greater evidence verifying it, were forthcoming in the following months.

The Western world's response to North Korea's development of an intercontinental range nuclear deterrent notably mirrored prior responses to the Soviet Union and China's nuclear weapons programs. Much like North Korea, both had faced serious threats of Western nuclear attacks before developing their own nuclear deterrents, and had seen Western political and military leaders widely advocate bombing raids to set back their nuclear programs. The three states' nuclear programs were all intended primarily as means to end Western attempts at nuclear coercion and deter potential attacks, thus directly impeding Western militaries' ability to secure objectives through military force. All three programs were accordingly portrayed in the West as unacceptable and as threats to peace, in contrast to those of Britain, France and the United States which were depicted positively as forces for good, and those of South Africa, Israel, India and Pakistan which were depicted ambiguously – as they neither upheld nor directly threatened Western hegemony.

The threats North Korea faced before completing its nuclear deterrent were far from unprecedented, and as early as 1945 the Pentagon had planned for nuclear strikes against 66 Soviet cities using 204 nuclear warheads, which Britain in particular had persistently lobbied for to prevent the USSR from developing its own nuclear bomb.[171] The Soviets achieved such a capability six years earlier than expected, which was key to deterring use of nuclear weapons either against their country or against neighboring China during the Korean War. Subsequently in the 1960s conventional and nuclear attacks on China were seriously considered by the John F. Kennedy and Lyndon Johnson administrations, and were widely advocated in the West to prevent the country from developing a nuclear deterrent.[172] As summarized by U.S. Naval War College Professor Lyle J. Goldstein: "Infiltration, sabotage, invasion by Chinese Nationalists, maritime blockades, South Korean invasion of North Korea, conventional air attacks on nuclear facilities, and the use of tactical nuclear weapons on selected targets" were among the means considered to destabilize China and set back its nuclear development.[173] These attack plans mirrored the widespread calls in the West up to late 2017 either for a limited "bloody nose" strike to set back North Korean weapons development, or for what lawmakers referred to as an "an all out war against the regime" intended "to take the regime completely down."[174]

Calls in the United States for a military assault on North Korea provided valuable insight into the implications the KPA's nuclear missile deterrent had for broader Northeast Asian security. Such calls consistently highlighted a strong willingness to place China and allied South Korea and Japan at risk of historically unprecedented catastrophe in order to achieve American objectives. The argument for doing so was prominently summarized by Senator Lindsey Graham, one of the Republican Party's most influential lawmakers, who preceding the KPA's demonstration of an ICBM capability repeatedly reiterated that an assault remained feasible precisely because the fallout would be confined to Northeast Asia. Regarding the consequences of the attack he was advocating, Graham elaborated: "It would be terrible, but the war would be over there [in Northeast Asia] it wouldn't be here. It would be bad for the Korean peninsula. It would be bad for China. It would be bad for Japan. It would be bad for South Korea. It would be the end of North Korea, but what it would not do is hit America."[175]

Graham elaborated in a subsequent interview: "There's a military option – to destroy North Korea's program and North Korea itself… If there's going to be a war to stop it, it will be over there. If thousands die, they're going to die over there. They're not going to die here." When asked about his thoughts on the U.S. initiating an attack, the senator responded: "it's inevitable unless North Korea changes because you're making our president pick between regional stability [in Northeast Asia] and homeland security."[176] Graham had been far from alone in lobbying for an attack on North Korea throughout much of 2017,[177] with his and others' statements consistently highlighting that only the ability to strike the American mainland would be sufficient to fully shift Washington's calculus against an attack.

Prominent figures in the military leadership advocating an attack similarly repeatedly stated that the devastation of allies in Northeast Asia was a price worth paying. Assistant to the President for National Security Affairs Lieutenant General H. R. McMaster, for one, stressed that Washington could not tolerate North Korea developing an ICBM, and should take measures to prevent it even if it meant a "human catastrophe" in South Korea.[178] McMaster strongly lobbied for such an attack during his time in office.[179] Chairman of the Joint Chiefs of Staff General Joseph Dunford in much the same vein stated that North Korea obtaining a nuclear-tipped ICBM was a far more "unthinkable" reality than a major war in Northeast Asia, and that initiating the latter to prevent the former was a real option. "Many people have talked about military options with words like 'unimaginable'… I would shift that slightly and say it would be horrific. It would be a loss of life unlike any we have experienced in our lifetimes. Anyone who has been alive since World War II has never seen the loss of life that could occur if there's a conflict on the Korean peninsula," he stated. The chairman concluded: "It is not unimaginable to have military options to respond to North Korean nuclear capability… What's unimaginable to me is allowing a capability that would allow a nuclear weapon to land in Denver, Colorado."[180]

Consultant to the Office of the Secretary of Defense, the State Department, and the National Security Council Edward Luttwak, who also separately consulted to the U.S. Army, Navy and Air Force and several European defense ministries, was among the most vocal influential proponents of an attack. As one of the last to publicly advocate for war, Luttwak in January 2018 authored the *Foreign Policy* article: "It's Time to Bomb North Korea," in which he blamed South Korea for failing to sufficiently fortify its cities to handle the fallout from an American attack on its neighbor. He on this basis claimed that the southern population's vulnerability was "very largely self-inflicted," arguing that this "cannot be allowed to paralyze" the U.S. and deter it from launching an assault. The risk to South Korean civilians, he stressed, was not "a good reason to hesitate before ordering an attack on North Korea." Luttwak otherwise stated that North Korea and other similar challengers to Western power should be prevented not only from fielding nuclear weapons, but should also have access to even basic firearms restricted.[181]

Summarizing the central issue raised by calls to attack North Korea, and the rationalization of putting citizens of allied states at risk, former strategist and policy adviser at the Office of the Secretary of Defense and Group Chair of the U.S.–ROK Extended Deterrence Policy Committee Van Jackson observed:

> Nuclear war, the very thing preventative war advocates claimed to want to prevent, was almost inevitable if the United States launched a war of choice in Korea. The way war advocates coped with that contradiction was by drawing a false distinction between nuclear weapons used in the Asia-Pacific versus nuclear weapons used against the U.S. homeland... to say nothing of the hundreds of thousands of non-U.S. citizens who would become victims of nuclear conflict in the event of preventive war.[182]

While an assault on North Korea, including one using nuclear weapons, had been seriously considered multiple times throughout the Cold War and in its aftermath, it was the country's development of a viable deterrent putting the U.S. mainland within reach that permanently seriously limited the possibility of open war. As made clear repeatedly by figures across the American leadership, the threat of strikes against the U.S. mainland were viewed entirely differently to those on allied populations and U.S. forces overseas, and only the ability to do the former could provoke a fundamental shift across the American political spectrum in the calculus for launching a war. While Seoul and Tokyo both perceived the possibility of a U.S. attack on North Korea with much apprehension in the mid-2010s, and attempted to dissuade Washington from pursuing such action,[183] it was only North Korea's demonstration to Washington that any war that put the Koreas and Japan in the firing line would also harm the American homeland which ensured their security. Pyongyang had deterred their ally from putting them in harm's way.

A conservative estimate of the death toll in Seoul from a single day of conventional hostilities was around 20,000,[184] although far higher figures have been quoted and overall casualties could realistically exceed 100,000 every 24 hours. The Center for the

National Interest's Director of Korea Studies Harry Kazianis referred to North Korean artillery aimed at Seoul as able to "start a 9/11-style crisis hundreds of times over in minutes,"[185] with even the most optimistic projections for U.S.-led destruction of KPA artillery predicting that bombardment would still continue for weeks.[186] This was aside from the death tolls from weapons of mass destruction, missile strikes, and other hostilities, with the close proximity of American military facilities to South Korean population centers and deployment of air defense systems at these facilities further increasing risks to civilians.[187] This was also the case in Japan, with notable examples including the Yokata and Tachikawa air bases in Tokyo and the base of the U.S. Navy's 7th Fleet in the city of Yokosuka, all of which would be targeted as key staging grounds for American offensives. The danger to civilians would be further exacerbated by the widespread use of depleted uranium munitions by U.S. forces, which were extensively employed in Yugoslavia, Syria and Iraq including in heavily populated areas, and contaminated surrounding environments with highly detrimental consequences for public health.[188]

The North Korean ICBM's contribution to South Korean, Japanese and broader regional security was summarized as follows by Van Jackson in his study of the 2016–2018 crisis:

> Everything that helped resolve the crisis in 2018 looked superficially like the decisions of bold leaders taking history in their hands. But their initiatives were only unlocked because North Korea attained its goal of demonstrating a viable nuclear deterrent at the end of 2017. Without North Korea realizing the first principle of its security strategy when it did… Trump would have had little choice but to succumb to the arguments of preventative war advocates.[189]

It was on this basis that North Korean references to its nuclear deterrent as protecting "the security of the Korean nation from the U.S. threat of aggression and averting a new war," and not only the Koreans north of the 38th parallel, had significant foundation to it.[190] Had North Korea failed to develop an ICBM capability when it did, the possibility of the United States initiating a war in Northeast Asia, to the severe detriment of the interests of all regional states and populations, would have been considerably greater.

Endnotes

1 'North Korean Missile Launches & Nuclear Tests: 1984–Present,' Missile Defense Project, Center for Strategic and International Studies (https://missilethreat.csis.org/north-korea-missile-launches-1984-present/) (accessed July 20, 2019).

2 '朝鲜成功研发新型洲际导弹KN-14？ 美媒 — 朝鲜成功研发针对美国本土的新型洲际弹道导弹' ['North Korea successfully developed a new ICBM KN-14? U.S. Media: North Korea Successfully Develops New Intercontinental Ranged Ballistic Missile Against U.S. Mainland'], *People's TV,* 2016 (http://tv.people.com.cn/n1/2016/0401/c67816-28245618.html).

3 'North Korea's fifth nuclear test prompts U.S. calls for more sanctions,' *Reuters*, September 10, 2016.

4 Mullen, Mike and Nunn, Sam and Mount, Adam, *A Sharper Choice on North Korea: Engaging China for a Stable Northeast Asia*, Council on Foreign Relations, Independent Task Force Report No. 74, September 2016.

5 Stewart, Phil, 'U.S. urges China to pressure North Korea after nuclear test,' *Reuters*, September 10, 2016.

6 Kerry, John, 'Remarks at the U.S. Navy Academy,' *U.S. Department of State Official Website*, January 10, 2017.

7 'Kim Jong Un's 2017 New Year's Address,' *KCNA,* January 2, 2017.

8 Haberman, Maggie and Sanger, David, '"It Won't Happen!" Donald Trump Says of North Korean Missile Test,' *New York Times,* January 2, 2017.

9 Ibid.

10 *Background Briefing by Senior Administration Officials on the Visit of President Xi Jinping of the People's Republic of China*, Washington, DC, April 4, 2017.

Baker, Gerard and Lee, Carol and Bender, Michael, 'Trump Says He Offered China Better Trade Terms in Exchange for Help on North Korea,' *The Wall Street Journal,* April 22, 2017.

11 Lee, Dong Hyuk, 'Analysis: What Trump Inherited from Obama,' *VOA*, June 7, 2018.

12 'Western spy agencies being outgunned by "bad actors," ex-CIA operative James Olson warns,' *ABC News*, July 29, 2019.

'Killing CIA Informants, China Crippled US Spying Operations,' *New York Times*, May 20, 2017.

Mai, Jun, 'CIA spy-killing claims "show China's strength in counter-espionage,"' *South China Morning Post,* May 22, 2017.

Murphy, Margi, 'Dozens of US spies killed after Iran and China uncovered CIA messaging service using Google,' *Telegraph,* November 3, 2018.

13 'Satellite Spots Cross-border Tunnels,' *CRI News,* August 25, 2014.

14 Hastings, Justin, 'How North Korea keeps its economy humming despite the sanctions,' *South China Morning Post,* September 24, 2017.

15 Anna, Cara and Pennington, Matthew, 'Lax enforcement weakens UN sanctions on nuclear North Korea, '*AP News*, January 10, 2016.

'EU warns Thailand on N.Korea sanctions,' *Bangkok Post*, October 18, 2017.

16 Albright, David et al., '56 countries involved in violating UNSC Resolutions on North Korea during last reporting period,' *Institute for Science and International Security*, June 6, 2019.

Obe, Mitsuru, 'Forty-nine nations breached North Korea sanctions: report,' *Nikkei*, December 8, 2017.

Ramani, Samuel, 'North Korea's Enduring Economic and Security Presence in Africa,' *38 North*, June 24, 2021.

Anna, Cara and Pennington, Matthew, 'Lax enforcement weakens UN sanctions on nuclear North Korea,' *AP News*, January 10, 2016.

Ham, Ji-ha and Kim, Seon-myung, 'Despite UN Sanctions, North Koreans at Work in Senegal,' *VOA*, September 24, 2019.

'EU warns Thailand on N.Korea sanctions,' *Bangkok Post*, October 18, 2017.

'North Korean Workers Remain in Africa Months After Sanctions Deadline to Repatriate,' *Radio Free Asia*, April 9, 2020.

Jewell, Ethan, 'Top Sri Lankan official admits to arms deal with North Korea, then backtracks,' *NK News,* February 7, 2022.

17 Berger, Andrea, 'A Familiar Story: The New UN Report on North Korean Sanctions Implementation,' *38 North*, March 16, 2017.

18 'China will never seek hegemony: white paper,' *Xinhua,* July 24, 2019.

19 Kelly, Robert E., 'A "Confucian Long Peace" in pre-Western East Asia?,' *European Journal of International Relations,* vol. 18, no. 3, 2011 (pp. 407–430).

20 Jackson, Van, *On the Brink: Trump, Kim, and the Threat of Nuclear War,* Cambridge, Cambridge University Press, 2018 (p. 21).

21 Evans, Stephen, 'How might Donald Trump deal with North Korea's Kim Jong-un?,' *BBC News,* November 11, 2016.

22 'Donald Trump Warns China the US Is Ready to Tackle North Korea,' *Financial Times*, April 3, 2017.

23 Alexander, Harriet and Boyle, Danny and Henderson, Barney, 'US Launches Strike on Syria – How it Unfolded,' *The Telegraph*, April 7, 2017.

24 Baker, Gerard and Lee, Carol E. and Bender, Michael C., 'Trump Says He Offered China Better Trade Terms in Exchange for Help on North Korea,' *The Wall Street Journal*, April 12, 2017.

25 Baker, Peter, 'The War That Wasn't: Trump Claims Obama Was Ready to Strike North Korea,' *New York Times*, February 16, 2019.

26 Bowden, John, 'Trump hits Obama, Biden over "mess" with China and North Korea,' *The Hill*, July 5, 2019.

Jackson, David, 'Trump blames Hillary Clinton for North Korea nuclear weapons program,' *USA Today*, September 20, 2017.

27 Fitzpatrick, Mark, 'North Korea: Obama's Prime Nonproliferation Failure,' *Arms Control*, December 2016.

Shaffer, Tony, 'Donald Trump puts past presidents to shame with North Korea policies,' *The Hill*, March 2, 2019.

28 McMaster, H. R., *Battlegrounds: The Fight to Defend the Free World*, New York, Harper, 2020 (Chapter 11).

29 Song, Jiwon, 'U.S. Official Encourages Plan for N. Korea Collapse,' *NK News*, May 4, 2016.

30 Yi, Yong-in, 'Hillary's Campaign Team Signals Hardline Stance on North Korea,' *Hankyoreh*, October 17, 2016.

31 Shorrock, Tim, 'Hillary's Hawks Are Threatening Escalation Against North Korea,' *The Nation*, October 28, 2016.

32 Yi, Yong-in, 'Hillary's Campaign Team Signals Hardline Stance on North Korea,' *Hankyoreh*, October 17, 2016.

33 'Clinton's Likely Defense Secretary Says U.S. Should Intensify Sanctions on N.K. Rather Than Negotiate,' *Yonhap*, October 16, 2016.

34 Jackson, Van, *On the Brink: Trump, Kim, and the Threat of Nuclear War*, Cambridge, Cambridge University Press, 2018 (pp. 83–84).

35 'Transcript of the Democratic Presidential Debate,' *New York Times*, February 5, 2016.

36 Evans, Stephen, 'How might Donald Trump deal with North Korea's Kim Jong-un?,' *BBC News*, November 11, 2016.

37 Ko, Dong-hwan, 'Trump up for "hamburger talk" with Kim Jong-un,' *Korea Times*, June 16, 2016.

38 'North Korean media paints Trump as "wise politician," Clinton as "dull,"' *Fox News*, June 1, 2016.

39 Pramuk, Jacob, 'What Trump said about Afghanistan before he became president,' *CNBC*, August 21, 2017.

Herman, Steve, 'Trump Comments on Withdrawing US Forces from Asia Raise Alarm,' *Voice of Asia*, July 21, 2016.

40 Gladstone, Rick, 'In Harvard Speech, Merkel Rebukes Trump's Worldview in All but Name,' *New York Times,* May 30, 2019.

Aleem, Zeeshan, 'Macron just slammed Trump's worldview in a rare address to Congress,' *Vox,* April 25, 2018.

Dathan, Matt, 'An EU army is even MORE necessary with Trump as President, EU chief Jean-Claude Juncker says as he presses ahead with plans to build a European military "superpower,"' *Daily Mail,* November 11, 2016.

41 Gearan, Anne, 'Clinton slams Trump as a dangerous isolationist in American Legion speech,' *Washington Post,* August 31, 2016.

42 Lee, MJ, 'Donald Trump vs. the Republican establishment,' *CNN,* October 26, 2015.

Reilly, Katie, 'Both Former Presidents Bush Won't Endorse Trump,' *Time,* May 4, 2016.

43 Hemmer, Nicole, 'After the Syria strikes, right-wing non-interventionists are back in the wilderness,' *Vox*, April 15, 2017.

Steinhauer, Jennifer, 'Trump's Opposition to "Endless Wars" Appeals to Those Who Fought Them,' *New York Times,* November 1, 2019.

Thomsen, Jacqueline, 'Trump supporters slam decision to launch strikes against Syria,' *The Hill,* April 14, 2018.

44 Weiner, Tim, 'When Trump savages his intelligence chiefs, the "deep state" has reason to worry,' *Washington Post,* January 31, 2019.

45 Jencks, Harlan W., *Some Political and Military Implications of Soviet Warplane Sales to the PRC*, Sun Yat Sen Center for Policy Studies, National Sun Yat Sen University, Paper no. 6, April 1991 (p. 21).

Larrabee, F. Stephen, 'Gorbachev and the Soviet Military,' *Foreign Affairs*, Summer 1988.

46 Stewart, Phil, 'As Trump warned North Korea, his "armada" was headed towards Australia,' *Reuters*, April 19, 2017.

'Strategic Confusion,' *The Economist*, April 22, 2017 (pp. 47–48).

47 Caldwell, Leigh Ann, 'Breakdown in North Korea Talks Sounds Alarms on Capitol Hill,' *NBC News*, October 25, 2017.

48 Dionne Jr., Eugene J., 'Trump picked Kim Jong Un over the CIA. Is anyone surprised?,' *Washington Post,* June 12, 2016.

49 Barnes, Tom, 'John Bolton contradicts Trump by saying Syria withdrawal depends on defeating Isis,' *The Independent,* January 6, 2019.

50 Transcript: 'House Judiciary Committee Holds Evidence Hearing on Trump Impeachment,' *CNN,* aired December 9, 2019.

51 Dönmez, Beyza Binnur, 'France to maintain troops in Syria,' *Andalou News Agency*, January 17, 2019.

'Syria conflict: Macron criticises Trump's withdrawal decision,' *BBC News*, December 23, 2018.

'UK, France Wanted to Send Their Own Troops to Syria After Trump Ordered Withdrawal Report,' *Sputnik News*, November 28, 2019.

Huggler, Justin, 'Germany "in secret talks to send aircraft to patrol Syrian safe zone,"' *The Telegraph*, May 30, 2019.

52 Williams, Katie Bo, 'Outgoing Syria Envoy Admits Hiding US Troop Numbers; Praises Trump's Mideast Record,' *Defense One,* November 12, 2020.

53 Choe, Sang-hun, 'Kim Jong-un's Half Brother Is Reported Assassinated in Malaysia,' *New York Times,* February 14, 2017.

54 Asmolov, Konstantin, 'Kim Jong-nam Murder Case is Closed, or More Precisely Falls Apart,' *New Eastern Outlook,* April 16, 2019.

55 Bernama, 'Dr M hails Seoul's "Look South" policy; affirms rapprochement with Pyongyang,' *New Straits Times,* November 26, 2019.

56 Jackson, Van, *On the Brink: Trump, Kim, and the Threat of Nuclear War,* Cambridge, Cambridge University Press, 2018 (pp. 100–102).

57 Strobel, Warren P., 'North Korean Leader's Slain Half Brother Was a CIA Source,' *The Wall Street Journal*, June 10, 2019.

58 Shesgree, Deirdre and Dorell, Oren, 'U.S. college student released by North Korea arrives back in Ohio,' *USA Today,* June 14, 2017.

59 Nedelman, Michael, 'Coroner found no obvious signs of torture on Otto Warmbier,' *CNN,* September 29, 2017.

60 'US court orders North Korea to pay $500 million for Otto Warmbier's death,' *Deutsche Welle,* December 24, 2018.

61 Tinker, Ben, 'What an autopsy may (or may not) have revealed about Otto Warmbier's death,' *CNN,* June 22, 2017.

Nedelman, Michael, 'Coroner found no obvious signs of torture on Otto Warmbier,' *CNN,* September 29, 2017.

62 'N.Korea successfully tests new high-thrust rocket engine: KCNA,' *NK News*, March 18, 2017.

63 Kim, Jeongmin, 'North Korean media marks three years since 2017 high-thrust rocket engine test,' *NK News*, March 18, 2020.

64 Lewis, Jeffrey, 'North Korea's Hwasong-12 Missile: Stepping Stone to an ICBM,' *Nuclear Threat Initiative*, July 20, 2017.

65 Ibid.

66 'A Conversation with General John Hyten, Vice Chairman of the Joint Chiefs of Staff,' *CSIS*, January 17, 2020.

67 Warrick, Joby and Nakashima, Ellen and Fifield, Anna, 'North Korea now making missile-ready nuclear weapons, U.S. analysts say,' *Washington Post,* August 8, 2017.

68 Panda, Ankit, 'US Intelligence: North Korea's ICBM Reentry Vehicles Are Likely Good Enough to Hit the Continental US,' *The Diplomat*, August 12, 2017.

69 'Did Ukraine Provide Rocket Engines to North Korea For Its Nuclear Missile Program?,' *Newsweek*, September 1, 2017.

70 Landay, Jonathan, 'North Korea likely can make missile engines without imports: U.S.,' *Reuters*, August 16, 2017.

71 Kim, Kyu-won, 'Most of December Rocket Was Produced within North Korea,' *Hankyoreh*, January 22, 2013.

72 Lewis, Jeffrey, 'Domestic UDMH Production in the DPRK,' *Arms Control Wonk*, September 27, 2017.

73 Fisher, Max, 'Remote Textile Plant May Secretly Fuel North Korea's Weapons,' *New York Times*, September 27, 2017.

74 Sanger, David E. and Choe, Sang-Hun, 'U.S. Urges Fuel Cutoff for North Korea, Saying It's "Begging for War,"' *New York Times*, September 4, 2017.

Choe, Sang-Hun, 'Putin Rejects Cutting Off Oil to North Korea,' *New York Times*, September 6, 2017.

75 Fisher, Max, 'Remote Textile Plant May Secretly Fuel North Korea's Weapons,' *New York Times*, September 27, 2017.

76 Panda, Ankit, 'No, North Korea Isn't Dependent on Russia and China for Its Rocket Fuel,' *The Diplomat*, September 28, 2017.

77 Baker, Peter and Choe, Sang-Hun, 'Trump Threatens "Fire and Fury" Against North Korea if It Endangers U.S.,' *New York Times*, August 8, 2017.

78 Serhan, Yasmeen and Gilsinian, Kathy, 'North Korea Answers Trump's Vague Threats With Specific Ones,' *The Atlantic*, August 10, 2017.

79 Baker, Peter and Choe, Sang-Hun, 'Trump Threatens "Fire and Fury" Against North Korea if It Endangers U.S.,' *New York Times*, August 8, 2017.

80 'USAF completes flight tests of B61-12 gravity bombs from F-15E,' *Air Force Technology*, August 30, 2017.

'The U.S. Military's Development and Testing of the B61-12 Tactical Nuclear Bomb; Why it is Cause for Concern in Russia and North Korea: Part Two,' *Military Watch Magazine*, August 31, 2017.

81 'N.Korea says it has developed advanced hydrogen bomb ready for ICBM,' *Reuters*, September 3, 2017.

82 Ibid.

83 Rogoway, Tyler, 'North Korea Shows H-Bomb Warhead Design, Says It Will Use It In EMP Strike,' *The War Zone*, September 3, 2017.

84 Albert, Eleanor, 'North Korea's Military Capabilities,' *Council on Foreign Relations*, January 3, 2018.

85 Freeman, Colin, 'North Korea: How did a small, dirt-poor pariah state build its own H-bomb?,' *The Telegraph*, September 28, 2017.

86 'U.S. nuclear commander assumes North Korea tested H-bomb Sept. 3,' *CBS News*, September 15, 2017.

87 'North Korea's Military Capabilities,' *Council on Foreign Relations*, June 28, 2022.

88 '2017 North Korean nuclear test order of magnitude larger than previous tests, new study finds,' *Advancing Earth and Space Sciences*, June 3, 2019.

Tucker, Patrick, 'North Korea's Nuclear Bomb Is Much Bigger than Previously Thought,' *Defense One*, June 4, 2019.

89 Rogin, Josh, 'Opinion Inside the drive to "make a deal" with North Korea,' *Washington Post*, November 9, 2017.

90 Jackson, Van, *On the Brink: Trump, Kim, and the Threat of Nuclear War*, Cambridge, Cambridge University Press, 2018 (p. 143).

Choe, Sang-Hun and Sanger, David E., 'North Korea Fires Missiles Over Japan,' *New York Times,* August 28, 2017.

91 Jackson, Van, *On the Brink: Trump, Kim, and the Threat of Nuclear War*, Cambridge, Cambridge University Press, 2018 (pp. 141–142).

92 McCaskill, Nolan D., 'Trump Says "Fire and Fury" Warning to North Korea Maybe Not "Tough Enough,"' *Politico,* August 10, 2017.

93 Kiernan, Ben and Simon, David, 'Donald Trump just threatened to commit genocide,' *Washington Post,* September 26, 2017.

94 Jackson, Van, *On the Brink: Trump, Kim, and the Threat of Nuclear War*, Cambridge, Cambridge University Press, 2018 (p. 146).

95 'Kim Jong Un calls Trump "deranged," says he will "pay dearly" for comments,' *CBS*, September 21, 2017.

96 'D.P.R. Korea denounces US President's "reckless and violent" comments,' *United Nations* (YouTube Channel), September 24, 2017.

97 Luttwak, Edward, 'It's Time to Bomb North Korea,' *Foreign Policy,* January 8, 2018.

98 'U.S. Must Invade North Korea to Wipe Out Kim Jong Un's Nuclear Weapons, Military Leaders Say,' *Newsweek*, November 5, 2017.

99 Hurst, Daniel, 'Former US military commander warns against "bloody nose" strike on North Korea,' *The Guardian*, February 20, 2018.

100 DeLuce, Dan and McLaughlin, Jenna and Groll, Elias, 'Armageddon by Accident,' *Foreign Policy*, October 18, 2017.

101 Baynes, Chris, 'US "to put nuclear bombers on 24-hour alert" for first time since Cold War,' *The Independent,* October 23, 2017.

102 Smith, Nicola, 'US Navy Seals tasked with North Korea "decapitation" strike could be part of exercises,' *Telegraph,* October 17, 2017.

103 Trevithick, Joseph, 'The South Koreans Want Kim Jong Un to Live in Fear of "Decapitation,"' *The Drive*, June 29, 2019.

'South Korea Plans "Decapitation Unit" to Try to Scare North's Leaders,' *New York Times,* September 12, 2017.

104 Weiner, Tim, *Legacy of Ashes: The History of the CIA*, New York, Anchor Books, 2008 (Chapter 6).

105 Ahn, JH, 'Veterans: S.Korean Special Forces can't infiltrate North Korea,' *NK News*, October 22, 2015.

106 Willis, Gerald, 'Andersen receives 1.5M pounds of munitions during annual in-shipment,' *Defense Visual Information Distribution Service*, October 18, 2017.

107 Gady, Franz-Stefan, '3 US Carrier Strike Groups Hold Massive Naval Drill with South Korea, Japanese Navies in Western Pacific,' *The Diplomat*, November 13, 2017.

108 Kristensen, Hans M. and Norris, Robert S., 'A history of US nuclear weapons in South Korea,' *Bulletin of Atomic Scientists,* vol. 73, no. 6, 2017 (pp. 349–357).

109 'U.S. military stokes N Korea flames with "secret nuclear silos" claim,' *RT*, November 16, 2017.

110 Lee, Yong-soo, 'Top. U.S. Official in Charge of Evacuations Visited S. Korea,' *Chosun Ilbo*, September 20, 2017.

111 Gamel, Kim, 'US Forces Korea warns of fake evacuation messages,' *Stars and Stripes*, September 21, 2017.

112 Wadhams, Nick and Epstein, Jennifer, 'Trump Says North Korea's Kim Is "Starting to Respect" America,' *Bloomberg,* August 23, 2017.

113 'U.S., South Korea to hold joint air force drill in early December,' *Reuters*, November 24, 2017.

114 Dominguez, Gabriel, 'USFK confirms North Korea's Hwaseong-15 ICBM can target all of US mainland,' *Janes,* July 11, 2019.

115 'US missile expert: N. Korean missile larger than thought, could carry decoys,' *Asia Times,* December 2, 2017.

116 Kim, Christine and Stewart, Phil, 'North Korea says "breakthrough" puts U.S. mainland within range of nuclear weapons,' *Reuters*, November 29, 2017.

117 Ambassador Nikki Haley, Remarks at an Emergency UN Security Council Meeting on North Korea, United States Mission to the United Nations, November 29, 2017.

118 Ibid.

119 'Russia calls U.S. threat to destroy North Korea a "bloodthirsty tirade,"' *Reuters,* December 1, 2017.

Gehrke, Joel, 'North Korea ready to negotiate on nukes with Russia's help,' *Washington Examiner,* December 1, 2018.

120 Shinkman, Paul D., 'China's "Freeze for Freeze" Plan for North Korea Gets Chilly Reception in U.S.,' *U.S. News*, September 5, 2017.

121 'How to Interpret Russia's Growing Surface-to-Air Missile Deployments Near the North Korean Border,' *Military Watch Magazine,* August 11, 2017.

122 'Vicious Circle: How to Prevent "Guam Missile Crisis" Between US, N Korea,' *Sputnik News,* August 12, 2018.

'Russian East Asian Expert Indicates that Russia's Air Defence Systems Cover North Korea to Deter American Attacks; Could Moscow's Actions Avert War on the Korean Peninsula?,' *Military Watch Magazine,* August 12, 2018.

123 'CNN: Россия «сдружилась» с КНДР назло США,' ['CNN: Russia "became friends" with the DPRK in spite of the USA'], *RT,* March 15, 2015.

124 Azanov, Roman, '«Лисья гончая» с «Кинжалом»: как МиГ-31 стал носителем гиперзвукового оружия' ['"Foxhound" with "Dagger": How the MiG-31 became a carrier of hypersonic weapons], *TASS*, May 11, 2018.

'Russia picks MiG-31 fighter as a carrier for cutting-edge hypersonic weapon,' *TASS*, April 6, 2018.

125 Blanchard, Ben and Olipahnt, James, 'Chinese State Media Says China Should be Neutral if North Korea Attacks the U.S.,' *Time,* August 11, 2017.

126 Luttwak, Edward, 'It's Time to Bomb North Korea,' *Foreign Policy,* January 8, 2018.

Schneider, Jacquelyn, 'Chinese Military Involvement in a Future Korean War,' *Strategic Studies Quarterly*, 2010 (pp. 50–67).

127 Lo, Kinling, 'China "shoots down incoming missiles" during exercise over waters close to North Korea,' *South China Morning Post,* September 5, 2017.

128 Nevett, Joshua, 'Vladimir Putin orders 1,000 Russian marines to OPEN FIRE close to North Korea border,' *Daily Star,* December 5, 2017.

129 'Pilots suppress hostile manpower at drills, Primorsky Krai,' *Ministry of Defence of the Russian Federation,* December 21, 2017.

130 McInnis, Kathleen J. et al., The North Korean Nuclear Challenge: Military Options and Issues for Congress, CRS Report, R44994, Washington, DC, Congressional Research Service, November 6, 2017 (p. 25),

131 Snyder, Scott A., '"Toughest Sanctions Ever": UN Security Council Resolution 2321,' *Council on Foreign Relations*, December 2, 2016.

132 'Allied navies conduct strike exercise against N.K. nuke facilities,' *Yonhap*, October 11, 2016.

133 'S. Korean fighter jets return from 3-week joint exercise in Alaska,' *Yonhap,* October 26, 2016.

134 Foley, Hamilton, *Woodrow Wilson's Case for the League of Nations*, Princeton, Princeton University Press, 1923 (p. 71).

135 Norrlöf, Carla, 'The Dollar Still Dominates,' *Foreign Affairs*, February 21, 2023.

136 Demarais, Agathe, 'The End of the Age of Sanctions?,' *Foreign Affairs*, December 27, 2022.

137 Hass, Richard N., 'Economic Sanctions: Too Much of a Bad Thing,' *Brookings Institute*, June 1, 1998.

138 'Do Sanctions Really Work on North Korea? The Impossible State Live!,' *Center for Strategic and International Studies* (YouTube Channel), March 8, 2023.

139 Yi, Yang, 'Commentary: U.S. should stop blaming China for trade deficit, Korean nuclear issue,' *Xinhua,* July 31, 2017.

140 Panda, Ankit, *Kim Jong Un and the Bomb: Survival and Deterrence in North Korea*, Oxford, Oxford University Press, 2020 (Chapter 11, Section 3).

Jackson, Van, *On the Brink: Trump, Kim, and the Threat of Nuclear War,* Cambridge, Cambridge University Press, 2018 (p. 199).

141 Remarks by LTG H.R. McMaster at U.S.-UK Policy Exchange Event, The White House, Secretary of the Press, December 12, 2017.

142 Democratic People's Republic of Korea, Food and Agriculture Organization of the United Nations, World Food Program Joint Rapid Food Security Assessment, May 2019 (p. 14).

United Nations Security Council Resolution 2397, 8151st meeting of UNSC, Adopted on December 22, 2017.

143 Crude Oil Consumption by Country, *Index Mundi* (accessed September 14, 2019).

144 Kim, Byung-Kook and Vogel, Ezra, *The Park Chung Hee Era: The Transformation of South Korea*, Cambridge, MA, Harvard University Press, 2011 (pp. 483–510).

Burr, William, 'Stopping Korea from Going Nuclear, Part I,' *National Security Archive,* March 22, 2017.

Ide, William, 'How the US stopped Taiwan's bomb,' *Taipei Times*, October 14, 1999.

Weiner, Tim, 'How a Spy Left Taiwan in the Cold,' *New York Times,* December 20, 1997.

145 Rubin, Michael, 'Why Taiwan needs nuclear weapons,' *The National Interest,* May 31, 2020.

Lyon, Rod, 'The Next Nuclear Weapons State: Australia?,' *The National Interest,* October 27, 2019.

'Australia debates developing nuclear weapons,' *Bangkok Post*, July 8, 2019.

Stangarone, Troy, 'Is Trump Right to Suggest that South Korea and Japan Should Go Nuclear?,' *Korea Economic Institute of America.*

146 Mueller, John and Mueller, Karl, 'Sanctions of Mass Destruction,' *Foreign Affairs*, vol. 78, no. 3, 1999 (pp. 43–53).

147 Ibid. (pp. 43–53).

148 'Sanctions Blamed for Deaths of Children,' *Lewiston Morning Tribune*, December 2, 1995.

Stahl, Lesley, 'Interview with Madeline Albright,' *60 Minutes*, May 12, 1996.

149 'How Sanctions Affect Iran's Economy,' *Council on Foreign Relations*, May 22, 2012.

Peterson, Sabrina M., 'Iran's Deteriorating Economy: An Analysis of the Economic Impact of Western Sanctions,' *International Affairs Review*, July 1, 2012.

'The harm that sanctions do to the vulnerable,' *Financial Times*, May 4, 2023.

Buncombe, Andrew, 'US sanctions on Venezuela responsible for "tens of thousands" of deaths, claims new report,' *The Independent,* April 26, 2019.

'Economic Sanctions as Collective Punishment: The Case of Venezuela,' *Center For Economic and Policy Research*, April 25, 2019.

150 Pearson, James and Park, Ju-Min, 'Despite sanctions, North Korea prices steady as Kim leaves markets alone,' *Reuters*, August 8, 2016.

151 Ibid.

152 Lankov, Andrei, 'Sanctions working? Not yet…,' *Korea Times*, May 29, 2016.

153 Mullen, Mike and Nunn, Sam and Mount, Adam, *A Sharper Choice on North Korea: Engaging China for a Stable Northeast Asia*, Council on Foreign Relations, Independent Task Force Report No. 74, September 2016 (p. 14).

154 Kim, Christine and Chung, Jane, 'North Korea 2016 economic growth at 17-year high despite sanctions: South Korea,' *Reuters*, July 21, 2017.

155 Dorell, Oren, 'North Korean Economy Keeps Humming Despite Ever-Tighter Sanctions,' *USA Today*, November 24, 2017.

156 'North Korea's Stable Exchange Rates Confound Economists,' *Associated Press*, November 16, 2018.

Kim, Christine and Chung, Jane, 'North Korea 2016 economic growth at 17-year high despite sanctions: South Korea,' *Reuters*, July 21, 2017.

157 Ibid.

158 'North Korea's Stable Exchange Rates Confound Economists,' *Associated Press*, November 16, 2018.

159 'Former unification minister criticizes Bank of Korea statistics on North Korean growth rate,' *Hankyoreh,* January 1, 2019.

160 Maresca, Thomas, 'Report: North Korea economy developing dramatically despite sanctions,' *UPI,* December 4, 2019.

Choi, Eun-joo, '21st Colloquium of 2019: Changes in the North Korean Economy Observed at Field Investigation of 2019 to China–North Korea Borders,' *Sejong Institute,* November 12, 2019.

161 'North Korea's Stable Exchange Rates Confound Economists,' *Associated Press*, November 16, 2018.

162 Baron, Jeff, 'What if Sanctions Brought North Korea to the Brink? "Well, in 1941…,"' *38 North*, September 7, 2017.

163 Ansley, Rachel, 'Tillerson's Take on US. Foreign Policy: A Year in Review,' *New Atlanticist,* December 13, 2017.

164 Riley-Smith, Ben, 'Exclusive: US Making Plans for "Bloody Nose" Military Attack on North Korea,' *The Telegraph,* December 20, 2017.

Seib, Gerald F., 'Amid Signs of Thaw in North Korea, Tensions Bubble Up,' *The Wall Street Journal*, January 9, 2018.

Jackson, Van, *On the Brink: Trump, Kim, and the Threat of Nuclear War,* Cambridge, Cambridge University Press, 2018 (pp. 163, 228).

165 'Tillerson a voice of reason in Trump's Cabinet,' *Los Angeles Times,* December 12, 2017.

Von Nahmen, Alexandra, 'With Tillerson's firing, White House loses a voice of reason,' *Deutsche Welle,* March 13, 2018.

166 'White House Contradicts Tillerson on North Korea,' *BBC News*, December. 14, 2017.

167 Donald J. Trump on Twitter: 'I told Rex Tillerson, our wonderful Secretary of State, that he is wasting his time trying to negotiate with Little Rocket Man....,' October 1, 2017.

168 Warrick, Joby and Nakashima, Ellen and Fifield, Anna, 'North Korea now making missile-ready nuclear weapons, U.S. analysts say,' *Washington Post,* August 8, 2017.

169 Sanger, David E. and Choe, Sang-Hun, 'North Korea Tests a Ballistic Missile That Experts Say Could Hit California,' *New York Times*, July 28, 2017.

170 Warrick, Joby and Nakashima, Ellen and Fifield, Anna, 'North Korea now making missile-ready nuclear weapons, U.S. analysts say,' *Washington Post,* August 8, 2017.

171 Ham, Paul, *Hiroshima Nagasaki: The Real Story of the Atomic Bombings and their Aftermath,* New York, Doubleday, 2012 (pp. 488–490, 494).

'Winston Churchill wanted to nuke Kremlin "to win Cold War," FBI memo reveals,' *RT*, November 9, 2014.

172 Burr, William and Richelson, Jeffrey T., 'Whether to "Strangle the Baby in the Cradle": The United States and the Chinese Nuclear Program, 1960–64,' *International Security*, vol. 25, no. 3, winter 2000–2001 (pp. 54–55, 58).

Gady, Franz-Stefan, 'How a State Department Study Prevented Nuclear War With China,' *The Diplomat*, October 25, 2017.

Goldstein, Lyle J., 'When China was a "rogue state": the impact of China's nuclear weapons program on US–China relations during the 1960s,' *Journal of Contemporary China*, vol. 12, issue 37, 2003 (p. 740).

173 Ibid. (p. 742).

174 Beavers, Olivia, 'Graham: 30 percent chance Trump attacks North Korea if it conducts another missile test,' *The Hill,* December 14, 2017.

175 Friedman, Uri, 'Lindsey Graham Reveals the Dark Calculus of Striking North Korea,' *The Atlantic*, August 1, 2017.

176 Ortiz, Erik and Yamamoto, Arata, 'Senator Lindsey Graham: Trump Says War with North Korean an Option,' *NBC News,* August 2, 2017.

177 McMahon, Patrick, 'Senator calls for "preemptive strike" on North Korea and offers a jaw-dropping justification for war,' *Rare News*, April 20, 2017.

178 'Lt. Gen. H. R. McMaster on foreign policy; Sen. Schumer on President Trump's first 100 days,' *Fox News*, April 30, 2017.

179 Dreazen, Yochi, 'Here's what war with North Korea would look like,' *Vox,* February 8, 2018.

180 Friedman, Uri, 'Lindsey Graham Reveals the Dark Calculus of Striking North Korea,' *The Atlantic*, August 1, 2017.

181 Luttwak, Edward, 'It's Time to Bomb North Korea,' *Foreign Policy,* January 8, 2018.

182 Jackson, Van, *On the Brink: Trump, Kim, and the Threat of Nuclear War,* Cambridge, Cambridge University Press, 2018 (p. 195).

183 'Seoul warns Trump: U.S. must not strike North Korea without our consent,' *The Guardian*, November 15, 2017.

Bandow, Doug, 'Honoring the Man Who Prevented the Second Korean War,' *CATO Institute*, November 30, 2015.

184 Daniels, Jeff, 'Pentagon Scenario of a New Korean War Estimates 20,000 Deaths Daily in South Korea, Retired US General Says,' *CNBC*, September 25, 2017.

Demick, Barbara, 'Escalating tension has experts simulating a new Korean War, and the scenarios are sobering,' *Los Angeles Times,* September 25, 2017.

185 Kazianis, Harry J., 'America Must Move Past Its "Sputnik" Moment on North Korea – Or Else,' *The National Interest,* March 4, 2019.

186 Peck, Michael, 'Here's Exactly Why War With North Korea Would Be Hell, According To New War Games,' *Task and Purpose*, June 9, 2018.

187 'Saudi Arabia's U.S.-made Patriot Missile Defense System "Malfunctions", Crashes in Residential Area,' *Haaretz,* March 27, 2018.

188 '"Up to 15 tons of depleted uranium used in 1999 Serbia bombing" – lead lawyer in suit against NATO,' *RT,* June 13, 2017.

Oakford, Samuel, 'The United States Used Depleted Uranium in Syria,' *Foreign Policy*, February 14, 2017.

Edwards, Rob, 'U.S. fired depleted uranium at civilian areas in 2003 Iraq war, report finds,' *The Guardian*, June 19, 2014.

189 Jackson, Van, *On the Brink: Trump, Kim, and the Threat of Nuclear War,* Cambridge, Cambridge University Press, 2018 (pp. 12–13).

190 'DPRK Foreign Ministry Clarifies Stand on New Measure to Bolster War Deterrence,' *KCNA*, October 3, 2006.

CHAPTER 6

North Korea Wins: Coming to Terms with a New Status Quo

Deescalation

The beginning of 2018 saw the end of a two-year standoff between North Korea and the United States, during which two American administrations had brought unprecedented pressure to bear both on China and Russia to allow the world's harshest economic sanctions regime to be imposed, and on Pyongyang itself with military maneuvers that were both massive and intense. The DPRK had during this time escalated the modernization of its nuclear deterrent with three tests of miniaturized warheads, while demonstrating an improved capability to strike Guam and then the continental United States. A combination of factors including formidable and significantly improved conventional capabilities, an "intelligence black hole" complicating possible operations, a WMD and missile deterrent, heretofore unseen resilience to economic warfare efforts, and indications by neighboring China and Russia that they would defend their neighbor, had by late 2017 left Washington and its allies with very few options.

Even before the testing of the Hwasong-15, it appeared by the late summer that North Korea had come out on top in this stage of its standoff with the United States. On August 9, a day after U.S. intelligence confirmed the country's intercontinental range nuclear strike capabilities,[1] *Foreign Policy* summarized the emerging realization in the title of its article: "The Game Is Over, and North Korea Has Won." Based on the latest intelligence estimates it observed: "North Korea has a large stockpile of compact nuclear weapons that can arm the country's missiles, including its new intercontinental ballistic missiles that are capable of hitting the United States. That's another way of saying: game over."[2] This new consensus would grow stronger in the following months both in the United States and abroad, with Russian President Vladimir Putin similarly highlighting the achievements of North Korean weapons programs, stating: "I believe Mr. Kim Jong Un has certainly won this round. He has a nuclear weapon and a missile with a range of up to 13,000 kilometers [Hwasong-15] that can reach almost any place on Earth or at least any territory of his potential adversary. He is already an absolutely shrewd and mature politician."[3]

In his January 1, 2018 new year's address exactly a year after announcing the imminent completion of ICBM development, Chairman Kim summarized the shift which advances in his country's strategic nuclear arsenal had caused over the past year as follows:

> We attained our general orientation and strategic goal with success, and our Republic has at last come to possess a powerful and reliable war deterrent, which no force and nothing can reverse. Our country's nuclear forces are capable of thwarting and countering any nuclear threats from the United States, and they constitute a powerful deterrent that prevents it from starting an adventurous war. In no way would the United States dare to ignite a war against our country. The whole of its mainland is within range of our nuclear strike and the nuclear button is on my office desk all the time; the United States needs to be clearly aware that this is not merely a threat but a reality.[4]

Confirming that all fundamental design issues had been solved, the chairman stated that what was left was only to "mass-produce nuclear warheads and ballistic missiles… to give a spur to the efforts for deploying them for action." With this stage of the strengthening the country's deterrent able to be pursued far less conspicuously than missile test launches or nuclear warhead detonations, it was an optimal time to pursue détente from a position of strength. The speed at which the Hwasong-12, Hwasong-14 and Hwasong-15 had been tested to readiness for mass production had been a vital contributor to regional security. Had this testing been protracted over several years not only would the United States have been much less likely to be deterred from initiating a war in late 2017, but the West's construing of missile testing as provocations meant a shorter more successful testing period contributed to significantly shortening the period of high tensions.

Able to press for deescalation from a position of strength, following the Hwasong-15 test North Korea would cease all ballistic missile testing for 18 months, all strategic missile testing for 23 months, and all ICBM testing for four years and four months. Contrasting sharply with his 2017 new year's address. Chairman Kim accordingly emphasized that he was not making a threat, while his allusion to a "nuclear button" was interpreted abroad as an intentional indication of his centralized command and control of the country's nuclear arsenal. The speech was widely seen in Western assessments to have been conciliatory, heavily defensively focused, and intentionally non-threatening.[5]

Chairman Kim's address included unusually conciliatory language towards South Korea, notably a singling out the significance of the Winter Olympic Games set to be hosted in Pyeongchang the following month, and calling on Seoul to "respond positively to our sincere efforts for a détente," "discontinue all the nuclear war drills they stage with outside forces," and "refrain from any acts of bringing in nuclear armaments and aggressive forces from the United States." The address otherwise appeared to recognize that the new Moon Jae In administration, inaugurated in May 2017, represented a potential channel through which to reduce tensions with Washington.[6]

President Moon's government was quick to respond with a well-timed diplomatic initiative precisely as Washington needed a way to deescalate. In contrast to the derailing of Secretary Tillerson's call for talks two months prior, the Trump administration took no steps to undermine Seoul's diffusing of the situation, indicating that the consensus in Washington had indeed further shifted. A landmark in this regard was Seoul's request to delay the massive Key Resolve and Foal Eagle military exercises for the Olympic Games, which Chairman Kim's address had called for, and which the U.S. quickly assented to. With Pyongyang maintaining a self-imposed moratorium on nuclear and missile testing, this represented the informal reaching of a "freeze for freeze" agreement – something Washington had dismissed totally out of hand the previous year.

On February 9 North Korean Head of State and President of the Presidium of the Supreme People's Assembly Kim Yong Nam led a high-level delegation to Seoul, with the 89-year-old being the highest level official to make foreign visits and by some accounts the most powerful man in North Korea when the young Kim Jong Un was being groomed for leadership. The president was accompanied by Chairman Kim's sister, Kim Yo Jong, who *CNN* reported "stole the show" at the Olympics with her charm and positive message of reconciliation. While comparing North Korea to Nazi Germany, and referring to Chairman Kim as a "brutal dictator," the American outlet nevertheless departed from the staples of Western coverage of the country by highlighting: "If 'diplomatic dance' were an event at the Winter Olympics, Kim Jong Un's younger sister would be favored to win gold. With a smile, a handshake and a warm message in South Korea's presidential guest book, Kim Yo Jong has struck a chord with the public just one day into the PyeongChang Games."[7] A North Korean cheerleading team with Korean unification flags, described by the *BBC* as "mesmerizing"[8] and elsewhere as an "army of beauties," also stole the show, and was described by *USA Today* as "one of the most indelible memories of these Olympics."[9] President Moon was personally presented with a hand-written invitation to North Korea from Chairman Kim, and an exchange of envoys and symbolic gifts began soon afterwards. Forty-five days into the new year the mood on the Korean Peninsula had transformed entirely, with Pyongyang's objective of peace through strength appearing to have been attained.

Having suspended joint military exercises, President Trump appeared pleased to accept praise for the success of the Olympic détente, with unconfirmed reports of his behind-the-scenes role in the inter-Korean reconciliation providing a possible basis for this. While President Moon had been elected pledging inter-Korean reconciliation, after taking office in May his administration had been strongly dissuaded by Washington from pursuing this, with the sudden very significant turnaround and progress on this front indicating an American green light had been given. The Trump administration would subsequently clearly demonstrate that when Moon's reconciliation efforts were seen to infringe on American interests, such as through moves towards loosening economic sanctions or constructing an inter-Korean railway, they could quickly and decisively be blocked.[10] As President Trump would summarize in October in response to Seoul's efforts to reduce its unilateral sanctions: "They won't do it without our approval. They do nothing without our approval."[11,i] The perfect timing from Washington's perspective of Moon's olive branch to Pyongyang was thus likely far form coincidental. The Olympics were immediately followed by inter-Korean talks, after which the Blue House announced on March 8: "The North expressed its willingness to hold heartfelt dialogue with the United States on the issues of denuclearization and normalizing relations with the United States… while dialogue is continuing, it will not attempt any strategic provocations, such as nuclear and ballistic missile tests."[12]

Pyongyang had made no changes to its position, with even its moratorium on missile launches being clearly stated as a consequence of the testing phase of its programs being over and mass production beginning. The United States by contrast had shown a new willingness for dialogue, abandoning the harsh preconditions imposed since the Obama years, suspending military exercises in South Korea, and subsequently accepting one-to-one talks

---

i Leading American scholar on Korea Bruce Cumings observed to this effect that persistent and successful efforts by Washington "to keep South Korea in line – following American policy. The United States is the only major power that keeps interfering in Korean affairs – other countries do not do this," stressing that as a result Seoul's peace initiatives "can't get anywhere without American support." ('Moon has done more for inter-Korean peace than any other president, US professor says,' *Hankyoreh,* June 29, 2020.)

missile testing efforts was realized on April 2 with the first test launch of the Hwasong-16B ballistic missile – a successor to the intermediate range Hwasong-12 featuring not only a solid fuel engine, but also a hypersonic glide vehicle. The launch notably followed the unprecedented testing of a prototype AGM-183 air launched hypersonic missile from a U.S. Air Force B-52 bomber over Guam on March 17. The American missile had previously been reported canceled due to technical issues, before reportedly being revived due to the lack of viable alternative programs, and afterwards again being dropped from the Pentagon budget.[174] The timing of the Korean launch raised allusions to a new stage in a hypersonic arms race between Washington and Pyongyang, as both modernized both their strike capabilities and their missile defenses. Intermediate range ballistic missiles were North Korea's last ballistic missile category not to have seen a solid fuel platform introduced, with ground testing of a solid fuel engine having been reported in November 2023 and again on March 20, 13 days before the Hwasong-16B's test launch.[xxii]

With South Korean sources stressing that the missile had "different flight features from the missiles the North previously tested,"[175] development of the Hwasong-16B was a further major milestone in the transformation of the balance of power in the U.S.-DPRK conflict. Even without hypersonic glide vehicles or nuclear warheads, assessments by RAND Corporation among multiple other sources consistently highlighted that military facilities on Guam were "seriously threatened" by and extremely vulnerable to ballistic missile attacks, concluding that even if missiles

---

xxii A great deal of importance appeared to be attributed to improving the ability to strike Guam and other mid-Pacific facilities, with Chairman Kim having gone so far as to state on March 20: "The military strategic value of this weapon system is appreciated as important as ICBM from the security environment of our state and the operational demand of the People's Army." A separate missile, the Hwasong-16A, was thought to integrate a conical maneuvering reentry vehicle rather than a hypersonic glide vehicle, although it remained uncertain whether this simpler missile would enter service. ('Respected Comrade Kim Jong Un Guides Ground Jet Test of Solid-fuel Engine for New-type Intermediate-range Hypersonic Missile,' *KCNA*, March 20, 2024.)

deployed conventional warheads "the prospects are grim" for the bases' survival.[176] The Pentagon had initiated extensive measures to mitigate the vulnerability of facilities on Guam in response to potential adversaries' growing strike capabilities against them, with plans announced from mid-2022 to install up to 23 new air defense sites hosting a range of complementary systems, making the island's airspace among the best and most densely defended in the world.[177] Against this network, further supported by the Aegis anti-missile systems on nearby warships, the ability to deliver nuclear strikes by hypersonic glide vehicle was invaluable to guaranteeing North Korea's ability to disrupt or end American use of the territory for power projection into East Asia. The first launch of the Hwasong-16B thus appeared to mark the latest case of North Korea's counter to upcoming U.S. missile defense measures being ready before these defenses were even deployed.

While tensions remained high, a new status-quo on the Korean Peninsula appeared set to remain indefinitely, with Pyongyang expected to continue to strengthen its position as a shifting geopolitical environment rapidly brought an end to its isolation, while its nuclear capabilities continued to be cemented. In the United States, meanwhile, the unpopularity and perceived unacceptability of dealing with Pyongyang to achieve anything less than a one sided capitulation meant the country was also unlikely to shift from its position on talks, which only became more unfeasible as North Korea's position strengthened.

The Biden administration's tenure in many respects marked a return to the Cold War era status quo for U.S.-DPRK relations, in the respect that the United States had returned to a time when its ability to shape world order was far more constrained and serious challenges to its power were made from around the world. Where North Korea from the 1990s came under intense pressure as one of the few states outside the Western sphere of influence, and as a holdout from a time when a broader Soviet Bloc had challenged Western dominance, by the mid-2020s Pyongyang was far less of an outlier in world order. Beyond North Korea's nuclear and missile programs and improving economic resilience, the subsiding of Pyongyang's isolation, and America's fast diminishing ability to focus attentions on it, had a transformative effect on the two states' three-quarter century long conflict that left Washington's position increasingly unfavorable.

Endnotes

1 Warrick, Joby and Nakashima, Ellen and Fifield, Anna, 'North Korea now making missile-ready nuclear weapons, U.S. analysts say,' *Washington Post,* August 8, 2017.

2 Lewis, Jeffrey, 'The Game Is Over, and North Korea Has Won,' *Foreign Policy,* August 9, 2017.

3 Macdonald, Hamish, 'Putin praises Kim Jong Un, says N. Korean leader has "won this round,"' *NK News,* January 11, 2018.

4 'Kim Jong Un makes New Year Address,' *KCNA,* January 1, 2018.

5 Haggard, Stephan, 'Kim Jong-un's 2018 New Year's Address: The Nuclear Program, the Economy, and the Challenge to the South,' *Peterson Institute For International Economics*, January 2, 2018.

6 'Kim Jong Un makes New Year Address,' *KCNA,* January 1, 2018.

7 Sterling, Joe and McKenzie, Sheena and Todd, Brian, 'Kim Jong Un's sister is stealing the show at the Winter Olympics,' *CNN,* February 10, 2018.

8 'Winter Olympics: North Korean cheerleaders mesmerise crowds,' *BBC News,* February 10, 2018.

9 Madhani, Aamer and Rogers, Martin, 'North Korea cheerleaders making quite an impression at Winter Olympics,' *USA Today*, March 2, 2018.

10 Hass, Benjamin, 'Train project linking North and South Korea stopped in its tracks by US,' *The Guardian,* August 21, 2018.

Asmolov Konstantin, 'South Korea: "They Do Nothing Without Our Approval!,"' *New Eastern Outlook*, October 27, 2018.

Choe, Sang-Hun, 'South Korea Backtracks on Easing Sanctions After Trump Comment,' *New York Times*, October 11, 2018.

11 Kim, Bo-eun, 'Trump's remarks infringe national sovereignty,' *Korea Times,* October 11, 2018.

Choe, Sang-Hun, 'South Korea Backtracks on Easing Sanctions After Trump Comment,' *New York Times,* October 11, 2018.

12 Choe, Sang-hun and Landler, Mark, 'North Korea Signals Willingness to "Denuclearize," South says,' *New York Times,* March 6, 2018.

13 Sanchez, Luis, 'White House: "Maximum Pressure" Campaign on North Korea is Working,' *The Hill*, March 27, 2018.

14 Transcript of the Press Conference by the Secretary-General with the Prime Minister of Sweden, Stockholm, April 23, 2018.

15 Jackson, Van, *On the Brink: Trump, Kim, and the Threat of Nuclear War,* Cambridge, Cambridge University Press, 2018 (p. 201).

16 Kazianis, Harry J., 'America Must Move Past Its "Sputnik" Moment on North Korea – Or Else,' *The National Interest,* March 4, 2019.

17 Donald J. Trump on Twitter: 'Possible progress being made in talks with North Korea. For the first time in many years, a serious effort is being made by all parties concerned. The World is watching and waiting! May be false hope, but the U.S. is ready to go hard in either direction,' March 6, 2018.

18 Donald J. Trump on Twitter: 'Kim Jong Un talked about denuclearization with the South Korean Representatives, not just a freeze. Also, no missile testing by North Korea during this period of time. Great progress being made but sanctions will remain until an agreement is reached. Meeting being planned!,' March 6, 2018

19 Pompeo, Mike, *Never Give an Inch: Fighting for the America I Love*, Northampton, MA, Broadside Books, 2023 (Chapter 8).

20 'North Korea rejects Pompeo from nuclear dialogue: KCNA,' *Reuters,* April 18, 2019.

'Tick Tock: Pyongyang Warns Time is Running Out For Denuclearization Deal with US,' *Sputnik News*, June 27, 2019.

21 Pompeo, Mike, *Never Give an Inch: Fighting for the America I Love*, Northampton, MA, Broadside Books, 2023 (Chapter 1).

22 Ibid. (Chapter 8).

23 Ibid. (Chapter 1).

24 Jeong, Sophie and Ripley, Will and McKirdy, Euan, 'Kim Jong Un: North Korea no longer needs nuclear tests,' *CNN*, April 22, 2018.

25 Rampton, Roberta and Brunnstrom, David, 'Upbeat Trump welcomes U.S. prisoners released by North Korea,' *Reuters,* May 10, 2018.

26 Kim, So-hyun, 'Korean American pastor says he was spying in NK,' *Korea Herald*, July 30, 2019.

27 Albright, David, Institute Statement on the Dismantlement of Punggye-ri, Institute for Science and International Security, May 25, 2018.

28 Ko, Dong-hwan, 'Trump up for "hamburger talk" with Kim Jong-un,' *Korea Times,* June 16, 2016.

29 Press Conference by President Trump, Capella Hotel, Singapore, June 12, 2018.

30 De Luce, Dan and Dilanian, Ken, 'China eases economic pressure on North Korea, undercutting the Trump admin,' *NBC News*, September 5, 2018.

31 Brunnstrom, David, 'China appears to relax North Korea sanctions: report to U.S. Congress,' *Reuters,* November 15, 2018.

32 Press Conference by President Trump, Capella Hotel, Singapore, June 12, 2018.

33 Snodgrass, Guy M., *Holding the Line: Inside Trump's Pentagon with Secretary Mattis*, New York, Sentinel, 2019 (Chapter 18).

34 Pompeo, Mike, *Never Give an Inch: Fighting for the America I Love*, Northampton, MA, Broadside Books, 2023 (Chapter 8).

35 Donald J. Trump on Twitter: 'Just landed – a long trip, but everybody can now feel much safer than the day I took office. There is no longer a Nuclear Threat from North Korea. Meeting with Kim Jong Un was an interesting and very positive experience. North Korea has great potential for the future!,' June 13, 2018.

36 Donald J. Trump on Twitter: 'Before taking office people were assuming that we were going to War with North Korea. President Obama said that North Korea was our biggest and most dangerous problem. No longer – sleep well tonight!,' June 13, 2018.

37 Jackson, Van, *On the Brink: Trump, Kim, and the Threat of Nuclear War,* Cambridge, Cambridge University Press, 2018 (p. 187).

Crowley, Michael and Nelson, Louis, '"Ludicrous": Pompeo Snaps at Reporters Seeking Clarity on North Korea Deal,' *Politico*, June 13, 2018.

38 Panda, Ankit, 'Exclusive: North Korea Has Continued Ballistic Missile Launcher Production in 2018, Per US Intelligence,' *The Diplomat,* June 30, 2018.

Cheng, Jonathan, 'North Korea Expands Key Missile-Manufacturing Plant,' *The Wall Street Journal*, July 1, 2018.

39 Ri, Yong Ho, 'Press Statement by Ri Yong-ho, Hanoi, Vietnam,' *Global News*, March 1, 2019.

40 Oberdorfer, Don, *The Two Koreas: A Contemporary History*, Boston, Addison-Wesley, 1997 (p. 352).

41 Ibid.

42 Shorrock, Tim and Richards, Kathleen Ok Soo, 'The Trump-Kim Talks Ended Abruptly – but Negotiations Will Continue,' *The Nation*, February 18, 2019.

정세현 '합의문 괄호만 메우면 됐는데..볼턴때문에 사달난 듯' [Jeong Se Hyun, 'All I had to do was fill in the parenthesis of the agreement'], 노컷뉴스, February 28, 2019.

43 Pompeo, Mike, *Never Give an Inch: Fighting for the America I Love*, Northampton, MA, Broadside Books, 2023 (Chapters 4, 8).

44 Taylor, Adam, 'Nukes and sanctions: What actually went wrong for Trump and Kim Jong Un?,' *Washington Post,* March 1, 2019.

45 Wroughton, Lesley and Brunnstrom, David, 'Exclusive: With a piece of paper, Trump called on Kim to hand over nuclear weapons,' *Reuters,* March 29, 2019.

Byrne, Leo, 'North Korean FM says Pyongyang asked for "partial" sanctions relief,' *NK News,* February 28, 2019.

46 LeTourneau, Nancy, 'Kim Jong Un Played Trump Like a Fiddle,' *Washington Monthly,* February 28, 2019.

47 Ri, Yong Ho, 'Press Statement by Ri Yong-ho, Hanoi, Vietnam,' *Global News*, March 1, 2019.

48 'Supreme Leader Kim Jong Un Makes Policy Speech at First Session of 14th SPA,' *KCNA*, April 13, 2019.

49 Ward, Alex, 'A top Trump official may have just doomed US–North Korea talks,' *Vox,* March 8, 2019.

Johnson, Jesse, 'North Korean denuclearization possible during Trump's first term: U.S. official,' *Japan Times,* March 8, 2019.

50 Rampton, Roberta, 'Trump decides against more North Korea sanctions at this time – source,' *Reuters,* March 22, 2019.

51 Smith, Josh and Lee, Joyce, 'North Korea's Kim Jong Un gives U.S. to year-end to become more flexible,' *Reuters*, April 12, 2019.

52 'Supreme Leader Kim Jong Un Guides Power Demonstration Fire of New-Type Tactical Guided Weapon,' Ministry of Foreign Affairs of the Democratic People's Republic of Korea, April 18, 2019.

53 Yi, Wonju, 'N. Korea says it test-fired new tactical guided missiles,' *Yonhap*, March 26, 2021.

54 Yu, Yong-weon, 'Aegis Ships Missed N. Korea's Recent Missile Launches,' *Chosun Daily*, October 11, 2019.

55 'Japanese radar stations and MSDF crews failed to track recent North Korean missiles launches,' *Japan Times*, September 23, 2019.

56 Cloud, David S., 'U.S. officials say new North Korean missile appears aimed at evading missile defenses,' *Los Angeles Times*, May 15, 2019.

57 'Japan says North Korea developing warheads to penetrate missile defenses,' *Reuters*, August 28, 2019.

'New North Korean Projectiles Could Reach Japan Without Being Intercepted – Military,' *Sputnik News*, June 27, 2019.

58 Kim, Suk Hi and Roehrig, Terence and Seliger, Bernhard (eds.), *The Survival of North Korea: Essays on Strategy, Economics and International Relations*, Jefferson, NC, McFarland & Co., 2011 (p. 49).

59 Lewis, Jeffrey, 'KN-11 AND THAAD,' *Arms Control Wonk,* August 28, 2016.

60 'Iskander är så mycket mer än bara en ballistisk robot' ['Iskander is so much more than just a ballistic robot'], *SVD*, February 23, 2020.

'Swedish Military Intel Boss Sees "Threat" From Russian Missiles, Chinese Bases,' *Sputnik News*, March 20, 2019.

61 Abrams, A. B., 'Russia's Iskander Ballistic Missile System Has Long Worried NATO: Its North Korean Cousin is Much More Dangerous,' *Sino NK*, October 13, 2022.

Abrams, A. B., 'KN-23B deployments against Ukraine could be major boon for North Korea's wider defence exports,' *Daily NK*, January 8, 2024.

62 Mullen, Mike and Nunn, Sam and Mount, Adam, *A Sharper Choice on North Korea: Engaging China for a Stable Northeast Asia*, Council on Foreign Relations, Independent Task Force Report No. 74, September 2016.

63 Johnson, Jesse, 'North Korea calls Bolton "warmonger" and says halting missile tests means giving up right to self-defense,' *Japan Times,* May 27, 2019.

64 Remarks by President Trump and Prime Minister Abe of Japan in Joint Press Conference, Akasaka Palace, Tokyo, Japan, May 27, 2019.

65 Ibid.

66 Shin, Hyonhee, 'North Korea says time running out for talks as U.S. envoy due in South,' *Reuters,* June 27, 2019.

67 Bowman, Michael, 'US Senate Approves New North Korea Sanctions,' *Voice of Asia,* June 27, 2019.

68 Donald J. Trump on Twitter: 'After some very important meetings, including my meeting with President Xi of China, I will be leaving Japan for South Korea (with President Moon). While there, if Chairman Kim of North Korea sees this, I would meet him at the Border/DMZ just to shake his hand and say Hello(?)!,' June 28, 2018.

69 Rampton, Roberta and Lee, Joyce, 'Trump holds historic meeting with Kim with a tweet, handshake and "flowers of hope,"' *Reuters*, July 1, 2019.

70 'Trump meets Kim Jong Un at DMZ and becomes first sitting U.S. president to enter North Korea,' *Los Angeles Times*, June 29, 2019.

71 McCurry, Justin, 'Donald Trump invites Kim Jong-un to US after entering North Korea,' *The Guardian,* June 30, 2019.

72 'In June summit, Kim told Trump he won't make unilateral concession: N.K. TV,' *Yonhap,* January 10, 2020.

73 Friedman, Uri, 'The Day Denuclearization Died,' *The Atlantic,* July 2, 2019.

74 Maresca, Thomas, 'Report: North Korea economy developing dramatically despite sanctions,' *UPI,* December 4, 2019.

75 Snodgrass, Guy M., *Holding the Line: Inside Trump's Pentagon with Secretary Mattis*, New York, Sentinel, 2019 (Chapter 23).

76 Bolton, John, *The Room Where It Happened: A White House Memoir*, New York, Simon & Schuster, 2020 (pp. 94–95).

77 Ibid. (p. 125).

78 Howell, Edward, *North Korea & The Global Nuclear Order: When Bad Behaviour Pays*, Oxford, Oxford University Press, 2023 (p. 208).

79 Ibid. (p. 221).

80 Kim, Suk Hi, *The Survival of North Korea: Essays on Strategy, Economics and International Relations*, Jefferson, NC, McFarland & Co., 2011 (p. 46).

Funabashi, Yoichi, *The Peninsula Question: A Chronicle of the Second Korean Nuclear Crisis*, Washington, DC, Brookings Institution Press, 2007 (p. 143).

81 Oprysko, Caitlin, 'Clinton predicts Trump's North Korea deal will be like putting "lipstick on a pig,"' *Politico,* February 26, 2019.

82 Oprysko, Caitlin, 'Biden dings Trump for his handling of North Korea and Iran,' *Politico,* July 1, 2019.

83 DePetris, Daniel R., 'How Joe Biden Became John Bolton on North Korea,' *The National Interest,* July 15, 2019.

84 DePetris, Daniel R., 'Watch the Video: Would Joe Biden Launch a War Against North Korea?,' *The National Interest,* May 7, 2019.

85 Sganga, Nicole and O'Keefe, Ed, 'Potential 2020 Democratic hopefuls are biggest skeptics of North Korea deal,' *CBS News,* June 13, 2018.

86 'Trump Officials Block U.N. Meeting on Human Rights Abuses in North Korea,' *New York Times*, December 9, 2019.

87 Regan, Helen and Ripley, Will and Browne, Ryan and Kwon, Jake, 'North Korea says it test fired a new type of submarine-launched ballistic missile,' *CNN,* October 3, 2019.

88 Panda, Ankit, 'North Korea Tests New Type of Short-Range Ballistic Missile,' *The Diplomat,* August 12, 2019.

89 *North Korea's Nuclear Weapons and Missile Programs,* Congressional Research Service, July 14, 2020.

90 'N. Korean foreign ministry advisor calls on Trump to make "bold decision,"' *Hankyoreh,* September 30, 2019.

91 Ibid.

92 Peltz, Jennifer, 'North Korea complains at UN about US "provocations,"' *Associated Press*, September 30, 2019.

93 Ahlander, Johan and O'Connor, Philip, 'North Korea breaks off nuclear talks with U.S. in Sweden,' *Reuters*, October 6, 2019.

94 Howell, Edward, *North Korea & The Global Nuclear Order: When Bad Behaviour Pays*, Oxford, Oxford University Press, 2023 (pp. 245–246).

95 'Statement of Spokesman for DPRK State Affairs Commission,' *KCNA*, November 13, 2019.

96 'U.S. postpones military exercises with South Korea in nod toward North Korea,' *Politico*, November 17, 2019.

97 Yang, Seung-sik, 'S. Korea, U.S. to Practice Stabilizing N.Korea,' *Chosun Daily*, August 9, 2019.

98 Lee, Haye-ah, 'U.S. has never abandoned military options for N. Korea: Pentagon official,' *Yonhap*, December 5, 2019.

99 Panda, Ankit, 'North Korea Announces Completion of "Very Important" Test at Satellite Launching Ground,' *The Diplomat*, December 8, 2019.

100 Dilanian, Ken, 'Satellite photos show work on North Korean site linked to long-range missiles,' *NBC News,* December 22, 2019.

101 'North Korea's Kim holds military meeting as tension rises under looming deadline,' *Reuters,* December 22, 2019.

102 'North Korea's Kim convenes party plenary as deadline looms,' *Al Jazeera,* December 29, 2019.

103 Millward, David, 'Kim Jong-un says North Korea ending moratoriums on tests – and touts "new strategic weapon,"' *The Telegraph,* January 1, 2020.

104 Jo, Hak Chol, 'Basic Idea and Spirit of the 5th Plenary Meeting of the 7th C.C., WPK,' *Rodong Sinmun,* January 6, 2019.

105 Panda, Ankit, 'Trump-Kim Relationship No Longer Sufficient for US–North Korea Diplomacy: NK Official,' *The Diplomat,* January 14, 2020.

106 Berlinger, Joshua, 'North Korea says US "deceived" Pyongyang on nuclear talks after Trump sends Kim birthday letter,' *CNN,* January 11, 2020.

107 Lee, Haye-ah, 'N. Korea may be ready to test more advanced ICBM: U.S. general,' *Yonhap,* March 13, 2020.

Cotton, Shea, 'Expect a surge in North Korean missile tests, and of greater range,' *Defense News,* March 10, 2020.

108 Shorrock, Tim, 'Washington Hawks Are Softening Their Hard Line on Sanctions Against North Korea,' *The Nation,* March 5, 2020.

109 Nichols, Michelle, 'Europeans, Britain raise North Korea missile launches at U.N. Security Council,' *Reuters,* March 5, 2020.

Lederer, Edith M., '6 European nations condemn North Korean missile launches,' *Associated Press,* April 1, 2020.

110 Koettl, Christoph, 'Coronavirus Is Idling North Korea's Ships Achieving What Sanctions Did Not,' *New York Times,* March 26, 2020.

111 'The Capital Cable #54: Recent Developments on the Korean Peninsula,' *Center for Strategic & International Studies* (YouTube Channel), September 8, 2022.

112 Cha, Victor, 'Opinion North Korea could become one of Biden's biggest challenges – and not just because of its nukes,' *Washington Post,* January 15, 2021.

113 'Do Sanctions Really Work on North Korea? The Impossible State Live!,' *Center for Strategic and International Studies* (YouTube Channel), March 8, 2023.

114 'Kim says last five years "worst of the worst" for North Korea,' *Al Jazeera,* January 6, 2021.

115 Maresca, Thomas, 'Report: North Korea economy developing dramatically despite sanctions,' *UPI,* December 4, 2019.

Lee, Jong-seok and Choi, Eun-ju, *Demystifying the North Korean Economy,* The Sejong Institute, November 2019.

116 Staracqualursi, Veronica and Davis, Richard, 'Commerce secretary says coronavirus will help bring jobs to North America,' *CNN,* January 30, 2020.

117 Bradsher, Keith, 'Coronavirus Could End China's Decades-Long Economic Growth Streak,' *New York Times,* March 16, 2020.

Rapoza, Kenneth, 'Coronavirus Could Be The End Of China As A Global Manufacturing Hub,' *Forbes,* March 1, 2020.

Davidson, Helen, 'Coronavirus deals China's economy a "bigger blow than global financial crisis,"' *The Guardian,* March 16, 2020.

118 'WHO Says China Actions Blunted Virus Spread, Leading to Drop,' *Bloomberg,* February 24, 2020.

Nebehay, Stephanie and Farge, Emma, 'WHO lauds Chinese response to virus, says world "at important juncture,"' *Reuters,* January 29, 2020.

Lau, Stuart, 'Coronavirus: WHO head stands by his praise for China and Xi Jinping on response to outbreak,' *South China Morning Post,* February 13, 2020.

119 Inkster, Ian, 'In the battle against the coronavirus, East Asian societies and cultures have the edge,' *South China Morning Post,* April 10, 2020.

Cha, Victor, 'South Korea Offers a Lesson in Best Practices,' *Foreign Affairs,* April 10, 2020.

'Once the biggest outbreak outside of China, South Korean city reports zero new coronavirus cases,' *Reuters,* April 10, 2020.

Graaham-Harrison, Emma, 'Coronavirus: How Asian countries acted while the West dithered,' *The Guardian,* March 21, 2020.

120 Lister, Tim and Shukla, Sebastian and Bobille, Fanny, 'Coronavirus sparks a "war for masks" as accusations fly,' *CNN,* April 3, 2020.

121 'US Seizes Ventilators Destined for Barbados,' *Telesur,* April 5, 2020.

Willsher, Kim and Holmes, Oliver and McKernan, Bethan and Tondo, Lorenzo, 'US hijacking mask shipments in rush for coronavirus protection,' *The Guardian,* April 3, 2020.

122 Chandler, Kim, 'Some states receive masks with dry rot, broken ventilators,' *Associated Press,* April 4, 2020.

123 Robertson, Harry, 'Almost a fifth of ALL US dollars were created this year,' *CITYAM*, October 8, 2020.

Lynch, David, 'Inflation has Fed critics pointing to spike in money supply,' *Washington Post,* February 6, 2022.

Franck, Thomas, 'The ballooning money supply may be the key to unlocking inflation in the U.S.,' *CNBC*, August 5, 2020.

Levy, Mickey D., 'America's Money Supply Has Ballooned. What Should We Expect Next?' *Manhattan Institute,* July 7, 2020.

124 Ahn, Sung-mi, 'Trump says open to third summit with Kim: report,' *The Korea Herald,* July 8, 2020.

Kim, Jeongmin, 'U.S. committed to renewed diplomacy with North Korea, envoy says,' *NK News*, July 9, 2020.

125 Johnson, Jesse, 'North Korea says U.S. is seeking December nuclear talks, warns of "trick" to buy time,' *Japan Times*, November 15, 2019.

126 Zwirko, Colin, 'North Korean leader's sister rules out another "useless" summit with U.S.,' *NK News,* July 9, 2019.

'New Department Director General of DPRK Foreign Ministry for Negotiations with U.S. Issues Statement,' *KCNA*, March 30, 2020.

Hotham, Oliver, 'North Korea has no interest in more talks with the U.S., senior diplomat says,' *NK News,* July 4, 2020.

127 'North Korea says no more photo ops for Donald Trump,' *Nikkei*, November 19, 2019.

Taylor, Adam, 'North Korea says it doesn't want Trump meeting if it's just something to brag about,' *Washington Post*, November 18, 2019.

128 Pollack, Joshua, 'Peeking Under the Shroud of North Korea's Monster Missile,' *Arms Control Wonk*, November 5, 2020.

129 Ibid.

130 'Press Statement by the Permanent Representative of the Democratic People's Republic of Korea to the United Nations,' *DPRK Ministry of Foreign Affairs*, December 8, 2019.

131 'Statement of First Vice Foreign Minister of DPRK,' *KCNA*, March 18, 2021.

132 'Kim Yo Jong, Deputy Department Director of CC, WPK, gives statement to media,' *Voice of Korea*, March 16, 2021.

133 Gomez, Eric, 'Kim Jong Un Lays Out Stark Nuclear Choice for the Biden Administration,' *CATO Institute*, January 9, 2021.

134 Brewer, Eric and Terry, Sue Mi, 'It Is Time for a Realistic Bargain With North Korea,' *Foreign Affairs,* March 25, 2021.

135 'Remarks by President Biden in Press Conference,' *The White House*, March 25, 2021.

136 Bandow, Doug, 'Wake Up: Pushing De-nuking on N. Korea Is a Dream with a Nightmare Ending,' *CATO Institute*, July 22, 2023.

137 Bandow Doug, 'Why Trump Is Right about North Korea,' *CATO Institute*, December 19, 2023.

138 'On Report Made by Supreme Leader Kim Jong Un at 8th Congress of WPK,' *KCNA*, January 9, 2021.

139 'Respected Comrade Kim Jong Un Makes Speech at Military Parade Held in Celebration of 90th Founding Anniversary of KPRA,' *Rodong Sinmun*, April 26, 2022.

140 'Academy of Defence Science Test-fires New-type Tactical Guided Missiles,' *KCNA*, March 26, 2023.

141 Shin, Hyonhee and Smith, Josh, 'N. Korea tests first "strategic" cruise missile with possible nuclear capability,' *Reuters*, September 13, 2021.

142 Bermudez Jr., Joseph S., 'What is the Significance of North Korea's Rail-mobile Ballistic Missile Launcher?,' *CSIS*, September 29, 2021.

143 'Secretary Pak Jong Chon guides launching drill of Railway Mobile Missile Regiment for inspection,' *Voice of Korea,* September 16, 2021.

144 Cordesman, Anthony H., 'The Other Side of the North Korean, Iranian, Hezbollah, and Yemeni Missile Threat,' *CSIS*, November 30, 2017.

145 'Kim Jong Un Watches Test of New-type Anti-Aircraft Guided Weapon System,' *KCNA*, May 28, 2017.

146 'Anti-aircraft Missile Newly Developed by Academy of Defence Science Test-fired,' *KCNA*, October 1, 2021.

147 Abrams, A. B., 'North Korea's Leap Forward in Air Defence Modernisation,' *Sino NK*, April 5, 2024.

148 Diepen, Vann H., 'A Strong Military Warning: Four Key Implications of North Korea's October 10 Missile Statement,' *38 North*, October 14, 2022.

'North Korea's missile launch over Japan shows increased payload, distance: exclusive analysis,' *Breaking Defense*, February 15, 2023.

149 Lewis, Jeffrey, *North Korea's Ballistic Missile Program*, April 2024 Edition, The National Committee on North Korea, April 2024.

150 'North Korea claims US has put "nuclear script" into "Final Stage,"' *RT*, November 1, 2022.

151 Jeter, Kelley, 'U.S. Air Force and ROK Air Force Conduct Large-Scale Joint Air Training Event Vigilant Storm,' *U.S. Indo-Pacific Command*, October 31, 2022.

152 'WPK Solemnly Declares Its Immutable Will to React to Enemy's Nuke and Full-frontal Confrontation in Kind: Respected Comrade Kim Jong Un Guides Test-fire of New-type ICBM of DPRK's Strategic Forces,' *Rodong Sinmun*, November 19, 2022.

153 Murphy, Francois and Smith, Josh, 'Second North Korean nuclear reactor appears to be operational, IAEA says,' *Reuters*, December 22, 2023.

154 'DPRK Foreign Ministry Declares Strong Counter-Measures against UNSC's "Resolution 1874,"' *KCNA*, June 13, 2009.

155 Hecker, Siegfried S., 'A Return Trip to North Korea's Yongbyon Nuclear Complex,' *NAPSNet Special Reports*, November 22, 2010.

156 'North Korea Makes Significant Progress in Building New Experimental Light Water Reactor (ELWR),' *38 North*, November 14, 2011.

Braun, Chaim et al., 'North Korean Nuclear Facilities After the Agreed Framework,' Center for International Security and Cooperation, May 27, 2016 (pp. 18–19).

157 Hecker, Siegfried S., 'A Return Trip to North Korea's Yongbyon Nuclear Complex,' *NAPSNet Special Reports*, November 22, 2010.

158 Byrne, Leo, 'North Korea Completes 10 Hydro Plants,' *NK News*, November 18, 2015.

Williams, Martyn, 'North Korea's Energy Sector: Hydropower Stations and Policy,' *38 North*, June 14, 2023.

'Huichon Power Station Goes Operational,' *KCNA*, April 6, 2012.

'Orangchon Power Station No. 4 Completed,' *KCNA*, July 11, 2020.

'나라의 전력공업발전을 위한 또 하나의 토대 구축 내평3호발전소 준공식 진행' ['Naepyeong Power Plant No. 3 construction ceremony held to establish another foundation for the development of the country's electric power industry'], *Rodong Sinmun*, December 24, 2023.

159 Lewis, Jeffrey and Pollack, Joshua and Schmerler, David, 'North Korea Resuming Construction at the Yongbyon 50 MW(e) Reactor,' *Arms Control Wonk*, May 10, 2022.

Lewis, Jeffrey, 'New Construction at Yongbyon,' *Arms Control Wonk*, May 13, 2022.

160 Cohen, Zachery, 'New satellite images reveal North Korea has restarted construction on long-dormant nuclear reactor,' *CNN*, May 13, 2022.

161 W. Bennett, Bruce et al., 'Countering the Risks of North Korean Nuclear Weapons,' *RAND Corporation*, April 12, 2021.

162 Seo, Yoonjung and Register, Larry and Chen, Heather, 'North Korea declares itself a nuclear weapons state, in "irreversible" move,' *CNN*, September 9, 2022.

163 'North Korea's Military Capabilities,' *Council on Foreign Relations*, June 28, 2022.

164 Reif, Kingston and Bugos, Shannon, 'New ICBM Interceptor to Cost $18 Billion,' *Arms Control Association*, June 2021.

165 Panda, Ankit and Narang, Vipin, 'Trump's Overconfidence in US Missile Defense Could Lead to a Deadly War With North Korea,' *The Diplomat*, October 17, 2017.

Pelopidas, Benoit, 'The unbearable lightness of luck: Three sources of overconfidence in the manageability of nuclear crises,' *European Journal of International Security*, vol. 2, 2017 (pp. 240–262).

Sankaran, Jaganath, 'The Delusions and Dangers of Missile Defense,' *Arms Control Today*, September 2023.

'US Missile Defense,' Union of Concerned Scientists (https://www.ucsusa.org/nuclear-weapons/missile-defense).

166 'We Can't Count on Missile Defense to Defeat Incoming Nukes,' *Scientific American*, June 2014.

Willman, David, 'The nation's missile-defense system has serious flaws. So why is the Pentagon moving to expand it?,' *Los Angeles Times*, December 13, 2016.

Ground-based Midcourse Defense, GMD, Director Operational Test and Evaluation, 2016.

Cirincione, Joe, 'No, We Cannot Shoot Down North Korea's Missiles,' *Defense One*, September 17, 2017.

Hitchens, Theresa, 'No US missile defense system proven capable against "realistic" ICBM threats: Study,' *Breaking Defense*, February 22, 2022.

167 Zwirko, Colin, 'Kim Jong Un and daughter inspect mass-produced missiles at Pyongyang factory,' *NK News*, January 1, 2023.

168 Zwirko, Colin, 'North Korea's rapid weapons plant construction betrays urgent production push,' *NK News*, May 23, 2024.

169 'DPRK Missile Administration Conducts Test of New Important Technology,' *KCNA*, June 27, 2024.

170 'The U.S. and South Korea staged a joint air exercise after the North's missile launch,' *NPR*, February 19, 2023.

171 'Underwater Strategic Weapon System Tested in DPRK,' *KCNA*, April 8, 2023.

172 'Hypersonic Missile Test-fire Conducted in DPRK,' *KCNA*, January 15, 2024.

173 'New IRBM Solid-fuel Engine Test Conducted in DPRK,' *KCNA*, November 15, 2023.

174 Losey, Stephen, 'US Air Force drops Lockheed hypersonic missile after failed tests,' *Defense News,* March 30, 2023.

'ARRW Hypersonic Weapon Again Appears Headed For Cancellation,' *Aviation Week*, March 11, 2024.

175 Oh, Seok-min, 'N. Korea fires one short-range missile into East Sea: JCS,' *Yonhap*, September 28, 2021.

176 Heginbotham, Eric and Nixon, Michael and Morgan, Forrest E., *The U.S.-China Military Scorecard,* Santa Monica, CA, RAND Corporation, 2015 (Chapter Three, Scorecard 1, 'Chinese Capability to Attack Air Bases').

177 Mahshie, Abraham, 'Guam Would Get Command Center With Integrated Air Picture in Missile Defense Agency Budget,' *Air and Space Forces Magazine,* May 25, 2022.

Grady, John, 'Pentagon Starts Work to Build Ballistic Missile Defense Capability in Guam,' *UNSI News*, May 10, 2023.

CHAPTER 7

The Second Cold War: A New Era For North Korea

China's Rise and the Geopolitical Shift

The balance of power in North Korea's conflict with the United States has since its inception in the 1950s been heavily influenced by geopolitical trends far beyond the Korean Peninsula and North America, with the Cold War having seen an unprecedented growth in the globalization of conflicts worldwide. Thus, while Pyongyang had benefited from significant socialist bloc support at the height of the Sino-Soviet Alliance in the 1950s, the beginnings of Soviet economic decline, followed by its disintegration, had weakened its position considerably. One notable indicator was the growing discrepancy in the economic opportunities available to North and South Korea, with the latter given favorable access to Western and international markets and capital. Although North Korea's living standards and tech sector had been far ahead of the south in the 1950s and 1960s, South Korea was able to gain a strong lead in the 1980s as the Soviet economy stagnated, and more so from the 1990s as Pyongyang lost access to Soviet Bloc trade and came under intensive siege. The economic discrepancy between the two Koreas was proportional to the degree of the U.S.-led Western Bloc's influence over the global economy, and was thus most extreme in the post–Cold War period.

While the Cold War never ended on the Korean Peninsula, the rapprochement of North Korea's former strategic partners with the Western Bloc from the 1990s left them increasingly sensitive to Western pressure to isolate the country. By contrast, the Obama administration's overseeing of widespread escalation of tensions and deterioration of relations with countries outside the Western sphere of influence fueled a bifurcation of global order, leaving

Pyongyang with a greater range of potential partners. As summarized by Defense Secretary James Mattis in June 2017, there had been "a return to Great Power competition," forcing America to "look on the prospect of a new era, one governed by today's economic realities and returning once again to a balance of powers."[1] The beginning of a new global Cold War would lead a growing number of countries to attribute greater value to partnerships with America's oldest adversary, as the DPRK had throughout the post–Cold War years remained a fortress unlike any other.

A primary driver of geopolitical change against Western interests in the post–Cold War era has been the rise of China as a dominant economic, technological and military power. This not only had immediate benefits for North Korea as its ally and trading partner, but also globally as Beijing's emergence as an alternative for tech and trade partnerships loosened Western influence over the wider world. From 1991 to 2021 China achieved a tenfold growth in income and labor productivity and a thirteen-fold increase in GDP,[2] with a system of growth driven by savings, investment, productivity gains and domestic consumption contrasting sharply with the heavily debt reliant systems seen in the West.[3] China surpassed the United States as the world's largest trading nation around 2013, and Chinese GDP, as measured by the International Monetary Fund and CIA using purchasing power adjusted figures, overtook America's as the world's largest in 2014.[i] In the preceding seven years, from the year of the global financial crisis in 2007, China's incremental GDP growth exceeded that of the next seven countries (U.S., Brazil, India, Russia, Australia, Germany, Indonesia) combined, gaining $6.85 trillion.[4] By the end of 2020 the Chinese economy was fully one sixth larger than that of the United States.[5]

From the 2010s China increasingly showed signs of strong advantages over its closest economic rivals in terms of general education and the concentration of skills and talent among its

i This is considered a superior measure of the size of an economy by the majority of economists, and is based directly on a country's productivity while avoiding incidents where the size of an economy on paper changes by double digits within weeks based on fluctuations in currency markets.

citizens which were vital to its ability to compete in high tech. This could be measured in a number of ways, including the quantity of patents being filed, the number of science and technology related papers being published and cited, and the performances of children in schools, with almost all metrics consistently pointing to a fast-growing Chinese edge. Taking as an example the number of peer-reviewed papers published in scientific journals, which is considered the most basic barometer of a country's research and development activity, China overtook the U.S. in the 2016–2018 period, publishing 19.9 percent of the world's total at 305,927. This was 18 times the country's average for 1996–1998, and 3.6 times that from the 2006–2008 period, with the rate of growth indicating that China would likely double the U.S. figure before 2030.[ii] Like in many metrics of technological competition the two countries were very much in a league of their own, with third place held by Germany at just 67,041 papers – less than a quarter of the U.S. figure of 281,487 papers.[6]

Rapid growth in the number of Chinese publications came on the back of fast growth in its still developing economy, in research funding, in the proportion of its population working in research, and in the number and rankings of its institutions. Chinese primacy in patent applications was significantly more distinct still, and by 2022 the country accounted for 47 percent of the global total followed by America at 17, Japan at 10 and South Korea at 6 percent.[7] This was reflected in the Australian Strategic Policy Institute's findings in 2023 that China was succeeding in "establishing a sometimes stunning lead in high-impact research across the majority of critical and emerging technology domains," and of 44 tracked strategic technology areas was leading the world in 37 of them.[8]

Where Western Bloc countries' dominance of high tech and centrality in the global economy after the Cold War had allowed

---

ii A much higher proportion of Chinese papers were notably in materials science, chemistry, engineering, computer science and mathematics. The difference between the numbers published in China and the U.S. in these fields was much greater, with a far larger proportion of American papers being in clinical medicine and basic life sciences.

them to deny adversaries opportunities for growth and trade, while providing favorable conditions for the economies and tech sectors of a number of allies, the rise of China's economy and tech sector would increasingly undermine this. North Korea was among the countries most affected, and after the West had effectively cut it off from most meaningful potential industrial, trade or tech partnerships in the 1990s, China's rise had from the 2010s provided fast expanding trade opportunities and access to technologies previously monopolized by its adversaries, improving its economic standing significantly.[9] Without actively itself opposing Western power, China through its politically neutral trade policies seriously limited the pain that the West could inflict on states across the world – whether actual adversaries like Pyongyang, Khartoum, Moscow or Harare – or others which were taking some policy decisions that were out of line with Western interests such as Budapest, Jakarta or Pretoria. The result of this dilution of Western influence was a fundamental shift in world order.

Pyongyang's long moratorium on missile and nuclear testing from November 2017, demonstrating its willingness to make sacrifices for deescalation, closely coincided with a more rapid deterioration of Sino-U.S. relations from late 2018, and led Beijing to show a growing willingness to strengthen ties with its neighbor. Signs of stronger ties ranged from indications of considerable Chinese investment in the North Korean economy, to a major concert by Korean artists in Beijing in January 2019 attended by President Xi Jinping.[10] The president visited Pyongyang in June and was treated to a special Chinese version of the Arirang Mass Games, the largest show on earth, with multiple agreements on improving of bilateral ties made at the time.[11]

Subsequently in mid-August Director of the General Political Bureau of the Korean People's Army Kim Su Gil led a delegation to Beijing, stating after talks that Pyongyang was ready to "strengthen friendly exchanges between the two armed forces in various fields and mutual learning," and to promote the relations between the two armed forces to a "higher level." Vice chairman of China's Central Military Commission General Zhang Youxia announced: "The Chinese People's Liberation Army is ready to work alongside North Korea to implement the important consensus, which was achieved by the leaders of our nations." He added that Beijing was "ready to contribute to peace and stability in the region together" with Pyongyang.[12] The North Korean moratorium on missile and nuclear testing was key to politically facilitating such open pursuit of security cooperation, without which Beijing's actions would have risked being seen as undermining global non-proliferation norms.

As the only major part of North Korea's economy not covered by UNSC sanctions, the tourism industry saw the most conspicuous signs of booming through cooperation with China.[13] Considerable investments had been made in the further expansion of tourist activities, beach resorts,[14] ski resorts[15] and other facilities,[16] and demand was such that airlines were seeking to open a number of new flight routes to the country – with Pyongyang increasingly suffering from a shortage of hotels in high season.[17] Chinese imports from North Korea also increased significantly in 2019, with this trend having been expected to continue before trade was disrupted by the COVID-19 pandemic.[18] Chinese support and technology transfers were widely speculated to have supported a range of technological advances and achievements in the North Korean economy, the scope of which would grow more rapidly into the 2020s. These ranged from the introduction of smartphone e-banking and online payment services in 2020, to 4G internet using second hand Huawei equipment in 2023, increasingly sophisticated domestic smartphones, accelerated progress at hydroelectric dams, and the introduction of cutting-edge new trains on the underground railway system.[19]

Pyongyang's position of advocating concessions in stages appeared to enjoy significant international support, including both within South Korea and in China,[20] with a freeze on ground-based strategic missile launches for over 25 months leaving Beijing among many others more inclined to blame Washington for missing several opportunities to make a deal. China had alongside Russia made a first major push towards easing sanctions at the UN Security Council in September 2018, which was argued for both on humanitarian grounds and as a reward for the testing moratorium. This and similar efforts the following year were blocked by Western council members.[21] All Western-led efforts to pass further resolutions against North Korea after 2017, however, were blocked by Beijing and Moscow, leaving the council at an impasse.[22]

On December 1, 2020, U.S. Deputy Assistant Secretary for North Korea Alex Wong accused China of "flagrant violation" of its obligation to enforce sanctions, alleging that tens of thousands of North Koreans continued to be allowed to work in the country, while on at least 555 occasions ships carrying sanctioned North Korean goods docked in China. He stressed that Beijing "increasingly allows" its firms to trade with North Korea in a broad spectrum of areas sanctioned by the UNSC including seafood, textiles, iron and steel, industrial machinery, vehicles, sand and gravel. China was "seeking to revive trade links and revenue transfers to the North," he stated, threatening new unilateral U.S. sanctions against China-based individuals and entities, and offering rewards of up to $5 million for information about sanctions evasion. The Chinese Foreign Ministry responded that Beijing always implemented the sanctions seriously, and that countries should care more about how the sanctions regime had affected North Koreans' "humanitarian livelihood."[23]

Beijing would in turn increasingly condemn American actions towards its neighbor, including by joining Pyongyang in objecting to U.S.-led military exercises simulating attacks on the country. On August 16, 2022, for example, the Chinese Foreign Ministry condemned the launch of the first joint U.S., South Korean and Japanese missile defense drills since 2017 for exacerbating tensions on the Korean Peninsula.[24] In April the following year, after Pyongyang responded to a new round of U.S.-led exercises with a ballistic missile launch, the Chinese Foreign Ministry again stressed: "the current round of tension on the peninsula has its causes. The negative impact of the U.S. military drills and deployment of strategic weapons around the peninsula is obvious to all."[25]

As Sino-U.S. relations further worsened moving into the 2020s, Pyongyang would increasingly propose closer cooperation to bolster ties and counter a perceived common threat from the U.S. Such cooperation was described in a March 2021 statement by Chairman Kim as "required by the times that call for intensifying the strategic communication between the two parties on the basis of deep comradeship."[26] Cooperation with China provided North Korea with access not only to the world's largest markets, but also to by far the world's largest and one of its most high tech industrial bases. This increased manifold the opportunities for modernization of the DPRK's economy while allowing its future specialists to be educated across the border at a world leading level. In the cultural sphere as well Chinese media imports, including popular films and documentaries, supported Pyongyang's efforts to limit Western and South Korean penetration of its information space by providing far more options of media content conveying similar cultural and political values than the DPRK's own limited media industry could produce alone. Translation of Chinese media on a significant scale, and its uploading onto local streaming services, was highly valuable in this regard.[27]

Beijing's willingness to increase cooperation will likely only grow as economic and political ties with the West worsen, meaning an incident such as a new Taiwan Strait conflict could lead to an exponential growth in Pyongyang's opportunities to bolster ties, much as the escalation of war in Ukraine in February 2022 facilitated a rapid expansion of cooperation with Russia. The tremendous growth in Chinese military capabilities, the vast majority of them focused in the Western Pacific, was also a major boon to North Korean security interests as its ally became one of the world's two preeminent military powers. By the early 2020s China's top destroyer, the Type 055, was widely considered in the West to be the world's most capable surface combatant,[28] while its air force pilots were flying fighter planes on average several decades newer than their American counterparts and getting significantly more hours training in the air. These were among a multitude of issues U.S. military leaders raised with serious concern.[29] China's top stealth fighter, the J-20, had seen combat units deployed near the Korean Peninsula in growing numbers from February 2018, and boasted over double the range and significant other performance advantages over its American counterparts. While North Korea's fighter fleet and surface navy were considered by far the weakest parts of its armed forces, the country's treaty ally had very clear supremacy in the region in both these areas.

A Partnership of Convenience with Russia

In parallel to the strengthening of ties with China, North Korea's other northern neighbor Russia would also become more amenable to improving relations following the Western-backed overthrow of the Ukrainian government in 2014, and significantly moreso as the Russian-Ukrainian War escalated into full scale hostilities from February 2022. Russia's value as a strategic partner to Pyongyang was significantly lower than it had been during the Soviet era, with the country's international standing having been very severely diminished in all areas. From 1992–1999 Russian GDP had contracted by 45 percent, with life expectancy, public health and education levels all declining fast,[30] while a 900 percent rise in drug addiction, doubling of the suicide rate and emergence of HIV and tuberculosis as nationwide epidemics, were among changes seen.[31] Life expectancy for men fell to under 60, while HIV cases were in 2007 estimated at 1–1.3 million and rising.[32] *The Economist* observed in 1999 that rather than joining the G7, Russia could join a "P7" grouping of financial pariahs alongside Sudan, Liberia, Congo, Somalia, and other "poor, war-ridden places, some barely existing as states."[33] Russian analysts highlighted that the economic destruction seen in the post-Soviet years was comparable to that from a large nuclear attack in terms of the scale of loss of life and destruction of industry and agriculture.[34]

As summarized by armored warfare expert Yu. P Kostenko in 2001 regarding the contrast between the first generation of post-Soviet Russian military personnel and their predecessors: "As a result of 'perestroika,' the physical, moral and psychological level of training of the contingent of possible future tankers dropped sharply. The level of general education has also dropped. There are cases when freshmen in higher educational institutions do not know the multiplication tables." This seriously reduced

Russia's ability to operate a modern military.[35] Expert on Russian security at the Foreign Policy Research Institute Pavel Luzin similarly observed in 2021 that "Russia today is far lower on economic, technological and human resources than the Soviet Union was,"[36] with the country having largely devolved from a leading player in industry and high tech into a rentier economy propped up primarily by energy exports.

Where during the Cold War the Soviet Union had consistently been able to supply North Korea with military equipment on par with or superior to U.S. counterparts deployed in South Korea, from MiG-15 fighters in 1950, to MiG-29s in 1988, the standing of Russian weapons systems in most areas was far poorer by the 2010s. This was particularly true in aviation where North Korea's own defense sector was most deficient. Where Soviet industrial imports such as machine tools had also been highly valued at the cutting edge, most industries either disappeared or fell far behind their leading foreign competitors in the post-Soviet years, meaning they were of far more limited value for North Korea. Security guarantees provided by Russia were also far less valuable than those of the USSR had been, and by the mid-2020s it increasingly appeared that any joint war effort in Northeast Asia would see Moscow rely on Pyongyang's support much more than vice versa.

While Russia's much weakened position limited its value as a strategic partner, it also provided North Korea with significant opportunities as its neighbor became unprecedentedly dependent on its support. Although Moscow had been very far from supportive of Pyongyang in the two decades after the Cold War,[iii] to the extent that it was considered a possible participant in Western operations against North Korea such as sanctions and blockade in the 1990s,[37] the DPRK proved to be among Russia's most reliable

---

iii Russia had otherwise abrogated the two states' mutual defense treaty in 1995 and seriously restricted defense exports to the country, while offering a wide range of top end weaponry to South Korea. This forced North Korea to take extreme measures, such as looking to black markets in other post-Soviet states, with the most prominent example being its acquisition of 30 MiG-21bis fighters from Kazakhstan.

supporters in its conflict with NATO and Ukraine from 2022.[iv] On July 13, 2022 North Korea recognized the independence of the self-proclaimed people's republics of Donetsk and Luhansk, which had launched an armed war of independence from Ukraine in the spring of 2014, five months after Russia had provided recognition in February. Russian state media would shortly afterwards claim that North Korean workers would be dispatched to support reconstruction efforts in Donetsk and Luhansk and would potentially support and participate in war crimes tribunals in Donetsk.[38] Russian Ambassador to North Korea Alexander Matsegora further raised this possibility in an interview in July,[39] with Russian state media reporting the following month that Pyongyang had confirmed its intention to dispatch workers.[40] U.S. state funded media outlet *Daily NK* would report that the first Korean workers arrived in early 2024, as Pyongyang had hesitated to dispatch its citizens until the military situation in the area stabilized.[41]

The Russian-Ukrainian War emerged as the latest in a long line of conflicts in which North Korea made significant contributions to oppose U.S. and Western Bloc interests. Ukrainian forces received tremendous Western material and manpower support, ranging from aid in the hundreds of billions of dollars, which came to support almost all functions of the Kiev government, to access to a broad array of satellite and airborne surveillance assets.[42] The *New York Times* on June 25, 2022 referred to the U.S. as setting up within Ukraine's borders "a stealthy network of commandos and spies rushing to provide weapons, intelligence and training... CIA personnel have continued to operate in the country secretly, mostly in the capital, Kiev, directing much of the massive amounts of intelligence the United States is sharing with Ukrainian forces." "Commandos from other NATO countries, including Britain, France, Canada and Lithuania, also have been

iv On March 2, 2022, for example, North Korea was one of just five countries to vote against a Western-sponsored UN General Assembly resolution calling on Russia to withdraw its forces from Ukraine. Other than Russia itself, and Syria and Belarus which were both heavily dependent on Russian military protection, North Korea and Eritrea were the only states to provide such support.

working inside Ukraine... training and advising Ukrainian troops and providing an on-the-ground conduit for weapons and other aid," it added, stressing the sheer "scale of the secretive effort to assist Ukraine that is underway."[43] Further details on the extent of Western operations, which played an increasingly central role in the war effort, would emerge over the following years, including volunteer units, military contractors and active personnel from Western militaries and intelligence services.[44] On December 13, for example, British Deputy Chief of Defense Staff Royal Marines Lieutenant General Robert Magowan revealed that the Marines had been carrying out high-risk frontline operations alongside Ukrainian government forces from April 2022.[45]

For North Korea, contributing to the Russian war effort thus provided a means of both countering Western forces in an area vital to their security interests, while at the same time strengthening ties with its resource rich but militarily and economically much diminished neighbor and gaining firsthand experience of modern warfare. This mirrored the rationales seen in theaters from Vietnam in the 1960s to Syria in the 2010s. With the Russian government's overthrow, and possibly the country's partitioning, being highly possible should it be defeated, the existential nature of the conflict Moscow faced provided Pyongyang with further strong incentives to support its war effort. Doing so could help to prevent instability across both China's northern borders and its own, and to ensure that the relatively friendly Vladimir Putin administration would not be replaced by a Western-aligned government that would inevitably downgrade relations. Thus, while presenting North Korea with considerable opportunities, the Russian-Ukrainian War also presented very significant dangers should it end unfavorably.

In response to NATO members' supplies of a range of rocket artillery systems such as the M142 HIMARS and M270 to Ukraine in mid-2022, analysts at *Military Watch Magazine* observed from July 23 that imports of North Korea's much longer ranged KN-25 and smaller KN-09 systems could provide Russian forces with the optimal counter to these assets. These could be accompanied by Korean specialists to facilitate their faster integration into Russian forces.[46] With China unable to supply its own systems for political reasons, North Korea could be highly valued for its ability to provide Russian artillery units with a clear range advantage. The KN-25, its predecessor the KN-09 introduced in the 2010s, and the KN-23 and KN-24 ballistic missile systems, were among eight North Korean weapons systems which Russia was expected to be most interested in urgently importing.[47]

In August editor in chief of Russia's Defense journal and host on the Rossiya 1 channel, reserve colonel Igor Korotchenko, observed: "If North Korean volunteers with their artillery systems, wealth of experience with counter battery warfare and large caliber multiple launch rocket systems, made in North Korea, want to participate in the conflict, well let's give the green light to their volunteer impulse."[48] Subsequently on September 5 a newly declassified U.S. intelligence report indicated that Russia was purchasing "millions of North Korean artillery shells and rockets," with assessments consistently stressing the sheer quantities which Pyongyang had the capacity to provide.[49] Multiple figures in the U.S. military leadership had by then highlighted that artillery assets were playing a particularly central role in the Ukrainian theater,[50] with this remaining a field where North Korea's defense sector was particularly strong with significant quantitative and range advantages over pre-war Russia. Senior research fellow at the Royal United Services Institute Jack Watling claimed at the time that Moscow had sought Pyongyang's support, with this "not just limited to supplying ammunition."[51] Other experts widely observed that North Korea's military stockpiles were "sizeable enough to accommodate large orders without additional production for many types of weaponry."[52]

Where in the final year of the Cold War, 1989, the Soviet Army had fielded 1184% as much towed artillery as North Korea, 350% as much self-propelled artillery and 284% as much rocket artillery, by contrast in 2021 North Korea at a conservative estimate fielded 412% as much towed and self-propelled artillery and 625% as much rocket artillery as the Russian Army did.[53] This reflected the extent to which Russian forces had contracted, and that to which the KPA had sustained vast conventional ground capabilities past the Cold War era. The extreme contraction of Russia's frontline forces and stockpiles, its defense sector and its general military readiness resulted in a very different balance of power between the two states, which yielded dividends for Pyongyang as its neighbor came to depend on it heavily.

Reports of arms transfers, in particular large transfers of artillery shells, would continue to emerge from mid-2022, with the White House from November citing satellite footage showing a surge in railcar transits across the Russian-Korean border as one of multiple indicators.[54] This culminated in the announcement by the White House on January 4, 2024 that North Korean KN-23 ballistic missiles and KN-25 rocket artillery had begun to be utilized by Russian forces in Ukraine, fueling speculation that KPA personnel could be deployed to support Russian employment of these assets and observe their effectiveness under combat conditions.[55] With Pyongyang able to arm Russia in ways that Beijing could not, but nevertheless significantly benefited from, the arms transfers highlighted how in the context of a new global Cold War North Korea's two northern neighbors now had a very strong incentive to strengthen defense industry collaboration with it, including with technology transfers.

The Russian-Ukrainian War represented a new phase in the escalation of a global Cold War, and demonstrated that lines could not be cleanly drawn between theaters of conflict. Ukraine's Western-trained special forces, for example, deployed to target Russian forces from Syria to Africa,[56] while its far-right militias had previously marched with Western-sponsored forces in Hong Kong against the Chinese government.[57] Considering North Korea's history of supporting war efforts against Western interests globally, it would have been highly unusual for the country not to back the Russian war effort. Beyond pushing back against Western Bloc interests, and further bogging U.S. and allied forces down in Eastern Europe, its intervention in Ukraine marked a major turning point for Pyongyang's relations with Moscow, which had significant implications for its economic, military and international political standings.

Where Russian representatives had even in the late 2010s referred to Pyongyang's weapons tests as "defiance of the international law norms and the world community's opinion" which "deserves the strongest condemnation," and frequently in similar terms, Moscow's rhetoric transformed to strongly support its neighbor.[58] A major milestone was the first ever visit by a Russian defense minister to North Korea since the Soviet era, with Sergei Shoigu arriving in Pyongyang on July 25, 2023, and being toured around and positively commenting on an exhibition of North Korean defense products, at the center of which were its Hwasong-15, 17 and 18 ICBMs. This caused serious concerns in the Western world, and was interpreted as an unprecedented endorsement by a permanent UNSC member of North Korea's weapons programs. U.S. intelligence reports would subsequently state that the Russian delegation had pitched a deal on increasing arms acquisitions from North Korea.[59]

Two months after Shoigu's visit to Pyongyang, Chairman Kim in September visited the Russian Far East, and on the 15th led a delegation to the Komsomolsk-on-Amur Aircraft Plant where they closely inspected production lines and aircraft on display, including Russia's two most sophisticated fighters the Su-35 and Su-57. They also observed the final assembly room for the SSJ-100 airliner. Pyongyang was considered likely to be interested in acquiring all three aircraft, one of the former two to succeed the MiG-29 as its top fighter class, and the latter to replace refurbished Tu-204s and Il-62Ms as the main airliner of its flag carrier Air Koryo. Although a number of loopholes to the UN arms embargo could facilitate a North Korean Su-35 or Su-57 acquisition,[v] it appeared more likely in the near term that a modernized variant of the MiG-29 could be transferred, with outward differences from the KPA's existing older MiG-29s being few and attributable to domestic upgrades. With North Korea having previously produced MiG-29s under license, there remained ambiguity as to the size of the fleet, with the first locally-built models having flown in April 1993 before assembly ended sometime in the 2000s.[60,vi]

v This was explored by the writer in detail in the article: 'Legal Barriers to the North Korea-Russia Arms Trade – and the Loophole That Could Allow it to Expand,' *The Diplomat,* January 10, 2024.

vi The unveiling of what appeared to be cutting-edge indigenous North Korean

Significant work done to expand and modernize Sunchon Airfield near Pyongyang in the early 2020s, which hosted the country's top fighter units, may have indicated an intention to field more capable aircraft than the country's existing Cold War era jets.

While North Korea's defense sector had gone a very long way towards bridging technological gaps with that of Russia in many key areas, with the capabilities of indigenous air defense systems, ballistic and cruise missiles, and tanks appearing to be far narrower in the 2020s than it had been in the 1980s, technology transfers from Russia could nevertheless be highly valued. Regarding the technology areas where Pyongyang was believed by U.S. intelligence to be most interested in receiving Russian support, U.S. National Security Council Spokesman John Kirby stated on January 4, 2024 that these included "fighter aircraft, surface-to-air missiles, armored vehicles, ballistic missile production equipment or materials" among "other advanced technologies."[61] Space technologies remained an area where Russia had retained a strong international standing into the post-Soviet era, with Chairman Kim's visit to Russia's newest spaceport, the Vostochny Cosmodrome, in September 2023, having fueled speculation that technology transfers could be sought to support plans for a North Korean military satellite network.

Moscow's permanent seat at the UN Security Council made partnership particularly valuable for Pyongyang, with Russia having pressed the council for sanctions on the DPRK to be renewed annually, rather than put in place indefinitely, which would provide it as well as Beijing with some say in their severity.[62] With this consistently firmly rejected by Western council members, the standoff at the Security Council over sanctions culminated on March 28, 2024 with Moscow's vetoing of the annual renewal of the Panel of Experts which monitored enforcement of UNSC

air-to-air missiles in 2021 raised the possibility that newly delivered MiG-29s would not need to deploy Russian weaponry, removing what would otherwise be an irrefutable external indicator of new deliveries since 21st century MiG-29 models used visibly different missiles to Soviet era ones. (Abrams, A. B., 'Air-to-Air Missiles Could Be the North Korean Defense Sector's Next Breakthrough: Why It Matters,' *38 North*, October 27, 2022.)

sanctions on North Korea, effectively disbanding the panel. Preceding this, Western assessments had long accused Moscow, as well as Beijing, of constraining the panel's activities and blocking or obfuscating unfavorable findings.[63]

Echoing Pyongyang's own rhetoric on the sanctions regime, Russian ambassador to the UN Vassily Nebenzia stated regarding the panel: "Its work is increasingly being reduced to playing into the hands of Western approaches, reprinting biased information and analyzing newspaper headlines and poor quality photos."[64] Regarding Russia's position on the panel and on the sanctions regime more broadly, Foreign Ministry spokeswoman Maria Zakharova stated on March 29: "The Group of Experts of the UN Security Council Committee 1718 has lost all standards of objectivity and impartiality, which should be integral characteristics of its mandate," and had instead "turned into an obedient tool of the DPRK's geopolitical opponents."[65,vii] With the panel having since 2009 reported to the Security Council twice a year and recommended action to improve implementation, its disbanding significantly strengthened Pyongyang's position and caused considerable concern in the Western world, with former members of the panel concluding that "the future is grim for the DPRK sanctions regime."[66,viii]

---

vii Highlighting an opposition to the sanctions regime itself, she added: "The United States and its allies have clearly demonstrated that their interest does not extend beyond the task of 'strangling' the DPRK by all available means, and a peaceful settlement is not on the agenda at all." This echoed prior criticisms by Russian officials that a refusal to reduce sanctions in response to Pyongyang's long weapons testing moratoriums had been far from conducive to resolving the issue. (Faulconbridge, Guy, 'After veto, Russia says big powers need to stop "strangling" North Korea,' *Reuters*, March 29, 2024.)

viii Reflecting the extent of the issue, U.S. ambassador to the United Nations Linda Thomas-Greenfield on April 17 stated that Washington would work with "like-minded" countries on alternatives either within, or if necessary outside the UN to sustain pressure. "The point here is that we cannot allow the work that the panel of experts were doing to lapse," she stated, providing an indication of the extent to which Moscow had undermined efforts to target Pyongyang's economic activities. Regarding Moscow and Beijing's expected future positions, she elaborated: "I don't expect that they will cooperate or agree with any efforts that we make to find another path,

Where the non-Western international community had already consistently proven unwilling to implement sanctions on North Korea (see Chapter 5), the loss of an ability to monitor implementation would further disincentivize countries from complying with the sanctions regime. As noted by former British member of the UN panel of experts on sanctions enforcement Aaron Arnold: "Without an effective monitoring mechanism, countries may have little incentive to implement sanctions as robustly." An inability to make new designations since 2017, he noted, had already had the effect of "leaving sanctions implementation in a state of limbo... What's left is ultimately a sanctions regime with no enforcement or monitoring mechanism, and enough political disagreement to ensure stagnation for the foreseeable future." "Of course, Western governments and civil society will step in to provide intelligence on North Korea's activities and shore-up unilateral sanctions," Arnold observed, although "many countries will still view them with suspicion, seeing them as instruments of Western intelligence propaganda. They will not enjoy the near universal trust that Panel reports have been able to garner." He concluded by referring to Russia's veto as "so devastating," highlighting that there was little doubt Pyongyang would be able to exploit the openings it provided to reap considerable benefits.[67] Other experts similarly highlighted that "journalists, private companies and individual governments lack the authority or clout" to obtain the kind of information that the panel of experts had been able to.[68,ix]

---

but that is not going to stop us from finding that path moving forward." (Remarks by Ambassador Linda Thomas-Greenfield at a press conference in Seoul, ROK, *United States Mission to the United Nations*, April 17, 2024.)

ix In sharp contrast to the previous decade, Russian officials would from 2022 become increasingly outspoken in support of North Korea. An example was Ambassador Vassily Nebenzia's statement on March 28, 2024 slamming the "increasingly blatant involvement of Washington's nuclear potential in the allied maneuvers" on and around the Korean Peninsula, alleging that other NATO members "located tens of thousands of kilometers away from North Korea" were contributing to militarizing the region around the country. ('Involvement of US nuclear potential in drills around DRPK affects Russia's interests,' *TASS*, March 29, 2024.)

Further signs of growing Russian–North Korean ties ranged from special screenings of Korean films in Moscow in April 2024,[69] to the deployment of Russia's largest strategic airlifter class, the scarce An-124, for supply runs to the country the previous month,[70] and a visit to Pyongyang by the head of Russia's Foreign Intelligence Service (SVR) Sergei Naryshkin the preceding month to meet Minister of State Security Ri Chang Dae. There KCNA reported they discussed "deepening Russian–North Korean cooperation in the face of attempts to increase pressure from external forces," as well as options for further boosting cooperation to deal with the "ever-growing spying and plotting moves by the hostile forces."[71] Strengthening ties caused considerable concern in the Western world, with the U.S. State Department's senior official for North Korea Jung Pak warning on April 23 that, Moscow's "complete embrace" could provide Pyongyang with a "luster of legitimacy that it does not deserve, and it should not have."[x] He highlighted that arms sales could set a precedent which would allow more states to begin purchasing North Korean armaments.[72]

One week later on April 30 Defense Secretary Lloyd Austin informed lawmakers that improvements to Russa-DPRK relations were "very concerning," with Pyongyang "becoming more confident because of its affiliation with Putin."[73] On May 6 a U.S. Congressional Research Service report highlighted that strengthening ties with Russia would "potentially embolden North Korea to expand illicit activities and engage in provocations," terms widely used in the West to refer to actions such as missile testing, while also warning that ties "may improve DPRK military capabilities."[74]

---

x References to the DPRK's illegitimacy remained widespread in the Western world, as despite it being a UN member state the vast majority of Western countries continued to deny the country's right to exist and to varying degrees supported the official South Korean position that Seoul was the sole legitimate Korean government. The strong tendency to perceive westernized political systems as the sole provider of legitimacy, allowing all states with different systems to be deemed illegitimate, had particularly significant implications for Western perceptions of North Korea as it remained among the very least westernized countries in the world.

Russia would intensify its use of North Korean ballistic missiles against Ukrainian targets from late July, while footage released at the time, corroborated by a number of Ukrainian sources, indicated that the country had made its first ever acquisition of North Korean combat vehicles.[75] The vehicle in question was a specialized derivative of an armoured personnel carrier built to accommodate eight Bulsae-4 Non Line of Sight anti-tank guided missiles. Although Soviet anti-tank missile systems had consistently led the world in performance during the Cold War, Russia's position in the field had deteriorated from the 1990s, leaving its top anti-tank missiles in the 2020s still reliant on line of sight for targeting. This seriously limited their potency and the kind of tactics they could be employed for compared to top Chinese, North Korean and U.S. counterparts, including American FGM-148 Javelins supplied to Ukraine. With the Javelin having gained near mythic status in the West due to its effectiveness in destroying Russian armor in 2022, the introduction of the Bulsae-4 in Russia, which had similar 'fire and forget' capabilities provided by electro-optical guidance, but also boasted over double the engagement range of its American counterpart, was likely to have been highly prized for more than bridging the performance gap.[76]

The Bulsae-4 was well optimized for the kind of conflict being waged in Ukraine, and was seen exploiting its range and mobility to neutralize Ukrainian artillery around 10 kilometers behind the frontlines, before then quickly withdrawing.[77] With Beijing's embargo on arming either party in the war preventing Russia from acquiring the similarly capable HJ-12 anti-tank missile system, which had long been considered the asset the Russian Army would likely be most interested in acquiring from China,[78] North Korea's provision of the Bulsae-4 provided a further example of its tremendous value as an arms supplier, as well as the rise in its defensce sector's standing relative to that of Russia.[79] The transfer of Bulsae-4s and associated armoured vehicles was widely referred to in the West as a development that "marks a turning point in Pyongyang's involvement in the conflict" and in similar terms.[80]

As tensions between Russia and the West further worsened considerably in 2024, with Western states more openly expanding their military contingents in Ukraine and facilitating Ukrainian strikes against sensitive targets deep within Russian territory, Moscow's inclination to deepen ties with Pyongyang appeared only to grow.[xi] A landmark in this process was the visit by President Putin to North Korea on June 18–19, which was his first in 24 years. While in Pyongyang the president highlighted the possibility of further "development of military-technical cooperation" between the two countries,[81] as well as plans to "develop alternative mechanisms of trade and mutual settlements that are not controlled by the West."[82] Both countries signed a "comprehensive strategic partnership" treaty, Article 4 of which bound each to "provide military and other assistance with all means" and "without delay" should the other "fall into a state of war." The treaty highlighted that a great deal had changed in the relationship, with Moscow no longer being the senior partner as it had been in the Cold War era, nor the distant neighbor with westernizing aspirations as it was in the subsequent two decades, but a country for which ties with Pyongyang had become unprecedentedly vital to its security interests.

While China's rise transformed global order, with Beijing's position as the sole high-tech economy outside the Western Bloc's sphere of influence being a vital boon to the positions of all potential Western adversaries, Russia's actions and its distancing form the West also had a transformative impact. The worsening of Russia ties with the Western Bloc from 2014 had had wide ranging

xi Former president and Deputy Chairman of the Security Council Dmitry Medvedev, for one, stated that the West had declared a "war without rules" on Russia, stressing on June 13 that Russia should "transfer our arms to the enemies of the Western world" and "send every kind of weapon, except nuclear (for now)!" With Russia having largely allowed the Western world to attack and dismantle the Iraqi and Libyan states, candidates to receive such arms were few and far between, with North Korea standing out as the most suitable. Although Medvedev had made several outspoken statements in the past, they were considered to represent growing sentiments within the Russian leadership which had potentially highly positive implications for Pyongyang. ('West has declared "war without rules" on Russia – Medvedev,' *RT*, June 13, 2024.)

reverberations that were highly beneficial for North Korea, an example being Russia's military intervention in Syria from August 2015 to support counterinsurgency efforts against Western-backed militias, which North Korea and Damascus' regional allies had been combating for years.[83] Russia's tremendous resource wealth made its willingness to enter into closer partnerships from 2022 highly welcome, with opportunities for North Korean goods, services and labor exports expected to grow considerably due in part to the far greater levels of trust Moscow had in the country relative to its other neighbors.

North Korea in a New Global Order

Following the demonstration of a nuclear ICBM capability in 2017, a primary factor in the strengthening of North Korea's position relative to the United States in subsequent years was the escalation of tensions between Washington and major states outside its sphere of influence, accelerating the trend towards a new cold war that had begun under the Obama administration. The result was both a growing willingness by Beijing, Moscow and a rising number of others targeted by the West to work more closely and openly with Pyongyang, ending its post–Cold War period of isolation, as well as a stretching of Western resources and attentions between multiple fronts, further undermining the viability of achieving hardline objectives against North Korea.

Writing for the *National Interest,* instructor at the Republic of Korea Air Force Academy and researcher at the Korea Institute for Defense Analyses Cha Tae Suh observed that the beginning of a new Cold War had provided a "fundamentally altered strategic context" for Pyongyang's long war with Washington. "The nature of the nuclear conundrum has profoundly altered, as we face an era of renewed great power competition. During the last three decades of U.S. hegemony, North Korean nuclear pursuit was defined as the problem of a rogue state against the U.S.-led world order," where by contrast by the early 2020s "the favorable time when the U.S. was a unipole freely shaping the Korean Peninsula's strategic milieu and imposing liberal norms on others has come to an end are now unhappy but inevitable realities." He highlighted that growing numbers in Washington "believe that conventional liberal interventionist or neoconservative goals – including comprehensive, verifiable, irreversible dismantlement; final, fully verifiable denuclearization; and regime change – are simply impossible in the current strategic environment," stressing that this would be "a pill hard to swallow" in the West. There was a growing acceptance that North Korea would "keep its nuclear stockpiles for a while."[84]

As otherwise observed by former RAND Corporation policy analyst specializing in Indo-Pacific security issues Soo Kim: "It's not just North Korea that we're dealing with right now. It's China, it's Russia, and other countries, and Covid, and the economy, so there are different buttons so that when you push one, the other buttons kind of go helter skelter." This, she observed, had limited Washington's ability to maximize pressure on North Korea or "bring enough sticks to the table." Regarding the implications of America's inability to enact any serious policies to roll back progress in the North Korean nuclear program, Kim lamented that "wittingly or not we've sort of acknowledged the existence of North Korean nuclear weapons. We've not formally acknowledged North Korea as a nuclear weapons state, but I think we're almost there. We're not doing anything about it."[85]

As global tensions escalated, growing signs pointed to a diminishing of Western influence over the international community, boding very positively for Pyongyang and reducing the West's ability to pressure states to shun ties with its oldest adversary. A central factor in this shift was the impact of China's emergence as not only a leading supplier of high tech products across the non-Western world, but also more generally as the world's largest trading nation which it achieved in 2013, with annual trade exceeding $4 trillion that year.[86] By 2023 China was the leading trading partner of over 120 countries out of 195 in the world,[87] which came largely at the expense of the position of the United States. The U.S. had seen over 80 percent of countries trade more with it than with China before 2000 – but by 2018 saw this figure fall to just 30 percent.[88] As trade continued to represent a fast growing portion of global GDP, reaching 59 percent in 2013 as China gained first position compared to just 35 percent 30 years prior, the geopolitical significance of this shift was tremendous.[89]

Signs of Western isolation from the international community would become evident over a number of geopolitical issues from the late 2010s. Three primary issues demonstrating this included the U.S.-led campaigns to pressure states to deny contracts to the Chinese telecoms giant Huawei, to press the world to condemn China for what Western sources alleged was a genocide in Xinjiang province, and to gain global support for the war against Russia in Ukraine. All three campaigns would be met with overwhelming failure. Huawei was able, with few exceptions such as Japan and Singapore, to rapidly gain contracts across the non-Western world, with very extensive U.S. efforts ranging from threatening to deny countries aid and disaster relief,[90] to threats to downgrade trade and security ties,[91] and outright offers of billion-dollar payments to block Huawei,[92] widely failing.

The Xinjiang campaign faced similar failures, as demonstrated repeatedly at the United Nations. Of the 22 countries which launched a joint statement to the High Commissioner of the UN Human Rights Council in July 2019 condemning Chinese policies, the only non-Western country was Japan.[93] At the same Council session 50 countries from across the non-Western world, including 23 Muslim-majority countries, defended China's position,[94] sparking outraged responses from Western commentators and media outlets accusing countries supporting China of human rights abuses.[95] In October a bloc of 22 Western countries and Japan launched another round of criticism of alleged abuses in Xinjiang at the UN, which was again countered by support for China from across the non-Western world as 54 countries issued a joint statement supporting its Xinjiang policies.[96] The 54 had all sent delegations to Xinjiang to observe the reality on the ground, and described policies there as having "effectively safeguarded the basic human rights of people of all ethnic groups," leaving the West again isolated from the international community.[97]

A similar effort in October 2020 led by the U.S., Germany and Britain again gained no non-Western supporters except Japan, while nearly 70 countries voiced their support for China's position. Pakistan, Kuwait and Cuba each led separate groupings of nations to issue joint statements praising Beijing's human rights and rebutting Western allegations.[98] The same trend could be seen the following year, when in June 2021 more than 90 countries expressed support for China's stance and 65 declared their opposition to interference in China's domestic affairs in Xinjiang and Hong Kong. This represented a clear rebuke of the Western campaign by the international community.[99] Three months prior in July 2020, at the 47th session of the United Nations Human Rights Council, envoys of 30 countries, among them Saudi Arabia, Pakistan and Iran, voiced support for China's policies in Xinjiang while slamming Western efforts to fabricate claims of humanitarian abuses.[100] Opposition to interference in China's internal affairs had been voiced by 70 countries at the 46th session of the Council in March.[101] Thus while Western media outlets continued to refer to "the international community's attempt to challenge its [China's] policy in Xinjiang," this represented a serious misuse of the term to describe a very isolated Western position.[102] The Xinjiang campaign marked a watershed moment in the post–Cold War era highlighting a wholly unprecedented degree of Western isolation from the remainder of the world.

Western efforts to gain global support for the war effort against Russia in Ukraine would similarly be met with resounding failure. A year into hostilities in February 2023 *Bloomberg* highlighted that: "Western political and media classes are only just becoming aware of the problem and its magnitude: how, for instance, the majority-white nations of Europe and North America appear more and more isolated in their accelerating military and economic campaign against Russia."[103] The West's growing isolation was repeatedly raised as a key theme in Western discourse at the Munich Security Conference that month. The conference's final report warned: "Many countries in Africa, Asia, and Latin America have steadily lost faith in the legitimacy and fairness of an international system which has neither granted them an appropriate voice in global affairs, nor sufficiently addressed their core concerns. To many states, these failures are deeply tied to the

West. They find that the Western-led order has been characterized by post-colonial domination, double standards, and neglect for developing countries' concerns."[104] The Security Conference's final report stressed that "countries in the Global South can become crucial 'swing states.' They can tip the balance between systemic competitors and therefore determine the fate of the international rules-based order."[105]

Reporters from the *Financial Times*, writing from Munich, observed that "Western pleas over Ukraine fail to sway African and South American leaders," and while a "clutch of senior U.S. and European officials sought to convince the rest of the world of the threat… there was little evidence their message got through," with leaders of non-Western states showing "palpable frustration."[106] Stressing that the West needed to be more successful in getting non-Western states "to participate in the world reaction against Russia for the war in Ukraine," EU High Representative for Foreign Affairs Joseph Borrell stated at the time that the West had to "face this deep resentment in Africa… Or in Latin America and the anti-imperialism feeling."[107] French President Emmanuel Macron stressed at the time that he was "shocked by how much credibility we are losing in the Global South."[108] Writing from *Bloomberg* Indian scholar Panjak Mishra observed: "Make no mistake: Moral condemnation of Western powers has not been so widespread since the mid-20th century… it is again shaping mass perceptions and straining geopolitical relations across the globe." Regarding the grounds for peoples from across the non-Western world, from Indonesia to Africa, to tend strongly towards support for Russia's position, Mishra noted: "Their memories of exploitation and disastrous interventions by Western Europeans and Americans remain too strong… they see that the former masters of Asia and Africa are still refusing to address their past of violence, dispossession and plunder."[109] The *National Interest* concluded at the time: "the Ukraine crisis, as prosecuted by NATO, has moved the 'neutral camp' to inch closer to China and Russia. Whereas Washington made supporting Ukraine against Russian aggression a fundamental foreign policy priority, many neutral countries and China have seen the world eye-to-eye."[110]

The tremendous escalation in Western efforts to target Russia with economic sanctions from 2022, including threatening secondary sanctions on its trading partners across the non-Western world, fueled significant efforts by states to "sanctions proof" their economies. An example of this prevailing trend was Indonesian policy, with President Joko Widodo calling in March 2023 for reduced reliance on Western payment networks like MasterCard and Visa and increased dependence on the new Domestic Government Credit Card payment system. "Be very careful. We must remember the sanctions imposed by the U.S. on Russia. Visa and Mastercard could be a problem," he warned, adding that without them "we can be independent." "If we use our own platforms, and everybody is using them, from ministries and local administrations to municipal governments, then we can be more secure," he elaborated regarding the benefits of pursuing this.[111] Board member of the Indonesian Credit Cards Association Dodit Proboyakti was among the local sources adding that Russia's experience developing the Mir payment system to insulate itself from Western sanctions from 2014 would be learned from to develop local equivalents – in an apparent effort to ready the economy to endure similar Western economic attacks.[112] President Widodo's statement came five months after Bank Indonesia urged a transition to use of national currencies for international payments to reduce Indonesian financial markets' reliance on the U.S. dollar,[113] and as the country was expanding two-way payment systems based on national currencies with China, Japan, Thailand, Malaysia and others.[114] Similar measures could be seen across much of the non-Western world from India to Brazil.

As summarized in a 2023 *Foreign Affairs* assessment reflecting the growing consensus view in the West: "sanctions against Russia are contributing to a realignment of global currency holdings," with Western unilateralism in imposing sanctions, often at considerable cost to uninvolved third parties, seen to be a key factor undermining the dollar. "Imposing sanctions to pursue narrow U.S. interests raises legitimate fears among countries that they could be targeted next and therefore motivates them to find alternatives to the dollar," it added.[115] As otherwise summarized in an *Atlantic Council* assessment: "Western sanctions in particular that on Russia's central bank… has violated the presumed sanctity of central bank reserves. This will lead to efforts by a number of non-Western countries, especially those feeling vulnerable to sanctions, to develop an alternative payment system to evade and dilute the full impact of sanctions."[116]

As the incentives rapidly increased for a growing number of countries to develop means of trading internationally that circumvented the Western world, with a shift in global trade away from Western currencies being key to this, the potential diminishing of the West's ability to shape the world through sanctions was widely alluded to with considerable concern by a growing number of European and American sources. *Foreign Affairs* accordingly in December 2022 hailed "the end of the age of sanctions" in the title of a prominent article that month, highlighting that the rapid growth in means of insulating trade from Western attacks was quickly stripping the West of its potency in economic warfare.[117] One of the most notable summaries of the issue was given by U.S. Senator Marco Rubio, who warned in an interview in March 2023:

> Just today, Brazil, the largest country in the Western Hemisphere, cut a trade deal with China… They're going to, from now on, do trade in their own currencies, get right around the dollar. They're creating a secondary economy in the world totally independent of the United States. We won't have to talk about sanctions in five years, because there'll be so many countries transacting in currencies other than the dollar that we won't have the ability to sanction them.[118]

In parallel to moves to circumvent Western currencies in international trade was a move to avoid firms or institutions under Western jurisdiction. The most prominent example was the Society for Worldwide Interbank Financial Telecommunication (SWIFT) headquartered in Belgium, which was heavily relied on to enable banks to communicate transaction information. A blocking of Iran from SWIFT in 2012, credited with causing a 30 percent decline in its foreign trade that year,[119] followed by threats to block Russia from 2014, fueled the beginning of a growth in the awareness among non-Western states of the need for alternatives.[120] As observed by chief foreign affairs columnist for the *Financial Times* Gideon Rachman: "the devastating effect of the SWIFT ban was noted all over the world… It revealed some of the hidden wiring that makes the global economy work. It also highlighted how much of this wiring is still centered in the West."[121] The Chinese Cross-Border Interbank Payment System (CIPS) began construction in 2012 as an alternative, and after being founded in 2015, escalated sanctions on Russia from February 2022 were widely described as "a wake-up call for Beijing" that added urgency to its expansion.[122]

China was also seen to be "leading the charge among major economies" to develop a digital version of its currency,[123] and by mid-2023 transactions in the digital yuan trial had reached $5.3 billion with 21 million individual users, with successes in trials indicating the country would lead the way in achieving widespread adoption of central bank digital currencies.[124] This was seen by some economists to threaten a "new global monetary order" contributing to undermining the dollar's position, and would further seriously limit the West's ability to isolate and otherwise harm targeted economies with sanctions.[125] The internationalization of the Digital Yuan was as early as January 2020 highlighted by Western experts as a potential key facilitator of North Korean international trade and underminer of the U.S.-led sanctions regime.[126,xii]

The more countries "sanctions proofed," the weaker the West's leverage over them became. Although North Korea's

---

xii As observed by Harvard University professor and economist Kenneth Rogoff in November 2019: "If, however, the digital currency were run out of China, the U.S. would have far fewer levers to pull. Western regulators could ultimately ban the use of China's digital currency, but that wouldn't stop it from being used in large parts of Africa, Latin America, and Asia... Just as technology has disrupted media, politics, and business, it is on the verge of disrupting America's ability to leverage faith in its currency to pursue its broader national interests." (Kharpal, Arjun, 'China's digital yuan could help North Korea evade US sanctions, launch missiles, experts say,' *CNBC*, January 24, 2020.)

trading profile was far too small to stimulate such measures, sanctions on Russia, and the very real threat of these being expanded to China as well, provided the non-Western world with very strong incentives to pursue them. Where the geopolitical trends of the 1990s had left North Korea isolated, those of the 2020s were very highly favourable, and while the Western Bloc states that had for decades sought the country's erasure from the map had had tremendous power over the world at the center of the preceding economic order, the new order left them in a far weaker position to pursue this objective.

Much as Western diplomats had for years described Pyongyang as "emboldened by the deterioration in relations between Russia and China and the U.S.," stressing that "the worse it gets, the stronger they feel," so too was a rift between the West and more of the international community expected to further bolster the North Korean position.[127] This geopolitical shift was alluded to multiple times in North Korea itself, with Chairman Kim Jong Un observing when addressing the 14th Supreme People's Assembly in September 2022: "the change from a unipolar world advocated by the U.S. into a multipolar world is being accelerated significantly. Our Republic will develop foreign relations proactively in line with the development trend of the current international situation and its position as a powerful independent country."[128] The strong geopolitical trend towards a decline in Western political and economic influence over the non-West was set to facilitate a significant increase in North Korean integration into the global economy, including through systems such as CIPS, as the West's primary tools for bringing harm to countries over their ties to Pyongyang fast lost their potency.

Endnotes

1 Secretary of Defense Jim Mattis, Senate Armed Services Committee, Written Statement for the Record, Tuesday June 13, 2017.

2 'Reskilling China: Transforming the World's Largest Workforce into Lifelong Learners,' *McKinsey,* January 12, 2021.

3 Sanderson, Jihong, 'China's Economic Growth and International Standing,' *ISPI*, November 3, 2010.

4 Figures from the October 2014 update of the International Monetary Fund's World Economic Outlook Database.

5 Allison, Graham, 'China Is Now the World's Largest Economy. We Shouldn't Be Shocked,' *Belfer Center*, October 15, 2020.

6 Koshikawa, Noriaki, 'China passes US as world's top researcher, showing its R&D might,' *Nikkei,* August 8, 2020.

7 World Intellectual Property Indicators 2023, Geneva, World Intellectual Property Organization, 2023.

8 Gaida, Jamie et al., 'ASPI's Critical Technology Tracker: The global race for future power,' Australian Strategic Policy Institute, Policy Brief, Report No. 69, 2023.

9 'Former unification minister criticizes Bank of Korea statistics on North Korean growth rate,' *Hankyoreh,* January 1, 2019.

Maresca, Thomas, 'Report: North Korea economy developing dramatically despite sanctions,' *UPI,* December 4, 2019.

Choi, Eun-joo, '21st Colloquium of 2019: Changes in the North Korean Economy Observed at Field Investigation of 2019 to China–North Korea Borders,' *Sejong Institute,* November 12, 2019.

Feron, Henri, 'Pyongyang's Construction Boom: Is North Korea Beating Sanctions?,' *38 North,* July 18, 2017.

10 Shin, Elizabeth, 'North Korean performers feted after China concert, state media says,' *UPI,* January 31, 2019.

Lee, Jeong-ho, 'What Xi Jinping attending North Korean pop concert signals to Donald Trump,' *South China Morning Post,* January 28, 2019.

11 Goldman, Russel, 'In Pictures: For Kim Jong-un and Xi Jinping, Small Talk and Mass Games,' *New York Times,* June 21, 2019.

12 'China & N. Korea 'to boost military ties & provide security in Asia-Pacific' amid tensions with US,' *RT*, August 17, 2019.

'N. Korea, China demonstrate military ties in high-level talks,' *Yonhap,* August 18, 2019.

13 O'Carroll, Chad, 'How a massive influx of Chinese visitors is changing North Korean tourism,' *NK News,* November 1, 2019.

'North Korea enjoying tourism boom after summit between Kim Jong-un and Moon Jae-in in April,' *South China Morning Post,* July 29, 2018.

Jang, Seul Gi, 'Has thriving Chinese tourism emboldened North Korea?,' *Daily NK,* October 28, 2019.

O'Carroll, Chad, 'As Chinese tourism to North Korea soars, local operators feel the strain,' *NK News,* October 31, 2019.

14 'North Korea's new beach resort will soon be ready for tourists,' *South China Morning Post,* January 17, 2019.

15 Choe, Sang-Hun, 'North Korea Touts New Resort, Seeking to Blunt U.N. Sanctions,' *New York Times*, December 3, 2019.

16 Choe, Sang-Hun, 'Kim Jong-un Orders "Shabby" South Korean Hotels in Resort Town Destroyed,' *New York Times*, October 23, 2019.

17 Zwirko, Colin, 'Qingdao Airlines awaiting approval to run three new routes to Pyongyang,' *NK News,* January 16, 2020.

Zwirko, Colin, 'North Korean airline begins twice-weekly Pyongyang-Macau route following delay,' *NK News,* October 1, 2019.

18 Fromer, Jacob, 'China's imports, exports to North Korea grew in 2019: data,' *NK News,* January 31, 2020

19 A Capitalist in North Korea on Facebook: 'North Korean citizens can now use e-banking on their phones. http://arirangmeari.com provides online payment services for DPRK citizens. This will surprise mainstream media consumers because North Korea has always been portrayed by them as a backward country,' October 25, 2020.

Onag, Gigi, 'North Korea rolls out 4G service with secondhand Huawei gear,' *Light Reading*, January 9, 2024.

Park, Soong-joo, 'North Korea's newest smartphone "Samtaesong 8" mirrors Samsung Galaxy phones,' *The Korea Herald*, July 13, 2023.

20 'Lee Jong-seok calls for easing of sanctions under "snapback" provision,' *Hankyoreh,* January 21, 2020.

Bernama, 'Dr M hails Seoul's "Look South" policy; affirms rapprochement with Pyongyang,' *New Straits Times,* November 26, 2019.

21 Alexander, Harriet, 'Russia and China's calls to lift North Korea sanctions rejected by Mike Pompeo,' *Telegraph*, September 27, 2018.

Smith, Josh, 'U.S.-led pressure fractures as China, Russia push for North Korea sanctions relief,' *Reuters*, December 17, 2019.

22 Lederer, Edith M., 'Russia, China block UN from saying N Korea violated sanctions,' *Associated Press,* June 19, 2019.

23 Brunnstrom, David, 'U.S. accuses China of "flagrant" North Korea violations, offers $5 million reward,' *Reuters*, December 2, 2020.

24 'China urges parties to stop fueling tensions on Korean Peninsula,' *CGTN*, August 16, 2022.

25 Sabes, Adam, 'China faults "negative impact" of US military drills for Korean Peninsula tensions,' *Fox News*, April 13, 2023.

26 'N.K. leader calls for communication, unity with China against "hostile forces' all-round challenges,"' *Yonhap*, March 23, 2021.

27 Lee, Sang-yong, 'After Zhao Leji's Visit, What's Next for China–North Korea Relations?,' *The Diplomat*, April 26, 2024.

28 International Institute for Strategic Studies, *The Military Balance, Volume 120, Chapter 6: Asia,* 2020 (p. 236).

29 Tirpak, John A., 'New Study: USAF Needs Big Cash Infusion to Overcome Aging Fighter Fleet,' *Air & Space Forces Magazine*, June 29, 2023.

Guastella, Joseph and Birkey, Douglas and Gunzinger, Eric and Poling, Aidan, 'Accelerating 5th Generation Airpower: Bringing Capability and Capacity to the Merge,' *Mitchell Institute,* vol. 43, June 29, 2023.

30 Menshikov, S., 'Russian Capitalism Today,' *Monthly Review,* vol. 51, no. 3, 1999 (pp. 82–86).

Millar, James R., 'Can Putin Jump-Start Russia's Stalled Economy?,' *Current History*, vol. 99, no. 639, October 2000 (pp. 29–33).

31 Klein, Naomi, *The Shock Doctrine: The Rise of Disaster Capitalism*, London, Penguin, 2008 (Chapter 11).

32 *Russia Air Force Handbook Volume 1: Strategic Information and Weapon Systems*, Washington, DC, International Business Publications, 2011 (pp. 21, 22, 29).

33 *The Economist*, February 6, 1999 (p. 21).

34 Millar, James R., 'Can Putin Jump-Start Russia's Stalled Economy?,' *Current History*, vol. 99, no. 639, October 2000 (pp. 329–333).

35 Kostenko, Yu. P., *Танк: Человек, Среда, Машина* [*Tank: Human, Environment, Machine*], Moscow, Arkhangelsk, 2001.

36 Luzin, Pavel, 'Russia's Defense Industry and Its Influence on Policy: Stuck in a Redistributive Feedback Loop,' *Russia Matters*, November 3, 2021.

37 Cushman, John H., 'Military Options in Korea's End Game,' *Nautilus Institute*, May 23, 1994.

38 Glebova, Diana, 'North Korea Offers Russia 100,000 "Volunteers" for War on Ukraine, Russian State TV Says,' *National Review*, August 5, 2022.

39 'Experts Say Russia Turns to Sanctioned North Korea to Break Rules,' *Voice of Asia*, July 27, 2022.

40 Zwirko, Colin, 'North Korea confirms plan to send workers to Russia-occupied Ukraine,' *NK News*, August 2, 2022.

41 Jang, Seulkee, 'N. Korea sends workers to eastern Ukraine to help reconstruction efforts,' *Daily NK*, April 12, 2024.

42 'NATO's entire military infrastructure, satellites working against Russia – Kremlin,' *TASS*, February 1, 2023.

43 'Commando Network Coordinates Flow of Weapons in Ukraine, Officials Say,' *New York Times*, June 25, 2022.

44 'La guerre d'Ukraine vue par nos képis' ['The Ukrainian war as seen through our picture'], *Causeur*, August 4, 2022.

'Mercenaries or Ideologues? Examining the Most Famous Foreign Militia in Ukraine the Georgian National Legion,' *Military Watch Magazine*, November 8, 2022.

'U.S. Special Forces Chief Gives New Details on British Ground Forces' Frontline Ops. in Ukraine,' *Military Watch Magazine*, May 14, 2022.

'Russian Missile Strike on French Contractor Base in Ukraine Highlights Heated Franco-Russian Cold War,' *Military Watch Magazine*, January 19, 2024.

45 Grylls, George, 'Royal Marines deployed on 'high-risk covert operations' in Ukraine,' *The Times*, December 14, 2022.

46 'Asian Allies Could Equip Russia with Rocket Artillery for Ukraine Outperforming America's HIMARS: These Are The Leading Candidates,' *Military Watch Magazine*, July 23, 2022.

47 'Four North Korean Weapons Types Russia Could Seek to Import Urgently: How Each Could Shift the Balance in Ukraine,' *Military Watch Magazine*, August 20, 2023.

48 Stewart, Will, '100,000 North Korean soldiers could be sent to bolster Putin's forces fighting Ukraine,' *News.au*, August 5, 2022.

49 Bremer, Ifang, 'North Korea able to supply vast quantities of ammunition to Russia: Experts,' *NK News*, September 6, 2022.

50 Larson, Caleb, 'Lessons Learned: U.S. Army Is Laser-Focused on Long-Range Weapons,' *The National Interest*, May 15, 2022.

51 Bremer, Ifang, 'North Korea able to supply vast quantities of ammunition to Russia: Experts,' *NK News*, September 6, 2022.

52 Ibid.

53 International Institute for Strategic Studies, *The Military Balance*, Volume 89, 1989 (pp. 34, 164).

International Institute for Strategic Studies, *The Military Balance*, Volume 121, 2021 (pp. 192, 275).

54 'Do Sanctions Really Work on North Korea? The Impossible State Live!,' *Center for Strategic and International Studies* (YouTube Channel), March 8, 2023.

55 'Press Briefing by Press Secretary Karine Jean-Pierre and NSC Coordinator for Strategic Communications John Kirby,' *The White House*, January 4, 2024.

56 Lovett, Ian, 'Ukraine Is Now Fighting Russia in Sudan,' *The Wall Street Journal*, March 6, 2024.

Ajala, Olayinka, 'Russia-Ukraine war spills into west Africa: Mali attacks signal dangerous times ahead,' *The Conversation*, August 16, 2024.

'Ukrainian Special Forces and Syrian Rebels Decimate Russian Mercenaries in Syria,' *Kyiv Post*, June 3, 2024.

57 Hume, Tim, 'What the Hell Are Ukrainian Fascists Doing in the Hong Kong Protests?,' *Vice News*, December 5, 2019.

Xu, Keyue and Chen, Qingqing, 'HK police probes alleged neo-Nazis,' *Global Times*, December 4, 2019.

58 'Moscow voices serious concern over North Korea nuclear test,' *TASS*, September 9, 2016.

59 Madhani, Aamer, 'White House says top Russian official pitched North Korea on increasing sale of munitions to Moscow,' *AP News*, August 4, 2023.

60 Joo, Sung Ho and Kwak, Tae Hwan, 'Military Relations Between Russia and North Korea,' *Journal of East Asian Affairs*, vol. 15, no. 2, Fall/Winter 2001 (p. 301).

'MiG-29s reach North Korea for assembly,' *Flight Global*, September 8, 1999.

International Institute for Strategic Studies, *The Military Balance*, Volume 101, 2001 (p. 197).

61 'Press Briefing by Press Secretary Karine Jean-Pierre and NSC Coordinator for Strategic Communications John Kirby,' *The White House*, January 4, 2024.

62 Nichols, Michelle, 'Russia blocks renewal of North Korea sanctions monitors,' *Reuters*, March 29, 2024.

63 Smith, Josh, 'Russian veto points to "grim future" for North Korea sanctions enforcement,' *Reuters*, March 29, 2024

64 Nichols, Michelle, 'Russia blocks renewal of North Korea sanctions monitors,' *Reuters*, March 29, 2024.

65 Faulconbridge, Guy, 'After veto, Russia says big powers need to stop "strangling" North Korea,'*Reuters*, March 29, 2024.

66 Smith, Josh, 'Russian veto points to "grim future" for North Korea sanctions enforcement,' *Reuters*, March 29, 2024

67 Arnold, Aaron, 'Russia Just Gutted the UN Panel of Experts on North Korea – What Now?,' *Royal United Services Institute*, April 3, 2024.

68 O'Carroll, Chad, 'What if the UN shuts down the Panel of Experts overseeing North Korea sanctions?,' *NK News*, May 27, 2022.

69 'North Korean film shown in Moscow to mark anniversary of Putin-Kim meeting,' *TASS*, April 24, 2024.

70 Zwirko, Colin, 'Massive Russian cargo plane linked to missile trade flies to North Korea,' *NK Pro*, March 27, 2024.

71 'Putin's spy chief visited North Korea, Russian intelligence service says,' *Reuters*, March 28, 2024.

72 'Russia's North Korea Embrace Could Embolden Kim Jong Un, US Says,' *Bloomberg*, April 23, 2024.

73 'Sec. Austin, Chairman Of The Joint Chiefs Testify At House Armed Service Committee Hearing | Part 1,' *Forbes Breaking News* (YouTube Channel), May 1, 2024.

74 North Korea-Russia Relations: Current Developments, Congressional Research Service, May 6, 2024.

75 Kriegsforscher on Twitter: 'Seems like NK delivered to Russia not only millions of artillery rounds but also some quite specific vehicles. I hope that SK will respond,' July 29, 2024.

Kriegsforscher on Twitter: 'Well, I didn't expect that someone will publish the photo that fast. But new U have seen it. That ATGM managed to launch six rockets before leaving,' July 30, 2024.

76 Abrams, A. B., 'North Korea Closes Russia's Anti-Tank Missile Gap With Ukraine,' *The Diplomat,* August 6, 2024.

77 Clash Report on Twitter: 'Destruction of Ukrainian 155mm AS-90 howitzer by what is most likely North Korea's Bulsae-4 ATGM. –This footage was released this spring, at the time was unclear what type of munition was used. – Javelin-Spike like trajectory, working engine, relatively low speed. – The same Kharkiv frontline on which Bulsae-4 system was spotted recently. – The howitzer was located at a distance of about 10 km from the front line (which fits within the estimated flight range of the Bulsae-4 NLOS missile),' July 30, 2024.

78 'One Chinese Weapon Russia Needs For What is Coming: Why HJ-12 Missiles Are the Best Answer to Ukrainian Armoured Offensives,' *Military Watch Magazine,* February 26, 2023.

79 Abrams, A. B., 'North Korea Closes Russia's Anti-Tank Missile Gap With Ukraine,' *The Diplomat,* August 6, 2024.

80 'North Korean Bulsae-4 Anti-Tank Missile Vehicle Reportedly Spotted in Ukraine for First Time,' *Army Recognition Group,* July 30, 2024.

81 Smith, Josh and Park, Ju-min, 'Russia's Putin and North Korea's Kim sign mutual defence pact,' *Reuters,* June 20, 2024.

82 Putin, Vladimir, 'Russia and the DPRK: Traditions of Friendship and Cooperation Through the Years,' *Rodong Sinmun,* June 18, 2024.

83 Mansourov, Alexandre, 'North Korea: Entering Syria's Civil War,' *38 North,* November 25, 2013.

Gady, Franz-Stefan, 'Is North Korea Fighting for Assad in Syria?' *The Diplomat*, March 24, 2016.

'DPRK Ambassador affirms his country's readiness to support health sector in Syria,' *Syrian Arab News Agency*, July 25, 2016.

'Report: North Korea wants to help Syria rebuild,' *Washington Post*, May 1, 2019.

84 Cha, Taesuh, 'Confronting the North Korean Question in a Post-Unipolar World,' *The National Interest*, November 6, 2022.

85 'Do Sanctions Really Work on North Korea? The Impossible State Live!,' *Center for Strategic and International Studies* (YouTube Channel), March 8, 2023.

86 Monaghan, Angela, 'China surpasses US as world's largest trading nation,' *The Guardian*, January 10, 2014.

87 Green, Mark A., 'China Is the Top Trading Partner to More Than 120 Countries,' *Wilson Center*, January 17, 2023.

88 Ghosh, Iman, 'How China Overtook the U.S. as the World's Major Trading Partner,' *Visual Capitalist*, January 22, 2020.

89 Trade, % of GDP, The World Bank Official Website (https://data.worldbank.org/indicator/NE.TRD.GNFS.ZS).

90 Pate, Durrant, 'US warns Jamaica against Chinese 5g,' *Jamaica Observer,* October 25, 2020.

91 Stewart, Heather and Proctor, Kate, 'Mike Pence hints UK's Huawei decision could jeopardise trade talks,' *The Guardian,* February 7, 2020.

Kharpal, Arjun, '"Our special relationship is less special": UK-US bond tested by Britain's Huawei 5G decision,' *CNBC,* January 29, 2020.

Geddie, John, 'Britain "reasonably confident" of U.S. trade deal despite Huawei concerns,' *Reuters,* February 10, 2020.

92 Kharpal, Arjun, 'U.S. tries to get Huawei blocked from Brazil's 5G networks with $1 billion financing pledge,' *CNBC,* October 21, 2020.

93 Putz, Catherine, 'Which Countries Are For or Against China's Xinjiang Policies?,' *The Diplomat,* July 15, 2019.

94 Yellinek, Roie and Chen, Elizabeth, 'The "22 vs. 50" Diplomatic Split Between the West and China Over Xinjiang and Human Rights,' *Jamestown Foundation,* December 31, 2019.

'Ambassadors from 50 countries voice support to China's position on issues related to Xinjiang,' *Xinhua,* July 27, 2019.

Putz, Catherine, 'Which Countries Are For or Against China's Xinjiang Policies?,' *The Diplomat,* July 15, 2019.

95 Berlinger, Joshua, 'North Korea, Syria and Myanmar among countries defending China's actions in Xinjiang,' *CNN,* July 15, 2019.

96 'Joint Statement on Xinjiang at Third Committee Made by Belarus on Behalf of 54 Countries,' October 30, 2019.

97 Westcott, Ben and Roth, Richard, 'China's treatment of Uyghurs in Xinjiang divides UN members,' *CNN*, October 30, 2019.

98 'Nearly 70 countries voice support for China on human rights issues,' *CGTN,* October 8, 2020.

99 Liu, Xin, 'More than 90 countries express support to China amid rampant anti-China campaign at UN human rights body,' *Global Times,* June 22, 2021.

100 Fan, Anqi, 'UN envoys attend event highlighting ethnic group solidarity in Xinjiang, condemn West for fabricating lies,' *Global Times,* July 8, 2021.

101 'Belarus represents 70 countries to call for non-interference in China's internal affairs,' *Xinhua,* March 6, 2021.

102 'Muslim nations are defending China as it cracks down on Muslims, shattering any myths of Islamic solidarity,' *CNN,* July 17, 2019.

103 Mishra, Panjak, 'The West Shouldn't Be Losing So Many Hearts and Minds,' *Bloomberg*, February 14, 2023.

104 Bunde, Tobias and Eisentraut, Sophie, Munich Security Conference Report 2023 (Chapter 1 – Introduction: Re:vision, Munich Security Conference Official Website).

105 Kump, Isabell and Mudie-Mantz, Amadée, Munich Security Conference Report 2023 (Chapter 4 – Development Cooperation, Strings Attached, Munich Security Conference Official Website).

106 'Western pleas over Ukraine fail to sway African and South American leaders,' *Financial Times*, February 19, 2023.

107 'Munich Security Conference: Speech by High Representative/Vice-President Josep Borrell on the European Security Architecture,' *The Diplomatic Service of the European Union Official Website*, February 19, 2023.

108 Yuichi Hosoya, 'Why Japan and the G7 must take notice of the Global South,' *Japan Times*, April 13, 2023.

109 Mishra, Panjak, 'The West Shouldn't Be Losing So Many Hearts and Minds,' *Bloomberg*, February 14, 2023.

110 Rabil, Robert G., 'Has Russia's Invasion of Ukraine Doomed the Dollar?,' *The National Interest*, December 23, 2022.

111 'Jokowi wants local governments to ditch Visa, Mastercard,' *Jakarta Post*, March 16, 2023.

112 'Indonesia ready to bypass Visa and Mastercard – media,' *RT,* April 24, 2023.

Weir, Fred, 'A new Russian bank card? Priceless... for the Kremlin,' *Christian Science Monitor*, March 28, 2014.

113 'Widodo urges Indonesia to abandon Visa, MasterCard to be "independent,"' *Al Mayadeen,* March 16, 2023.

114 'Bank Indonesia calls against payments in US Dollars,' *Al Mayadeen,* October 15, 2022.

115 Norrlöf, Carla, 'The Dollar Still Dominates,' *Foreign Affairs*, February 21, 2023.

116 Tran, Hung, 'Internationalization of the Renmibi via bilateral swap lines,' *Atlantic Council*, March 18, 2022.

117 Ibid.

118 'US needs to "wake up" about the threat from China: Marco Rubio,' *Fox News* (YouTube Channel), March 30, 2023.

119 Shagina, Maria, 'How Disastrous Would Disconnection From SWIFT Be for Russia?,' *Carnegie Endowment for International Peace,* May 28, 2021.

120 Rachman, Gideon, *Easternisation, War and Peace in the Asian Century*, New York, Vintage, 2017 (Chapter 14).

121 Ibid. (Chapter 14).

122 Wang, Orange, 'China's yuan-centered payment network no match yet for US-dominated global financial system: experts,' *South China Morning Post*, November 24, 2022.

123 Fonda, Daren, 'Why Cryptocurrencies Are a Threat to Central Banks,' *Barrons,* May 3, 2021.

124 'Has China released a digital currency?,' *World Economic Forum*, September 18, 2023.

125 Bianco, Jim, 'A New Global Monetary Order Threatens the Dollar,' *Bloomberg,* May 12, 2021.

'Will China's digital yuan vanquish the dollar?,' *Nikkei,* August 11, 2021.

Hasenstab, Michael, 'China's digital currency is a threat to dollar dominance,' *Financial Times,* April 14, 2021.

Bansal, Rajesh and Singh, Somya, 'China's Digital Yuan: An Alternative to the Dollar-Dominated Financial System,' *Carnegie Endowment for International Peace*, August 2021.

Bambrough, Billy, 'Bitcoin "Undermining The Dollar" – Hillary Clinton Issues A Surprise Crypto Warning As El Salvador Helps The Bitcoin Price Suddenly Surge,' *Forbes*, November 21, 2021.

The Nixon Seminar on Conservative Realism and National Security, April 6, 2021

126 Kharpal, Arjun, 'China's digital yuan could help North Korea evade US sanctions, launch missiles, experts say,' *CNBC*, January 24, 2020.

127 'Kim Jong Un toughens nuclear policy to allow pre-emptive strikes,' *Financial Times*, September 9, 2022.

128 Kim, Jong Un, Policy Speech at Seventh Session of the 14th Supreme People's Assembly of DPRK, September 10, 2022.

CHAPTER 8

Future Trajectories in the U.S.-DPRK Conflict

Escalation Dominance and a New Military Balance

In parallel to the modernization of its strategic nuclear forces, which saw their capabilities revolutionized from 2016 to 2024 in particular, a much broader modernization of North Korean military capabilities from the mid-2010s totally transformed the country's ability deter and if necessary engage in conflict with the United States and its allies. The modernization of conventional capabilities was significant for multiple reasons and highly complementary to the modernization of strategic forces. A key reason for this was that conventional forces were needed to defend nuclear assets from enemy strikes, meaning the tremendous enhancement of North Korean air defense and sea denial capabilities made enemy strikes far more difficult and reduced the chances of a successful attack being able to destroy nuclear assets before launch. A second key reason was that it significantly improved Pyongyang's ability to manage escalation with the United States and its allies.

In March 2016 former U.S. National Security Council Director for Asian Affairs and leading American DPRK expert Victor Cha observed: "For North Korea the escalation ladder is only artillery, and then nuclear weapons."[1] While this was a gross exaggeration, it did serve to highlight the fact that U.S. analysts believed an attack on the country was possible through dominance of the escalation ladder. By promising a full scale invasion and nuclear strikes to completely wipe out the state should Pyongyang use its nuclear weapons, it was believed that more limited attacks could be carried out without leading to nuclear escalation and would leave the KPA with limited options to respond. Possessing strategic nuclear weapons was much like an ability to wipe a chessboard clean should an enemy threaten to capture one's king – they deterred attacks which threatened a state's fundamental existence such as carpet bombing of population centers, full scale invasions, or attempts to wipe out the leadership, but were limited in their utility to respond to more minor strikes, for which lower rungs on an escalation ladder were needed. Without this, Pyongyang's adversaries could continue to contemplate provocations such as "bloody nose" strikes.

Western attacks on other states with formidable missile deterrents, but insufficient capabilities to manage limited escalation, provided significant warnings to Pyongyang in this regard. Notable examples were the U.S., European, Turkish and Israeli attacks on Syria in the 2010s, which although fielding a formidable ballistic missile arsenal, previously tipped with chemical weapons, was deterred from using it to respond to anything short of a full scale assault. Damascus was unable to respond proportionally with more limited attacks using other kinds of assets. Another notable example was Russia, which struggled to retaliate against its Western adversaries as their satellites, advisors and equipment were used to facilitate Ukrainian strikes on sensitive targets deep inside its territory. By contrast, highly effective escalation management was demonstrated by the Lebanese militia group Hezbollah, which in clashes with Israel from 2023–2024 was able to respond proportionally to attacks and deter its adversary from escalating due to its very wide range of options for retaliating against a range of strategic, military and civilian targets.

At the center of efforts to provide a multi-tiered arsenal for response was North Korea's ballistic missile program, which provided options for retaliation on multiple levels, ranging from limited firings into South Korean waters as shows of force, up to a full scale thermonuclear attack on cities across the U.S. mainland. By the early 2020s a limited American attack could be responded to with missile strikes, possibly even with tactical nuclear warheads, against U.S. military bases from Tokyo Bay and Okinawa to Guam and Wake Island, with North Korea conserving full scale retaliatory options with multiple megatons of force to deter escalation by the U.S. to full scale war. Thermonuclear warheads and

ICBMs provided a top tier of the escalation ladder, which allowed lower tier assets to be used more freely, with the improvement of capabilities on the lower tiers playing a central role in ruling out Western options for limited attacks.

A landmark in North Korea's development of more effective options for escalation management was the unveiling of the country's first tactical nuclear warhead, the Hwasal-31, on March 24, 2023. Its very small estimated diameter of just 40 to 50 centimeters allowed it to be deployed using KN-23 and KN-24 tactical ballistic missiles, and even rocket artillery systems and cruise missiles.[2] This was considered vital to provide a proportional response to growing deployments of U.S. assets such as F-35 fifth generation fighters across the region, which could carry B61 tactical nuclear bombs, and were officially certified to do so seven months later on October 12.[3,i] Considerations for the use of tactical nuclear weapons against North Korea dated back to the Korean War, and in the post–Cold War years were widely seen as necessary to counter the country's vast conventional forces and deep fortifications. The lack of a similar capability had left North Korea vulnerable to U.S. escalation dominance, with the Hwasal-31 providing a proportional means of nuclear retaliation short of escalating to employing strategic nuclear assets.[ii]

---

i Developed under the Joint Strike Fighter program, the F-35 had been designed in the post–Cold War era when, with the disappearance of the Soviet combat aviation sector, it was presumed that U.S. air superiority would not be challenged. The new fighter was thus developed primarily for strike missions and to suppress enemy ground-based air defenses, which made it especially dangerous for North Korea which depended particularly heavily on such assets. Systems such as the KN-23 and KN-25 were at the core of its response, with the maintenance-intensive and often problematic American stealth fighters requiring particularly long periods on the ground for every hour in the air, making the ability to attack their air bases highly valuable.

ii As North Korea's defense sector began to provide significantly more sophisticated equipment in a wide range of areas, the revival of KPA conventional capabilities played a further significant role in strengthening Pyongyang's ability to manage escalation. A major landmark and show of force in this regard was the deployment of North Korean drones for an incursion into South Korean airspace on December 26, 2022, during a period of high inter-Korean tensions under the new Yoon administration.

Where Western and South Korean assessments of North Korean military capabilities consistently indicated the need for a very high degree of caution, military officials' assessments of America's own readiness for war against the country were consistently far from optimistic. This was highlighted by a report submitted to Congress by former deputy commander of U.S. Forces Korea Lieutenant General Jan-Marc Jouas,[iii] which when leaked in early November 2017 as tensions between the two countries came to a head painted a grim picture of American prospects. It did so despite discounting the then high possibility of Chinese or Russian intervention. U.S. forces "are vastly outnumbered by North Korean forces, as well as (allied) forces that will conduct the overwhelming majority of the fighting," he observed, adding that deploying reinforcing personnel would be extremely difficult due to missile, chemical weapons and special forces attacks far behind friendly lines. American forces "may well find their bases subject to attack by conventional or chemical weapons, which will further delay their entry into the war," while ports and incoming ships and airfields would all be vulnerable.[4]

Perhaps the most significant issue highlighted in the leaked assessment was that there was a high possibility of North Korea neutralizing American facilities on Guam, Hawaii and Okinawa, and the Navy's 7th Fleet based in Japan, which could leave the war

---

Although the south's Joint Chiefs of Staff had dismissed early reports that one of these drones had loitered over sensitive areas in Seoul as "untrue and groundless," this was conceded the following month to be true. Over 100 rounds fired by South Korean attack helicopters failed to damage the aircraft, while a KA-1 attack jet launched to intercept crashed before reaching its target, allowing the northern aircraft to conduct reconnaissance with near impunity.

iii Jouas had previously served as Commander of the Seventh Air Force permanently stationed in South Korea, as well as Pacific Air Forces Director of Operations, Plans, Requirements, and Programs, making him one of the best acquainted former air force officials with the realities of the conventional balance on the Korean Peninsula. From January 2012 to December 2014, he was a central figure influencing the redrawing of plans for a U.S.-led military campaign in Korea, summarizing afterwards that "planning for it was the most challenging problem I'd encountered in my 35-year career."

effectively over for the isolated American forces on the ground. Chemical and nuclear strikes would leave American naval assets and bases across the Pacific vulnerable, further seriously limiting personnel on the ground's access to air support, supplies or reinforcements. One hundred thousand non-combatant American citizens in South Korea would also depend on the military for evacuation, further stretching its forces.[5]

Not only was the KPA far better prepared and in a much stronger position to engage U.S. and allied forces than it had been at the start of the Korean War, but the United States Armed Forces were also far from what they had been during the Cold War. While already in 1993 U.S. military leaders such as Air Force Chief of Staff Merrill McPeak and Joint Chiefs of Staff Chairman John Shalikashvili had indicated that a North Korean counteroffensive could allow it to capture Seoul,[6] this had preceded both the fallout from deep post–Cold War budget cuts on the U.S. Armed Forces and the KPA's rapid and comprehensive modernization from the mid-2010s. Downsizing of the services was such that the U.S. Air Force fell from 158 combat squadrons during Operation Desert Storm to just 55 in the mid-2020s, with a similar decline seen across the services.

Aside from the immense downsizing of the services, by the 2020s a more serious issue for the U.S. was the significant dulling of capabilities for a state-on-state conflict as a result of two decades of focus on counterinsurgency. This point gained prominent coverage following the escalation of Russian-Ukrainian hostilities in February 2022, where American veterans of the wars of the post–Cold War era who fought in the theatre consistently highlighted that Western militaries' training and preparation for a peer level conflict fell very far short. One such veteran in April 2024 stressed: "In the U.S. military, we mostly have been focusing on a guerilla war and battling insurgents, with places like Iraq and Afghanistan... We've gotten so used to the idea of just fighting guerilla wars and f*cking fighting terrorists and everything else that we kind of forgot what it means to actually fight a war." He highlighted that training in the post–Cold War years provided little preparation for war with a peer level adversary. "A little bit of talking about it and just a little bit of training, but nothing to the point that would have prepared me for the war in Ukraine... I believe that a lot of the training that we have is tailored more to fighting in a guerilla warfare nowadays than it is to actually fighting a near-peer adversary."[7]

The veteran stated that this was an issue widely affecting NATO members, with many Western veterans having struggled in Ukraine as "they already have a set idea about how things should be and everything, and it's just not that way out in Ukraine," without the kind of overwhelming equipment and manpower advantages they were used to in counterinsurgencies. "We haven't fought a conventional war in f*cking forever," he concluded regarding NATO militaries.[8] Another American veteran fighting in Ukraine observed at the time regarding the stark difference between the kind of wars Western militaries had become accustomed to, and peer level conflicts, was that "nowhere is safe." In Afghanistan and Iraq, by contrast, "you could stand outside and have a barbecue, a sandwich, and drink" just a mile behind the frontlines.[9] Similar statements from Western combatants were widespread for over two years from March 2022.

While Western sources from the mid-2010s increasingly widely reiterated that a core advantage the U.S. and its NATO allies would have in war with North Korea or China was that they had experience in wartime operations,[10] it appeared increasingly evident that the opposite was true. There were no adversaries more disparate than the Taliban and the Chinese People's Liberation Army in terms of capabilities, and experience fighting precisely the opposite kind of war, while North Korean and Chinese forces were very heavily focused on preparing for possible war with the Western Bloc states, was a major disadvantage.[iv]

iv A less extreme example of the detrimental impacts which preparations for the wrong kind of war could have was demonstrated during the Gulf War, when Iraqi military thought was overwhelmingly shaped by experience fighting Iran in a protracted eight year war that had ended two years prior. Iraqi forces hunkered down in trenches and fortifications expecting a massed ground assault, while leaving their western flank totally unprotected in the expectation that Western forces, much like the Iranians, would be unable to navigate the desert regions to engage from that direction. With

In June 2017 as tensions between North Korea and the United States came to a head, the newly appointed Secretary of Defense James Mattis expressed shock at the very poor state of preparation for a possible war with a major power. "I have been shocked by what I've seen with our readiness to fight. For all the heartache caused by the loss of our troops during these wars [Iraq and Afghanistan] no enemy in the field has done more to harm the readiness of our military than sequestration... It took us years to get into this situation. It will require years of stable budgets and increased funding to get out of it." This was despite the country having at the time been at war for 16 years – what Mattis referred to as "the longest continuous stretch of armed conflict in our Nation's history."[11]

As defense secretary, bolstered by a significant surge in defense spending, Mattis oversaw a number of efforts to improve the military's readiness, albeit with consistently very limited success.[12] A notable example was the setting of a goal on September 17, 2018 for the Navy and Air Force's F-35, F-22, F-16 and F-18 fighter units to attain 80 percent combat readiness by the end of September the next year, calling on other military departments to "also set and pursue aggressive targets for our other enduring fixed wing and rotary wing aviation assets." This followed his acknowledgement on September 17 that "budget constraints and shortfalls in aviation squadrons across the force" have led to "systemic underperformance, overcapitalization and unrealized capacity."[13] Meeting these goals in the air force appeared highly unviable from the outset, however, since not only was the bulk of the fleet comprised of fourth generation aircraft worn out from

---

air power having played a very limited role in the Iran-Iraq War, this was also seriously undervalued. Where Iran had executed much of its air force's officer corps and many more of its skilled airmen were jailed or in exile, this was far from the case for NATO militaries built up to face the Warsaw Pact. Had the Iraqi Armed Forces gone into the Gulf War with no combat experience, and with training tailored to no specific kind of warfare, they likely would have fared much better than they did going in with the wrong kind of experience. For NATO militaries, two decades of focus on counterinsurgency and attacks on very poorly armed states would likely be even more of a hindrance if fighting China or North Korea.

decades of operations, but newly built fifth generation F-22s and F-35s were so problematic that their availability rates were consistently much worse still.[14] Nine months after missing the Defense Secretary's deadline, the Air Force on May 8 released an official statement that it would no longer work to meet the 80 percent readiness target, to which it had not even come close.[15] By the early 2020s, as the issue continued to worsen, senior air force officials increasingly warned that force readiness could "fall off a cliff," and was already having a seriously detrimental impact on training hours, allowing Chinese pilots to on average train in the air for significantly longer.[16] The case of fighter availability rates, which was one of the first issues Secretary Mattis attempted to address, reflected maladies affecting the Armed Forces and defense sector very broadly that had worsened considerably since the Cold War ended. The full extent of issues that emerged to hamper the American defense sector and the military overall are best detailed in another volume, but were extremely detrimental to and seriously limited the country's ability to engage in conventional wars against major militaries.

By the mid-2020s North Korea was no longer facing the America at the height of its power of the 1950s, or of the immediate post–Cold War unipolar moment, but instead a much weakened superpower in a world where Western dominance was facing challenges unprecedented in centuries. U.S. government debt had by mid-2024 reached 35 trillion dollars, and was increasing unsustainably with annual deficits of close to $2 trillion, while for the first time in history, the U.S. Armed Forces admitted they were short 40,000 personnel as recruiting goals were missed by wide margins despite a significant reduction in both numerical and qualitative requirements.[17] The disorderly withdrawal from Afghanistan in 2021, leaving collaborators' fates at the hands of the Taliban, taking significant casualties to terrorist attacks while in retreat, and abandoning $7 billion worth of military equipment, was one notable indicator. Growing social unrest and political divisions within the U.S. were increasingly at the forefront of discourse, raising concerns regarding the country's future. Conservative military historian Victor David Hanson, for one, observed in mid-2024: "never have we been faced with such existential challenges in a period where we are so weak.... when you look at crime, when you look at debt, when you look at the border, when you look at our universities... we are not the same people who stormed Omaha Beach."[18] The United States had changed much more than North Korea had both since 1950 when the war began, and since the turn of the century, with political, societal, economic, and military trends, both in the two countries and more broadly worldwide, very strongly favoring Pyongyang's position.

The Possibility of a Peace or an Arms Control Agreement

On October 25, 2016 the Obama administration's Director of National Intelligence James Clapper stated: "I think the notion of getting the North Koreans to denuclearize is probably a lost cause." The best the U.S. could settle for, he said, was a negotiated limit on the types of nuclear weapons North Korea could deploy.[19] As the first such admission by a senior U.S. official, Clapper proved to be well ahead of his time – if not in his conclusions then in his willingness to publicly state the reality of the situation. While considerable emphasis was placed on denuclearization as the end goal of negotiations, realistically the prospects for both states agreeing to sufficient stages of concessions to bring this about, although having been viable during the period of the Agreed Framework, were by the mid-2000s already extremely slim. While North Korea is set to remain a nuclear weapons state indefinitely, with their possession seen as inseparable from the state's right to independence and self-defense and codified in the constitution, the timescale for and circumstances of the normalization of the state's nuclear capabilities in the Western world remains highly uncertain. An assessment of Western relations with and perceptions of North Korea, and the state's place in the Western worldview, indicates that such normalization is highly unlikely to proceed smoothly or quickly if at all.

The difficulties for the Western psyche in accepting North Korea as a nuclear weapons state have been and will continue to be considerable, with the country's continued existence in and of itself representing one of the most direct contradictions to the idea of a new world order centered on the economic and military power of the Western world and the global triumph of Western values. With the Western world envisaging a global order built in its own image, even China and Iran appeared somewhat westernized next to North Korea, with its political philosophy and social system firmly rooted in Confucian thought, Marxism and Asian values. Described by its leading American critics as the "ultimate outlier in world order,"[20] and an imminent threat to "the moral structure on which global order is built,"[21] the fact that this small state developed and will retain the military capacity to devastate cities across the Western world with thermonuclear strikes is considered particularly unacceptable. Under the protection of this nuclear deterrent, a growing economy independent of Western trade or investment, and a society almost untouched by Western values, can continue to exist seemingly indefinitely.

One of the best summaries of the difficulties the American psyche in particular would face in coming to terms with a nuclear North Korea was provided by the Director of Korea Studies at the Center for the National Interest Harry J. Kazianis, who observed:

> Our own national psychology that reinforces over and over our own need for primacy in all parts of the world and our "exceptional" nature surely means we should not have to accept a nuclear North Korea. That psychology declares that we can make Pyongyang bend to our will and that the Kim regime simply has no way to resist our demands. And yet, every intelligence report that breaks puts cracks in our own collective sense of invulnerability. Those reports that a nation as economically backward such as North Korea can kill millions of Americans rocks us to our core and challenges how Americans think of themselves. That might explain why so many of us here in Washington – including yours truly – reacted with such shock and anger over North Korea's nuclear weapons and missile tests back in 2017. It was, and still is, our twenty-first-century "Sputnik"

> moment, a series of events that shattered our sense of security, our perceptions of how powerful our nation is mixed with the dreadful realization that a country with the human rights record such as North Korea has and will continue to build even more dangerous weapons of mass destruction. We want to believe that this is unacceptable, and yet the facts tell us otherwise.

Observing a strong case of cognitive dissonance, Kazianis referred to the constant denial of both North Korea's capabilities and its newfound position of strength as a "foreign policy fantasyland."[22] Where even the Agreed Framework, which had stopped North Korea's nuclear program decisively, had seen widespread opposition within the U.S. described as "vociferous" and been viewed as "tantamount to an act of appeasement," and as imposing "a high political price" domestically for every concession made,[23] an agreement reflecting the realities three decades later would likely only be less politically feasible.

The longer the nuclear standoff between Pyongyang and Washington has continued, the greater nuclear capability the former is expected to retain in the event of a deal. With denuclearization off the table, possibilities for a deal could include a freeze on the construction of additional heavy water facilities, such as the 50 MW(e) second Yongbyon facility, and international monitoring to prevent nuclear weapons production at existing facilities. This and a moratorium on nuclear weapons testing could well be leveraged to roll back multiple rounds of sanctions at the United Nations Security Council. Further concessions could include a cap on the number of medium and intermediate range ballistic missiles, which would be far more difficult to monitor, as well as a moratorium on their launches, in return for relief from more UNSC sanctions. As North Korea brings a growing range of new nuclear delivery capabilities into service, from unmanned submarines to hypersonic glide vehicles, the concessions it can expect to receive for placing limits on their production and further development will only grow. With the United States having gradually lost its position of strength in negotiations, which was at its height in the 1990s but dissipated from 2003, a failure to shift its negotiating position to accommodate these new realities, and the diminishing of the importance Pyongyang attaches to sanctions relief as UNSC resolutions are increasingly ignored, will nevertheless likely remain key barriers to a breakthrough.

A number of factors seriously impede the possibility for a reduction of tensions between Pyongyang and the Western world through arms control and peace agreements. One of the foremost among these is the nature of the political system in the United States, which has allowed administrations to consistently annul, withdraw from, or ignore commitments made by preceding administrations from opposing political parties. From Bill Clinton to Donald Trump, every single administration since the end of the Cold War broke one or more major security related agreements made by its immediate predecessor, seriously compromising the interests of a country which had previously placed a degree of trust in the United States. In the 1990s the Bill Clinton administration ignored "iron clad guarantees" its predecessor had made to Moscow that NATO's expansion would go "not one inch eastward," taking advantage of the Soviet trust and renunciation of its sphere of influence in Eastern Europe to rapidly expand the U.S.-led alliance closer to Moscow.[24] The George W. Bush administration in the early 2000s subsequently abandoned the Agreed Framework and ongoing denuclearization talks with North Korea for a hard line on regime change. Pyongyang was at the time fortunate that talks had not progressed to a stage of irreversible concessions such as the dismantling of Yongbyon or its position would have been seriously compromised.

In the summer of 2010 a paper by the U.S. National Academy of Engineering by leading experts on the North Korean nuclear program summarized: "during the past 20 years, diplomacy has left Pyongyang with only a handful of bombs, instead of the 100 or more it might have had by now, and essentially no significant nuclear-generated electricity."[25] The paper highlighted that Pyongyang's repeated entry into talks with the U.S., suspending work on its civilian reactors and carrying out multiple years-long freezes on its nuclear activities under the Clinton and Bush administrations, had ended poorly for the country, as even when Washington had agreed on concessions it had consistently failed to meet its obligations. Preceding the Agreed Framework, North Korea had been expected to open its 50 MW(e) reactor as early as late 1995, and certainly long before the turn of the century, while its 200 MW(e) factory was expected to be finished in 1996. Work on both had been described as "intense," but was suddenly abandoned for hopes of normalization of economic and political relations and provision of light water reactors that was never seen through.[26]

Following the trend set by preceding administrations, the Barack Obama administration in 2011 entirely ignored security guarantees provided by its predecessor to the government of Libya, which had renounced its missiles and weapons of mass destruction and allowed for intrusive inspections of its military facilities in return for these guarantees and normalization of economic and diplomatic relations. Sanctions were re-imposed under Obama, with Libyan assets across the Western world frozen or seized, before the now near-defenseless state[v] was devastated by Western air attacks. Director of National Intelligence James Clapper would be among many officials to later observe regarding the consequences: "[Libyan leader Muammar] Gaddafi pleaded

---

v Perhaps one of the most ominous warnings directed towards North Korea came from the son of Libyan leader Muammar Gaddafi, Saif Al Islam Gaddafi, who while naming the country specifically referred to the circumstances of Libya's downfall as "a good lesson for everybody." Noting that Pyongyang had in the 2000s advised his country against disarmament, he stated in a televised interview in 2011 while his country was under Western bombardment: "*You give up your weapons of mass destruction, you stop developing long range missiles, you become very friendly with the West and this is the result. So what does this mean, it means this is a message to everybody that you have to be strong. You never trust them, and you have to be always on alert. Otherwise those people, they don't have friends. Overnight they change their mind and they start bombing us, and the same thing could happen to any other country... One of our big mistakes was that we delayed buying new weapons, especially from Russia, it was a big mistake. And we delayed building a strong army because we thought that we will not fight again, the Americans, the Europeans are our friends.*" ('Gaddafi's son: Libya like McDonald's for NATO – fast war as fast food,' *RT* (YouTube Channel), July 1, 2011.)

for the United States and then NATO to stop the attacks, citing his cooperation with weapons inspectors, his voluntary disarmament of his nuclear program, and his restraint from using chemical weapons in his current civil struggle. It was far too late, and no one in the West paid attention. However, I believe North Korea and Iran took careful note of what happens when you give up your nuclear program."[27]

In 2018 the Donald Trump administration unilaterally withdrew from the Joint Comprehensive Plan of Action multilateral agreement with Iran, which had placed limits on its nuclear activities in exchange for sanctions relief. A renegotiation of terms was demanded, with harsh economic sanctions and threats of military action soon following. Reflecting widely held concerns regarding the message this sent to Pyongyang, Russian Foreign Minister Sergei Lavrov observed at the time: "If the United States drops out of this deal, it won't be very credible in the eyes of those who are now requested to drop their (own) nuclear program like North Korea."[28] Had Iran's Supreme Leader Ali Khamenei not personally overseen a major expansion in missile deterrent, insisting that any deal should not affect these capabilities, the possibility of U.S. military action would have been considerably greater.[29]

Statements from Pyongyang indicate a strong awareness of these precedents and the resulting difficulties in reaching agreements with the United States.[30] A notable example was the following DPRK Foreign Ministry statement regarding the lessons from the Western air assault on Libya: "Libya's nuclear dismantlement much touted by the U.S. in the past turned out to be a mode of aggression by which the latter coaxed the former with such sweet words as 'guarantee of security' and 'improvement of relations' to disarm and then swallow it up by force." In exchange for a lifting of sanctions and normalization of diplomatic ties, Libya "took the economic bait, foolishly disarmed themselves, and once they were defenseless, were mercilessly punished by the West."[31] Referring to the example of Iraq, which comprehensively disarmed and allowed inspectors extensive access to its facilities, the Foreign Ministry stated on a separate occasion: "The Iraqi war shows that to allow disarming through inspection does not help avert a war but rather sparks it."[32] A similar awareness of the risks of comprehensive disarmament were expressed on several other occasions.

The Trump administration's Director of National Intelligence Daniel Coats appeared to reach a similar conclusion, affirming that it was strongly against Pyongyang's national security interests to disarm. The North Korean leadership, he stated, "has watched, I think, what has happened around the world relative to nations that possess nuclear capabilities and the leverage they have and seen that having the nuclear card in your pocket results in a lot of deterrence capability." "The lessons that we learned out of Libya giving up its nukes ... is, unfortunately: If you had nukes, never give them up. If you don't have them, get them," he concluded.[33] Coats' predecessor James Clapper in much the same vein referred to the Korean deterrent as "their ticket to survival," highlighting that it was one which Pyongyang was not realistically going to yield.[34]

Throughout Pyongyang's 75-year conflict with the U.S. and the wider Western Bloc, instances where it has observed its adversaries breaking defense-related agreements have been manifold, both in East Asia and worldwide. Examples have ranged from America's unilateral abrogation of article 13(d) of the Korean War Armistice Agreement without legal premise to deploy nuclear weapons in South Korea in June 1957, to European leaders' admitted use of the 2014 Minsk Agreements to buy time with the intention of renewing hostilities in the Ukrainian Civil War once they built up government forces to greater strength.[35] Thus while predominant perceptions in the Western world of its place in the international system, and of North Korea's, made a realistic approach to an arms control agreement difficult, precedents for Western adherence to agreements ensured that Pyongyang was highly unlikely to make concessions that were not quickly reversible unless technical factors, such as the UNSC's mechanism for imposing sanctions, ensured that Western concessions were similarly irreversible.

North Korea and the Fundamentals of the Western Worldview

At the center of the longevity of the conflict between North Korea and the U.S.-led Western world is the latter's longstanding objective of achieving the total destruction of the former, which has on a fundamental level been motivated not only by geopolitics, but by ideology and the perception of a civilizing mission to politically westernize the world. As leading international relations scholar John Mearsheimer was among many to observe, the perception of a right and responsibility for interventionism, including with military force, to reshape countries outside Western influence, remained "the mentality that most people have in the West."[36] As the world's least westernized country, and one of the few places in the world where Western states had never imposed their rule, the zeal behind the perceived need to impose such change on North Korea was proportionally strong.

As was the case with all major Western adversaries, a massive metanarrative was created surrounding North Korea casting it as an intolerable evil in the world using fabricated stories of atrocities. This had a very long history dating back to the early days of the Korean War, with one of the most notable fabrications at the time being the widely publicized allegation that entire South Korean population centers were being massacred and buried in mass graves. Images taken by American personnel were widely publicized showing mass killings on a tremendous scale and women holding babies in mass graves, with the Pentagon sponsoring the film *The Crime of Korea* among other media to further spread this message.[37] The U.S. Army reported regarding the site of one such alleged massacre: "for murderous barbarism, the Taejon massacre will be recorded in the annals of history along with the rape of Nanking, the Warsaw Ghetto and other similar mass exterminations... Those responsible... must be brought to judgement before the tribunal of civilized peoples." Similar descriptions were widespread across Western reporting.[38] With mass slaughter of the South Korean population being one of several early atrocity stories which shaped the Western world's core understanding of North

Korea, it was only 50 years later that it declassified Pentagon documents quietly revealed that the massacres had been perpetrated across South Korea by Western-backed local government forces often under U.S. supervision. The collection of footage and its misattribution to the North Koreans was a highly effective form of war propaganda.[39] Stories of massacres of American prisoners of war, and their torture, were also widely propagated only to later prove to have been entirely fabricated.[40]

Atrocity fabrication and propagation of other false information in the West not only built up very considerable antagonism towards North Korea, but would also leave the Western world far out of touch with its realities on multiple levels. Fantastical Western portrayals of a failed and despotic "Kim Regime" cast it as holding its people back from all forms of progress, intentionally starving them to enforce submission, and regularly executing them with Bondesque methods ranging from piranha tanks to anti-aircraft guns, and for crimes ranging from watching the wrong movies, to failing to clean Kim Jong Il's photos, and even for falling asleep.[41] The fact that the majority of the most successful stories came from sources that were either directly or indirectly funded by Western governments, Radio Free Asia being a notable example, meant this delusion was largely self-inflicted. The country was widely portrayed as dysfunctional and deeply corrupt, comparable to Somalia, Afghanistan and other near failed states,[42] which resulted in its resilience, economic progress and technological advances, most conspicuously in its missile programs, consistently surprising Western observers.

The metanarrative created around North Korea in the West would grow more extreme when the country returned to the center of Western attentions after the end of the Cold War, with new fabricated atrocities further reinforcing the state's image as an ultimate evil, and its population as living among the worst lives of all the world's peoples. From the 1990s Western media described all manner of atrocities in Nazi-style concentration camps, an example being former British naval covert operations specialist and writer James Barrington's description, based on unspecified "documentary evidence," of chemical weapons experiments:

> some fifty women were selected at random and fed cabbage leaves laced with an unidentified poison that resulted in them vomiting blood and suffering agonizing deaths within about twenty minutes. In other instances, entire families were gassed simultaneously, the parents desperately trying to protect their children as the lethal concoction began its work... Those who aren't put in the gas chamber, or tortured to death for the pleasure of the guards, are forced to work on the land or in the nearby Chungbong coal mine. Many there die from their regular beatings or simply through exhaustion because of the appalling conditions... guards are instructed to kill all newborn children by stamping on their heads and necks.[43]

Portrayals of the country ranged from such extremes to seemingly trivial but ludicrous false stories such as mandatory Kim Jong Un haircuts for all males, published by the U.S. state run Radio Free Asia and widely republished,[44] or claims that North Korean state media had reported the existence of unicorns within the country.[45]

Although the longevity of the conflict between Pyongyang and the Western world allowed a particularly strong metanarrative to be built up over time, atrocity fabrication was common to the campaigns against almost all Western adversaries.[vi] Notable examples included stories of 400,000 Iraqis being found in mass graves,[46] Iraqi soldiers massacring Kuwaiti babies in hospitals,[47] and Iraqi dissidents being fed feet first into plastic shredders,[48] Yugoslav soldiers slaughtering Albanian minority civilians and burying them in mass graves,[49] Libyan Army units distributing Viagra to its personnel in order to commit mass rapes,[50] or Chinese soldiers gunning down thousands of peaceful students in central Beijing.[51] All of these narratives would later be debunked as fake once they had served their purposes, usually after the targeted state had been defeated. Such narratives created a strong consensus

---

vi For a detailing of the Western use of atrocity fabrication in conflict see the writer's work: *Atrocity Fabrication and Its Consequences: How Fake News Shapes World Order*, Atlanta, Clarity Press, 2023.

view in the Western world that, in line with its perceived responsibility to shape the world in line with its values, a hardline policy of forcing change on North Korea was necessary. This consensus was perhaps best summarized by Director of Korea Studies at the Center for the National Interest Harry J. Kazianis, who observed: "North Korea is a stain on human history that needs to be expunged."[52,vii]

For the Western world's deeply rooted sense of ideological and civilizational superiority and civilizing mission, North Korea as an ultimate other that had defied all odds to successfully reject the West for decades has long evoked particularly deep antagonism from both Western populations and their leaders. President George W. Bush, for one, had famously stated in 2002: "I loathe Kim Jong Il!," shouting and waving his finger in the air before stating: "I've got a visceral reaction to this guy." "It is visceral. Maybe it's my religion, maybe it's my – but I feel passionate about this," stressing that the world couldn't tolerate such a country. "They tell me, we don't need to move too fast, because the financial burdens on people will be so immense if we try to – if this guy were to topple. Who would take care of – I just don't buy that. Either you believe in freedom, and want to – and worry about the human condition, or you don't." He stated explicitly that there was a similar rationale to ending the Iraqi government's alleged abuses against its population.[53,viii]

---

vii Indicating the degree of animosity felt towards North Korea in the West, even in apolitical content the country could very seldom be mentioned without harsh rebuke, whether it be a travel guide, a book on flag designs or a collection of mountain scenery. Commentary labeling it as something along the lines of the "most vicious, paranoid, murderous dictatorship," as a British book on flag designs referred to it, appeared almost mandatory. (Marshall, Tim, *Worth Dying For: The Power and Politics of Flags*, London, Elliott & Thompson, 2016 (p. 165).)

viii Referring to the need for action against Pyongyang, Bush further elaborated: "There is a value system that cannot be compromised – God-given values. These aren't United States-created values. There are values of freedom and the human condition and mothers loving their children. What's very important as we articulate foreign policy through our diplomacy and military action, is that it never look like we are creating – we are the author of these values." (Woodward, Bob, *Bush at War*, New York, Simon & Schuster, 2002

Such sentiments were far from isolated to President Bush or to the American leadership, for whom atrocity stories had played a central role in winning both public support and votes on Capitol Hill for war efforts from Iraq to Yugoslavia and beyond. Taking Iraq as an example, preceding the U.S.-led invasion polls showed that 82 percent of Americans said they would support an attack regardless of whether weapons of mass destruction were found,[54] with 64 percent stating that "Saddam Hussein should be removed from power in Iraq, regardless of whether U.N. inspectors find evidence of weapons of mass destruction."[55] The vilification of the state was such that its destruction was seen as favorable regardless of whether or not its weapons programs – the primary pretext for attacking – existed or not. This trend was far from isolated to Iraq, with visceral reactions to adversary states, and a public consensus on the need to destroy them, being widespread in the West. President Bush's perceptions were far from confined to his administration. Two decades after his statement on Chairman Kim, State Secretary Mike Pompeo, who headed the Trump administration's talks with North Korea, would in his memoir refer to the inter-Korean border as "the border of diametrically opposed worlds of light and darkness,"[56] and to Chairman Kim Jong Un as "a bloodthirsty toad," with similar terms widely used.[57]

The strong consensus view in the Western world towards a similar moral obligation for action against the North Korean state, much like for Iraq, Yugoslavia and others before it, was far from relegated to political leaders alone. This was perhaps best summarized by British comedian and writer Jimmy Carr as follows:

> People still think, well: if slavery was going on today, I'd fight it. And if Hitler was around today, I'd fight him. And you go, but he is, and there is. Its horrific. Look at North Korea… America's original sin is slavery, and there's no way to change the past. But one thing you could do, if you can't work out reparations, is make America's foreign policy: why don't we just stop

(p. 113).)

> slavery. Who couldn't get behind that. Globally. You've got an incredible military. There's injustice going on in the world. That idea of being the world's policeman, freeing slaves. Who could disagree with that?[58]

The Western world's strong tendency to equate almost any adversary with a new Hitler, combined with what some experts such as former Singaporean UN ambassador Kishore Mahbubani referred to as a "messianic desire" to reshape the world in its own image, created deep antagonism and very strong tendencies towards aggression that in turn left little possibility for co-existence.[59] As observed by Pyongyang's senior diplomat for negotiations with the U.S. Kwon Jong Gun in 2019: "American politics are dominated by the policy-makers who have an inveterate antagonism towards the DPRK," which made it "difficult to look forward to the improvement of bilateral relations and denuclearization of the Korean Peninsula."[60]

Chairman Kim Jong Un was not infrequently likened to Hitler in the West,[61] and his country to Nazi Germany, with a number of reports published in a range of Western media sources going so far as to claim that he was a secret admirer of the German leader, who distributed copies of *Mein Kampf* to officials.[62] This followed the persistent tendency of Western officials and media to liken adversaries to the Führer, from Egypt's President Nasser[63] and Iran's supreme leaders Khomeini[64] and Khamenei,[65] to Iraqi President Saddam Hussein[66] (whom U.S. print media likened to Hitler 1,035 separate times preceding the Gulf War[67]), Yugoslav President Solobodan Milosevic,[68] Chinese President Xi Jinping,[69] and Russian President Vladimir Putin[70] among a multitude of others. While this reflected the Western world's ideological commitment to the total destruction of adversary states, North Korea's degree of resistance was particularly outstanding and long, and made Western antagonism towards the country especially virulent.

Western antagonism towards North Korea's existence seriously limits room for détente. Even the strongest advocates in the West of a more realist policy of loosening sanctions in exchange for arms control limitations have consistently highlighted that this would be a temporary measure until a more accommodating international climate facilitated a resumed focus on full disarmament and the state's destruction.[71] An example was Executive Director of the International Institute for Strategic Studies in North America Mark Fitzpatrick, who observed that while circumstances meant the Korean state's elimination could no longer be an "immediate answer," it needed to remain long-term goal. "There is only one happy ending to this long-running tragedy: unification of the Korean Peninsula as a democratic, free-enterprise-based republic that would be free of nuclear weapons," he concluded.[72] It remains clear that even if the state were to fully and verifiably denuclearize and disarm, a full lifting of Western economic sanctions would remain effectively impossible, much as governments across the world far more geopolitically accommodating to the West and with no nuclear programs have been sanctioned under a wide range of pretexts. Much as many of the U.S. sanctions on Iran over its nuclear program that were lifted following Iranian nuclear concessions in 2016 were then re-imposed within 24 hours for different reasons,[73] so too is the West's desire to sanction Pyongyang expected to see little change regardless of its weapons programs.

North Korea's weapons programs could, in the long term, result in fewer Western sanctions as it provided some leverage for pursuing sanctions relief – leverage which the majority of targets for Western economic warfare lack. Pyongyang's incentive not to abandon this leverage through disarmament only grew as the Western world's pretexts for applying sanctions on states outside its sphere of influence expanded, including making fuller westernization of countries' political systems a precondition for sanctions relief or normalized relations. Envoys of the United Kingdom visiting Caracas, for example, in early 2024 "repeatedly made clear there can be no hope of normalization in relations until Venezuela fully embraces democracy,"[74] with legislation sponsored in the U.S. Congress two weeks later ensuring Cuba would continue to be listed as a State Sponsor of Terror unless it similarly adopted a Western-style political system.[75] Across targeted countries from Myanmar to Sudan, specific institutions and figures in the leadership seen in the West to be impeding transitions to Western style liberal democracy were also singled out for sanctioning.[76] Beyond sanctions, a lack of sufficient Western-style democratization has been highlighted as a pretext for measures ranging from full scale invasions to illegal appropriation of natural resources and arbitrary treatment at sporting events.[77]

Other more specific targeting of countries for their domestic policies ranged from U.S. sanctioning of Uganda, after it imposed stricter penalties for homosexual activities domestically,[78] to Georgia for its passing of a transparency law that would force NGOs to reveal foreign sources of funding – something seen as unfavorable since much of this funding came from the West.[79] Sanctions over foreign relations were even more diverse, ranging from threatening Egypt and India over purchases of Russian fighter planes and air defense systems,[80] to a wide range of secondary sanctions applied on Russian trading partners.[81] Thus with or without nuclear weapons, the nature of Western foreign policy, particularly from the 2010s, left little possibility of North Korea not being heavily sanctioned or having normalized relations with the West.

The fact that Western designs for North Korea go well beyond its disarmament has been widely attested to, with a prominent indication of the very limited possibility of improved relations provided by the influential 2016 Council on Foreign Relations task force report *A Sharper Choice on North Korea*. It highlighted that even if the DPRK fully denuclearized:

> Full normalization of relations and sanctions relief will require major progress on North Korea's human rights position, including the release of all political prisoners and their families, a full accounting and voluntary repatriation of all persons abducted from foreign countries, nondiscriminatory food aid distribution monitored by aid workers who are guaranteed full nationwide access, freedom to leave the country and return without punishment, and ending the information blockade imposed on North Korea's citizens by the government.[82]

These conditions were broadly consistent with those listed in Sec. 402 of the North Korea Sanctions and Policy Enhancement Act of 2016, HR 757. The CFR's statement itself appeared to be closely based on Title III of the Act, which enshrined the fulfillment of unrealistic demands for domestic changes in and Western penetration of the DPRK into U.S. law as necessary preconditions for any relief of unilateral sanctions. While many of the allegations of human rights abuses were based on highly questionable evidence, maintaining them provided pretext for continued sanctions and pressure until North Korea's ultimate defeat could be engineered, much as fabricated narratives against Iraq, Libya, Yugoslavia and a multitude of others had been.

As the Council on Foreign Relations assessment made clear in its conclusion regarding the final Western goal:

> Finally, let us be clear about the essence of the North Korean nuclear threat: that threat is the North Korean government itself. So long as the real existing North Korean government holds power, that threat will continue. It is therefore incumbent upon the United States and its allies to plan for a successful Korean reunification that does not include the DPRK.[83]

As otherwise summarized by observers over a decade prior, the only way to dispel American hostility appeared to be "for North Korea to dismantle its very self," with offers to dismantle the nuclear and missile programs alone at the time consistently seen as far from sufficient.[84] Head of the CIA's Korea Mission Center Andrew Kim would similarly emphasize in early 2019: "The conflict is not only about denuclearization, it is also about redrawing the geopolitical and geo-economic map for North Korea."[85] Senior fellow at the Yale University Foreign Policy Research Institute Professor Paul Bracken, similarly noted that moves to force inspections and denuclearization "must surely be seen as only the first moves to open up the entire North Korean state." Beyond "bargaining around a military and nuclear negotiation where the gains of one side do not necessarily come at the expense of the other," he stressed, there was a "state survival competition" which was "more important" and "zero sum."[86,ix]

Against a Western world ideologically committed on a fundamental level to its destruction, nuclear weapons provided a barrier forcing an at least temporary policy reevaluation. For Pyongyang, the most optimistic projection for its adversaries' long term response would be for it to follow the Arab-Israeli precedent, as Israel's development of nuclear weapons led Arab states that had for decades denied its right to exist to increasingly accept that its removal from the map was no longer achievable, recognizing Israeli statehood either tacitly or officially.[87] Nevertheless, a similar Western coming to terms with North Korea's existence, easing of pressure and normalization of relations, appears unlikely, and unlike Israel's adversaries, the Western world is likely to maintain the objective of the state's destruction and pursue wide ranging means to achieve this. The prior nuclearization of the Soviet Union set a strong precedent for this, and while it forced a revision of prior plans for a mass U.S.-led military offensive to destroy the state, the West continued to persistently target the USSR with a wide range of economic and information warfare means until its destruction was achieved. As summarized by former British Prime Minister Tony Blair regarding the mission of "Western policy" from the early 1980s: "we sought the final collapse of the Soviet Union and the triumph of liberal democratic values," with success

---

ix Further insight into the objective of the sanctions regime was provided by the President of the Association of Korean Political Studies in North America Park Kyung Ae, who observed that the objective of Western policy remained "a transition to democracy, resulting in the termination of authoritarianism or socialism," noting that sanctions could serve as "the catalyst of regime collapse." Regarding the nature of the desired change in government, she stressed: "Any efforts to change the North Korea regime should involve attempts to destroy the fundamental values and structures of Kim's government, and alter the governing principles and norms, including the socialist values and the Juche (self-reliance) ideology." This reflected the Western consensus towards the necessity for a complete ideological, economic, social and cultural remaking of the country. (Park, Kyung-Ae, 'Regime Change in North Korea?: Economic Reform and Political Opportunity Structures,' *North Korean Review,* vol. 5, no. 1, Spring 2009 (pp. 23–45).)

in achieving this meaning that "things got better. The West was strong."[88] In much the same way, while North Korea's nuclear program rules out a quick military solution for the Western Bloc, the Western world is expected to sustain longer term efforts to gradually weaken the country with the aim of achieving a similar "final collapse."

Thus, the conflict between the Western world and North Korea will likely remain ongoing until either global geopolitical trends, in which the Korean Peninsula plays only one part, cause one of two outcomes. Either a sufficient collapse in the Western world's power forces a fundamental reevaluation of the the objective of placing all states in the world under its influence, or else some unforeseen breakthrough allows the West to achieve its goal of North Korea's destruction.

Endnotes

1 'North Korea's Nuclear Threat: VICE News Interviews Victor Cha,' *Vice News* (YouTube Channel), March 10, 2016.

2 '화산-31' 전술핵탄두 전격 공개한 북한...7차 핵실험 임박했나?' ['North Korea suddenly reveals "Hwasal-31" tactical nuclear warhead... Is the 7th nuclear test imminent?'], *SBS News*, March 28, 2023.

3 Marrow, Michael, 'F-35A officially certified to carry nuclear bomb,' *Defense News*, March 8, 2024.

4 Sharman, Jon, 'America could lose a war against North Korea, former US commander says in leaked letter,' *The Independent*, November 10, 2017.

5 Ibid.

6 'Trepidation at Root of U.S. Korea Policy,' *Washington Post*, December 12, 1993.

Transcript of General Shalikashvili's first press conference, Office of the Assistant Secretary of Defense, Public Affairs, December 14, 1993 (p. 2).

7 Baker, Sinead, 'The US spent so much time fighting insurgents that it forgot "what it means to actually fight a war," a US vet in Ukraine says,' *Business Insider*, May 2, 2024.

8 Ibid.

9 Ibid.

10 Heath, Timothy R., 'China's Military Has No Combat Experience: Does It Matter?,' *RAND Corporation*, November 27, 2018.

Sacks, Steve, 'China's Military Has a Hidden Weakness,' *The Diplomat*, April 20, 2021.

Gale, Alastair, 'China's Military Is Catching Up to the U.S. Is It Ready for Battle?,' *The Wall Street Journal*, October 20, 2022.

Dibb, Paul, 'Be alert to China's military weaknesses,' *The Strategist*, December 1, 2023.

11 Secretary of Defense Jim Mattis, Senate Armed Services Committee, Written Statement for the Record, June 13, 2017.

12 Crilly, Rob, 'Donald Trump orders £43 billion boost to defence spending,' *The Telegraph*, February 27, 2017.

13 Mehta, Aaron, 'Mattis orders fighter jet readiness to jump to 80 percent – in one year,' *Defense News*, October 10, 2018.

14 Losey, Stephen, 'Wittman says patience wearing thin on F-35 sustainment plan,' *Defense News*, October 3, 2023.

15 'Why the U.S. Air Force Admitted Defeat in its Efforts to Attain 80% Combat Readiness for its Fighter Fleet,' *Military Watch Magazine*, May 13, 2020.

16 Tirpak, John A., 'New Study: USAF Needs Big Cash Infusion to Overcome Aging Fighter Fleet,' *Air & Space Forces Magazine*, June 29, 2023.

Guastella, Joseph and Birkey, Douglas and Gunzinger, Eric and Poling, Aidan, 'Accelerating 5th Generation Airpower: Bringing Capability and Capacity to the Merge,' *Mitchell Institute,* no. 43, June 29, 2023.

17 Vanden Brook, Tom, 'Army lifts ban on waivers for recruits with history of some mental health issues,' *USA Today*, November 12, 2017.

Lacdan, Joe, 'Army eases tattoo restrictions with new policy,' *U.S. Army Official Website,* June 23, 2022.

Myers, Meghann, 'Nearly 70% of active service members are overweight, report finds,' *Military Times*, October 14, 2023.

18 '"The End of Everything," with Victor Davis Hanson,' *Hoover Institution* (YouTube Channel), April 9, 2024.

19 Brunnstrom, David, 'Getting North Korea to Give Up Nuclear Weapons Probably "Lost Cause": U.S. Spy Chief,' *Reuters*, October 26, 2016.

20 Lindsey Graham on Twitter: 'North Korea is the ultimate outlier in world order. It is a country built around the philosophy of the divinity of a family. And the person who's inherited the mantle is, on a good day, unstable,' December 15, 2017.

21 Mullen, Mike and Nunn, Sam and Mount, Adam, *A Sharper Choice on North Korea: Engaging China for a Stable Northeast Asia*, Council on Foreign Relations, Independent Task Force Report No. 74, September 2016 (p. xiii).

22 Kazianis, Harry J., 'America Must Move Past Its "Sputnik" Moment on North Korea – Or Else,' *The National Interest,* March 4, 2019.

23 Howell, Edward, *North Korea and the Global Nuclear Order: When Bad Behaviour Pays*, Oxford, Oxford University Press, 2023 (p. 127).

24 Shifrinson, Joshua R. Itzkowitz, 'Op-Ed: Russia's got a point: The U.S. broke a NATO promise,' *Los Angeles Times,* May 30, 2016.

25 Hecker, Siegfried S. and Lee, Sean C. and Braun, Chaim, 'North Korea's Choice: Bombs over Electricity,' *The Bridge*, Summer 2010.

26 Albright, David, 'How Much Plutonium Does North Korea Have?,' *Bulletin of the Atomic Scientists*, September/October 1994 (pp. 46–53).

27 Clapper, James R., *Facts and Fears: Hard Truths from a Life in Intelligence*, New York, Viking, 2018 (Chapter 6).

28 'Russia calls U.S. threat to destroy North Korea a "bloodthirsty tirade,"' *Reuters*, December 2, 2017.

29 Karami, Arash, 'Rafsanjani missile tweet draws fire from Khamenei,' *Al Monitor*, March 31, 2016.

30 'North Korea cites "tragedy" of countries that give up nuclear programs,' *Reuters,* February 21, 2013.

'North Korea cites Muammar Gaddafi's "destruction" in nuclear test defense,' *Reuters*, January 9, 2016.

31 Bandow, Doug, 'Thanks to Libya, North Korea Might Never Negotiate on Nuclear Weapons,' *The National Interest*, September 2, 2015.

32 French, Howards W., 'A Nation At War: Nuclear Standoff; North Korea Says Its Arms Will Deter U.S. Attack,' *New York Times*, April 7, 2003.

33 Schwarz, Jon, 'Trump Intel Chief: North Korea Learned From Libya War to "Never" Give Up Nukes,' *The Intercept*, July 29, 2017.

34 Snaith, Emma, 'Trump claim Obama begged for Kim Jong Un meeting dismissed by former US intelligence chief: "I don't know where he's getting that,"' *The Independent,* July 1, 2019.

35 'Real intention behind Minsk agreements further destroys credibility of the West,' *Global Times*, December 12, 2022.

Prouvost, Theo, 'Hollande: "There will only be a way out of the conflict when Russia fails on the ground,"' *The Kyiv Independent,* December 28, 2022.

36 'John Mearsheimer on Gaza, The Israel Lobby & More,' *The Katie Halper Show* (YouTube Channel), June 12, 2024.

37 Cumings, Bruce, *The Korean War: A History*, New York, Modern Library, 2010 (p. 177).

38 Shaines, Robert A., *Command Influence: A story of Korea and the politics of injustice*, Denver, Colorado, Outskirts Press, 2010 (p. 54).

39 '"Kill 'em All": American War Crimes in Korea,' *Timewatch,* Season 21, Episode 4, aired February 1, 2002.

Hanley, Charles J., 'No Gun Ri: Official Narrative and Inconvenient Truths,' *Critical Asian Studies*, vol. 42, no. 4, 2010 (pp. 589–622).

40 Stone, I. F., *The Hidden History of the Korean War*, Amazon Media, 2014 (Chapters 45, 46).

New York Times, November 12, 1951.

The Commander in Chief, Far East, Ridgway, to the Chief of Staff, United States Army, Tokyo, November 17, 1951, *Foreign Relations of the United States, 1951, Volume VII, Part 1, Korea and China,* Document 720.

41 Howard, Harry, 'North Korean leader Kim Jong-un "executes a general accused of plotting a coup by throwing him into a piranha-filled fish tank,"' *Daily Mail*, June 9, 2019.

42 Logan, Justin, 'Calling North Korea a "Failed State" Shows How Useless the Concept of "Failed State" Is,' *CATO Institute*, January 31, 2022.

43 Barrington, James, *Foxbat*, London, Macmillan, 2007 (Author's note).

44 'North Korean University Students Copy Kim Jong Un's Hairstyle,' *Radio Free Asia*, March 25, 2014.

'North Korea: Students required to get Kim Jong-un haircut,' *BBC News*, March 26, 2014.

Asmolov, Konstantin, 'How the Radio Free Asia released the whole set of baloney,' *New Eastern Outlook*, November 26, 2016.

Macdonald, Hamish, 'Why men's Kim Jong Un hairstyle requirement is unlikely true,' *NK News*, March 26, 2014.

45 'North Korea Says It's Found a "Unicorn Lair,"' *U.S. News*, November 30, 2012.

'Unicorns' Existence Proven, Says North Korea,' *Time*, November 30, 2012.

46 Beaumont, Peter, 'PM admits graves claim "untrue,"' *Observer*, July 18, 2004.

Beal, Tim, *North Korea: The Struggle Against American Power*, London, Pluto Press, 2005 (p. 129).

47 MacArthur, John R., *Second Front: Censorship and Propaganda in the 1991 Gulf War,* Berkeley, University of California Press, 2004 (pp. 49–55).

Sriramesh, Krishnamurthy and Vercic, Dejan, *The Global Public Relations Handbook: Theory, Research, and Practice*, Mahwah, Lawrence Erlbaum, 2003 (p. 418).

Rowse, Arthur E., 'How to build support for war,' *Columbia Journalism Review,* September–October 1992.

Krauss, Clifford, 'Congressman Says Girl Was Credible,' *New York Times*, January 12, 1992.

Pratt, Cornelius, 'Hill & Knowlton's two ethical dilemmas,' *Public Relations Review*, vol. 20, no. 3, 1994 (p. 288).

48 Clwyd, Ann, 'See men shredded, then say you don't back war,' *The Times,* March 18, 2003.

'Truth and fairness stuffed down the shredder,' *Sydney Morning Herald,* March 22, 2003.

Phillips, Melanie, 'This war IS about good versus evil,' *Daily Mail,* March 24, 2003.

O'Neill, Brendan, 'Not a shred of evidence,' *Spectator,* February 21, 2004.

49 Nelson, Lars-Erik, 'Numbers in Kosovo Don't Add Up,' *Orlando Sentinel,* October 28, 1999.

Hammond, Philip and Herman, Edward S., *Degraded Capability: The Media and the Kosovo Crisis*, London, Pluto Press, 2000 (p. 139).

Pilger, John, 'Kosovo Killing Fields?,' *New Statesman,* November 21, 1999.

Kouchner, Bernard, *Les Gurriers de la Paix* [*The Peace Warriors*], Paris, Grasset, 2004 (pp. 374–375).

Harper, Stephen, *Screening Bosnia: Geopolitics, Gender and Nationalism in Film and Television Images of the 1992–95 War,* New York, Bloomsbury, 2017 (pp. 40–43).

50 MacAskill, Ewen, 'Gaddafi "supplies troops with Viagra to encourage mass rape" claims diplomat,' *The Guardian,* April 29, 2011.

Ross, Chuck, 'Sid Blumenthal Floated Disputed Gaddafi Viagra Rape Rumor In Confidential Memo To Hillary,' *Daily Caller,* December 31, 2015.

51 'Latin American Diplomat Eyewitness Account of June 3–4 Events on Tiananmen Square,' US Embassy Telegram, Confidential, *Wikileaks,* July 12, 1989 (https://wikileaks.org/plusd/cables/89BEIJING18828_a.html).

Mathews, Jay, 'The Myth of Tiananmen,' *Columbia Journalism Review,* June 4, 2010.

Clark, Gregory, 'Birth of a massacre myth,' *Japan Times*, July 21, 2008.

52 Kazianis, Harry J., 'A U.S. Invasion of North Korea Would Be Like Opening the Gates of Hell,' *The National Interest,* May 13, 2019.

53 Woodward, Bob, *Bush at War*, New York, Simon & Schuster, 2002 (p. 293).

54 *Los Angeles Times*, Poll Study 484, April 2–3, 2003.

Gershkoff, Amy and Kushner, Shana, 'Shaping Public Opinion: The 9/11-Iraq Connection in the Bush Administration's Rhetoric,' *Perspectives on Politics*, vol. 3, no. 3, 2005 (pp. 525–537).

55 Ibid.

Based on four-poll average. Sources: Los Angeles Times Poll Study 481, January 30–February 2, 2003; Los Angeles Times Poll Study 482, February 7–8, 2003; CNN/ USA Today/Gallup Poll, March 22–23, 2003; ABC News/ Washington Post Poll, March 20, 2003.

56 Pompeo, Mike, *Never Give an Inch: Fighting for the America I Love*, Northampton, MA, Broadside Books, 2023 (Chapter 17).

57 Ibid. (Chapter 2).

58 'Jimmy Carr: "There are MORE SLAVES now than anytime in HISTORY!" JRE 2045,' *JRE Shorts Daily* (YouTube Channel), October 8, 2023.

59 Mahbubani, Kishore, 'Has the West Lost it?' (lecture), *Lee Kuan Yew School of Public Policy*, June 26, 2018.

60 'North Korea rejects Pompeo from nuclear dialogue: KCNA,' *Reuters*, April 18, 2019.

61 Furchtgott-Roth, Harold, 'Time To Take On Kim Jong Un,' *Forbes*, December 22, 2014.

Gamel, Kim, 'Biden calls North Korean leader a "thug" but says he'd meet Kim if denuclearization is agreed,' *Stars and Stripes*, October 23, 2020.

Martirosyan, Lucy, 'Trump-Kim summit gave "master manipulator" a global platform, says defector,' *PRI*, June 13, 2019.

Weiss, Bari, 'Kim Jong-un Isn't Tough. North Koreans Are,' *New York Times*, June 14, 2018.

62 Tertitskiy, Fyodor, 'Why Kim doesn't love Hitler, and why this matters,' *NK News*, February 11, 2015.

Fisher, Max, 'Report: Kim Jong Un handing out copies of "Mein Kampf" to senior North Korean officials,' *Washington Post,* June 17, 2013.

63 Braun, Lindsay Frederick, 'Suez Reconsidered: Anthony Eden's Orientalism and the Suez Crisis,' *The Historian,* vol. 65, no. 3, Spring 2003 (pp. 535–561).

'Hitler On the Nile,' *New York Times*, February 25, 2003.

64 MacArthur, John R., *Second Front: Censorship and Propaganda in the 1991 Gulf War*, Berkeley, University of California Press, 2004 (p. 70).

65 Knipp, Kersten, 'Ayatollah Khamenei and the "final solution" in the Middle East,' *Deutsche Welle*, May 24, 2020.

66 Raum, Tom, 'Bush Says Saddam Even Worse Than Hitler,' *AP News,* November 1, 1990.

Phillips, Melanie, 'This war IS about good versus evil,' *Daily Mail*, March 24, 2003.

67 Keeble, Richard, *The Myth of Saddam Hussein: New Militarism and the Propaganda Function of the Human Interest Story*, New York, Routledge, 1998 (p. 73).

68 Ascherson, Neal, 'Words fail us as the world drifts towards disorder,' *The Independent*, October 23, 1993.

Harper, Stephen, *Screening Bosnia: Geopolitics, Gender and Nationalism in Film and Television Images of the 1992–95 War*, New York, Bloomsbury, 2017 (p. 40).

'German Minister Warned Milosevic of Sea of Blood,' *Reuters*, April 11, 1999.

Pilger, John, 'US and British officials told us that at least 100,000 were murdered in Kosovo. A year later, fewer than 3,000 bodies have been found,' *New Statesman,* September 4, 2000.

69 Kolb, Charles, 'Xi Jinping's China and Hitler's Germany: Growing parallels,' *The Hill*, January 6, 2021.

70 Delfs, Arne, 'German Defense Chief Compares Putin to Hitler at Churchill Event,' *Bloomberg,* April 11, 2024.

'Prince Charles Compares Putin to Hitler,' *NBC News*, May 22, 2014.

Kayali, Laura and Chiappa, Claudia, 'Hitler didn't quit in 1938 and Putin won't stop at Ukraine, Lithuanian leader warns,' *Politico,* March 13, 2024.

Motyl, Alexander J., 'Is Putin's Russia a Nazi state?,' *The Hill*, March 10, 2024.

71 Cha, Taesuh, 'Confronting the North Korean Question in a Post-Unipolar World,' *The National Interest*, November 6, 2022.

Bandow, Doug, 'Why Trump Is Right about North Korea,' *CATO Institute*, December 19, 2023.

72 Fitzpatrick, Mark, 'North Korea: Is Regime Change the Answer?,' *Survival*, vol. 55, no. 3, May 29, 2013.

73 'Iran condemns new US sanctions over missile test,' *BBC News*, January 18, 2016.

74 'Boris Johnson flew to Venezuela for unofficial talks,' *BBC News*, March 10, 2024.

75 LeoGrande, William, 'Watching US Cuba policy in the theater of the absurd,' *Responsible Statecraft*, April 2, 2024.

76 'Executive Order on Imposing Sanctions on Certain Persons Destabilizing Sudan and Undermining the Goal of a Democratic Transition,' *The White House*, May 4, 2023.

'U.S. blacklists Myanmar official ahead of Obama visit,' *Reuters*, November 1, 2014.

'U.S. Restrictions on Relations with Burma,' U.S. Congressional Research Service, May 22, 2017.

Fang, Alex, 'US hits Myanmar junta with $1bn asset freeze and other sanctions,' *Nikkei*, February 11, 2021.

'Treasury Sanctions Military Leaders, Military-Affiliated Cronies and Businesses, and a Military Unit Prior to Armed Forces Day in Burma,' *U.S. Department of Treasury*, March 25, 2022.

77 Coman, Julian, '"We want them to be nervous," That means you Ali, Bashar and Kim),' *The Telegraph*, April 13, 2003.

'US secretly building airport in Syria near oil field,' *The News With Rick Sanchez, RT America* (YouTube Channel), February 15, 2021

'UPMC vs. Paris 2024: Paris mayor wants Russian athletes banned from Olympics,' *Reuters*, March 13, 2024.

78 Fortinsky, Sarah, 'Biden calls for repeal of Uganda's anti-gay law, threatens sanctions,' *The Hill*, May 29, 2023.

79 Solender, Andrew, 'U.S. lawmakers threaten sanctions over Georgia's "foreign agents" bill,' *Axios*, May 13, 2024.

80 Dizboni, Ali and El-Baz, Karim, 'Understanding the Egyptian Military's Perspective on the Su-35 Deal,' *Washington Institute*, July 15, 2021.

Pubby, Manu, 'Will not bow to US pressure on Russian sanctions: MOD,' *Economic Times*, July 14, 2018.

Miglani, Sanjeev, 'Exclusive: India's friction with U.S. rises over planned purchase of Russian S-400 defense systems,' *Reuters*, January 15, 2021.

81 Cook, Chris and Seddon, Max, 'US unveils tougher Russia sanctions for foreign banks,' *Financial Times*, June 12, 2024.

Flatley, Daniel, 'US Wields Risky Bank Sanctions in New Bid to Deny Putin Cash,' *Bloomberg*, December 23, 2023.

Putz, Catherine, 'US Puts Additional Central Asian Companies on Russia Sanctions List,' *The Diplomat*, February 28, 2024.

82 Mullen, Mike and Nunn, Sam and Mount, Adam, *A Sharper Choice on North Korea: Engaging China for a Stable Northeast Asia*, Council on Foreign Relations, Independent Task Force Report No. 74, September 2016.

83 Ibid. (p. 46).

84 Leupp, Gary, 'Basic Facts Good People Should Know,' *Counterpunch*, January 5, 2004.

85 Kim, Andrew, *Remarks delivered at Stanford's Shorenstein Asia-Pacific Research Center*, February 22, 2019 (https://aparc.fsi.stanford.edu/news/transcript-andrew-kim-north-korea-denuclearization-and-us-dprk-diplomacy).

86 Bracken, Paul, 'The North Korean nuclear program as a problem of state survival,' in: Macck, Andrew, *Asian Flashpoint: Security and the Korean Peninsula*, Canberra, Allen and Unwin, 1990.

87 Heikal, Mohamed, *Illusions of Triumph: An Arab View of the Gulf War*, New York, HarperCollins, 1993 (p. 219).

88 Blair, Tony, 'Tony Blair's Speech: After Ukraine, What Lessons Now for Western Leadership?,' *Tony Blair Institute For Global Change*, July 16, 2022.

Index